The New Utopian Politics of Ursula K. Le Guin's *The Dispossessed*

The New Utopian Politics of Ursula K. Le Guin's *The Dispossessed*

Edited by
Laurence Davis and
Peter Stillman

LEXINGTON BOOKS

A Division of
ROWMAN & LITTLEFIELD PUBLISHERS, INC.
Lanham · Boulder · New York · Toronto · Oxford

LEXINGTON BOOKS

A division of Rowman & Littlefield Publishers, Inc.
A wholly owned subsidiary of The Rowman & Littlefield Publishing Group, Inc.
4501 Forbes Boulevard, Suite 200
Lanham, MD 20706

PO Box 317
Oxford
OX2 9RU, UK

British Library Cataloguing in Publication Information Available

Library of Congress Cataloging-in-Publication Data

The new utopian politics of Ursula K. Le Guin's The dispossessed / edited by
  Laurence Davis and Peter Stillman.
    p. cm.
  Includes bibliographical references and index.
  ISBN 13: 978-0-7391-0862-8 (cloth : alk. paper)
  ISBN 10: 0-7391-0862-X (cloth : alk. paper)
  ISBN 13: 978-0-7391-1086-7 (pbk. : alk. paper)
  ISBN 10: 0-7391-1086-1 (pbk. : alk. paper)
    1. Le Guin, Ursula K., 1929- Dispossessed. 2. Le Guin, Ursula K., 1929—Political
and social views. 3. Politics and literature—United States—History—20th century. 4.
Political fiction, American—History and criticism. 5. Utopias in literature. I. Davis,
Laurence, 1967- II. Stillman, Peter G.
PS3562.E42D576 2005
813'.54—dc22   2005011066

Printed in the United States of America

♾™ The paper used in this publication meets the minimum requirements of
American National Standard for Information Sciences—Permanence of Paper
for Printed Library Materials, ANSI/NISO Z39.48-1992.

Contents

Editorial Note

*I*n print continuously since its original publication in 1974, *The Dispossessed* has appeared in a variety of differently paginated editions. All references to *The Dispossessed* in this book have been standardized to the recent (and identically paginated) 387-page HarperCollins paperback editions. The following table, which includes some of the most readily available editions of *The Dispossessed*, is meant to assist those readers who do not have a 387-page edition of the novel.

chap.	Harper & Row cloth 1974[1]	Harper & Row book club cloth 1974[2]	Avon pbk. 1975[3]	HarperCollins pbks. 1991, 1994, 2001, 2003[4]	Gollancz cloth 1974, 1991 Millennium pbk. 1999[5]	Granada pbk. 1975[6]
	pp.	pp.	pp.	pp.	pp.	pp.
1	1–22	1–22	1–20	1–25	5–24	9–28
2	23–55	23–55	21–50	26–62	25–54	29–58
3	56–80	56–79	51–73	63–90	55–77	59–81
4	81–111	80–110	74–101	91–125	78–105	82–109
5	112–136	111–134	102–124	126–153	106–128	110–132
6	137–169	135–167	125–154	154–191	129–159	133–162
7	170–205	168–203	155–187	192–232	160–193	163–195
8	206–238	204–235	188–217	233–270	194–223	196–225
9	239–270	236–267	218–246	271–307	224–253	226–254
10	271–295	268–292	247–269	308–335	254–276	255–277
11	296–309	293–306	270–282	336–351	277–289	278–290

(continued)

				Gollancz	
Harper			HarperCollins	cloth	
& Row	Harper & Row	Avon	pbks.	1974, 1991	Granada
cloth	book club cloth	pbk.	1991, 1994,	Millennium	pbk.
1974[1]	1974[2]	1975[3]	2001, 2003[4]	pbk. 1999[5]	1975[6]
chap. pp.	pp.	pp.	pp.	pp.	pp.
12 310–334	307–331	283–305	352–379	290–312	291–313
13 335–341	332–338	306–311	380–387	313–319	314–319

1. New York: Harper & Row, 1974.
2. New York: Book Club Edition, Harper & Row, 1974.
3. New York: Avon, 1975.
4. New York: HarperCollins pbks. (HarperPaperbacks, 1991; HarperPrism, 1994; Eos, 2001; Perennial, 2003).
5. London: Gollancz, 1974; Gollancz, 1991; Gollancz Millennium, 1999.
6. London: Granada, 1975.

Note: The full title of the book has varied. The 1974 Gollancz edition and the 2003 Perennial edition list the title of the book as *The Dispossessed: A Novel.* The 1991 and 1999 Gollancz editions read simply *The Dispossessed.* The 1975 Avon edition has on its cover a subtitle or banner: "The Magnificent New Epic of an Ambiguous Utopia." The others listed above read *The Dispossessed: An Ambiguous Utopia* on their title pages.

Introduction

Laurence Davis

$\mathcal{F}$irst published in 1974, Ursula K. Le Guin's powerful utopian novel *The Dispossessed: An Ambiguous Utopia* immediately received widespread acclaim, including both the Hugo and Nebula awards. More recently, the influential social and political thinker André Gorz commented that *The Dispossessed* is "The most striking description I know of the seductions—and snares—of self-managed communist or, in other words, anarchist society."[1] To date, however, the radical political ramifications of the novel remain woefully under explored.

In *The New Utopian Politics of Ursula K. Le Guin's* The Dispossessed, the first ever collection of original essays devoted to Le Guin's novel, we aim to help right this state of affairs. Among the pertinent questions we consider are the following. Is Gorz's characterization of the novel an accurate one? To what extent may *The Dispossessed* be read as an anarchist, ecological, anticapitalist, or revolutionary utopia? Which political themes emerge most strongly from the story, and to what extent do they engage with contemporary political debates or important ideas in the history of political thought? To what extent does Le Guin's "ambiguous utopia" represent a challenge to traditional models of utopian literature and thought? Does it have anything distinctive to say about the relationship between literature and politics, history and politics, science and politics, or art and society? Does the book have anything distinctive to say about the relationship between individuality and community, or about the nature and role of politics in general? In what ways does the work challenge the reader's sense of conventional temporal relationships? What connections does it suggest between conceptions of time and ideas of human freedom? What roles do moral, social, and political conflict play in the story? Is it fair to describe *The Dispossessed* as a "dynamic," "pluralistic," or "revolutionary" utopia?

The scholarly core of the book is composed of sixteen chapters grouped in six major sections, each of which focuses on a particular aspect of the novel's politics.

As editors of the volume, Peter Stillman and I are particularly pleased to note not only the exceptional quality of the individual contributions, but also the many stimulating ways in which they speak to one another. We are also delighted to draw the reader's attention to the concluding essay by Le Guin, written specially for this volume, in which she reassesses the novel in light of the contributors' analyses and the development of her own thinking over the past thirty years.

The book opens with chapters by Laurence Davis and Simon Stow on the "open-ended utopian politics" of *The Dispossessed*. Both tackle head-on a question that recurs throughout the edited volume, specifically the extent to which Le Guin's "ambiguous utopia" poses a challenge to prevailing models of utopian literature and thought premised on an association between utopia and the idea of perfection. Both do so, moreover, by paying particular attention to the fact that Le Guin chose to write her utopia as a novel.

In chapter 1, "The Dynamic and Revolutionary Utopia of Ursula K. Le Guin," Davis argues that *The Dispossessed* demonstrates the viability of a type of utopianism that defenders and critics of utopia alike have difficulty even imagining: namely, a dynamic and revolutionary utopia premised on an acceptance of the enduring reality of social conflict and historical change. In support of this argument he offers an extensive analysis of the structure of the novel, some of its key metaphors, the psychological, intellectual, and political development of its main character, and the changing relationship between its two central worlds. The common thread binding together these diverse modes of analysis is a focus on the treatment of time and history in the novel.

According to Davis, Le Guin succeeds in *The Dispossessed* in representing utopia not as a timeless and unattainable state of perfection, but as a time-sensitive, revolutionary critical perspective that can expand the opportunities for free human choice and meaningful action by helping to break open the horizon of historical possibility. In so doing, he suggests, she redeems both the concept and fictional practice of utopia. She also dramatizes the dangers of dogmatic, mechanistic, Euclidean, and deterministic conceptions of history, and reminds us of the indispensable part played in historical change by individual choice, moral responsibility, and personal creativity. Davis concludes the chapter by restating his argument in metaphorical terms, "if the dominant form of utopian narrative is a timeless monument to Euclidean reason, *The Dispossessed* is a mighty wave of the imagination in the ocean of time, on the crest of which we are all buoyed up and provided with a glimpse of the farther shore."

Like Davis, Stow eschews a reductively didactic or ideological reading of the novel in favor of one that emphasizes some of the more subtle ways in which it succeeds in fostering critical perspective. According to Stow, Le Guin avoids the twin pitfalls of treating utopia as either escapist fantasy or political blueprint by recognizing the complexity of the relationship between what the anarchist theorist Paul Goodman called the "written" and the "unwritten" worlds. She does so, more specifically, by tapping into a long tradition of political thought based on the juxtaposition of realities as a source of critical insight. Like some of the classics of ancient Greek theater, epic literature, and utopian philosophy, Stow suggests, *The Dispossessed* should be read as an imaginative voyage of journey and return meant to provoke citizens into synthesizing the dueling perspectives represented on the one hand by the written world of the text, and on the other by the unwritten worlds of politics and their daily existence.

Ultimately, however, this function of the text pales in comparison to another, for Le Guin's work offers us a "doubly critical" perspective. It forces the reader not only to consider her world and the way that she lives, but also to reflect upon the possibility of utopia itself and its role in political thought and analysis. The central conclusion of the piece follows from this line of analysis, "*The Dispossessed* offers us not the limited opportunities of a specific critique or thought experiment, but something much more valuable: the experience and the demonstration of replicable critical method."

The opening chapters by Davis and Stow are for the most part complementary. However, there is at least one potential area of debate between them. From Stow's perspective, the anarchist, ecological, and revolutionary politics of the text are almost incidental. As he argues in respect of its anarchism, "Far from presenting a simple depiction of the promise and problems of anarchism as a political theory, the novel offers us instead a method for critical reflection." The question this raises is whether it is possible that the text does both, albeit in a fashion that is not simplistically moralistic or reductively ideological. To put the question slightly differently, is *The Dispossessed* concerned exclusively with teaching us how to think critically, or does it also challenge us to think critically about particular political issues and ideas? Stow seems to advocate the former position, while Davis would appear to subscribe to the latter.

One means by which the reader might adjudicate between these conflicting positions is to consider the degree of success achieved by the remaining contributors in their efforts to illuminate more substantive aspects of the novel's politics. In part II of the volume, three of our contributors consider the material dimensions of *The Dispossessed*, and more specifically its "post-consumerist politics." Peter Stillman does so from the perspective of political ecology, Andrew Reynolds from the perspective of Marxian political economy, and Douglas Spencer from the point of view of radical design theory and practice. All three authors approach the text with remarkably similar views about the value of material wealth. In one way or another they are all deeply critical of consumerist society, but wary of the perils of extreme economic scarcity and antimaterialism. Yet another important commonality is that all three pay close attention to the immediate historical context in which the novel was written. Finally, at least two of the three chapters directly challenge the oft-repeated but simplistic claim that *The Dispossessed* advances a "sociopolitical hypothesis about the inseparability of utopia and scarcity."

In chapter 3, "*The Dispossessed* as Ecological Political Theory," Stillman focuses on the insights into *The Dispossessed* that we may gain by using the perspectives of environmental issues. Among the issues that he considers are anarchy and the problem of scarcity; resource use and disposal; the psychological and spiritual dimensions of nature; species survival; time; place; and the relevance of the anarchist ecological thought of *The Dispossessed* to the world in which it was written and continues to be printed and read. According to Stillman, one of the most important accomplishments of the novel is to provide a "thought experiment" of how an anarchist society might realistically confront scarcities in a sustainable manner. Stillman puts the point as follows, "What liberal capitalism and Marxism cannot do, Le Guin's anarchy, as practiced on Anarres, can: establish and maintain a society of liberty, equality, and community despite severe shortages of resources."

Beyond this, the novel can lead the reader to a series of questions, three of which are particularly salient from the perspective of environmental and ecological issues. First, is anarchy the only social arrangement that can resolve important environmental issues of resource use and disposal? Second, what about environmental and ecological issues that go beyond resource use and pollution? Third, although *The Dispossessed* presents an imaginary anarchist society that continues on Anarres under conditions of scarcity, is anarchy possible under conditions of relative plenty? Fittingly, Stillman's answer to this last question is an ambiguous one. Like Le Guin herself, he suggests that we who live in contemporary industrial-capitalistic countries will only know when we start the journey, act, and make the attempt.

In chapter 4, "Ursula K. Le Guin, Herbert Marcuse, and the Fate of Utopia in the Postmodern," Reynolds achieves his main insights into the text by juxtaposing it with another post–World War II utopian work, Herbert Marcuse's *Eros and Civilization: A Philosophical Inquiry into Freud*. Both works, Reynolds hypothesizes, are examples of a new category of utopia that emerges with the tremendous increase in American material abundance after World War II. More specifically, they are instances of "the post-utopian imagination," defined as "the positive imagination of a resolution to the postmodern problematic without recourse to either production or consumption as the ultimately determining factors of human experience." As such, they have many affinities, most notably their imagined rehabilitations of some everyday experiences such as work and sex. Their philosophical premises remain distinct, however. While Marcuse presents a psychological theory of pleasure, Le Guin represents and analyzes the politics of anarchist freedom. Each, in other words, suggests a very different way of moving beyond postmodern consumer society. Whereas Marcuse replaces abundance with the satisfaction of the libido, Le Guin holds out the idea of the promise as a way of binding the individual in time, and thus transforming the pain and emptiness of human freedom into plenitude.

Both visions, Reynolds concludes, are coherent on their own terms and based on a genuine fear of commodified domination. More problematically, the authors of *Eros and Civilization* and *The Dispossessed* share what Reynolds characterizes as "an implicit distrust or disdain toward material goods as part of a program of liberation and revolution." It follows that "the future of the post-utopian imagination might lie in a less antagonistic stance toward the world of objects, the goal being neither to unrealistically bracket economic life nor to pose the problem of liberation within the context of the struggle for survival."

Whereas Reynolds assumes that Le Guin's decision to explore how an anarchist society might fare under conditions of extreme scarcity necessarily signals an aversion to material goods as part of a program of liberation and revolution, Douglas Spencer challenges precisely this assumption in chapter 5, "The Alien Comes Home: Getting Past the Twin Planets of Possession and Austerity in Le Guin's *The Dispossessed*." On Spencer's reading, the utopia of Anarres is not meant to be interpreted either as an unambiguous alternative to consumerism or, in itself, a viable model for a future society. Rather, it ought to be understood as an element in a larger fictional design that both articulates and calls into question the apparent dualisms of possession and dispossession. Spencer elaborates his point as follows, "Both Urrasti capitalism, where objects are the source of human identity and sociability, and Anarresti anarchism, where objects alienate and their absence allows for identity and sociability, represent polar positions; Le Guin brings the two worlds, and by implication the two positions, into a proximity that starts to undermine the stability of both."

He arrives at this conclusion not only by means of a refreshingly earthly analysis of the material and aesthetic dimensions of *The Dispossessed*, but also by situating the novel in the context of near contemporary accounts of consumerism by radical design theorists and practitioners. Most notably, he identifies some important parallels between Le Guin's novelistic treatment of objects, and the utopian architectural and design projects of radical design groups such as Utopie in France and Superstudio in Italy. He concludes by emphasizing the even more important differences between them, and in particular those that suggest the novel ways in which Le Guin succeeds in reframing utopian approaches to objects and aesthetics. Whereas Utopie and Superstudio responded to the excesses of consumer capitalism by equating renunciation with salvation and freedom, Le Guin (like William Morris before her) recognizes the related limitations of both austerity and opulence. She also gestures to a possibility that Reynolds claims Marcuse overlooks, namely that art might provide a context for the rehabilitation of the object, liberating it from its commodified form.

If the post-consumerist politics of *The Dispossessed* are an important but relatively neglected aspect of the novel, its unprecedented portrayal of an imaginary anarchist society and the characters that emerge from it is arguably the book's primary contribution to contemporary political discourse. Philip E. Smith has argued that Le Guin deserves special recognition not only for her novelistic artistry in *The Dispossessed*, but also for her imaginative Odonian embodiment and application of anarchist theory.[2] The three contributors to part III of our edited volume would no doubt agree, albeit from very different perspectives about the nature and relative merits of anarchism as a political theory. All three focus in particular on the novel's extraordinarily original and important contribution to the perennial political debate about the proper relationship between individuality and community, though each approaches the issue from a radically different perspective. Dan Sabia (chapter 6) does so very much like Le Guin herself, as a communal anarchist in the mold of Peter Kropotkin. Mark Tunick (chapter 7) does so as a Hegelian, and Winter Elliott (chapter 8) as an individualist anarchist.

Judging by her public comments about the novel in the years since its first publication, Sabia's reading of the anarchist politics of the text is probably the closest of the three to Le Guin's own. In his chapter, "Individual and Community in Le Guin's *The Dispossessed*," Sabia focuses on what he takes to be a key attraction of the ideology referred to by Kropotkin as "anarchist communism": namely, its emphasis on the equal and paramount value of both individualism and community. The main thesis of his chapter is that *The Dispossessed* offers not only an informed and sympathetic portrayal of anarchist communism in general, but also a stimulating and highly suggestive account of how the ideology's promise of reconciliation between individuality and community might be approximated, and an equally suggestive account of why that promise can never be wholly satisfied. What is more, Le Guin's novel even explains why this inadequacy serves, paradoxically, to recommend the theory.

In support of his thesis, Sabia analyzes some of the major norms and institutions of Anarresti anarchism. One of the more important conclusions that he draws is that the idea of enlightened self-interest lies at the bottom of Anarres's anarchist political theory, as well as its promise of reconciliation between individuality and community. As he goes on to argue, however, even with enlightenment total reconciliation is an impossibility, in part because the sources of disharmony between individuality and community are also sources of harmony. To her great credit, Sabia suggests, Le Guin chooses not to overlook this fundamental ambiguity in the human condition, but to recognize and celebrate it. He concludes his chapter as follows, "Shevek's successes require transgressing customary physical and psychic borders, and disrupting social harmony. Using this ending as a signpost, the message would appear to be that not even anarchist communism can reconcile completely the ideals of individualism and community, and this bad result is, also, good."

Like Sabia, Tunick focuses on the relationship between individuality and community in *The Dispossessed*. His conclusions differ dramatically, however. Whereas Sabia argues that the imaginary world of Anarres offers a stimulating example of how anarchist communism's promise of reconciliation between individuality and community might be approximated, Tunick emphasizes the shortcomings of Anarresti anarchism and characterizes them as "hypocrites" who fail to live up to their "one-sided" ideals. This is not merely his own view, he suggests, but the message implicit in the text itself. According to Tunick, *The Dispossessed* rejects the one-sided and simplistic ideals of both Anarres and Urras, and implies that only a dialectical mediation between them might provide what he refers to as a "political blueprint for freedom." He concludes, furthermore, that this blueprint for freedom is essentially neither anarchist nor utopian nor Marxian in character, but Hegelian.

Tunick elaborates his argument by proposing that the freedom Shevek seeks requires community, which in turn may require the preservation of individual autonomy and the building of some walls without creating a state of possessive individualism as exists on Urras. His most extensive analysis in this regard focuses on what he takes to be Le Guin's implicit defense of "the modern family." According to Tunick, both Hegel and Le Guin defend a particular family form as a necessary institutional means of mediating between the ideals of individual and community. Tunick concludes his chapter by celebrating his newly Hegelianized Anarresti, "The Anarresti need some protective walls between public and private to shelter them from the coercive force of public opinion. It may be that this will lead to possessiveness, and encourage conservative institutions like the nuclear family. But thanks to Shevek's journey and return, they can point to the excesses on Urras as a cautionary guide."

Like Tunick, Elliott is highly critical of the anarchist society depicted on Anarres. She too views it as deeply repressive and damaging to human well-being. However, whereas Tunick celebrates those "Hegelian" moments of the text that transcend the wishes of any given single individual, Elliott lauds its uncompromising individualism. According to her, *The Dispossessed* is not ultimately as interested in which of its two major worlds has the best, or even better, political system as it is in Shevek's role within those worlds. From Elliott's perspective the novel therefore represents not a social but a "personal" utopia, an idea both experienced and realized by one person, Shevek. His idea of anarchist freedom cannot ultimately be perpetuated on a social level. Nor does anarchy even require an anarchist society, although individual anarchism may develop into a society of anarchists if a sufficient number of individual anarchists happen to live in close proximity. Even in this case, however, only on an individual basis can anarchy be achieved and the natural progression of societies toward law and regulation—and power—be interrupted.

As evidence for her argument Elliott focuses in particular on the ways in which Shevek's creative potential is stunted by the social systems of both Anarres and Urras. She discusses the distinctive methods by which those systems thwart his pursuit of knowledge, and the process of rebellion by which he eventually frees his thinking from social control. In freeing his mind, Elliott notes, Shevek not only undermines the tendencies toward control and law that have begun to regulate even Anarres. He also achieves his own personal utopia, the "clear, unmixed happiness" that comes to those who think, choose, and act according to their own volition.

Perhaps because of her literary focus on the development of a single character, Elliott reminds us of a dimension of the text too often ignored or downplayed by those who treat it as a straightforward form of political theory or argument, namely its novelistic concern with development and change over time. In the next two parts of the edited volume, this aspect of the text, elucidated by Davis in his opening chapter, again comes to the fore. In part IV, on "Temporal Politics," all three authors treat Shevek's theory of time. They do so from very different perspectives: Ellen Rigsby (chapter 9) draws on Hannah Arendt's political thought to illuminate the novel's temporal politics; Jennifer Rodgers (chapter 10) explores the meanings for individual and social development of working with time; and Tony Burns (chapter 11) considers whether Le Guin is a realist or constructivist in science and in ethics. But all conclude by tying Shevek's scientific theory of time to the novel's ethical vision and anarchist politics.

Ellen Rigsby sees that, like Arendt, Le Guin depicts "a politics based on the human experience of being born into time." The complex theory of time on which this politics is constructed includes both linear time, or sequency, which follows an event or action from a beginning to an end (an arrow shot and hitting a target), and cyclical time, or simultaneity, where an event or action perpetuates itself (and the arrow never hits the target). Acting in accordance with this dual notion of time entails both freedom and ethics. Human freedom, on this interpretation, means the capacity for free, willed action. Ethics involves a willful, free human act that creates a new beginning that sustains itself in linear time.

In temporal terms, ethics means creating linear time—by action with a beginning and an end—out of cyclical time, with its patterns and repetitions, but also with its varieties, contingencies, and hence possibilities for new beginnings. When a linear narrative has no cyclical time with its variations and possibilities, then there is a kind of determinism which Arendt thinks characterizes much modern western thought. Shevek, on the contrary, chooses initiative, acts, and begins things—even though acting produces new contingencies that may undermine the action itself. When Shevek attempts to teach others about time and ethics, he fails. Rigsby points out that Shevek then faces a choice: to continue to exercise his initiative of unbuilding walls and sharing his ideas, or to retreat. Le Guin depicts an example of retreat: Keng's fatalism, a product of Terra's desolation, which means that she cannot believe Shevek's speech or imagine Anarres as a possible future. Shevek rejects the fatalism of a purely cyclical time, and continues to act to create new beginnings, even though there is no certainty about the outcomes. Le Guin's dual conception of time, Rigsby concludes, "opens the possibility of begetting something new."

Jennifer Rodgers also delineates Shevek's view of time as encompassing moral, ethical, and social (or political) aspects. But Rodgers employs different sources for insight and emphasizes different aspects of the text. She draws in particular on J. T. Fraser's extensive explorations of time in order to clarify the meaning of linear and cyclical time, the arrow of time and the circle of time. She then uses these understandings of time to interpret both individual and society. Le Guin's novel encompasses a series of journeys and returns. Shevek goes out to the Dust, to Urras, to Takver. Each journey turns out to be a "working toward"—

toward brotherhood, toward scientific truth, toward finding a life partner—where he discovers that "by changing, learning, growing—working with time—he has achieved another level of fulfillment in coming home." These journeys are "circular journeys of cyclical growth" that prepare Shevek for further action and change upon his return home.

Similar change occurs on the level of societies, which Rodgers contrasts in their attitudes to time. Urras, outwardly beautiful, works against time to maintain the status quo. Anarres at the beginning of the novel, with its wall, has cut itself off from its past and thus called into question its utopian future. Keng's Terra is a world that possesses only a past. Shevek's journey to Urras and return to Anarres may transform his home world by connecting Anarres to its Urrasti past; the Anarresti (and other peoples) can now see Urras not simply as an opposite to oppose but as a past which they can criticize and grow beyond to possible futures.

Shevek's journey to Anarres's past on Urras also enables his discovery of the General Temporal Theory, uniting linear and cyclical time as surely as his experiences on Urras mirror and reproduce his growth on Anarres. In *The Dispossessed*, individuals begin journeys, and return, generating change, evolution, or revolution in themselves, their societies, and their knowledge of the world. Working with time means individual, social, and scientific change, "a continual, never-ending (r)evolution—the process of utopia."

Tony Burns weaves together Le Guin's views of science and politics, and links them to the current "science wars" debate pitting realists against constructivists. Focusing first on natural science in *The Dispossessed*, Burns recounts but rejects the powerful arguments that Le Guin is a relativist in science. Le Guin presents Shevek (Burns refers to them interchangeably) as one who sees, like Plato, that mathematics gives true answers and, like Galileo, that numbers prevent rhetorical manipulation. Although Shevek develops a theory of time the elements of which may not be logically consistent with one another, these elements are, like the binaries in Hegelian dialectic, incorporated into a single inclusive outcome, which encompasses the paradoxes. Burns concludes that Le Guin is a realist in science, and he goes on to note that her scientific "realism" places her squarely within the classical anarchist tradition, whose members, like Shevek on Urras, sought to serve truth, not the state.

Focusing next on politics, Burns presents but rejects the substantial arguments that Le Guin is an ethical relativist. He sees Le Guin as committed to the moral law that human beings are subjects, not objects. When human beings are objectified, as they are in propertarian states, human relations can only be power relations. When on the other hand human beings treat each other as subjects, human relations are ethical relations. For Shevek, treating others as subjects—the law of reciprocity—underpins mutual aid, legitimates criticism of A-Io's many hierarchies, and sustains his commitment to the equality of women. In the "science wars," then, Le Guin is a realist. And her realism, Burns concludes, leads her to anarcho-communism both in science, which should serve truth rather than power, and in ethics, where human beings should treat one another as equal subjects rather than objectify the other in power relations.

In the section on "Temporal Politics," Rigsby's and Rodgers's discussions of time illustrate how Le Guin is open to and indeed underwrites change as an integral part of her ambiguous utopia. The emphasis on change and development is intensified in the chapters on "Revolutionary Politics," where the contributors take very different paths to some remarkably similar conclusions. All three read *The Dispossessed* as a radical departure from the static, perfectionist utopian tradition. All focus on the relationship between Urras and Anarres, and in particular on the novel's ultimate rejection of a static binary opposition between the two worlds in favor of a dynamic process of "permanent revolution." All point to striking parallels between political and personal relationships in *The Dispossessed*. Very important, they also remind us that Le Guin's utopia does not present the reader with a simple choice between contrasting value systems, because the sister moons exist simultaneously and are inextricably tied by a shared history.

As Everett Hamner's chapter 12 title suggests, he focuses on walls as a "central image" in *The Dispossessed*. Unlike many earlier commentators on the novel's wall imagery, he disputes the argument that the only important walls in the book are those that Shevek is determined to destroy. According to Hamner, while some of the story's walls are "absolute" and so enable exploitative relationships, others facilitate a dialectic through which interdependent opposites may be both distinct and unified. There are thus two concepts of walls at work in the novel, one closed and negative and the other relatively open and positive. In keeping with its Taoist spirit, *The Dispossessed* upholds the latter type of wall over either the former or any attempt to eliminate walls entirely. In other words, it implies that a certain type of "wall" is a valuable, indeed essential, component of all aspects of life. Such walls must be both sufficiently permeable and "mobile" to allow for change, yet also solid and stable enough to protect that change as it occurs.

In support of this thesis Hamner examines Le Guin's use of wall metaphors to describe the novel's personal relationships, Shevek's scientific career, and the bond between Urras and Anarres. He observes that when Le Guin portrays walls negatively, as obstacles, they separate two parties who view each other as mere objects for manipulation or domination. This is true of the dalliance between Vea and Shevek, the exploitative professional relationship between Shevek and Sabul, and the antagonistic political dynamic between Urras and Anarres. When on the other hand Le Guin portrays walls positively, they are a central component of freedom. This is the case in Shevek's partnership with Takver, "a relationship that represents the novel's most thorough expression of the positive potential of walls." It is also true of Shevek's rejection of binary thinking in the development of his unified theory of time, and his recognition that he must not destroy but rather reassert the "permeability" of the wall between Urras and Anarres in order to rejuvenate the latter's revolutionary spirit. Hamner concludes his chapter by stepping back from *The Dispossessed* in order to consider its significance in the contexts of both Le Guin's corpus as a whole and the utopian tradition. He notes that for Le Guin "utopia is sustainable . . . only through active, ongoing choices against the tangible possibility of dystopia" and against the failed past, and that these choices are possible "only if there remains a gap in the wall."

Like Hamner, Bülent Somay interprets *The Dispossessed* as a genuinely revolutionary utopia. Unlike him, he argues that it represents a complete and total break from the previous utopian tradition. According to Somay (chapter 13), the utopian tradition, up until what he refers to elsewhere as the "open-ended" utopias of the 1970s, was authoritarian in style and "totalitarian" in content. Because utopias invariably portray a social order described as something finally achieved, they leave no room for further change. As soon as change is excluded, however, any conflicts, differences, or even variations of style must be suppressed, since each of these may lead to a subversion of the existing (supposedly perfect) state of affairs. Le Guin's utopia, by contrast, upholds the value of difference. Like Samuel Delany's *Triton*, it is a heterodox rather than an orthodox book—in part because (again like *Triton*) it is not written from a singular ideological perspective, but even more importantly because of the ambiguous location of its utopian horizon.

Whereas the other contributors to the edited volume locate the novel's utopian "address" (the term is Somay's) on Anarres, or on Urras, or in the relationship between them, or in Odo's philosophy of freedom, or in Shevek's experiences as a free thinker and revolutionary voyager between worlds, or in the critical perspective that may emerge from the readers' reflection on all of the above, Somay locates it "in the void between Anarres and Urras, in the fantasy space which has no actuality." Drawing on the language of contemporary psychoanalytical theory, he argues that Anarres cannot be the correct address for the novel's utopian horizon because it is locked in a binary opposition with Urras, and has consequently projected all of the "otherness" that is inherent in itself onto its moon, leaving no room for any "other" within. Seeking only to be different from Urras, its goal is to maintain itself so that its future is like its past; and so it has expelled any new utopian horizon in favor of this meager goal. Anarres is able to revitalize its revolutionary potential only when Shevek "demolishes" the wall that has cut his home world off from contact with other worlds. His actions expose Anarres to the diversity of the wider universe, thus facilitating a degree of self-reflexivity and growth impossible so long as it continued to define itself only as the opposite of its Urrasti past.

Like Hamner and Somay, Chris Ferns (chapter 14) focuses on the destructive effects of Anarres's spatial and temporal isolation. Like Somay, he argues that the Anarresti have made an example of Urras as the "other" which they must at all costs resist turning into, and so created an environment where the prospect of any further change is seen as threatening. Unlike Somay or Hamner, he pays particular attention to the radical narrative innovations that Le Guin employs in *The Dispossessed*, and to the ways in which these point to a possible way out of the political impasse in which Anarres finds itself.

Ferns sets the stage for his central argument by noting that if read in isolation, the Anarres chapters of *The Dispossessed* bear a striking resemblance to both the perfectionist utopia and its dystopian parody. As in most utopias, the Anarresti attempt to preserve their cherished way of life by rationally organizing everything from town planning and food distribution to child-rearing practices and language. Moreover, they go to great lengths to maintain the "*separation* of the[ir] utopian society from the real world (or in this case, its analogue)." Like most dystopias, the Anarres chapters depict a process whereby a small group of individuals comes to rebel against the increasing conformity and bureaucratic centralization of their society. While Ferns acknowledges that Anarres is a long way from becoming the kind of totalitarian state imagined by Zamyatin and Orwell, he also observes that there is little doubt that it is headed in a less than desirable direction. It thus provides "an illuminating perspective on the frequently commented-upon tendency of revolutions to relapse into something all too similar to the social order they were designed to overthrow."

As Ferns goes on to argue, however, what makes *The Dispossessed* so very different from its utopian and dystopian antecedents is precisely the fact that it does *not* maintain the separation between utopia and reality commonly found in such works. Instead, it juxtaposes the potentially dystopian narrative of Shevek and his comrades' growing resistance to societal conformity with a counter-narrative in which Shevek returns to Urras to encounter at first hand the society whose "contradictions" generated the revolution that founded his own. What emerges as a result, Ferns submits, might best be described as a dialogic relationship between the alternating sections, whereby the developments in each episode take on a markedly different resonance in the context of their juxtaposition. This narrative dialogue includes a temporal dimension, and a temporal allegory, insofar as it implies that for the possibility of a future that is qualitatively different to emerge there has to be a dynamic relationship between past and present. As Ferns demonstrates such a relationship does emerge by the end of the novel, at both the personal and the political levels. He concludes, therefore, that while Shevek's voyage to Urras may be seen in one sense as a return to the past, it is a return whose effect is ultimately to restore the possibility on both Urras and Anarres of genuine change. It follows that *The Dispossessed* not only "resolves some of the narrative problems inherent in the traditional utopia," but also makes a powerful case for the necessity of permanent revolution.

Ferns's analysis of the theme of permanent revolution in *The Dispossessed* brings us back almost full circle to where we began our study of the novel, with an assessment of its open-ended utopian politics. In the final two chapters of the volume, Claire Curtis and Avery Plaw resume the earlier discussion of the novel's open-ended utopianism with a particular emphasis on its contemporary political implications. Both respond directly to the anti-utopian criticisms articulated by some of the later twentieth century's most influential political philosophers, most notably Isaiah Berlin. According to these liberal or conservative critics of utopia, there is a necessary connection between utopian political thought and the single-minded, ruthless pursuit of dogmatic social goals. Curtis and Plaw rebut this suggestion by demonstrating that *The Dispossessed* is an open-ended utopia concerned with highlighting the perils of perfectionism and underscoring the perpetual need for free individual choice and respect of diversity and dissent. In contrast to those critics who have portrayed the novel as moralistic, monistic, or drearily didactic, they characterize it as a gently persuasive affirmation of the relative merits of Anarresti values over their Urrasti counterparts.

In chapter 15, "Ambiguous Choices: Skepticism as a Grounding for Utopia," Curtis directly confronts the anti-utopianism of political philosophers Michael Oakeshott, John Rawls, and Isaiah Berlin and argues that they misunderstand the possibilities inherent in the concept of utopia. All three are repelled by the dogmatic perfectionism that they associate with utopian thinking, and so reject it in favor of a messier world of rules, procedures, and deliberation with no guarantee of success. As Curtis points out, however, they fail to notice that their own critical arguments may lay the philosophical foundations for a new sort of utopianism premised on skepticism rather than perfectionism. Le Guin's Anarres, Curtis observes, is precisely such a skeptical utopia. Far from being a vision of final perfection of the sort condemned by Berlin and company, Anarres is a relatively ideal society whose necessarily imperfect ideals must be constantly re-interpreted in the light of changing circumstances.

In order to establish her thesis Curtis first outlines some of the key anti-utopian arguments of Oakeshott, Rawls, and Berlin. Specifically, she discusses Oakeshott's critique of rationalism, Rawls's concern with teleology, and Berlin's advocacy of pluralism and the politics of compromise. She then shows how these arguments are inapplicable to *The Dispossessed*. With respect to the charge of teleology, for example, she points out that the guiding principles of Odonianism are not intended as appeals to a shared future outcome, but as a common ground always open to interpretation. When Odo's writings are misused teleologically to simply mold Anarresti into one shape, the principles fail. Berlin's critique of the uncompromisingly perfectionist bent of utopia is equally inapplicable to *The Dispossessed*, because Anarres is no Pollyanna picture of unblemished perfection. It is a recognizably human world with famine, violence, and suffering. What makes it utopian (and so a potential spur to radical change in the unwritten world of present-day Earth) is the effort of its inhabitants to uphold the principle that one cannot justify the happiness of some by the degradation of others. The Anarresti do not always live up to this ideal, but unlike their Urrasti counterparts they recognize it as the necessary foundation on which their society is built.

Like Curtis, Plaw rejects the suggestion that *The Dispossessed* is a dogmatic or perfectionist utopia. Whereas Curtis prefers to characterize it as a "skeptical utopia," however, Plaw refers to it as a pluralist book. His chapter 16 is divided into three main sections. The first deals with the theme of cross-cultural communication in the novel. In the second he turns his attention to the vexed question of which of the book's two major cultures is better or more desirable. Against those critics who contend that Le Guin offers a drearily and predictably didactic answer to this question, Plaw argues that the understanding of the worlds that Shevek's journey permits is fundamentally pluralistic and persuasive rather than monistic and moralistic. In the third part of the chapter, finally, he concludes by submitting that even if the book is more persuasive than didactic, Shevek's words and actions still do suggest some forceful (although not necessarily conclusive) reasons for choosing Anarres over Urras.

Again like Curtis, Plaw both draws from and ultimately moves beyond the theoretical framework of Berlin's liberal pluralist philosophy. The debt to Berlin is greatest in section two of the chapter. Here he argues that *The Dispossessed* offers a genuinely pluralist perspective on the worlds of Urras and Anarres inasmuch as they are portrayed as realizing incompatible but equally ultimate goods. The question of which goods, and therefore which world, ought to be preferred is not one about which reason alone can give a clear and definitive answer. Rather the answer depends in large part on which goods one values most, and on what possibilities one recognizes in human nature. This value pluralism does not mean, however, that there is no possibility for genuine discussion regarding which goods an individual does or should value. According to Plaw, the book opens such a discussion by engaging in a thought experiment concerning what an anarcho-syndicalist society might actually feel like.

This is not all it does. As he goes on to argue in section three of the chapter, the resolution of the story lends gentle affirmation to Shevek's ultimate decision to choose Anarres over Urras. For Shevek, and for Le Guin as well on Plaw's reading, what makes Anarres so special is its commitment to a distinctive form of human community. In contrast to the pallid liberal conception of community evident in Berlin's writings, Le Guin's novel "persistently portrays private property and political power interfering with human self-realization by disrupting genuine community, undermining equality, and constraining freedom." It also suggests that only a society without markets and governments can facilitate the kind of open communication that allows individuals to realize themselves freely. Importantly, it does not tell us whether Shevek's permanent revolution is ultimately viable. This is only appropriate, Plaw concludes, for "to dictate a solution to the reader, as if it could be known with certainty, would . . . run against the theme of the book. Le Guin, true to her theme, comes to the reader with empty hands."

Like Le Guin, the editors of this volume also come to the reader with empty hands. We do not pretend to offer a final, definitive analysis of the politics of *The Dispossessed*. Although our treatment of the subject matter is the most sustained and comprehensive to date, there are important aspects of it—such as the gender and sexual politics of the novel[3]—that merit more intensive consideration. Indeed, we welcome further discussion and debate on all of the topics explored in this book. Our intention is not to foreclose scholarly dialogue on the politics of

The Dispossessed, but to stimulate it. Hence the rich diversity of opinions and wide variety of perspectives in the pages that follow.

Perhaps the best way to characterize the spirit that animates this book is that of rigorous and politically engaged but fundamentally open scholarly dialogue. In this spirit we are particularly pleased to welcome the concluding contribution by Le Guin herself. In order to appreciate the extent of our pleasure, the reader may wish to imagine a particularly lively and vigorous roundtable discussion at an academic conference devoted to the work of a famous author. Unbeknownst to the participants, that author has been eavesdropping on the proceedings through the slightly open door to the neighboring seminar room. Suddenly the door swings open, the author takes to the podium, and we all turn to listen with rapt attention as she offers her own opinions about our divergent interpretations of her work.

Rather than spoil the reader's surprise by attempting to summarize Le Guin's response, we will limit ourselves here to a few comments about the intellectual significance of one element of it, namely her new and important reflections about the nature of her utopian literary craft. As Le Guin acknowledges at the very start of the piece, she has vehemently and consistently objected to the reduction of fiction to an exclusively rational presentation of "ideas." In a paper written in 1980 called "Some Thoughts on Narrative," for example, she suggests that reason is no more than a "support system" in the telling of a good story. She explains why as follows, "We cannot ask reason to take us across the gulfs of the absurd. Only the imagination can get us out of the bind of the eternal present, inventing or hypothesizing or pretending or discovering a way that reason can then follow into the infinity of options, a clue through the labyrinths of choice, a golden string, the story, leading us to the freedom that is properly human, the freedom open to those whose minds can accept unreality."[4]

Seven years later, in 1987, she sounds a similar theme in an important paper titled "Where Do You Get Your Ideas From?" Whereas in the earlier essay her primary focus is on the nature and uses of narrative, in "Where Do You Get Your Ideas From?" it is on the creative origin of her stories. Against those who assume that fiction writing originates in a single, rationally accessible idea, Le Guin emphasizes the complexity, mystery, and nonrational elements of the creative process. She observes that the conception and formation of what is going to be a story may not involve ideas in the sense of intelligible thoughts at all. It may not even involve words. Rather, it may be a matter of "mood, resonances, mental glimpses, voices, emotions, visions, dreams, anything." Reflecting on her own experience as a writer, she suggests that the deepest roots of a story lie in feeling and imagination, when "in the author's mind a feeling begins to connect itself to an image that will express it." Only later does that image lead to an idea that begins to find words for itself. It follows that the writer is not completely in control of her craft. A story "tells itself," and the writer is merely the "medium" for it. Emphasizing this point, Le Guin refers to the "blind, beautiful arrogance of the creative moment," a moment which eventually gives way to a more self-conscious and clear-sighted process of revision.[5]

Le Guin reaffirms and elaborates on her earlier position in her most recent collection of critical essays, *The Wave in the Mind*. In the 2002 paper "A Matter of Trust," for example, she advises writers to "trust the story" by relinquishing the effort to attain full control over it. In contrast to the 1987 essay just referred to, here she acknowledges explicitly that the approach stage of a story may in some cases involve "conscious planning" in the form of "sitting and thinking about the setting, the events, the characters, maybe making notes." However, having acknowledged that deliberate, conscious control may be invaluable in the planning and revision stages of composition, she emphasizes once again that "during the actual composition it seems to be best if conscious intellectual control is relaxed." Intentions, theories, and opinions must be set aside so that the story can tell itself. Moreover, and here she takes a definite stand against didactic fiction, to conceive a story or manipulate it to make it serve a purpose outside itself is "a failure of trust, of respect for the work." She elaborates as follows, "Writers want to right wrongs, or bear witness to outrages, or convince others of what they see as truth. But in so far as they let such conscious aims control their work, they narrow its potential scope and power."[6]

How then does she regard *The Dispossessed*, a literary utopia informed by an intellectually sophisticated political theory (anarchism) that she has repeatedly referred to approvingly? In 1975, just one year after the publication of *The Dispossessed*, Le Guin hazarded an answer to this question in a memorable lecture piece entitled "Science Fiction and Mrs. Brown." Roughly half way through the published version (1976) of the lecture, she turns from a general discussion of the role of character in science fiction to a more focused consideration of *The Dispossessed*. She begins at the beginning with a description of the story's creative origin. Consistent with her subsequent published remarks about the origin of her stories, she points out that the book did not come to her as an idea, or a plot, or an event, or a society, or a message, but as a vision of a person. Specifically, it originated as an intensely vivid mental image of Shevek's facial features and his strangely attractive personality. Eventually she realized that he must be a citizen of Utopia, and it then took her "years of reading and pondering and muddling" through the unfamiliar terrain of utopian and anarchist literature before she could begin to see where he came from and where he was going. In short, the effort to visualize and understand a compelling imaginary character preceded and set the course for the subsequent foray into the domain of didactic literature and political theory. Or, as Le Guin expresses the point, "Thus in the process of trying to find out who and what Shevek was, I found out a great deal else, and thought as hard as I was capable of thinking, about society, about my world, and about myself."[7]

Having articulated the creative process involved in the composition of *The Dispossessed*, she then goes on to evaluate her efforts. And it is here that the reader may be somewhat puzzled. By 1975 Le Guin had achieved the rare honor of both a Hugo and a Nebula award for her new utopian novel. Yet in the very same year she berates herself for failing fully to embody the moral proposition of the story in a mass of living experience. She also concedes that "the sound of axes being ground" is occasionally audible in the narrative. Finally, she feels compelled to defend the book's very credentials as a novel, "Yet I do believe that it is, basically, a novel, because at the heart of it you will not find an idea, or an inspirational message, or even a stone axe, but something much frailer and obscurer and more complex: a person."[8] What happened in the immediate aftermath of *The Dispossessed*'s publication to make her speak of a work that is unquestionably a masterpiece in such self-critical and defensive terms? Why in subsequent years has she continued to refer to the novel in such a puzzlingly guarded fashion?

Now, at last, we have an answer. And what an answer it is! In "A Response, by Ansible, from Tau Ceti," Le Guin exorcises the ghosts of the past and fully embraces her ambiguous creation. She is disarmingly forthright in speaking about the ways in which one-dimensional criticism of her work has distorted even her own perception and characterization of it. Over the years, she remarks, she has been driven to "slightly lunatic extremes" of protest by the tendency of many readers of science fiction novels to talk about them as if they were simply "rational presentations of ideas by means of an essentially ornamental narrative." Speaking more directly of her own experience with critics she acknowledges that when they treat her—even with much praise—as a "methodical ax-grinder," she is driven against her better judgment to deny that there is any didactic intention in her fiction. *The Dispossessed*, in particular, has given her much grief and cause for defensive and sometimes extreme counterreaction to criticism, because it has generally been discussed "as a treatise, not as a novel." Experience has taught her to expect criticism of it that, even if not actually accusing her of "preaching, moralising, political naivety, compulsive heterosexuality, or bourgeois cowardice," would prove essentially indifferent to how the book says what it says.

We refer the reader to the endnote itself to see how she now regards the novel. By way of conclusion to this Introduction we would like to offer two final observations about the character of Le Guin's present response to both the *The Dispossessed* and its critics. First, we find it humbling that Le Guin has chosen once again not to respond in kind to those of her critics who have done such an injustice to her work. Who would blame her if she did? As usual, however, she is generous to a fault.

Second, she is also characteristically much too modest about her creative accomplishments. Although notably more positive about *The Dispossessed* today than she was thirty years ago, she nevertheless concludes her response piece by likening the book to a "drafty and imaginary house." We prefer to speak of *The Dispossessed* in far more laudatory terms. If it is indeed a drafty house, then it is one such as that described in the chapters on Rivendell in Tolkien's *The Lord of the Rings*: a place of extraordinary beauty and wisdom, enlivened by ardent debate and tales of great moral courage in distant lands, as well as a source of strength

and guidance in difficult times. Le Guin's "ambiguous utopia" is certainly not perfect, but then neither is it meant to be. Rather, like Odo's revolutionary books, it
is intended as a focal point for creative, thought-provoking, and politically engaged discussion and debate. Judging by this standard it is already an unqualified
success. Whether the novel will continue to attract serious critical attention from
new generations of readers only time will tell. If the verve and vitality of the following sixteen chapters are any indication of the future, however, then we may
confidently predict that her "drafty and imaginary house" has a lease of life extending well beyond our own troubled times. So long as the injustices and oppressive wall building that gave rise to *The Dispossessed* continue unabated, then
Le Guin's novel will retain a prominent place in our imaginations as a compelling
reminder that we can do far better.

NOTES

I wish to thank Peter Stillman for kindly contributing the paragraphs of this Introduction
dealing with the "Temporal Politics" chapters by Ellen Rigsby, Jennifer Rodgers, and Tony
Burns.

   1. André Gorz, *Capitalism, Socialism, Ecology*, trans. Chris Turner (London and New
York: Verso, 1994), 81.
   2. Philip E. Smith II, "Unbuilding Walls: Human Nature and the Nature of Evolutionary and Political Theory in *The Dispossessed*," ed. Joseph D. Olander and Martin Harry
Greenberg, *Ursula K. Le Guin* (New York: Taplinger, 1979), 96.
   3. At the present time much of the scholarly commentary in this particular area is critical of Le Guin, in the opinion of the editors unfairly so. A number of our contributors attempt to correct the imbalance. We encourage other scholars to take up the challenge.
Those looking for a good introduction to the topic may wish to consult Chris Ferns, *Narrating Utopia: Ideology, Gender, Form in Utopian Literature* (Liverpool, UK: Liverpool University Press, 1999), 219–30.
   4. Ursula K. Le Guin, "Some Thoughts on Narrative," in her *Dancing at the Edge of the
World: Thoughts on Words, Women, Places* (New York: Grove Press, 1989), 45.
   5. Ursula K. Le Guin, "Where Do You Get Your Ideas From?" in *Dancing*, 193, 195, 198.
   6. Ursula K. Le Guin, "A Matter of Trust," in her *The Wave in the Mind: Talks and Essays on the Writer, the Reader, and the Imagination* (Boston: Shambhala, 2004), 224–26, 229.
   7. Ursula K. Le Guin, "Science Fiction and Mrs. Brown," ed. Peter Nicholls, *Science
Fiction at Large* (London: Victor Gollancz, 1976), 24–26.
   8. Le Guin, "Science Fiction and Mrs. Brown," 26.

WORKS CITED

Ferns, Chris. *Narrating Utopia: Ideology, Gender, Form in Utopian Literature*. Liverpool,
   UK: Liverpool University Press, 1999.

Gorz, André. *Capitalism, Socialism, Ecology.* Trans. Chris Turner. London and New York: Verso, 1994.

Le Guin, Ursula K. "A Matter of Trust." Pp. 223–34 in her *The Wave in the Mind: Talks and Essays on the Writer, the Reader, and the Imagination.* Boston: Shambhala, 2004.

———. "Science Fiction and Mrs. Brown." Pp. 13–33 in *Science Fiction at Large,* ed. Peter Nicholls. London: Gollancz, 1976.

———. "Some Thoughts on Narrative," Pp. 37–45 in her *Dancing at the Edge of the World: Thoughts on Words, Women, Places.* New York: Grove Press, 1989.

———. "Where Do You Get Your Ideas From?" Pp. 192–200 in her *Dancing at the Edge of the World: Thoughts on Words, Women, Places.* New York: Grove Press, 1989.

Smith, Philip E., II. "Unbuilding Walls: Human Nature and the Nature of Evolutionary and Political Theory in *The Dispossessed.*" Pp. 77–96 in *Ursula K. Le Guin,* ed. Joseph D. Olander and Martin Harry Greenberg. New York: Taplinger, 1979.

I

OPEN-ENDED UTOPIAN POLITICS

• / •

The Dynamic and Revolutionary Utopia of Ursula K. Le Guin

Laurence Davis

$\mathcal{O}$ne of the most powerful and persistent criticisms of utopian thinking is that it does not, and perhaps cannot, recognize the unending flow of the historical process. Unlike real societies, so this argument goes, utopias by definition have no historical roots, assume a universal consensus on values and institutional arrangements, and are isolated in space and devoid of processes tending to upset them or change their design. As a result, they are either politically irrelevant, or—if taken seriously as a model for political organization—potentially dangerous.

In this chapter, I assess the merits of the claim that utopias are necessarily static and unhistorical by considering the treatment of time in Ursula K. Le Guin's utopian novel *The Dispossessed*.[1] Looking for evidence to support the anti-utopian position, I find none. To the contrary, *The Dispossessed* demonstrates the viability of a type of utopianism that defenders and critics of utopia alike have difficulty even imagining: namely, a dynamic and revolutionary utopia premised on an acceptance of the enduring reality of social conflict and historical change. Belying the now common assumption that utopianism is dead, this nonperfectionist variant of the literary utopia demonstrates that the utopian tradition itself is not static and moribund but dynamic, endowed with the creative resources necessary to adapt to changing historical circumstances.

TIME AND FREEDOM

The Dispossessed is a utopia,[2] and it is intended as such.[3] It is not meant to be regarded as a utopia in the obsolescent perfectionist understanding of the term, however. Hence its intriguing subtitle, "An Ambiguous Utopia." We begin our analysis of the book in this chapter by considering one important respect in which

3

it is an ambiguous utopia, namely its treatment of time as an integral and enduring part of human life.

As even those who are most sympathetic to the utopian tradition are now likely to concede, the vast majority of literary utopias have been static states, seemingly devoid of processes tending to upset them or change their design. Naomi Jacobs, for example, argues that this is no less true of many progressive utopias written in the nineteenth century than it is of the bulk of those produced in the Renaissance period or Greek antiquity. According to Jacobs (and Lewis Mumford, on whose scholarship she relies to support this particular point), the stasis and symmetry of the classical utopias was a conscious product of the attempt to imitate an elegantly balanced and stable divine creation. While some utopias, such as Campanella's, attempt to incorporate progress by importing new ideas and technologies, their only movement is "that of a spinning wheel, a kind of stasis."[4] Even the so-called "dynamic" utopias of such late nineteenth-century or early twentieth-century utopian writers as Bellamy, Gilman, and Wells are unconvincing, because no future can be projected for them other than a larger or purer version of what they already have. This content-driven stasis is matched by the narrative stasis of the standard utopian form. As Jacobs rightly points out, the familiar narrative resolution of the conflict between the visitor to utopia and his or her utopian guide, in which the visitor's doubts are all quickly overcome, seems to promise a disturbingly final resolution of all residual conflict, questioning, and unhappiness.

In *The Dispossessed* Le Guin breaks radically from this static utopian tradition. She does so, I contend, by imagining a genuinely dynamic and revolutionary utopia in which the past never assumes a final shape and the future never shuts its doors. "We are the children of time" (13: 385), Shevek declares in the novel's final few pages, and by that point one requires little persuasion of the truth of his observation.

As evidence for this argument, consider, first, the novel's complex theoretical discussions about the nature of time. On an initial reading of the book the pages devoted to such speculation may seem baffling, especially to nonscientific readers unlikely to be familiar with the intricacies of Simultaneity theory, Einstein's theory of relativity, or quantum physics. Those interested in the political implications of the book are apt to ignore them altogether. I believe that this is a mistake, as careful study of the text reveals both a coherent pattern to its temporal theory and a plausible link between its conceptions of time and human freedom.

In order to understand the logic of these connections as clearly as possible, it may be helpful to pause for a moment to consider a somewhat esoteric philosophical paper on the nature of time published just a few years before Le Guin began composing *The Dispossessed*. The reason for focusing on this particular essay—entitled "Time as Succession and the Problem of Duration"—is suggested in a footnote to James Bittner's book-length study of Le Guin, *Approaches to the Fiction of Ursula K. Le Guin* (1984).[5] According to Bittner, J.T. Fraser's anthology

The Voices of Time (1968) "may be the single most important source, after the writings of several anarchists, of Le Guin's ideas in *The Dispossessed*."[6]

In support of this view Bittner quotes some remarks made by Le Guin in a 1975 interview conducted for the *Portland Scribe* newspaper. Asked by the interviewer how she "came up" with the novel's theory of Simultaneity, Le Guin answered: "there are shelves of books about space and space-time, but there's *one* main reference for thinking about time, either from a physics point of view or from philosophy. It's called *The Voices of Time*, an anthology. He's collected all the main articles. . . . Sequency and Simultaneity seem to be the basic question. As well as I understood it I tried to work it into the book. It got absolutely fascinating."[7] Turning to Fraser's weighty anthology, one is rewarded with a range of stimulating papers that shed some light on the genesis and human significance of the novel's temporal theory. Most helpful of all in this regard is Friedrich Kümmel's "Time as Succession and the Problem of Duration."

According to Kümmel, philosophers of time have traditionally conceived the nature of the relation between past, present, and future as essentially one of vanishing succession. They have assumed, in other words, that while a particular time exists at present, there is a time which "not yet" is, but which will sometime come into being, as well as a time which, already having been, "no longer" exists. From this perspective, time is never present as a whole, but is divided into the elements of a succession. It consists of two periods delimited by the present and continually passing into one another, so that what was previously a future is "now" a present and will soon be a past.

The problem with this view is that it fails to do justice to time's real, abiding quality. If something is to endure, then its past may never be simply "past," but must in some way also remain "present." It follows that an alternative theory of time is required, specifically one which accounts for duration without negating temporal succession. Toward this end, Kümmel proposes a conception of time as a correlation of future, past, and present in which past and future may *coexist* with the present *conjointly*. Granted their independent individual nature and determination, the coexistence of past and future is no longer in contradiction with the present. All periods may be conceived of as existing at one and the same time. This incessant interweaving of the "times" does not however, as in Bergson's philosophy, imply their fusion. For only the past *as* past and the future *as* future are able to make the present, entering into it and giving it foundation.

Being primarily concerned with metaphysical questions, Kümmel does not offer much in the way of social theory. He does, however, help lay the groundwork for such theory by speculating on the implications of his "life-sustaining" conception of time for a theory of human freedom. As he observes more than once, man[8] is unique among organic beings in his ability to condition the order of his time himself. Indeed, "the main difference" between animal and human life is the complete lack of time consciousness in the former.[9] The animal remains always limited to its spatial situation, living the strict correlation of organism and environment. Unable to put a distance between the past and its own being, or to imagine a future that might enable it to transcend itself, it is forever bound to the present. Man, by contrast, is able to transform his environment into a world in which he can act freely. Being a time-conscious organism, he is able to relate himself freely to both his past and his future. By this means, he is also able actively to mediate the present. The exercise of this freedom is by no means a precondition for his survival. He may, for example, struggle to "emancipate" himself from time by attempting to live only in the present moment. Ultimately, however, such efforts are self-defeating. They are products of a compulsive reaction rather than free agency, and invariably end in subjection to the tyranny of time.

The alternative is to work with time rather than against it. This one does by accepting the reality of past and future, and by recognizing the interconnections between them. What, specifically, does the latter of these conditions entail? Most importantly, it entails a recognition that no act of man is possible with reference solely to the past or solely to the future, but is always dependent upon their interaction. Thus, for example, the future may be considered as the horizon against which plans are made, the past a source of the means for their realization, and the present the time in which these plans and means are mediated and actualized. From this perspective, the future represents the possibility, and the past the basis, of a free life in the present. Both, according to this view, are always found intertwined with the present. As Kümmel memorably puts it, "in the *open circle* of future and past there exists no possibility which is not made concrete by real conditions, nor any realization which does not bring with it new possibilities. This interrelation of reciprocal conditions is a historical process in which the past never assumes a final shape nor the future ever shuts its doors."[10]

Returning now to Le Guin's work, we are able to see the marked influence of these ideas, and thus are in a better position to understand the novel's treatment of the themes of time and human freedom. Like Kümmel, *The Dispossessed*'s scientifically brilliant protagonist Shevek rejects the received and much too simplistic view that time is essentially vanishing succession. This is most clearly apparent in chapter 7 of the book, in which we find Shevek attending a party hosted by Vea, the beautiful and seductive sister of one of his host/captors at the Ieu Eun University in A-Io. Never having been exposed to alcohol before, he has drunk too much, is in fact drunk. As a result, he finds himself speaking freely about a subject he had previously been careful to keep to himself, his pursuit of a General Temporal Theory. The initial provocation for his talkativeness is an offhand comment by an overbearing and irritatingly insistent businessman named Dearri. "As I see it," he informs Shevek, "your Simultaneity Theory simply denies the most obvious fact about time, the fact that time passes." Shevek's reply is a classic defense of block time of the sort that would have made Einstein proud, "Within the strict terms of Simultaneity Theory, succession is not considered as a physically objective phenomenon, but as a subjective one" (7: 221). In other words, we think that time flows past us; but what if it is we who move forward, from past to future, always discovering the new? When Dearri replies in characteristically prag-matic fashion that any such theoretical speculation is irrelevant, since we in fact experience the universe only as a succession, Shevek points to the obvious limita-tions of this common misconception. As he observes correctly, "it is only in con-sciousness, it seems, that we experience time at all" (7: 222). In a dream, for ex-ample, there is no time. Succession is changed about, and cause and effect are mixed together. Myths and legends share this timeless quality. So, too, does mys-ticism, as when the mystic makes the reconnection of his reason and his uncon-scious, and sees all becoming as one being.

Significantly, Shevek does not defend Simultaneity theory in order to deny the reality of temporal succession. Rather, like Kümmel, he does so in order to make the point that although succession is a necessary feature of time, it is by no means a sufficient basis for understanding human life in its temporality. As he goes on to explain, his Simultaneity theory is an effort to strike a balance in our understanding of the nature of time. Sequency, he concedes, explains beautifully our sense of linear time, and the evidence of evolution. It includes creation, and mortality. There it stops, however. It deals with all that changes, but it cannot ex-plain why things also endure. It speaks only of the arrow of time, but never of the circle of time. A true chronosophy, on the other hand, would "provide a field in which the relation of the two aspects or processes of time could be understood" (7: 224). Hence Shevek's lifelong quest to reconcile Simultanist and Sequentist thinking in a model of the cosmos that includes not only duration but creation, not only being but becoming, not only geometry but ethics.

Consideration of Shevek's scientific quest suggests another respect in which Le Guin's treatment of time in *The Dispossessed* is similar to Kümmel's. Like him, she attempts to do justice to both the enduring and the successive as-pects of the cosmos by playing with the idea of an open conception of time in which past and future are always found intertwined with each other, and with the present. This unorthodox temporal philosophy is integrated into the text of the novel in a number of subtle, and fascinating, ways. Consider, for example, the evocative symbolism of the Odonian Circle of Life. Described by Le Guin in personal correspondence as "a circle—not quite closed,"[11] it immediately calls to mind Kümmel's characterization of the relationship between past and future as an "open circle" in which the past never assumes a final shape nor the future ever shuts its doors.

Note, as well, the striking image of the interstellar starship that transports Shevek on his return journey from Urras to Anarres, the *Davenant*. Like the Cir-cle of Life, the *Davenant* is replete with temporal symbolism. As Bittner points out, "If 'Davenant' comes from the French *avenement* (coming, advent), or French *avenir* (future, future ages), or both, then *d'avenant* may be Le Guin's French neologism meaning 'from the beginning' or 'of the future' (a synthesis of beginning and ending, of etiology and teleology)."[12] The plausibility of this in-terpretation is confirmed by the explicit contrast Le Guin draws between

Shevek's perception of time on the home-like *Davenant*, and on the prison-like *Mindful* (the freighter that originally transports him from Anarres to Urras). On the *Mindful*, Shevek passes the hours and days of his voyage in a feverish vacancy, "a dry and wretched void without past or future" (1: 9). The walls of the ship stand tight about him, and time appears to have stopped. When he looks at the clock set in the wall by his bed, he observes that its pointer moves "from one to another of the twenty figures of the dial, meaningless" (1: 9). On the *Davenant*, by contrast, Shevek experiences time contentedly and meditatively. Barely aware of his Hainish traveling companions, he ponders his home world's "hope deceived," its "promise kept," and "the sources within his spirit, unsealed at last, of joy" (13: 382).

These are hardly isolated examples. Even the narrative structure of the novel calls attention to its author's sustained reflection on the nature of time. Eleven of the book's thirteen chapters alternate between Urras and Anarres, generating a creative dialectic in which the relationship between the two worlds becomes a symbol for the interrelationship of past, present, and future. This is apparent in both the narrative time of the novel, in which Urras represents the present and Anarres the past, and in its historical time, in which Urras represents the past and Anarres the future. It is evident as well in the shape of the tale as a whole, a chiasmus[13] connecting the first chapter ("Anarres—Urras") with the last ("Urras—Anarres") in an open circle.

The human significance of these various temporal symbols is first explicitly flagged in chapter 3. Having just been introduced to Pae, Oiie, and his other "hosts" at the Ieu Eun University in A-Io, Shevek explains to them that he has come to Urras in order to "unbuild walls" between the sister worlds, "You are our history. We are perhaps your future. . . . We must know each other" (3: 75). Even at this early stage in the narrative, Shevek understands that the Odonians who left Urras in order to settle Anarres had been wrong to deny their history. In their "desperate courage" to forge a better future, they had "turned their backs on the Old World and its past." They had "opted for the future only," and in so doing, failed to appreciate that "as surely as the future becomes the past, the past becomes the future" (3: 89). He recognizes, in other words, that when his forebears attempted to make a clean break from their past on Urras by starting afresh on Anarres, they failed to reckon with the unending flow of the historical process. They cut themselves off from history, and in so doing, doomed themselves to the status of "exiles" and their dynamic anarchist ideal to inevitable ossification and decay.

What Shevek does not yet apprehend is how to reconnect past and future in order to realize the neglected utopian possibilities latent in his present. The reason for this incomprehension is that he has replicated the mistakes of the past. Just as the Odonian settlers of Anarres became exiles by denying their past on Urras, so he has become an exile by disavowing his past on Anarres. As he muses in his rooms at the Ieu Eun University at the close of chapter 3, "He was alone, here, because he came from a self-exiled society. . . . The Settlers had taken one step away. He had taken two" (3: 89–90).

Along with many other comparable passages later on in the book, this one alludes to what I take to be the primary *political* aspiration animating Le Guin's treatment of time in *The Dispossessed*: namely, to illuminate the ways in which different conceptions of the relationship between utopia and existing reality may either enrich or constrain the possibilities of free human choice and meaningful action. In the course of the novel, the reader is exposed to two very different such conceptions grounded in two very different understandings of the nature of time. The first is the static assumption that utopian ideals occupy a fixed space outside time and history. On this view, time is but a trifling and ephemeral element of human life. The second is the dynamic recognition that utopian ideals are intimately bound up with time and history. According to this point of view, time is an integral and enduring part of human life. The psychological, ethical, and political consequences of choosing one or another of these abstract positions is clarified for us by Le Guin in her concrete, literary description of the changing relationship between Urras and Anarres.

In roughly the first two-thirds of the work, a vivid account of Shevek's alienating experiences on both Anarres and Urras prompts the reader to observe that there has been a total break between the two worlds, with disastrous consequences for both. Deprived of the utopian promise of greater human solidarity, Urras has become soulless and hopeless, an unchanging and interminable war of each against all. Cut off from non-propagandistic knowledge of the human suffering in which its utopian ideals are rooted, Anarres has become as characterless and stagnant as its barren desert landscape. If on one world Shevek finds a rigid utopian ideal, on the other he discovers an equally rigid, idealless present. In later chapters, by contrast, Shevek's growing political awareness and increasingly sophisticated understanding of the nature of time move him to take action which opens up the possibility of a more interactive and dynamic relationship between the sister worlds. In this creative dialectic of utopia and existing reality, the Anarresti utopia provides the hope that is the catalyst for revolution on Urras, while the continuing reality of oppression and injustice on Urras reminds the Anarresti of why they must be eternally vigilant in testing, protecting, and renewing their anarchism. Each, in other words, gives the other what it lacks in isolation: the reason to go on changing.[14]

In the remainder of this chapter, we will consider in some detail the textual evidence for these propositions, starting with the novel's dramatic exploration of the consequences of pursuing a static and timeless conception of utopia. More specifically, we will consider first, Le Guin's portrayal in the early Anarres chapters of a timeless utopia cut off from its past; and second, her depiction in the early Urras chapters of a timeless present cut off from its possible utopian future. We will then conclude the chapter by elucidating the alternative, dynamic, and revolutionary utopian vision sketched in the book's final chapters.

THE STATIC UTOPIA

Perhaps the most direct and scathing indictment of the course taken by the Anarresti utopia since its founding settlers' decision to break from the past appears in chapter 6 of the novel, in a powerfully written dialogue between Shevek and his boyhood friend Bedap. As Bedap reminds Shevek, there is nothing more basic to Odonian thought than the notion that "change is freedom, change is life" (6: 166). Over time, however, the overwhelming majority of Anarresti have either forgotten or deliberately chosen to disregard this fundamental truth. Rather than risk public disapproval by challenging received wisdom and established practices, they have settled into comfortable, safe hierarchies. Rather than struggle to think critically about their society's development, they have opted for the easier alternative of allowing others to think for them. As a result, the dynamic and revolutionary anarchist utopia envisaged by Odo has degenerated into a static society characterized first and foremost by conformity and obedience.

Of the many dangerous consequences of this state of affairs, Bedap calls Shevek's attention to two. First, it has led to what John Stuart Mill famously referred to in his essay *On Liberty* as a "tyranny of the majority." According to Mill, those who wish to protect individual liberty must be vigilant against more than just the tyranny of the magistrate. They must guard as well against "the tyranny of the prevailing opinion and feeling; against the tendency of society to impose, by other means than civil penalties, its own ideas and practices as rules of conduct on those who dissent from them; to fetter the development, and, if possible, prevent the formation, of any individuality not in harmony with its ways, and compel all characters to fashion themselves upon the model of its own."[15] This, in effect, is the point made by Bedap, though in his case in the form of a story. The story he tells Shevek concerns their mutual friend Tirin, a nonconformist character who composes and performs a play that is misinterpreted by his dogmatic fellow Anarresti as anti-Odonian. As a result, he receives a public reprimand. Formerly used to "cut a bossy gang-foreman or manager down to size," this informal sanction is used in Bedap's day only "to tell an individual to stop thinking for himself" (6: 169–70). Tragically, it has precisely this effect on Tirin. Imbalanced by the experience, he becomes paranoid, and is shipped off for "therapy" to an insane asylum on some remote island. Thus is dissent neutralized, and the cozy social consensus preserved.

The second dangerous consequence cited by Bedap follows directly from the first. In refusing to think for themselves, the people of Anarres opened the door to those who would think and govern for them. In the early years of the settlement, people were well aware that the institutionalization of mutual aid created opportunities for those who wished to exercise power over others. They understood that the need for expertise and stable administrative institutions brought with it the danger of a creeping bureaucratization of Anarresti society. As a result, they took appropriate measures to guard against this possibility. So well did they succeed, however, that their progeny forgot that the will to dominance is as much a part of human beings as the impulse to mutual aid is, and has to be trained in each individual, in each new generation. They forgot, in other words, that "nobody's born an Odonian any more than he's born civilized!" (6: 168). This collective amnesia manifested itself in the changing nature of Anarresti education. If the educational system originally taught the young to become independent-minded, freethinking adults who would question, adapt, and develop their society's values and institutions, over time it taught them instead to "parrot Odo's words as if they were *laws*" (6: 168). As the educational system became rigid, moralistic, and authoritarian, so too eventually did society itself. Once a "living thing," the social conscience degenerated into what Bedap describes as a "power-machine" controlled by bureaucrats (6: 167).

In chapters 2, 4, 6, and 8 (what we referred to earlier as "the early Anarres chapters"), we gradually come to appreciate the truth of Bedap's remarks as we learn more about Anarres through Shevek's young eyes. If there is a prominent common theme in these chapters, it is Shevek's alienation from the ossifying utopian world into which he is born. In chapter 2, for example, we first encounter Shevek as a baby in the nursery. Denied his spot in the sun by another child, Shevek pushes the intruder away. This draws a reprimand from the matron of the nursery, who instructs him in typical Anarresti fashion, "Nothing is yours. . . . It is to share. If you will not share it, you cannot use it" (2: 27). Shevek's assertiveness is again an issue when we see him next as a schoolboy, aged eight years. Having volunteered to speak in a "Speaking-and-Listening" group, Shevek proceeds to describe to the assembled students his own invented variation of Zeno's paradox. This prompts a harsh reprimand from the bewildered director of the group, who informs him that "Speech is sharing—a cooperative art. You're not sharing, merely egoizing" (2: 29). On both occasions, Shevek breaks down in tears. A naturally assertive individual in a society bent on preserving the status quo by stamping out all forms of self-assertion, Shevek feels acutely his alienation from prevailing social norms. As a result, he withdraws into the fertile world of his own mind, and embarks upon a consoling quest for the assurance of permanence represented by mathematical certainty. He also rationalizes his plight by internalizing a rigid social morality. This is evident in a scene in the middle of chapter 2, in which we find Shevek and four other young science students aged fifteen or sixteen discussing Anarresti society. One of the four, the young Tirin, expresses a number of perfectly reasonable criticisms of his world's foreign policy. He questions, in particular, the restrictions on unauthorized communication with Urras, and the absence of up-to-date, non-propagandistic information about contemporary Urrasti society. Shevek's too quick, dogmatic reply (2: 45) reveals all too plainly his stubborn refusal to think critically about the very social norms that generate and perpetuate his alienation.

The pattern of alienation and rationalization set in Shevek's early years repeats itself as he grows to maturity. This is particularly evident in his psychologically and ethically damaging accommodation with his research supervisor at the prestigious Central Institute of the Sciences, the thoroughly distasteful Sabul. A domineering hypocrite who has exploited the mistrust between Urras and Anarres in order to establish his senior position at the Institute (he plagiarized untranslated Urrasti physics texts), Sabul pressures Shevek into concealing his supervisor's misdeeds. He also exploits him by making the publication of his work conditional on Sabul being named as coauthor. Despite his profound ethical misgivings, Shevek is complicit in these arrangements. He rationalizes his situation as follows: "But all I want to do is get the job done. . . . It's my duty, it's my joy, it's the purpose of my whole life. The man I have to work with is competitive, a dominance-seeker, a profiteer, but I can't change that; if I want to work, I have to work with him" (4: 117). In order to get on with his work, in other words, Shevek chooses to overlook the corrupt power that it is being made to serve.

Just as the original settlers of Anarres fled to Urras's moon rather than continue the revolutionary struggle on Urras, and just as their descendants agreed to make Anarres a mining colony of Urras in order to forestall an Urrasti invasion, so for the sake of his career does Shevek permit Sabul to violate all the Odonian principles he holds most dear. As it turns out, the sacrifice is in vain. Chapter 8 closes with Shevek's dismissal from his teaching post at the Institute. Fittingly, it is Sabul who, barely able to conceal his joy, hypocritically informs Shevek that one of the main reasons why he was let go was due to his "privatism" and "non-altruism." Having sacrificed his principles in a futile effort to avoid confronting the ultimate source of both his own psychological alienation and Sabul's exploitative power over him—namely, the terms of the Odonian settlement which effectively wall Anarres off from Urras—Shevek's reward is the loss of his one abiding consolation.

This last observation suggests the flip side of Le Guin's dramatization of the pitfalls of a timeless, or static, conception of utopia. If in the early Anarres chapters the recurring motif is Shevek's alienation from the isolated, ossifying utopia into which he is born, in the early Urras chapters (chapters 1, 3, 5, and 7) the primary focus is his alienation from the equally static, idealless present to which he flees as an exile.

In chapter 1, describing Shevek's journey from Anarres to Urras, the reader is introduced to the book's most frequently recurring symbol of both Shevek's alienation and the social sources of that alienation—namely, the metaphor of the wall. The novel opens with a vivid description of the wall that separates Anarres from its Space Port. Early on in the chapter, Shevek crosses this wall in order to board the freighter that transports him to Urras. Significantly, however, the wall remains standing after his departure. So, too, does the idea it represents: the damming back (to borrow a metaphor from the opening pages of H. G. Wells's *A*

Modern Utopia) of change and development on Urras and Anarres by their almost complete separation under the terms of the Odonian Settlement.

That this mutual isolation is a mistake quickly becomes apparent as the action of the first chapter unfolds. Unlike in many early modern utopias, where wall imagery conveys a sense of the security and permanence of utopia (think, for example, of the walls surrounding each of the seven concentric circles of Campanella's *City of the Sun*), in *The Dispossessed* this same image takes on a much more negative evaluative charge. On board the *Mindful*, Shevek regards the walls of his room as like those of a "prison" (1: 8). Loath to occupy his quarters, he acquiesces only after repeated pleadings and urgings from Kimoe, the ship's doctor. Later, as the hours and days of the journey pass by in a dry and wretched void "without past or future," the room's walls appear to stand "tight about him" (1: 9). This claustrophobia develops into a violent rage when he discovers that the door to the room has been locked from the outside (1: 10–11). In conversation with Kimoe, Shevek observes that "there were walls around all his thoughts" (1: 16). This is particularly apparent in their conversation about the social status of Urrasti women, in the course of which Shevek reflects that the poor doctor had been (metaphorically speaking) "pounding his hands against the locked door and shouting" (1: 17). Even after his arrival on Urras, Shevek notes that the lights of the car transporting him from the space port to the University "shone on the mist ahead as if on a wall that kept retreating before them" (1: 21).

By the end of the first chapter, Le Guin has sown the seeds of what will later develop into a mature literary challenge to the perfectionist conception of utopia as a timeless idyll dammed off forever against the wide river of history. Even at this early point in the novel, however, the familiar utopian image of the wall begins to take on a new, and more menacing, cast. Rather than convey a reassuring feeling of safety and security, it instead calls to mind Shevek's pointed comment to his caretakers when they finally unlock the door to his quarters on the *Mindful*, "To lock out, to lock in, the same act" (1: 11).

In chapters 3, 5, and 7, the focus of the novel shifts exclusively to Urras. Here, as in the early Anarres chapters, the problems generated or exacerbated by the terms of the Odonian Settlement are not spelled out directly and immediately for the reader. Rather, in keeping with the conventions of the novel, they are suggested indirectly and gradually through the story of Shevek's grudging and alienated perception of them. Importantly, Shevek must scale the walls damming back change and development in his own mind before he can even begin to pursue his professed aim of unbuilding the political and cultural walls separating Urras and Anarres.

In chapter 3, dealing with his introduction to Urras, we find him overwhelmed by what he sees. Having turned his back on Anarres, he idealizes its opposite as a kind of paradise. From his sheltered point of view in the cozy environs of the Ieu Eun University, Urras appears to be blessed with breathtaking natural beauty, limitless prosperity and technological sophistication, and a complex culture rooted in a rich and varied history. Even the most blatant warning signs that all is not as benign as it appears to be are disregarded, suppressed, or rationalized. This is true of the bowing and scraping of his servant (3: 66), the patronizing views of women articulated by his academic colleagues (3: 73–75), Chifoilisk's remark to him that the Ioti government is footing the bill of his stay (3: 70), Pae's falseness (3: 75), the restricted nature of his access to Urrasti society (3: 81–84), and the too keen interest shown by just about everybody in his General Temporal Theory. Near the end of the chapter, an unguarded comment made by the engineer supervising Shevek's tour of the Ioti Space Research Foundation alerts him to his keepers' far from altruistic motivations. This, in turn, leads him to reflect critically on the vivid contrast between the showy and colorful domes of the Space Research Foundation and the grim, black façade of the prison towers in which Odo had been imprisoned for nine years. In spite of his misgivings, however, Shevek clings desperately to his idealized picture of Urrasti society. What changes as a result of his experience at the Space Research Foundation is his state of mind. By the end of chapter 3 Shevek's familiar sense of alienation returns with a vengeance. He is overcome by self-pity, a paralyzing self-doubt, and the lonely feeling that he belongs to neither world.

These feelings persist in chapter 5, the main narrative focus of which is Shevek's acclimatization to life on Urras. As he begins to settle into a routine, he is exposed to fresh warning signs of the darker sides of Urrasti prosperity and hospitality. For example, he is appalled to discover the existence of a mechanical, university-level examination system that compels students to cram in information and then disgorge it on demand.[16] Equally troubling is the crudely utilitarian rationale for that system. As he soon discovers, all of his students are planning careers as academic or industrial scientists. Rather than take an interest in what he has to offer them for its own sake, they see it simply as a means to professional success (5: 128). Another warning sign is the commodified nature of the Ioti system of production and distribution. During his second week in A-Io, Shevek is taken shopping in the capital city's most elegant retail street. There he discovers "acres of luxuries, acres of excrement," a bewildering array of things "either useless to begin with" or ornamented so as to disguise their use (5: 132). Even more bewildering to Shevek is the fact that the producers of all these things are out of sight, "behind walls." Those in the shops therefore have no relation to the items on sale but that of possession. Despite all such indications that Urras is anything but the vibrant and dynamic land of the free he imagines it to be, however, Shevek persists in blaming himself and his Anarresti background for his inability to take in all the riches that his host world has to offer. He also continues to abide tamely the restrictions imposed upon him by the Urrasti authorities.

Not until the climactic chapter 7 does Shevek attempt to scale the walls erected by his captors and his own psyche in order to see Urras without the comfort of illusions. Jolted out of his complacency by, among other things, an anonymous letter sent to him by members of the Urrasti resistance movement, Shevek decides to take an unauthorized trip to the capital city of A-Io. The journey proves to be a revelation, not only for Shevek, but also for the unsuspecting reader suddenly confronted with a panoramic view of a world bereft of utopian promise and paralyzed in a deadly acquiescence to the given. Through Shevek's alienated and estranged eyes we are able to glimpse for the first time the sheer lifeless, mechanical ugliness and moral vacuousness of Urrasti society. With him we notice the "certain sameness" of expression on people's faces, all etched with unmistakable signs of anxiety, aggression, and loneliness (7: 207). We shudder with Morris-like revulsion at the degradation of art under capitalism when he escapes from "the moral claustrophobia" of the streets into an art gallery, only to be confronted there by an art dealer who remarks of a skillfully painted but outrageously priced nude that has caught the Anarresti's eye, "That's a Fei Feite. . . . We had five a week ago. Biggest thing on the art market before long. A Feite is a sure investment, sir" (7: 209). We are horrified and disgusted when Vea guides him through a palace preserved as a museum of the ancient times of royalty, and remarks casually of a Queen's cloak made of the tanned skins of rebels flayed alive, "It looks awfully like goatskin to me" (7: 217). Having read earlier in the chapter of the treatment meted out to the Benbili rebels, and being aware of the tragic fate that awaits the Ioti dissidents in chapter 9, we are sickened again when she attempts to reassure a visibly shaken Shevek, "But it's all just history. Things like that couldn't happen now!" (7: 217).

Even more disturbing than any of these individual examples of what life detached from utopian ideals may become is the fatuous natural law doctrine that rationalizes and legitimates such a sad state of affairs, and thus ensures that it remains closed to radical challenge and change. What is this anti-utopian doctrine? Vea sums it up succinctly when she declares to Shevek that "The law of evolution is that the strongest survives!" (7: 220). Fittingly, it is in Vea's company that Shevek finally challenges this Urrasti variant of our own Earthly social Darwinism.

He is still alienated and alone in the brilliantly satirical party scene that constitutes the final part of chapter 7, but he is no longer an uncritical observer. In a telling foretaste of things to come, he subjects the Urrasti "survival of the strongest" mentality to rigorous ethical criticism. This is apparent in the debate with Vea, when he counters her declaration that the law of evolution is the survival of the strongest with the observation, "Yes, and the strongest, in the existence of any social species, are those who are most social. In human terms, most ethical" (7: 220). It is clear in his magnificent drunken outburst to the stunned assemblage of Vea's party guests:

> On Anarres nothing is beautiful, nothing but the faces . . . the men and women. We have nothing but that, nothing but each other. Here you see the jewels, there you see the eyes. And in the eyes you see . . . the splendor of the human spirit. Because our men and women are free—possessing nothing, they are free. And you the possessors are possessed. (7: 228–29)

Most relevantly of all to our present effort to highlight the novel's dramatization of the dangers of a static conception of utopia, it is evident in his speculative remarks about the nature of time. As he points out in response to a question from one of the guests, chronosophy involves ethics. It does so because our sense of time involves our ability to separate cause and effect, means and end. Babies or animals do not see the difference between what they do now and what will happen because of it. Adult human beings can. Seeing the difference between now and not now, they can make the connection between the two. They can understand that actions undertaken in the present are necessarily entrained in a temporal trajectory that extends into the past and future. And if they can do this, then they can also understand the need for morality and responsibility. For, as Shevek comments persuasively, "To break a promise is to deny the reality of the past; therefore it is to deny the hope of a real future. If time and reason are functions of each other, if we are creatures of time, then we had better know it, and try . . . to act responsibly" (7: 225).

In other words, if we are who we are only over time, then the attempt to live in and for nothing but the present is a radically inadequate expression of our humanity. It represents not human freedom, but barbarism of the sort so ubiquitous among the so-called "civilized" peoples of Urras. This, in effect, is the point suggested by Le Guin in her frequent references to the beautiful wrappings and trappings of Urrasti life. Strip these away, she seems to be saying, and you are left with nothing but "States and their weapons, the rich and their lies, and the poor and their misery" (11: 346). You are left with a superficially sophisticated people reduced to its blind instincts and immediate needs, as Shevek is at the end of chapter 7 when he drunkenly ejaculates onto the white silk of Vea's pleated party dress and vomits into a silver platter dotted with tiny stuffed pastries delicately arranged in the shape of a flower.

THE DYNAMIC AND REVOLUTIONARY UTOPIA

Having now examined in some detail the novel's dramatization of the consequences of pursuing a static and timeless conception of utopia, let us proceed to elucidate the alternative, dynamic, and revolutionary utopian vision sketched in the book's final chapters. Before we do so, however, let us first contextualize the task by considering Le Guin's own characteristically wise, witty, and eloquent observations about utopia in an essay entitled "A Non-Euclidean View of California as a Cold Place to Be."[17]

Originally conceived as a lecture delivered in honor of the memory of the late utopian scholar Robert Elliott, Le Guin's essay takes its title in part from a term borrowed by Elliott from the work of Russian writers such as Dostoevsky and Zamyatin. The utopia of the Grand Inquisitor, she explains by quoting approvingly the following line from Elliott's book *The Shape of Utopia*, "is the product of 'the Euclidean mind' (a phrase Dostoevsky often used), which is obsessed by the idea of regulating all life by reason and bringing happiness to man whatever the cost."[18] Here, in a nutshell, is the vision of utopia that Le Guin is reacting against. Controlling in essence, the Euclidean utopia is a reaction of will and reason "against, away from, the here-and-now." It is "pure structure without content; pure model; goal." As a result, it is also static, mechanical, uninhabitable, and potentially destructive of both itself and existing reality. The Euclidean utopia, Le Guin observes damningly, is "a power trip . . . a monotheocracy, declared by executive decree, and maintained by willpower." As its premise is "progress, not process," it has no habitable present, and speaks only in the future tense. In the end, even "reason itself" must reject it.

Against this Euclidean conception of utopia, Le Guin outlines her own very different—let us call it "Le Guinean"—picture of utopia. Whereas the Euclidean utopia looks only to the future, the focus of the Le Guinean utopia is the temporally extended present, the "right here, right now" inhabited by living, breathing human beings. Paradoxically, it is such that if it is to come, then it must exist already. In fact, it has existed already, as a feature of many of the so-called "primitive" societies crushed under the wheels of European capitalism and technological "progress." Its essence was and is a state of society in which human beings are at peace with themselves and their environment. Animated by a generous Spirit of Place rather than an exclusive and aggressive Spirit of Race, the Le Guinean ideal society is concerned predominantly with preserving its existence. It has a modest standard of living, conservative of natural resources, as well as a low constant fertility rate and a political life based upon consent. [19]

From the perspective of those obsessed by technological "progress" and "modernization," such a social vision may appear to be regressive, politically naïve, Luddite, and antirational. However, such criticisms might be more appropriately leveled at the utopian vision of William Morris than Ursula Le Guin, for unlike him, she is sensitive to the need to maintain the conditions necessary to nourish a degree of social dynamism and change.[20] As she points out on a number of occasions in the course of the essay, she is not advocating an Arcadian, or pastoral, social vision. Her intent is "not reactionary, nor even conservative, but simply subversive."[21] Convinced that the utopian imagination is trapped, like capitalism and industrialism and the human population, in a one-way future consisting only of growth, she is, as she says quite memorably, simply trying "to put a pig on the tracks."

These claims are borne out, in particular, by her unusually nuanced attitude toward technology. Unlike those who reject all technology out of hand on the grounds that it is inherently control-oriented and antisocial, Le Guin recognizes that technology in one form or another is an essential element of all human cultures. It is also an important means of making life materially easier, and an "endless creative source."[22] Very important, she does not reject technology per se, but rather "faith in the continuous advance of technology as the way towards utopia."[23] As she quite rightly suggests, such a faith is one of the primary sources of the invasive, self-replicating, mechanical forward drive of modern civilization.[24] It is likely to lead not to the utopian vision of a world where machines do all the work while human beings sit back and play, but to the sort of terrifying dystopian vision depicted in E. M. Forster's science-fiction tale "The Machine Stops." As an alternative to this nightmare scenario, Le Guin offers us the realistic utopian vision of a low technology, organically evolving society at peace with itself and its environment.[25] She also redeems both the concept and fictional practice of utopia by following it "into the abyss which yawns behind the Grand Inquisitor's vision,"[26] and then emerging into a bright new world that turns out on closer inspection to be a long-neglected but always-present possibility of our own.

Returning now to the text of *The Dispossessed*, we are better able to appreciate the magnitude and precise nature of its break from the static utopian tradition. My main argument in what follows is that Le Guin succeeds in *The Dispossessed* in creating something that defenders and critics of utopia alike have difficulty even imagining: namely, a genuinely dynamic and revolutionary utopia premised on an acceptance of the enduring reality of social conflict and historical change. She does so, I contend, by representing utopia not as a timeless and unattainable state of perfection, but as a time-sensitive, revolutionary critical perspective that can expand the opportunities for free human choice and meaningful action by helping to break open the horizon of historical possibility.

As evidence for this argument, consider first the dramatic developments in chapter 9 that inject the novel with a fresh sense of life, possibility, and revolutionary urgency. Whereas in previous chapters Shevek experiences the passage of time as a wretched, continuous present without past or future, in the course of chapter 9 he begins the difficult process of reconnecting past and future in order to realize the neglected utopian possibilities latent in his present. He does so both as a scientist, and as an Odonian anarchist.

Influenced perhaps by the anarchist writer Paul Goodman's insight that "professionals, at least, become radicalized when they try to pursue their professions with integrity and courage—their professions are what they know and care about—and they find that many things must be changed,"[27] Le Guin plots Shevek's scientific breakthrough as the first major development in chapter 9. The chapter opens on a somewhat humorous note, with a disoriented Shevek waking the morning after the night of Vea's party to a pounding hangover and a burning sense of shame. This shame proves to be a revelation, as it spurs him to the pivotal realization that he made a terrible mistake in entrusting his fate to the Urrasti. Having done so, he reflects ruefully, he committed himself to serving not society, humankind, or the truth, but the state. Rather than wallow in guilt and self-pity, Shevek accepts and takes full responsibility for his mistakes. He also resolves to regain his independence and integrity by working for the betterment of humanity rather than for the enrichment and empowerment of a few. Given the circumstances, this involves a certain amount of distastefully non-Odonian possessiveness and secretiveness. Importantly from our perspective as analysts of the temporal dimensions of the novel, it also involves Shevek's exercise of his faculties of memory and creative imagination in such a way that he is able redeem the neglected intellectual promises of the past in a temporally charged and scientifically revolutionary present.

In concrete terms, he alters his professional behavior in at least four crucial respects, each of which helps to shed some light on the lineaments of Le Guin's time-sensitive, dynamic, and revolutionary conception of utopia. First, he engages seriously with ideas that are foreign to him. Unlike most of his fellow Anarresti, who so fear change that they barricade their world against all that is alien, Shevek achieves his scientific breakthrough only after careful study of the Terran "Ainsetain's" symposium on the theories of Relativity. Second, he abandons the quest for mathematical perfection and certainty that sustained and consoled him through all the years of alienation on Anarres. According to the omniscient narrator, "In the region of the unprovable, or even the disprovable, lay the only chance for breaking out of the circle and going ahead. . . . He had been groping and grabbing after certainty, as if it were something he could possess. He had been demanding a security, a guarantee, which is not granted, and which, if granted, would become a prison" (9: 280). Third, he recognizes the importance of perspective, or interval, as a means of surmounting the seemingly irreconcilable conflict between Sequentist and Simultanist points of view. As he muses to himself at the pivotal moment when he achieves his scientific breakthrough, "The fundamental unity of the Sequency and Simultaneity points of view became plain; the concept of interval served to connect the static and the dynamic aspects of the universe" (9: 280). Fourth, he redeems the revolutionary promises of the past by building imaginatively on theoretical aspirations that others had neglected because of their narrow power- and profit-driven focus on high technological yields. As we discover later on in chapter 11, Shevek retains an interest in the technological applications of his temporal theory, but in genuinely radical fashion does so because he wants his ideas to be used for the common good (rather than for private power), as a means of opening up a more interactive and dynamic relationship among all the known worlds.

The other major development in chapter 9 that nicely illustrates Le Guin's dynamic and revolutionary conception of utopia is Shevek's contact with the Ioti resistance movement. Just as he struggles in his professional life to remain true to his unique self by asserting his right to free creation, so too in his political activities Shevek struggles to remain true to his Odonian anarchist values by asserting the right of all human beings to free individual development. Specifically, he alters his political behavior in at least three important ways directly analogous to the process by which he achieves his scientific breakthrough.

First, rather than continue to idealize Urras, or to ignore and demonize it in the fashion of so many of his compatriots, Shevek strives to understand it in all its rich complexity. The occasion for doing so arises when Shevek's University-appointed servant, Efor, enters his rooms to serve him breakfast and finds him delirious with a high fever. Initially, Efor attends to Shevek's needs with the same formal courtesy and strict professionalism that characterized their relationship in previous chapters. After a couple of days, however, Efor begins to respond to his suffering at a more personal level, thus confirming the wisdom of Shevek's insight in chapter 2 that "brotherhood . . . begins in shared pain" (2: 62). In the course of one of their conversations, Efor attempts to explain to Shevek what life is like on Urras for its dispossessed. He describes in some detail, for example, the rat-infested hospital in which his daughter died at age two. He also refers in passing to a number of loathsome, but commonplace, features of Urrasti society that are completely foreign to his Anarresti interlocutor, including an army barracks, an insane asylum, a poorhouse, a pawnshop, an execution, a thief, a tenement, a rent collector, a man who wants work but cannot find any, and a dead baby in a ditch. In order to understand Efor at all, Shevek must "exercise his imagination and summon every scrap of knowledge he had about Urras" (9: 284). Ultimately, he is able to make the imaginative leap across the cultural divide separating the two worlds, and as the narrator observes pointedly, "he did understand." Rather than react to this understanding by condemning Urras in the same sort of absolute terms that he once idealized it, however, Shevek endeavors to survey Anarres's sister world in all its moral complexity. His thinking at this point in time is a model of balance and clarity, "This was the human suffering in which the ideals of his society were rooted, the ground from which they sprang. It was not 'the real Urras.' The dignity and beauty of the room he and Efor were in was as real as the squalor to which Efor was native. To him a thinking man's job was not to deny one reality at the expense of the other, but to include and to connect. It was not an easy job" (9: 284–85).

Second, Shevek doesn't just strive to imagine "the suffering in which the ideals of his society" are rooted. He goes out to see for himself what life is like for the dispossessed of A-Io, and in so doing achieves a radical critical perspective unavailable to those on both Urras and Anarres who are trapped in the prison of their more limited experience. Having acknowledged to himself that he made a grave mistake in entrusting his fate to the representatives of Urrasti state authority, Shevek resolves to escape from the confines of the Ieu Eun University and make contact with members of the Ioti resistance movement. With Efor's help he is whisked away in a taxi to a subway station in Nio Esseia, and from there makes his way to Old Town, home to the leaders of the resistance. En route to his destination of "Joking Lane," Shevek witnesses the terrible human price paid for all the beautiful wrappings and trappings of Ioti society. As he emerges from the marble subway station into the gloom of the city streets, for example, he stares into the worn and tired face of a woman aged well beyond her years:

> An old woman was coming up the stairs behind him, and he turned to her to
> ask his way. In the light of the yellow globe that marked the subway entrance

he saw her face clearly: white and lined, with the dead, hostile stare of weariness. Big glass earrings bobbed on her cheeks. She climbed the stairs laboriously, hunched over with fatigue or with arthritis or some deformity of the spine. But she was not old, as he had thought; she was not even thirty. (9: 290–91)

A little further on he notices a homeless man lying in a gutter:

There were many wineshops and pawnshops, some of them still open. A good many people were in the street, jostling past, going in and out of the wineshops. There was a man lying down, lying in the gutter, his coat bunched up over his head, lying in the rain, asleep, sick, dead. Shevek stared at him with horror, and at the others who walked past without looking. (9: 291)

He also exchanges words with a beggar, who responds to his request for directions to Joking Lane by extending an open hand and quipping, "Sure, joking, I'm joking, no joke I'm broke." At first, Shevek does not understand what the man wants from him. When he finally does understand, he is gripped by a fear "that was not fear for himself" (9: 292). Although the narrator never tells us exactly what Shevek is thinking at this precise moment, one may surmise that it is at this point in the novel that he achieves a radical critical perspective on Urrasti society similar in many ways to that held by the anarchist and libertarian socialist members of the resistance movement. As if in tacit confirmation of this point, Le Guin plots Shevek's encounter with a group of anti-centralist socialist activists almost immediately after his contact with the beggar.

Third, Shevek is not just a passive witness to injustice. He acts on his newfound critical understanding by serving as a living symbol of the links between past and future, existing reality and utopia. Once perceived by many on Urras as a symbol of capitulation to the state, Shevek becomes instead a symbol of hope for the resistance. In so doing, he helps to break open the horizon of historical possibility and unleash the revolutionary utopian energy latent in his present. The catalyst for this radical shift in Shevek's symbolic status is his initial meeting with some of the leaders of the Ioti resistance. One of them, a shopkeeper named Tuio Maedda, compares the current political climate in A-Io to the situation 150 years previously, when Odo led the General Strike that culminated in the settlement of Anarres. Having lamented the absence of contemporary rebel leaders of Odo's caliber, he attempts to convey to Shevek a sense of the scientist's symbolic importance in Urrasti politics, "I wonder if you fully understand why they've kept you so well hidden out there at Ieu Eun, Dr. Shevek. . . . It's not just because they want this idea of yours. But because you are an idea. A dangerous one. The idea of anarchism, made flesh. Walking amongst us" (9: 295). Another rebel, a young girl named Siro, interjects at this point with a remark that takes Maedda's train of thought to its logical conclusion, "Then you've got your Odo. . . . After all, Odo was only an idea. Dr. Shevek is the proof" (9: 295–96). Shevek responds to these honest expressions of need with great moral courage by agreeing to publish some material in the radical press. This, in turn, generates tremendous hope and enthusiasm among the dissidents, and helps to draw out those elements in Ioti society intent on redeeming the utopian promise of the Odonian past in the Urrasti present.

The revolutionary impact of Shevek's actions is illustrated in the final pages of chapter 9, in Le Guin's memorable description of the dissidents' protest march and its tragic aftermath. One of the most striking features of this description is the vivid way in which it suggests that utopian ideals are intimately bound up with time and history. As we have already seen, in previous chapters Shevek was alienated and alone, stranded on a temporal island cut off from both the past and the future. In the protest march, by contrast, he is surrounded by thousands of like-minded individuals. Working together, he and they are able to escape at least temporarily from the prison of the timeless present, and act freely in the landscape of time. The dissidents achieve this freedom by remaining loyal to the heritage of their radical Odonian past. As the narrator observes, "Anarres had no flag to wave, but among the placards proclaiming the general strike, and the blue and white banners of the Syndicalists and the Socialist Workers, there were many homemade signs showing the green Circle of Life, the old symbol of the Odonian Movement of two hundred years before" (9: 298). What is true of the banners and placards of the protestors is no less true of their choice of song, such as the Odonian Hymn of the Insurrection, a paean to radical promises kept. The momentous temporal implications of the moment are not lost on Shevek, who appears to be attuned to the resonance between the singing and his scientific theories about the nature of time:

> It was . . . indistinct, overwhelming, that lifting up of thousands of voices in one song. The singing of the front of the march, far away up the street, and of the endless crowds coming on behind, was put out of phase by the distance the sound must travel, so that the melody seemed always to be lagging and catching up with itself . . . and all the parts of the song were being sung at one time, in the same moment, though each singer sang the tune as a line from beginning to end. (9: 298)

In solidarity with the protestors, he joins in the singing of the Hymn of the Insurrection. In the speech that he delivers shortly thereafter, he also shares with them a glimpse of the open-ended utopian horizon represented by Anarres, and reminds them of the unfulfilled promises of their revolutionary past. In so doing, he acts as a bridge between past, present, and future, and helps to break open the horizon of historical possibility, much as did some of those who "demanded the impossible" in our own recent past in May 1968.[28]

It may appear from a cursory reading of the chapter that this revolutionary breach is abruptly sealed shut almost as soon as it is opened by Le Guin's subsequent description of the Ioti authorities' violent suppression of the demonstration. I read the scene differently, however. Rather than use it to bludgeon Le Guin with the charge of "defeatism," as some of her more ideologically dogmatic critics have done, I interpret it as a reflection of her sober historical realism. Influenced no doubt in part by the frequently brutal governmental responses to the peaceful demonstrations of the late 1960s, Le Guin is simply acknowledging the fact that even the most emancipatory utopian vision may bring hope and renewed promise, but no guarantee of immediate revolutionary change. To put the point in a slightly different way, she recognizes not only the neglected radical potential of utopian imagination as a means of galvanizing opposition to injustice, but also its limitations. The utopian imagination cannot dictate social change. Insofar as it misused in such a manner, moreover, it degenerates into its opposite, namely an instrument in the service of the will to power.

Le Guin seems to sense this fundamental truth, and so wields utopia not as a weapon to be deployed in violent combat with the authoritarian state, but as a tool to be used in constructing peaceful and consensual alternatives to it. This, at least, is how I interpret Shevek's admonition to the assembled crowd, "If it is Anarres you want, if it is the future you seek, then I tell you that you must come to it with empty hands. . . . You cannot buy the Revolution. You cannot make the Revolution. You can only be the Revolution. It is in your spirit, or it is nowhere" (9: 301). Speaking in terms that will be very familiar to those of Le Guin's readers who are versed in the pacifist anarchist tradition, Shevek is reminding his listeners that genuine revolution consists not in blind destruction or replacement of one ruling class by another, but in the never ending and in part very personal struggle to resist the will to power and domination in all its forms.

This reading of the text is confirmed by Le Guin's thoughtful reflections about power, imagination, and revolution in her recently published collection of essays *The Wave in the Mind* (2004). Near the end of the essay entitled "A War without End," she considers Audre Lorde's observation that you can't dismantle the master's house with the master's tools. Having acknowledged the richness and power of Lorde's metaphor, Le Guin hazards the following explanation of why revolutions generally fail, "I see their failure beginning when the attempt to re-build the house so everybody can live in it becomes an attempt to grab all the saws and hammers, barricade Ole Massa's toolroom, and keep the others out. Power not only corrupts, it addicts. Work becomes destruction. Nothing is built."[29] The point is a persuasive one, supported by an abundance of historical evidence. Of course, some might object to this analysis on the grounds that revolutionaries have no choice but to make use of the master's tools when the master resorts to violence in order to retain his privileges. This is the position articulated in *The Dispossessed* by Siro, in her heated exchange in chapter 9 with Tuio Maedda. Ultimately, the debate between the two is inconclusive, as is the meaning of the violent events depicted in the chapter's closing pages.

One thing is certain about this element of the narrative, however. It does not reflect a "defeatist" attitude on the part of Le Guin. This is made amply clear by her diametrically opposed treatment of the violence exercised by the state and the resistance to it expressed by the protestors. The former is described as follows:

> The noise of the rotating vanes of the machines in the huge stone box of Capitol Square was intolerable, a clacking and yapping like the voice of a monstrous robot. It drowned out the chatter of the machine guns fired from the helicopters. Even as the crowd noise rose up in tumult the clack of the helicopters was still audible through it, the mindless yell of weaponry, the meaningless word. (9: 301)

Now consider her account of the latter:

> When they [the soldiers] came, marching in their neat black coats up the steps among dead and dying men and women, they found on the high, grey, polished wall of the great foyer a word written at the height of a man's eyes, in broad smears of blood: DOWN.
> They shot the dead man who lay nearest the word, and later on when the Directorate was restored to order the word was washed off the wall with water, soap, and rags, but it remained; it had been spoken; it had meaning. (9: 302)

In both cases, Le Guin frames the narrative in terms of the metaphor of speech. Yet one form of speech has meaning, while the other does not. Both are suffused with blood and death. Yet one is paradoxically life affirming, and will give rise over time to further communication, and to further struggle for the utopian dream of a genuine human community that supports the right of every one of its members to free individual development. The other leads only to stasis and the silence of death.

Having explored both the nature and implications of Shevek's professional and political radicalization in chapter 9, what conclusions can we draw about the distinguishing features of Le Guin's dynamic and revolutionary variant of the literary utopia? Perhaps the most fundamental conclusion to be drawn is that whereas the perfectionist utopia abstracts from the time-bound features of our world in order to render an absolute and final moral judgment on them, the Le Guinean utopia engages dynamically with time and history in order to help transform the given confines of the here and now into an open landscape of historical possibility. It does so by inviting the reader to engage in an historically grounded and time-sensitive journey of the utopian imagination complete with fundamental moral conflict, meaningful choice, and continuing change, by the end of which she or he may return to the nonfictional present with a broader perspective on its latent emancipatory possibilities.

Unlike the didactic lessons of the perfectionist utopia, the insights to be gleaned from the Le Guinean utopia are ambiguous. For Le Guin does not tell her readers what to think. Rather, by using her fictional skills to enlarge the field of historical possibility, she challenges us to reevaluate our present from the perspective of the promises of, and aspirations to, emancipation that have not yet been realized. In *The Dispossessed*, this challenge takes the particular form of Shevek's journey from Anarres to Urras and back again, in the course of which he overcomes seemingly insurmountable obstacles in order to achieve a partial and provisional, but nonetheless revolutionary, critical perspective on his present. While few among us can realistically hope to emulate the heroic nature of Shevek's accomplishments, we can still learn from his experience by regarding him as what he is intended to be, namely an exemplar of honesty, integrity, and moral courage. Like him, we can strive to "include and connect" different social possibilities dynamically in the hope of generating a genuinely realistic and radical politics based on something more substantial than cynical platitudes and tired, either/or binary oppositions. Like him as well, we can choose to take responsibility for our convictions by acting conscientiously and courageously to oppose the will to power and domination whenever and wherever it raises its ugly head.

This last point is a particularly important one too often ignored or misunderstood by Le Guin's more ideologically inclined interpreters. Phillip Wegner, for example, spoils an otherwise thoughtful discussion of Le Guin by misleadingly characterizing the dynamic and revolutionary philosophy of history implicit in *The Dispossessed* as a messianic faith in history's rationality. According to Wegner, who interprets Le Guin critically through the lens of Gramsci's philosophy, the Odonian concept of permanent revolution is nothing more than a dogmatic, mechanistic, and deterministic forecast of the future that demolishes itself by not in fact coming true. Moreover, he concludes by quoting a passage from Gramsci's *Prison Notebooks*, "if such a 'naïve philosophy of strength' is forced to be sustained for too long, it invariably mutates into 'a cause of passivity, of idiotic self-sufficiency. This happens when they [the intellectuals] don't even expect that the subaltern will become directive and responsible.'"[30]

What Wegner neglects to mention is that Gramsci's target in the passage just quoted is the idea of historical inevitability, and in particular the belief in the inevitable spontaneous collapse of capitalism and its replacement by a socialist order.[31] It hardly needs to be said that this idea is completely alien to Le Guin's way of thinking. In fact, as we have already seen, *The Dispossessed* is first and foremost a novel concerned with the relationship between time and freedom. Far from expressing a messianic faith in history's rationality, it dramatizes the *dangers* of dogmatic, mechanistic, Euclidean, and deterministic conceptions of history, and calls attention to the indispensable part played in historical change by individual choice, moral responsibility, and personal creativity.

Like Tolstoy, Dostoevsky, and William James, Le Guin employs her formidable artistic talents in order to discredit deterministic conceptions of history, and deepen our appreciation of the fullness and openness of time. In a playful, appropriately self-critical, and lighthearted fashion so unlike the plodding, theory-heavy manner of her most dogmatic critics, she reminds us that past, present, and future all contain multiple possibilities far in excess of concretely realized actualities. As a result, choice and responsibility have value and meaning. Furthermore, like Bakhtin (and unlike Dostoevsky[32]), Le Guin recognizes that they have value and meaning at all moments of time, and not just during periodic moments of crisis. It follows that even seemingly more prosaic choices can have ethical significance, and that while the consequences and meanings of these choices may not be immediately apparent, they are nevertheless entrained in a temporal trajectory that extends into both the past and the future.

We see this quite clearly if we reconsider chapter 9 in light of the events of chapter 10. Read in isolation from the chapter that follows it, chapter 9 appears to be a revolutionary moment standing outside the flow of time. From this perspective, all the radical changes initiated by Shevek on Urras represent a complete and total break from everything that has gone before. As we discover when we read chapter 10, however, the courageous actions that he takes in chapter 9 have a clear precedent in choices made in his recent past on Anarres.

As on Urras, so on Anarres the catalyst for Shevek's radicalization is his perception of social injustice. Chapter 10 begins with a dialogue in which Shevek describes how, in the course of a four-year work posting during a time of drought and famine, he was assigned the soul-destroying task of drawing up lists to determine who among his fellows would be placed on subsistence rations. His interlocutor rightly replies that no society has the right to make such demands on its members. The other main instance in chapter 10 of Shevek's galvanizing perception of injustice is his recognition during a conversation with Takver that Bedap was right after all about their mutual friend Tirin. He had been destroyed by pressure to conform to prevailing social norms. Toward the end of this conversation Shevek makes the following telling observation about Anarresti society, "We have created crime, just as the propertarians did. We force a man outside the sphere of our approval, and then condemn him for it. We've made laws, laws of conventional behavior, built walls all around ourselves, and we can't see them, because they're part of our thinking" (10: 330–31). Moved by a shock of recognition to reflect critically on the gap between the idealistic promises of the Odonian past and the habitual betrayal of them in the Anarresti present, Shevek makes a brave decision. He resolves never again to permit his life choices to be dictated by convention, moralism, fear of social ostracism, fear of being different, or fear of being free. He resolves, in short, to become a true anarchist, and to act on this commitment by returning to Abbenay to start a radical printing syndicate (the Syndicate of Initiative).

In what are perhaps two of the most important (and potentially controversial) pages of the novel from the perspective of its temporal politics, he also thinks long and hard about the philosophical justifications for this decision. More specifically, he considers the nature of time, freedom, and responsibility. His thinking begins at the level of the individual, with an unflinching recognition of the strength of his own will. It then moves to the level of society, with the acknowledgment that a healthy society would be one that promotes individual growth and diversity, finding in the coordination of all such individualities its adaptability and strength. While such a society might legitimately demand "sacrifice" from its members in order to maintain the social preconditions of universal individual development, it has no right to demand "compromise" (presumably of one's personal integrity or fundamental humanity), for only "the individual, the person, had the power of moral choice—the power of change, the essential function of life" (10: 333). From Shevek's perspective, what links these two levels of thinking is the idea of responsibility, by which he means neither rigid adherence to atemporal moral truths nor the unencumbered exercise of present will, but the commitment to living one's life as a journey through the "landscape of time." In such a journey, every moment counts, for it is not the end of the journey that gives it value, but the very process of journeying itself. Fulfillment is thus a function of time. As he muses to himself before nodding off to sleep, an act only becomes a human act when it asserts "the continuity of past and future" (10: 335), thus binding time into a habitable whole.

When Shevek resolves to lead his life as a genuine anarchist he could not possibly have foreseen what impact his seemingly private and personal choices would have on the lives of others. He makes the choices he does simply because he believes them to be right. Only in hindsight does their complex political meaning and significance become more readily apparent, thus confirming the wisdom of his scientific insights about the simultaneously successive and enduring nature of time. As we discover in chapters 11, 12, and 13, Shevek's decision to found a radical printing syndicate sets off what appears to be "an uncontrollable chain of events" (12: 354), beginning with the reopening of radio contact between Urras and Anarres. On Urras, this energizes and gives hope to a group of post-settlement Odonians in Benbili, whom as we recall from earlier in the novel are the spearheads of an anarchist revolutionary uprising in which jails are thrown open and prisoners granted amnesty. On Anarres, it provokes a heated public debate about the terms of the Settlement. This in turn provides the impetus for Shevek's journey to Urras, which in turn leads to the demonstration and general strike in A-Io, his revolutionary scientific breakthrough (which, as we learn elsewhere in Le Guin's Hainish cycle, leads to the invention of the ansible and so makes possible the establishment of a league of all known worlds), and the renewal of the Odonian revolution on Anarres.

In stark contrast to the perfectionist utopia, there is no implication in *The Dispossessed* of a final resolution to all residual conflict nor any suggestion of an end to history and politics. If there is a recurring motif in the final three chapters of the novel, it is that the revolutionary Odonian philosophy brought to life by the founding settlers of Anarres remains a living, open-ended utopian promise the historical relevance of which will depend largely on unpredictable human action. This is evident in chapters 11 and 12 in Shevek's encounters with individuals who cannot or will not understand the dynamic and revolutionary utopian ideal that he attempts to share with them, and who by their fatalistic passivity or active opposition call attention to its radical historical contingency.

In chapter 11, Shevek meets with a fatalistic response in his dialogue with Keng, the Terran ambassador to the Urrasti Council of World Governments. Keng, it soon becomes evident, is the diplomatic representative of a dystopian future of our Earth. In this particular future the Earth is a ruin, a planet spoiled by the human species. Its inhabitants "multiplied and gobbled and fought" until there was nothing left. First they destroyed their environment, then they destroyed each other. They survived only thanks to the generosity of the Hainish, and to "the absolute regimentation of each life towards the goal of racial survival." From this bleak perspective the anarchist ideal represented by Anarres means "nothing" to Keng. It is an illusory hope, a mirage in a desert. Urras on the other hand appears to be a realistically attainable ideal, perhaps because of its centralization of authority in a sovereign state. To Keng, and to those of her fellow-Terrans who have seen the planet, it is "the world that comes as close as any could to Paradise" (11: 347–49).

From Shevek's perspective, Keng's view is based upon a misconception of the nature of time. Like the privileged elite on Urras whom she so envies, Keng rejects the reality of past and future embodied in Anarres. For her, only the present is real. Yet, as Shevek points out, such an understanding of time is terribly limited, "You cannot have anything. . . . And least of all can you have the present, unless you accept with it the past and the future. Not only the past but also the future, not only the future but also the past! Because they are real: only their reality makes the present real. You will not achieve or even understand Urras unless you accept the reality, the enduring reality, of Anarres" (11: 349).

The difference in perspective between the two is nicely symbolized by a brief but important passage that seems to have escaped the attention of previous commentators on the novel. Just before he makes the above quoted remarks about the nature of time, Shevek gets up from the chair in which he is seated and walks over to one of the embassy windows. Because the embassy is housed in an ancient river castle, the window is little more than a narrow horizontal slit in the side of a tower. Beneath the window slit is a niche into which an archer would have stepped up to look down and aim at assailants at the gate. Here is how the narrator very casually describes Shevek's approach to the window, "if one did not take that step up one could see nothing from it but the sunwashed, slightly misty sky. Shevek stood below the window gazing out, the light filling his eyes" (11: 349). In a blinding flash, the image conjures up some of the central metaphors of the novel: the wall, the radiant Tau Ceti sun shining through the window of Shevek's nursery and later through the observation port of the *Davenant*, and the plot's spiraling dialectic between the soulless militarism of Urras and the parched idealism of Anarres. It recalls the numerous allusions in previous chapters to the relativity of truth and the importance of perspective, be it the "ambiguous, two-faced wall" in chapter 1, the brief exchange in chapter 2 between young Tirin and young Bedap about the nature of truth, or Shevek's recognition in chapter 9 of the importance of perspective as a means of surmounting the seemingly irreconcilable conflict between Sequentist and Simultanist points of view. It also suggests that while it is sometimes possible to bridge widely varying points of view, it is not always possible to do so. Shevek seems to realize as much when he remarks to Keng, "My people were right, and I was wrong, in this: We cannot come to you. You will not let us. . . . You would destroy us rather than admit our reality. . . . We can only wait for you to come to us" (11: 349–50).

For all her shrewdness and sophistication, Keng is like those on present-day Earth who point to the inexorable spread of the "blessings" of capitalism as evidence of an impending end to world historical development. She is blinded by fatalism, and so cannot even conceive of the possibility of a world without (in Shevek's words) "States and their weapons, the rich and their lies, and the poor and their misery" (11: 346).

In chapter 12, Shevek meets with more active political opposition from Rulag, his estranged mother and one of the most outspoken critics of the fledgling Syndicate of Initiative. Throughout most of the narrative Rulag is a shadowy presence notable more for her absence from Shevek's life than for any distinguishing characteristics of her own. On the one occasion when we do get to know her personally, during a visit with Shevek in an Anarresti clinic at the end of chapter 4, she comes across as cold, calculating, rigid, and devoid of human feeling. Having abandoned Shevek and his loving father Palat when Shevek was just a boy, Rulag presumes that she can simply walk into her son's life nearly twenty years later and carry on as if nothing had ever happened. As her conversation with Shevek makes clear, life is for Rulag a solipsistic game, in which other people have value only insofar as they are useful to her in some way. Palat and Shevek ceased to be useful at some point, and so she left them. Impelled by a sense that the twenty-year-old Shevek might now be of use to her, she attempts to renew the bond between them.

Like Keng (and Vea), Rulag appears to be entirely unconcerned about the relationship between past, present, and future. For her, only the present moment is real, and it alone is of any consequence. She admits as much in her unfeeling appeal to the strictly rational and calculating side of Shevek's personality, "You don't remember me, and the baby I remember isn't this man of twenty. All that is time past, irrelevant. But we are brother and sister, here and now. Which is what really matters, isn't it?" (4: 124). From Shevek's perspective the contrast with Palat's unconditional love and loyalty is painfully apparent. Whereas his deceased father lives on in Shevek's memory as a shining symbol of "that clear constant love in which his life had taken root," his living mother stirs nothing in him but a deadening fear and resentment. As she departs Shevek gives way to the fear that came with her, the fear of the breaking of promises and the incoherence of time.

We encounter Rulag again in chapter 12, at a Production and Distribution Coordination (PDC) meeting on Anarres. In her public capacity as an experienced member of the PDC she is both one of the most influential critics of the Syndicate of Initiative and the personification of all the most conservative forces in Anarresti society. Set in her ways, she cannot, or will not, adapt and change. Nor will she permit the rest of Anarresti society to do so. In response to Bedap's proposal to welcome to Anarres a small group of post-Settlement Odonians from Benbili, she advocates a rigid and uncompromising adherence to the Terms of the Settlement. Later in the debate, when a particularly hot-tempered member of the PDC threatens violence against anybody who attempts to return home again from a voyage to Urras, it is Rulag who rationalizes the threat. "If there is violence," she remarks to Bedap, "you will have caused it. You and your Syndicate. And you will have deserved it" (12: 358).

Such inflammatory comments no doubt contribute to the escalating fear and hostility which culminates in the fatal violence described in the novel's opening pages. As we recall from chapter 1 (this is one of many occasions in the novel when we "recall" future events, thus prompting reflection on the inextricable relationship between past and future), matters reach such a fever pitch that a bloodthirsty mob assembles at the Port of Anarres just before Shevek's departure. One member of the crowd hurls a two-pound flint that misses Shevek, but ends up killing a member of the Defense crew escorting him. The threat of violence looms once again at the end of the novel, as Shevek prepares to land. On both occasions—as during Shevek's dialogues in chapters 11 and 12 with Keng and Rulag—we are reminded in graphic detail of the radical historical contingency of Odo's dynamic and revolutionary utopian ideal.

We are reminded of this fact once again in chapter 13, albeit in a more hopeful fashion. As Shevek prepares to land on Anarres he is joined by the first mate of the *Davenant*, a Hainishman named Ketho. Although a member of the oldest and most fatalistic race in the known universe, Ketho has been moved sufficiently by Shevek's moral courage to take a risk of his own. Having noted that he wishes to "explore and investigate" (13: 383) Anarresti society before eventually returning home, he requests and receives permission from Shevek to land with him.

The incident is significant in part because it suggests that just as there are always those who will turn a blind eye to injustice and inequality, there are others who will take a risk on behalf of the promise of human freedom and solidarity. Just as Shevek takes a risk by exposing himself to danger in order to rekindle the revolutionary flame on two worlds, so too Ketho knowingly puts himself in harm's way not only on behalf of disinterested scientific exploration, but also for the sake of what Shevek describes as "an idea, a promise, a risk" (13: 385). As is the case with all risks, this one comes without any guarantee of success. At the novel's close, social conflict and political struggle continue unabated on both Urras and Anarres. On Urras, the government of A-Io exploits its monopoly on high technology military power in order to suppress the Odonian opposition movements in Benbili and Nio Esseia. On Anarres, there are as many opponents as there are supporters of revolutionary change, and the outcome of the struggle between them is far from certain. And yet, in spite of all these confirmations of the

Hainish philosophy that there is nothing new under any sun in the universe, things have changed from the first page of *The Dispossessed* to the last. Whereas at the start of the novel Urras and Anarres were separated by a wall damming back change and development on both worlds, at its close the revolutionary promises of the past have been reasserted and the possibility of continuing revolutionary change renewed. Fittingly, the very end of the story is not an ending, but a radical new beginning. Ketho's journey begins where Shevek's leaves off, and the spiral of time continues.

As John Brennan and Michael Downs rightly point out in the conclusion to their essay on anarchism and utopian tradition in *The Dispossessed*, "Thomas More's King Utopus gave his islanders a blueprint for the future, as permanent and well-founded as human prescience would permit; Ursula Le Guin's founding mother gave her Odonian followers some thoughtful books and a place to begin, and a legacy of hope in every frustration. No more can be left to the children of time."[33] In *The Dispossessed*, Le Guin has given us, her readers, an exceptionally thoughtful and powerfully imagined work of art. Far more than just a wistful expression of hope or desire, the novel is an achieved example of something that defenders and critics of utopia alike have difficulty even imagining: namely, a dynamic and revolutionary utopia premised on an acceptance of the enduring reality of social conflict and historical change. An offshoot of the utopian tradition, *The Dispossessed* is also a radical new beginning. It reaffirms the revolutionary promises of the utopian past and reasserts the possibility of the tradition's continuing change and development. It does so first and foremost by acknowledging the unending flow of the historical process. If the dominant form of utopian narrative is a timeless monument to Euclidean reason, *The Dispossessed* is a mighty wave of the imagination in the ocean of time, on the crest of which we are all buoyed up and provided with a glimpse of the farther shore.

NOTES

I would like to thank Ursula K. Le Guin and Peter Stillman for their generous comments on an earlier draft of this chapter.

1. Ursula K. Le Guin, *The Dispossessed: An Ambiguous Utopia* (New York: Harper & Row, 1974), cited in the text by chapter and page to the 387-page Eos HarperCollins edition of 2001.

2. I take the defining feature of utopian thought to be the imagination of the norms, institutions, and individual relationships of a society meant to be regarded as radically better worth living in than that of its originator. I am skeptical of definitions of utopia that insist on its necessary association with the idea of perfection, because it seems to me that they fail to illuminate a good deal of the history of utopian thought. For further discussion of the relationship between utopianism and perfectionism, see my essay "Isaiah Berlin,

William Morris, and the Politics of Utopia," *Critical Review of International Social and Political Philosophy* 3, nos. 2/3 (Summer/Autumn 2000): 56–86. See also Peter Stillman's contribution to the same journal issue, "'Nothing is, but what is not': Utopias as Practical Political Philosophy," 9–24; Lyman Sargent, "The Three Faces of Utopianism Revisited," *Utopian Studies* 5, no. 1 (1994): 1–37; and Elisabeth Hansot, *Perfection and Progress: Two Modes of Utopian Thought* (Cambridge, MA: MIT Press, 1974).

3. Le Guin has consistently referred to the novel as a utopia. Note, for example, her remarks in the excellent essay "A Non-Euclidean View of California as a Cold Place to Be" (1982), in her *Dancing at the Edge of the World: Thoughts on Words, Women, Places* (New York: Grove Press, 1989), 93: "The major utopic element in my novel *The Dispossessed* is a variety of pacifist anarchism . . . though the utopia was (both in fact and in fiction) founded by a woman, the protagonist is a man." Only very recently has she wavered somewhat in this commitment, and then only to distance herself unambiguously from the obsolescent perfectionist understanding of the term as a rationalistic social plan or blueprint—the implementation of which is intended to end injustice and inequality once and for all.

4. Naomi Jacobs, "Beyond Stasis and Symmetry: Lessing, Le Guin, and the Remodeling of Utopia," *Extrapolation* 29, no. 1 (Spring 1988): 34.

5. James Bittner's *Approaches to the Fiction of Ursula K. Le Guin* (Essex, UK: Bowker, 1984) is one of the best existing studies of Le Guin's fiction. I warmly recommend it.

6. Bittner, *Approaches*, 148.

7. Barry Barth, "Ursula Le Guin Interview: Tricks, Anthropology Create New Worlds," *Portland Scribe* 4, no. 8 (May 17–23, 1975): 8–9.

8. I believe that Kümmel's argument would have been much stronger had he spoken of "human beings" rather than "man," since his argument is in no way gender specific. See chapter 6 ("Wet Round Time and Dry Linear Time") of Jay Griffiths, *Pip Pip: A Sideways Look at Time* (London: Flamingo, 1999) for a spirited discussion of the ways in which time has always been a highly genderized concept. According to Griffiths (119), "the way time is pictured, or described in any age, mirrors remarkably closely the way the feminine is treated then." See also Mario Klarer, "Gender and the 'Simultaneity Principle': Ursula Le Guin's *The Dispossessed*," *Mosaic* 25, no. 2 (Spring 1992) for a defense of the proposition that Le Guin's treatment of time in *The Dispossessed* anticipates recent anti-essentialist and dialogic trends in feminist thinking. According to Klarer, the novel is much more than progressive in gender terms than its early critics would have us believe. This is particularly true, he observes, of its structure, symbolism, and concern with simultaneity.

9. Friedrich Kümmel, "Time as Succession and the Problem of Duration," ed. J. T. Fraser, *The Voices of Time* (London: Allen Lane, Penguin Press, 1968), 50. Here again it may be worth pausing to note that I would be more inclined to draw a distinction between children and adult human beings (as Shevek does in *The Dispossessed*) rather than animals and human beings, since I just don't know whether nonhuman animals have a sense of time.

10. Kümmel, "Time," 50.

11. Bittner, *Approaches*, 149.

12. Bittner, *Approaches*, 96.

13. Bittner, *Approaches*, 119.

14. I owe this last point to Chris Ferns. See Chris Ferns, *Narrating Utopia: Ideology, Gender, Form in Utopian Literature* (Liverpool, UK: Liverpool University Press, 1999), 228.

15. John Stuart Mill, *On Liberty* (1859), in *John Stuart Mill: A Selection of His Works*, ed. John Robson (Indianapolis: Bobbs-Merrill Educational Publishing, 1966), 7.

16. Shevek's reaction recalls William Morris's response to the general education system of his day:

> I must say . . . that on the few occasions that I have been inside a Board-school, I have been much depressed by the mechanical drill that was obviously being applied there to all the varying capacities and moods. My heart sank before Mr. M'Choakumchild and his method, and I thought how much luckier I was to have been born well enough off to be sent to a school where I was taught—nothing; but learned archaeology and romance on the Wiltshire Downs.

See William Morris, "Thoughts on Education under Capitalism," in *William Morris: Artist, Writer, Socialist*, ed. May Morris (Oxford: Basil Blackwell, 1936), II: 498.

17. It may strike some readers as rather odd that I would choose to contextualize a novel published in 1974 by reference to an essay written in 1982. The reason for this choice is my considered conviction that Le Guin continued to struggle with many of the same fundamental questions raised by *The Dispossessed* about the nature and purposes of utopia in the years following its initial publication. While she no doubt modified some of her views in the interval separating the novel from the essay, I believe that there is sufficient continuity in her thinking during this period of time in order to justify the juxtaposition of the two. Interestingly, if I am correct in this hypothesis, then it proves that Le Guin is more serious about the fictional games she plays with the concepts of time and freedom in *The Dispossessed* than she may at times let on—serious enough, that is, to take on board some of their philosophical implications in the practice of her literary art.

18. Le Guin, "A Non-Euclidean View," 85. Subsequent quotations and descriptors in this paragraph may be found in Le Guin, "A Non-Euclidean View," 81, 89, 97, 81, 86–87, 82–83, and 87.

19. Le Guin, "A Non-Euclidean View," 93, 84, 96.

20. We learn in chapter 4 of *The Dispossessed* that while the communities of Anarres are decentralized, relatively frugal and conservative of natural resources, "they would not regress to pre-urban, pre-technological tribalism. They knew that their anarchism was the product of a very high civilization, of a complex diversified culture, of a stable economy and a highly industrialized technology that could maintain high production and rapid transportation of goods" (4: 95).

21. Le Guin, "A Non-Euclidean View," 85.

22. Le Guin, "A Non-Euclidean View," 96.

23. Le Guin, "A Non-Euclidean View," 96.

24. There is vast scholarly literature confirming this suggestion. See, for example, David Noble, *Forces of Production: A Social History of Industrial Automation* (New York: Oxford University Press, 1986), and Lewis Mumford, *Technics and Civilization* (New York: Harcourt Brace and Company, 1963 [1934]). See also the appendix to the 1996 paperback edition of Zygmunt Bauman, *Modernity and the Holocaust* (Cambridge, UK: Polity Press, 1996 [1989]), "Social Manipulation of Morality: The European Amalfi Prize Lecture."

25. To my mind, this is a far more realistic utopian vision than that proffered by those of her critics who insist on associating the idea of a radically better form of society with

an expectation of limitless abundance. One wonders whether those who make such an association have read even a single book or article about ecologism. As Andrew Dobson correctly points out in his *Green Political Thought*, 3rd edition, (London: Routledge, 2000), 62, "finitude" is the framework within which any putative picture of green society must be drawn, and "sustainability" is its guiding principle. Working within an ecological framework in *The Dispossessed*, one very interesting question raised by Le Guin is what level of material wealth is necessary to sustain a society in which people may resolve peacefully the inevitable material conflicts of interest arising from an economy of limited resources.

26. Le Guin, "A Non-Euclidean View," 85, quoting from Robert Elliott, *The Shape of Utopia: Studies in a Literary Genre* (Chicago: University of Chicago Press, 1970).

27. Paul Goodman, quoted by Victor Urbanowicz, "Personal and Political in *The Dispossessed*," *Science-Fiction Studies* 5, no. 2 (July 1978): 112. Urbanowicz's essay is one of the more interesting accounts of the novel's anarchist politics. On the same subject, see also the excellent pieces by Philip Smith II, "Unbuilding Walls: Human Nature and the Nature of Evolutionary and Political Theory in *The Dispossessed*," in *Ursula K. Le Guin*, ed. Joseph D. Olander and Martin Harry Greenberg (New York: Taplinger, 1979), 77–96; and John Brennan and Michael Downs, "Anarchism and Utopian Tradition in *The Dispossessed*," in *Ursula K. Le Guin*, ed. Olander and Greenberg, 116–52.

Those interested in exploring further the influence of Goodman's writings on the anarchist politics of *The Dispossessed* may wish to begin with Paul Goodman and Percival Goodman, *Communitas: Means of Livelihood and Ways of Life*, 2nd revised ed. (New York: Vintage, 1960), and Paul Goodman, *Art and Social Nature* (New York: Vinco, 1946). As Smith demonstrates persuasively, Kropotkin is one of the other major influences on the novel's anarchist politics. Those interested in pursuing this topic in greater depth may wish to consult the following works by Peter Kropotkin: *The Conquest of Bread* (New York: Vanguard, 1926), *Fields, Factories, and Workshops* (London: Nelson, 1912), and *Mutual Aid* (London: Heinemann, 1902).

28. See Eleni Varikas, "The Utopian Surplus," *Thesis Eleven* 68 (February 2002): 101–5, for an account of the historical meaning and significance of May 1968 that calls attention to its unsubdued utopian surplus.

29. Ursula K. Le Guin, *The Wave in the Mind: Talks and Essays on the Writer, the Reader, and the Imagination* (Boston: Shambhala, 2004), 217.

30. Phillip Wegner, *Imaginary Communities: Utopia, the Nation, and the Spatial Histories of Modernity* (Berkeley: University of California Press, 2002), 182.

31. This point is made abundantly clear by the editors of the very same edition of the *Notebooks* from which Wegner quotes, on the very same page. See Antonio Gramsci, *Selections from Prison Notebooks*, ed. Quintin Hoare and Geoffrey Smith (London: Lawrence and Wishart, 1971), 336.

32. It is interesting to note in this context Le Guin's very different treatment of Dostoevsky and William James in the introduction to her short story, "The Ones Who Walk Away from Omelas," in *The Wind's Twelve Quarters* (London: Victor Gollancz, 2000 [1975]), 275–76. According to Le Guin, "Dostoyevsky was a great artist, and a radical one, but his early social radicalism reversed itself, leaving him a violent reactionary. Whereas the American James, who seems so mild, so naïvely gentlemanly . . . was, and remained, and remains, a genuinely radical thinker."

33. Brennan and Downs, "Anarchism and Utopian Tradition," 152.

WORKS CITED

Barth, Barry. "Ursula Le Guin Interview: Tricks, Anthropology Create New Worlds." *Portland Scribe* 4, no. 8 (May 17–23, 1975): 8–9.

Bauman, Zygmunt. *Modernity and the Holocaust.* Cambridge, UK: Polity Press, 1996 (1989).

Bittner, James. *Approaches to the Fiction of Ursula K. Le Guin.* Essex, UK: Bowker, 1984.

Brennan, John, and Michael Downs. "Anarchism and Utopian Tradition in *The Dispossessed.*" Pp. 116–52 in *Ursula K. Le Guin,* ed. Joseph D. Olander and Martin Harry Greenberg. New York: Taplinger, 1979.

Davis, Laurence. "Isaiah Berlin, William Morris, and the Politics of Utopia." *Critical Review of International Social and Political Philosophy* 3, nos. 2/3 (Summer/Autumn 2000): 56–86. Reprinted in *The Philosophy of Utopia,* ed. Barbara Goodwin. London and Portland, OR: Frank Cass, 2001.

Dobson, Andrew. *Green Political Thought.* London and New York: Routledge, 2000 (third edition).

Elliott, Robert. *The Shape of Utopia: Studies in a Literary Genre.* Chicago and London: University of Chicago Press, 1970.

Ferns, Chris. *Narrating Utopia: Ideology, Gender, Form in Utopian Literature.* Liverpool: Liverpool University Press, 1999.

Goodman, Paul. *Art and Social Nature.* New York: Vinco, 1946.

Goodman, Paul, and Percival Goodman. *Communitas: Means of Livelihood and Ways of Life.* New York: Vintage, 1960 (second revised edition).

Gramsci, Antonio. *Selections from Prison Notebooks.* Ed. and trans. Quintin Hoare and Geoffrey Smith. London: Lawrence and Wishart, 1971.

Griffiths, Jay. *Pip Pip: A Sideways Look at Time.* London: Flamingo, 1999.

Hansot, Elisabeth. *Perfection and Progress: Two Modes of Utopian Thought.* Cambridge, MA, and London: Massachusetts Institute of Technology Press, 1974.

Jacobs, Naomi. "Beyond Stasis and Symmetry: Lessing, Le Guin, and the Remodeling of Utopia." *Extrapolation* 29, no. 1 (Spring 1988): 34–45.

Klarer, Mario. "Gender and the 'Simultaneity Principle': Ursula Le Guin's *The Dispossessed.*" *Mosaic* 25, no. 2 (Spring 1992): 107–21.

Kropotkin, Peter. *The Conquest of Bread.* New York: Vanguard, 1926.

———. *Fields, Factories and Workshops.* London: Nelson, 1912.

———. *Mutual Aid.* London: Heinemann, 1902.

Kümmel, Friedrich. "Time as Succession and the Problem of Duration." Pp. 31–55 in *The Voices of Time,* ed. J. T. Fraser. London: Allen Lane, Penguin Press, 1968.

Le Guin, Ursula K. *Dancing at the Edge of the World: Thoughts on Words, Women, Places.* New York: Grove Press, 1989.

———. *The Dispossessed: An Ambiguous Utopia.* New York: Eos, HarperCollins, 2001 (1974).

———. *The Wave in the Mind: Talks and Essays on the Writer, the Reader, and the Imagination.* Boston: Shambhala, 2004.

———. *The Wind's Twelve Quarters.* London: Victor Gollancz, 2000 (1975).

Mill, John Stuart. *On Liberty* (1859). In *John Stuart Mill: A Selection of His Works,* ed. John Robson. Indianapolis: Bobbs-Merrill Educational Publishing, 1966.

Morris, William. "Thoughts on Education Under Capitalism." Pp. 496–500 in *William Morris: Artist, Writer, Socialist* (vol. 2), ed. May Morris. Oxford: Basil Blackwell, 1936.

Mumford, Lewis. *Technics and Civilization*. New York: Harcourt Brace and Company, 1963 (1934).

Noble, David. *Forces of Production: A Social History of Industrial Automation*. New York and Oxford: Oxford University Press, 1986.

Sargent, Lyman. "The Three Faces of Utopianism Revisited." *Utopian Studies* 5, no. 1 (1994): 1–37.

Smith, Philip E. II. "Unbuilding Walls: Human Nature and the Nature of Evolutionary and Political Theory in *The Dispossessed*." Pp. 77–96 in *Ursula K. Le Guin*, ed. Joseph D. Olander and Martin Harry Greenberg. New York: Taplinger, 1979.

Stillman, Peter. "'Nothing is, but what is not': Utopias as Practical Political Philosophy." *Critical Review of International Social and Political Philosophy* 3, nos. 2/3 (Summer/Autumn 2000): 9–24. Reprinted in *The Philosophy of Utopia*, ed. Barbara Goodwin. London and Portland, OR: Frank Cass, 2001.

Urbanowicz, Victor. "Personal and Political in *The Dispossessed*." *Science-Fiction Studies* 5, no. 2 (July 1978): 110–17.

Varikas, Eleni. "The Utopian Surplus." *Thesis Eleven* 68 (February 2002): 101–5.

Wegner, Phillip. *Imaginary Communities: Utopia, the Nation, and the Spatial Histories of Modernity*. Berkeley: University of California Press, 2002.

Worlds Apart: Ursula K. Le Guin and the Possibility of Method

Simon Stow

> This is a work of fiction. Names, characters, places, and incidents are products of the author's imagination or are used fictitiously and are not to be construed as real. Any resemblance to actual events, locales, organizations, or persons, living or dead, is entirely coincidental.[1]

*D*espite this disclaimer, printed on the copyright page of Ursula K. Le Guin's *The Dispossessed*, the novel has almost always been regarded as an account of the promise and problems of an anarchist society.[2] In many of the critical and political responses to the novel there has, that is to say, been a conflation between the world of the text and the world in which that text is written—between what the anarchist theorist Paul Goodman called the *written* and the *unwritten* worlds[3]— one that makes the former stand in for the latter, undermining or simply ignoring the value of the legal claim made at the outset of the novel. In this moment of tension between the disclaimer and the conflation we see both the complexity of the relationship between Goodman's two worlds—how the distinction between them is less clear cut than some would have us believe[4]—and the problem of utopia in political theory: either the disclaimer is embraced, and the two worlds are seen as entirely separate, with utopia becoming little more than a thought experiment with minor import for our everyday lives; or it is ignored, and the utopia is seen as a detailed blueprint for a future society. In either case, something important in the way of critical reflection is lost. In her creation of two fully realized literary worlds, Anarres and Urras, Le Guin's novel shows us a way out of this binary opposition, one that taps into a long tradition in political thought—stretching all the way from Thucydides to John Rawls—of juxtaposing realities as a source of critical insight. In this instance, however, Le Guin's work offers us a doubly critical perspective: one that forces the reader not only to consider her world and the way that she lives, but also to reflect upon the possibility of utopia itself and its role in political thought and analysis. In this, *The*

Dispossessed offers us not the limited opportunities of a specific critique or thought experiment, but something much more valuable: the experience and the demonstration of replicable critical method.

That *The Dispossessed* is concerned in some way, shape, or form with anarchism cannot be denied. The description of life of the Anarresti population is remarkably close to the accounts of ideal societies in anarchist theory: "Members of a community, not elements of a collectivity, they were not moved by mass feeling; there were as many emotions as there were people. And they did not expect commands to be arbitrary, so they had no practice in disobeying them" (1: 4). Similarly, Shevek describes himself—albeit somewhat ironically—as an "anarchist" (1: 25) in his early encounters with the Urrasti. Even more tellingly, Le Guin, who has described anarchism as "the most idealistic, and to me the most interesting of all political theories," declared that her purpose in writing *The Dispossessed* was to embody anarchism "in a novel, which had not been done before."[5] In this context, the disclaimer that precedes the novel begins to look like an ironic form of *occupatio*, the rhetorical device by which one announces that one is not going to talk about a subject as a means of doing precisely that. It is an approach which is, of course, common to much fiction. No matter how fantastic the written worlds of literature, they must bear at least some resemblance to the unwritten world in which they are disseminated and published, otherwise we readers would not be able to make sense of them; as Wittgenstein observed in another context: "If a lion could talk, we could not understand him."[6] Despite the legal disclaimer that prefaces the novel then, the written world of fiction must stand in some relationship to the unwritten world to the extent that the resemblance of events, locales, organizations, or persons living or dead must be something more than "coincidental." Consciously or unconsciously, written world situations, events, and characters are constructed for the purpose of reflecting upon the unwritten world: they are ways of exploring, amongst other things, the politics, relationships and emotions of the unwritten world under different conditions. We might think, for example, of the Ring of Gyges in Plato's *Republic*, which is used to illustrate the alleged consequences of removing the fear of sanction from human behavior.[7]

The use of the literary as a realm of alternate possibility is especially common in the genres of science fiction, speculative fiction, and utopian literature. Margaret Atwood draws a distinction between the first two categories when she declares that science fiction deals with "technologies we don't yet have, other universes," whereas speculative fiction is concerned with "this planet. It doesn't use things we don't already have or are not already developing."[8] In its acceptance of relatively easy travel between planets, *The Dispossessed* seems to belong quite clearly to Atwood's first category of science fiction. However, in its concern with the unwritten world theory of anarchism, and in the tension on Urras between A-Io and Thu—a tension which clearly corresponds to the conflict between the United States and the Soviet Union in the period that the novel was written—*The Dispossessed* might also be regarded as speculative fiction: exploring the possibilities and implications of ideologies and political problems that we already have. In this alone, *The Dispossessed* might seem to be disqualified from the genre of utopian literature altogether. Resting on a Latin pun, the word utopia as coined by Thomas More suggests both no place and a better place, one that is divorced from current political formations. In the words of David Chidester and Edward T. Linenthal, "utopian space is unbounded, unfixed to any particular location, a place that can only be reached by breaking out of, or being liberated from the bonds of a prevailing social order."[9] If this is indeed the case, it is little wonder that Francis Bacon complained in *The Advancement of Learning* that, "As for the philosophers, they make imaginary laws for imaginary commonwealths, and their discourses are as the stars, which give little light because they are so high."[10] It is, however, precisely this notion of utopia that *The Dispossessed* calls into question, leading us back to an older tradition of social and political thought. It is a tradition that forces us to recognize the connectedness of utopia to the political context in which it is written, with critical leverage and theoretical insight emerging from the juxtaposition of the written world of utopia with the political problems of the unwritten world from which it springs.

For the Greeks, *Theoria*, the root of the modern word theory, was primarily connected to the noun *theoros*, meaning an "observer" or "spectator." As such it was inextricably associated with the theater: an alternative space in which, as many studies have shown, the Greeks addressed their most pressing social and political issues in comedic or tragic form.[11] Additionally, however, *theoros* had the implication of someone who travels to see other cities and places: an ambassador or official envoy sent by the city to other places to witness and testify on their actions. It is against this background that we should consider Shevek's oft-repeated claim that he is a "theoretician" (3: 86) concerned with "theoretical work" (12: 366). Shevek's role in the text is precisely that: one who travels between worlds to reflect on them both. This was certainly the role of the theater in Greek political life, with the citizens acting as spectators, reflecting upon the world depicted on stage, and then returning, potentially transformed, to their quotidian and political worlds. The aim of the exercise was not, of course, simply to repeat that which they had seen depicted on stage in their own lives—had they done so Greek life would have been as bloody as that of the Romans—but rather to incorporate that which they had seen into their lives by synthesizing the world of the theater with the world of politics and that of their daily existence. It was, on a much smaller scale, an opportunity for ordinary Greek citizens to engage in the epic tradition of journey and return that marked Homer's *Odyssey*.[12] The dual notions of journey and return and of synthesizing dueling perspectives are central to Shevek's life, and indeed, to the Odonian philosophy by which he attempts to live.

The connection between Odonian philosophy and the notion of homecoming—or what the Greeks called *nostos*—is evidenced by the inscription on Odo's tomb, the latter part of which reads "*true voyage is return*" (3: 84). Shevek, we are told, "would always be one for whom the return was as important as the voyage out. To go was not enough for him, only half-enough; he must come back" (2: 54). Indeed, one of Shevek's final observations in the novel is that "True journey is return" (13: 386). There is, nevertheless, something of a tension between the journey and the return. For Shevek is aware that the place to which he seeks to return will no longer be the same, revealing the implicit connection between the Greek *nostos* and nostalgia: longing for what is lost. We are told that Shevek believed that "the very nature of the voyage, like a circumnavigation of the globe, implied return. You shall not go down twice to the same river, nor can you go home again" (2: 54). Shevek's theoretical work is, perhaps, an attempt to compensate for this nostalgia. "You *can* go home again, the General Temporal Theory asserts, so long as you understand that home is a place where you have never been" (2: 55). In this, Shevek's work might be seen as belonging to the tradition of Epic Theory, what Peter Euben called "the attempt to redeem in thought what is denied in practice."[13] By seeking to reconcile the journey with the changed location of the return, Shevek's theoretical work might be thought of as the attempt to overcome the disconnect caused by the journey or to ameliorate the profound sense of loss that generates feelings of nostalgia. An alternative and more forward-looking response to such loss is, however, to embrace it, and to seek to reconcile the journey with the loss through critical reflection and the recognition of the transfiguration of self that produces the loss. Indeed, this second response seems to be a better account of Shevek's experience in the novel. The text appears to be profoundly concerned with the transfiguring nature of the journey between worlds, with the insight generated by the disorientation and unfamiliarity of travel. Many aspects of *The Dispossessed* echo Plato's *Republic*; Shevek's travel reverberates with the allegory of the cave.

Plato's *Republic* is, of course, a text that is replete with references to journey and return, from the Philosopher Kings who separate themselves from the Ideal City, only to return in order to rule; to Er who dies, goes down to the underworld, and returns with a message to for living. It is, however, in the allegory of the cave that we can see the strongest parallel between Le Guin's work and Plato's text. Shevek parallels Plato's cave dweller who is dragged upward into the light and who, as a result of his journey, experiences a profound sense of disorientation and discomfort. The first chapter of *The Dispossessed*—which, like Plato's *Republic*, begins in a port, traditionally a place for the influx of new ideas into a community—deals specifically with Shevek's debilitating sense of disorientation caused by the journey from Anarres to Urras. It is a disorientation caused by the experience of space travel itself, one that emerges from the inversion of his traditional perspective on his own world. "This blackness," we are told, "reversed the whole picture, made it negative. The real stone part of it was no longer concave and full of light but convex, reflecting, rejecting light. It was not a plain or bowl but a sphere, a ball of white stone falling down in blackness. It was his world. 'I don't understand,' he said aloud" (1: 6). It is a disorientation which affects Shevek physically: his mental state reflecting his geographical position. "His arms and buttocks ached from injections; he ran a fever that was never quite heightened to delirium but left him in a limbo between reason and unreason, no man's land" (1: 9). As with Plato's traveler, Shevek gradually becomes adjusted to his new circumstances—even if he is never entirely comfortable on Urras—and, again like the figure from Plato's text, decides that he must return. However, the disorientation caused by the journey makes Shevek an exile in both contexts—Urras and Anarres—and it is for this reason that he can no longer ever really go home again.

The connection between critical theory and exile is a strong one, both in the history of political thought and in Le Guin's text. Shevek recognizes that "he came from a self-exiled society" (3: 89), and, upon visiting the monument to Odo on Anarres, Shevek has a profound moment of realization. We are told that for "the first time in his life he comprehended" that "Odo was an alien: an exile" (4: 101). The very nature of exile makes one a spectator. It is this existence as a spectator—one who lives between worlds but never fully part of either—that generates the strong possibility of critical insight: we should think of Aristotle the Macedonian writing on Athens, Tocqueville the Frenchman writing on America, Marx the German writing on England, or Dante, whose political theorizing began only upon his exile from the actual practice of politics. It is, however, in the allegory of the cave that we once again find the strongest parallel between Shevek and the history of political theory. Having returned to the cave, the figure in Plato's allegory would, Socrates tells us, be mocked by those who had never left their posts, and they would deny the need to go upward toward the light of knowledge. So hostile would be their response, says Socrates, that were they not still chained to their posts, they would probably try to murder the traveler. The traveler on the other hand would, we are told, undoubtedly benefit from this experience. For, upon hearing opinions that differed from his own, he would not reject them outright, but would be forced to consider whether they came either from ignorance or from a brilliance greater than his own.[14] He would, that is to say, be opened up to the existence of conflicting perspectives, and with it, the possibility of dialectic.

Dialectic, according to Stanley Fish, is an experience that forces people into a "rigorous scrutiny of everything they believe in and live by."[15] His definition draws heavily on a reading of Plato's *Phaedrus*, in particular the discussion of the distinction between the good and bad lover. The bad lover, according to Socrates, merely flatters the object of his affections, intent solely on satisfying his most immediate and fleshly desires. The good lover, on the other hand, offers up criticism in the hope that the object of his affections might become more perfect.[16] It is in this possibility of being challenged—of being faced with the unfamiliar and unexpected—that the possibility of dialectic lies, for the object of the critic's affections must seek to reconcile the criticism with its aim. He must find, that is to say, a new way to think. Doing so, however, can be a profoundly disorienting experience: what we might refer to as the discomfort of dialectic. This is precisely what we see in Shevek's journey between worlds and indeed with his concern with dualist perspectives, and his attempts to reconcile them throughout the text.

The notion of competing perspectives dominates *The Dispossessed*. In only the second paragraph of the novel we are told about the dual nature of the boundary wall of the Port of Anarres. "Like all walls," we learn, "it was ambiguous, two-faced. What was inside it and what was outside it depended on which side you were on" (1: 1). Later, in the same chapter, Shevek responds to the suggestion that he has been locked up to keep others out of his quarters with the observation "To lock out, to lock in, the same act" (1: 11). Similarly in a passage that echoes Nietzsche's characterization of his genealogical project—seeing things as if from another planet[17]—Shevek observes that the "way to see how beautiful the earth is, is to see it as the moon. The way to see how beautiful life is, is from the vantage point of death" (6: 190). Nor is Shevek the only character who experiences—consciously or unconsciously—this dualism. As a young boy at the Northsetting Regional Institute of the Noble and Material Sciences, Shevek is the participant in the following conversation between two of his classmates:

> "I never thought before," said Tirin unruffled, "of the fact that there are people sitting on a hill, up there, on Urras, looking at Anarres, at us, and saying, 'Look, there's the Moon.' Our earth is their Moon; our Moon is their earth."
> "Where, then, is Truth?" declaimed Bedap, and yawned.
> "In the hill one happens to be sitting on," said Tirin. (2: 41)

Journeying between worlds as a source of different perspectives and potential critical insight is, perhaps, the central theme of the novel. In this instance the theme is somewhat tritely presented, hence Bedap's yawn, but the shifting of perspectives as a source of critical insight permeates even the structure of the novel, with each alternate chapter moving back and forth geographically and temporally to offer the reader an experience similar to those undergone by the characters in the text. That the final two chapters juxtapose the period immediately before Shevek's departure for Urras with his return from it, suggests that we have experienced, at the level of literature, something of what Shevek's General Temporal Theory seeks to achieve in space and time travel: some notion of synthesis or dialectic.

Dialectic occurs then when some way is found to reconcile two apparently conflicting positions, by locating some third position that both accounts for and explains the apparent conflict in such a way as to make the conflict disappear. Scientifically speaking, successful dialectic produces what Thomas Kuhn calls a "paradigm shift"[18]: a new way of looking at the world that allows us to do more than the previous way of conceiving of reality could. It is precisely this that Shevek is seeking in his General Temporal Theory; hence his exchange with Dearri at Vea's party:

"You can't assert two contradictory statements about the same thing," said Dearri, with the calmness of superior knowledge. "In other words, one of these 'aspects' is real, the other's simply an illusion."

"Many physicists have said that," Shevek assented.

"But what do you say?" asked the one who wanted to know.

"Well, I think it's an easy way out of the difficulty. . . . Can one dismiss either being, or becoming, as an illusion? Becoming without being is meaningless. Being without becoming is a big bore. . . . If the mind is able to perceive time in both these ways, then a true chronosophy should provide a field in which the relation of the two aspects or processes of time could be understood." (7: 224)

Or, more succinctly, it is later said about Shevek that: "To him a thinking man's job was not to deny one reality at the expense of the other, but to include and connect. It was not an easy job" (9: 284–85). In this instance, as with many others, Shevek's quest for a scientific theory that will incorporate and synthesize apparently conflicting positions runs parallel to the political aspects of Le Guin's novel. Far from presenting a simple depiction of the promise and problems of anarchism as a political theory, the novel offers us instead a method for critical reflection. It is a method that reflects a perennial tradition in political theory: that of offering dualistic accounts as a way of prompting ongoing critical thought and generating dialectic. In so doing, the tradition seeks to change *how* we think, not just what we *know*. Such an approach stands in stark contrast to the way in which literary works, utopias among them, are often read in political contexts: as the written world depiction of simple lessons or maxims to be applied unmediated to the unwritten world. Such maxims, as Plato tells us in the *Republic*, can easily become platitudes and, as such, the enemy of genuine critical thought.

The first book of Plato's *Republic* famously begins with Socrates systematically working his way through the then contemporary platitudes about justice: giving what is owed, or helping one's friends and hurting one's enemies, or simply the will of the stronger. The counterarguments that Socrates offers to these positions are, of course, notoriously weak.[19] John Seery, amongst others, has suggested that what we are witnessing in this first book of the *Republic*, is Plato, the author of the text, appealing over the heads of his characters to alert us the readers to the ways in which ill-thought-out conceptions, or simply the rote repetitions of platitudinous positions, are easily defeated by even the simplest and most wrong headed of counterarguments.[20] Against this background, Seery suggests, we might think of Socrates' shocking proposals for the Just City in the *Republic* as an attempt to generate critical political thought in the reader. On this account, it is the juxtaposition of the Just City with the Athenian polis, rather than the outlining of a literal blueprint for an Ideal City, that is central to the text.[21] Seery's argument is that what we are witnessing in the *Republic* is *Platonic* irony: a way of generating uncertainty in the reader, an uncertainty that disrupts the platitudes of everyday life, and paves the way for genuine critical thought. In *The Dispossessed* we see a similar relationship between Odonian philosophy as it is practiced on Anarres and Shevek's journey to Urras. For all the individual liberty promised on Anarres, it becomes clear that by Shevek's time the society has stagnated. In the words of Victor Urbanowicz: "Its prolonged isolation has made it xenophobic towards Urras, quite against anarchist ideals of human cooperation and solidarity across political boundaries; the administrative syndicates have developed informal hierarchies, hardening into bureaucracies and clinging to powers acquired during long-past emergencies; custom has made most persons ashamed to refuse postings even when acceptance means being separated for years from a mate or from one's chosen work."[22] Indeed, we see the strongest criticism of the Anarresti society in an intense exchange between Shevek and Bedap where the latter declares: "You can't crush ideas by repressing them. You can only crush them by ignoring them. By refusing to think, refusing to change. And that's precisely what our society is doing!" (6: 165) Later, in the same exchange, Bedap notes how Odonian philosophy has, like the Greek conceptions of justice depicted in the *Republic*, become simply platitudinous. "Kids learn to parrot Odo's words as if they were *laws*—the ultimate blasphemy!" (6: 168). Most tellingly, perhaps, from a theoretical viewpoint—given the genealogy of that word and its meaning to the Greeks—we see the stagnation of Anarres in the role of the Theater in its society.

Whereas the various arts taught on Anarres "served largely as elements of architecture and town planning" (6: 156–57), we are told that "only the theater stood wholly alone, and only the theater was ever called 'the Art'—a thing complete in itself" (6: 157). Indeed, there appears to have been a thriving theatrical community on the planet:

> There were many regional and traveling troupes of actors and dancers, repertory companies, very often with a playwright attached. They performed tragedies, semi-improvised comedies, mimes. They were as welcome as rain in the lonely desert towns, they were the glory of the year wherever they came. Rising out of and embodying the isolation and communality of the Anarresti spirit, the drama had obtained extraordinary power and brilliance. (6: 157)

As such, the claim that critical thought or reflection had stagnated on Anarres might be thought to be overstated. With a thriving theatrical community, the opportunities for *Theoria* on Anarres might seem to have been positively bountiful, until that is, one examines the *type* of plays that were presented on Anarres, plays that were said to be the "embodying [of] the isolation and communality of the Anarresti spirit." Turning again to Plato's *Republic*, we might recall the sort of poetry that Socrates advocates in his Ideal City, poetry that celebrates the virtues of the city at the expense of that which calls its central values into question. Such poetry serves only to reinforce the values of the city's rulers, without concern about artistic merit. We might think of the didactic art of the Soviet Union, or the thinly veiled moralizing of television's "after school specials." It is indicative that the conditions of life on Anarres were so dreary that even this form of stolid entertainment was so gratefully received, even to the extent of being regarded as extraordinarily powerful and brilliant. That plays on Anarres were actually of a drearily didactic variety is indicated by the treatment handed out to the rather more transgressive theater of Shevek's contemporary, Tirin. We are told that his play "made trouble for him" (10: 327). The play, in which an Urrasti smuggled himself onto Anarres, echoes, of course, the plot of the novel and Shevek's role in it, even down to the failed attempt at copulation caused by conflicting social mores. Shevek, who did not care for traditional Anarresti theater, describes Tirin as "a born artist. Not a craftsman—a creator. An inventor-destroyer, the kind who's got to turn everything upside down and inside out. A satirist, a man who praises through rage" (10: 328). For such acts of creativity and critical reflection—for producing theater in the Greek tradition—Tirin is forced into therapy. We are told that "he was destroyed as a person" (10: 328), and that all he could do thereafter was to write the same play over and over again, his creativity reduced to the rote-like repetition that plagued the stymied Odonian philosophy of Anarres. Critical reflection was, we are to conclude, not welcome on Anarres, with Odonian platitudes replacing genuine political thought. In her depiction of the costs of this decline in critical thought for life on Urras, Le Guin the author seems to appeal over the heads of her characters—as, Seery argues, Plato does in *The Republic*—to alert us, her readers, to the dangers of such a decline in our own lives. Indeed, she appears to warn us against reducing her text to the simple lessons of Anarresti theater. In so doing, Le Guin avoids the self-defeating paradox or potential hypocrisy of making this warning itself a simple platitude. She does so by making the warning part of a critical *method*, one that demands that we her readers take part in the process to think and reflect for ourselves. She encourages us as readers, that is to say, to engage in a potentially transfiguring journey between worlds—written and unwritten—by constantly alerting us to the fictionality of her own enterprise.

In only the second chapter of the novel, Shevek, in an argument with Bedap about the respective values of Anarres and Urras, responds angrily to his friend's rhetorical use of a scientific analogy. "Oh, you can prove anything using the analogy, and you know it," he declares (2: 43). It is a warning we readers, especially those of us concerned with reading Le Guin's novel in a political context, would do well to take seriously. In using literature as evidence in our political arguments we too run the risk of arguing by analogy, of holding that the written world is sufficiently similar to the unwritten world to make it good evidence for our arguments about unwritten world politics. Consequently, readings of *The Dispossessed*, or indeed *any* novel, which reduce that text to simple lessons about anarchism, communism, or indeed *any* political theory, run the risk of the conflation of worlds identified at the outset. Just as the worlds of Anarres and Urras are similar but different, the written world of *The Dispossessed* is similar but different from the unwritten world in which Le Guin wrote her text. Neither the simple conflation of worlds which marks certain types of utopia reading or political-literary criticism—the sort which looks for political lessons or maxims in the text—nor the extreme disassociation of worlds—that which we see in the legal disclaimer that prefaces the text and warns us that resemblance to actual events is coincidental—captures the relationship between the worlds accurately. Nor indeed could either of these approaches do so.

For, just as we cannot summarize a poem—the question "what is it about?" asks about themes but misses something crucial to the poetic form—we cannot give a scientific or even a discursively stable account of the relationship between the written and unwritten worlds. Rather the relationship between these worlds is something to be *experienced*. Le Guin reminds of this not only by depicting the experience of moving between worlds in Shevek's journey from Anarres to Urras and back again, but also by inviting us to experience it for ourselves as we read. She does so by a persistent baring of her device: drawing self-referential attention to the act of reading and the problems of fiction as critical thought.

The reference to reasoning by analogy is but one example of Le Guin's exposing the device. Other more obvious examples are to be found in the book's structure—which invites the reader to move back and forth in space and time and thereby to recreate for herself the *experience* of Shevek's journey—and Le Guin's multiple references to, and use of, reading analogies in her text. We see this when Shevek tries to explain his temporal theory, identifying the role of the agent in creating the experience:

> Well, we think that time "passes," flows past us, but what if it is we who move forward, from past to future, always discovering the new? It would be a little like reading a book, you see. The book is all there, all at once, between its covers. But if you want to read the story and understand it, you must begin with the first page, and go forward, always in order. So the universe would be a very great book, and we would be very small readers. (7: 221)

Similarly, early on in the text, in a passage reminiscent of the Wittgenstein of the *Tractatus*, we are told that: "If a book were written all in numbers it would be true. It would be just. Nothing said in words ever came out quite even. Things in words got twisted and run together, instead of staying straight and fitting together" (2: 31). The inadequacy of words in this context reminds of the inadequacy of books as a form of knowledge, something that Shevek acknowledges when he says of a certain aspect of life on Urras, "you know, I had not ever understood that, in all my reading of Urrasti books" (1: 15). Life on Urras, like reading and indeed thinking, are, we are reminded, not things to be experienced secondhand. When Le Guin draws attention to the fictionality of her enterprise she does so in such a way as to remind the reader of the partiality and incompleteness of the picture presented in the text. She reminds us of the inadequacy of literature by itself to capture the totality of the experience of some nonliterary reality and, as such, of the differences between the written and unwritten worlds. We are reminded, that is to say, to avoid the easy conflation of worlds which produces the trite lessons and maxims of reductive, politically motivated reading.

A particularly revealing example of Le Guin baring the device occurs in the second chapter with the introduction of an author footnote, the only one in the text. In this moment (2: 47), the narrative approach breaks down and the author collapses the fourth wall to speak in her own voice about the literary world that she has created. In this footnote concerning the written-world word "*tadde*" and its relationship to the unwritten-world word "Papa," the information she imparts could easily have been incorporated in the text of the novel in numerous other ways; certainly Le Guin is not shy about having characters explain more complex concepts in longer passages of dialogue. That she chooses to incorporate the information in a footnote momentarily plucks us from the written world of the narrative back into the unwritten world of the writing of the text. In this moment, Le Guin reminds us that this written world is the construction of a particular author with a particular purpose. She also shows us just how pervasive in her work is the notion of travel between worlds as a source of insight. We are once again invited to travel between worlds, and journey not from Anarres to Urras and back with Shevek, but rather from the unwritten world to the written world and back again. Just as Shevek develops the critical perspective of *Theoria* from his travels, to develop the same, by using the written world of literature to reflect upon the unwritten world in which we live.

The claim that literature can be a source of insight into the way we live our lives—political and otherwise—is, of course, not new: we can see it in the work of thinkers as diverse as Matthew Arnold and Martha Nussbaum.[23] Le Guin's work, however, differs from this rather didactic tradition by showing us that the reduction of texts to simple lessons, be they about Empire, empathy, or anarchism, though easily done, is not the way to generate meaningful critical thought. It suggests that, in this process of generating critical reflection, the *journey* not the *play* is the thing. Le Guin illustrates that insight comes not from simply applying the lessons of literature to the world in which we live, but by using both worlds to reflect upon and consider the other. In a highly ironic moment in the *Phaedrus*, Socrates suggests that texts can only remind us of what we already know (even as that text seeks to transfigure and change our understanding of the act of reading)[24]; and indeed, reading to confirm what we already believe to be the case is a danger in all politically motivated approaches to literary texts. In this instance Le Guin's work might, however, be thought of as a *positive* reminder, not of the pre-existing concerns we bring to the text, but of an older tradition in the history and methods of political thought, one that juxtaposes realities as a source of insight. We see such an approach in such seemingly disparate works as Thucydides' *History of the Peloponnesian War,* where the author juxtaposes the idealized Athens of Pericles' Funeral Oration with the dystopian Athens of the Plague in order to offer us a more rounded and complex vision of the city,[25] and John Rawls's *A Theory of Justice,* where the insights about justice gleaned in the Original Position are to be compared and contrasted with the agents' preexisting moral intuitions in a process that Rawls refers to as "Reflective Equilibrium."[26] In each instance, the critical insight of *Theoria* emerges not from simply constructing another world and reading-off the lessons for our own, but rather by traveling between them and using the perspectives gained from evaluating both realities in tandem with the other.

The subtitle of Le Guin's novel is *An Ambiguous Utopia,* whose meaning is, perhaps, as ambiguous as the utopia itself. The reading that has been offered here, however, suggests that we should read this subtitle as a reminder of the inherent ambiguity of the text—*any* text—as a source of insight into the political and that what we derive from the text depends crucially upon how it is read. In reminding us of this, however, and the role of the juxtaposition of realities in the creation of *Theoria,* Le Guin also offers us a method. It is one that has recently been revived in the work of Fredric Jameson, work in which Jameson, crucially and revealingly, cites Le Guin as an inspiration and an example. Jameson revives the argument that utopia is not simply a blueprint for a future but rather a method. What "utopian oppositions allow us to do, by way of negation," he writes, is "to grasp the moment of truth in each term. Put the other way around, the value of each term is differential, it lies not in its own substantive content but as an ideological critique of its opposite number."[27] Utopia, he suggests, should be seen as dialectical, not didactical. It is, he writes, "a negative dialectic in which each terms persists in its negation of the other; it is in their double negation that the genuine political and philosophical content is to be located."[28] In *The Dispossessed,* Le Guin offers us a powerful illustration of this method, one that shows us a much richer way of understanding the role of literature in critical reflection, and indeed, the function of utopia in political thought than that identified at the outset of this piece. She offers us a replicable critical method, and in so doing she connects her work to a long tradition in the history of political philosophy. Indeed, it is a testament to the complexity of her approach that Peter Euben's summary of the work of Hannah Arendt seems equally applicable to Le Guin's *The Dispossessed.* "What she teaches us," writes Euben of Arendt, "is as much a practice of reading as a set of doctrines or specific arguments."[29] Le Guin, in her complexity and nuance, offers political thinkers a similarly valuable gift.

NOTES

1. Ursula K. Le Guin, *The Dispossessed: An Ambiguous Utopia* (New York: Harper & Row, 1974), cited in the text by chapter and page to the 387-page Eos HarperCollins edition of 2001, copyright page.

2. See, for example, Victor Urbanowicz, "Personal and Political in *The Dispossessed*," *Science-Fiction Studies* 5, no. 2 (July 1978): 110–17.

3. Cited in Philip Roth, *Reading Myself and Others* (New York: Vintage, 2001), xiii.

4. "I find it more useful than the distinction between imagination and reality, or art and life, first, because everyone can think through readily enough to the clear-cut differences between the two, and second, because the worlds that I feel myself shuttling between every day couldn't be better described" (Roth, *Reading*, xiii).

5. Ursula K. Le Guin, *The Wind's Twelve Quarters* (New York: Harper & Row, 1975), 232.

6. Ludwig Wittgenstein, *Philosophical Investigations* (Englewood Cliffs, NJ: Prentice Hall, 1958), 223e.

7. Plato, *The Republic*, 359*d*–360*c*.

8. Mel Gussow, "Atwood's Dystopian Warning: Hand-Wringer's Tale of Tomorrow," *New York Times*, Tuesday 24 June 2003, B1–B5.

9. David Chidester and Edward T. Linenthal, Introduction to *American Sacred Space*, ed. David Chidester and Edward T. Linenthal (Bloomington: Indiana University Press, 1995), 15.

10. Francis Bacon, *The Advancement of Learning*, II.20.1, quoted in Sheldon Wolin's *Hobbes and the Epic Tradition of Political Theory* (Los Angeles: William Andrews Clark Memorial Library, 1970), 13.

11. See, for example, John J. Winkler and Froma I. Zeitlin, *Nothing to Do with Dionysos?: Athenian Drama in Its Social Context* (Princeton, NJ: Princeton University Press, 1990), especially the essays by Longo and Goldhill.

12. See Patrick J. Deneen, *The Odyssey of Political Theory: The Politics of Departure and Return* (Lanham, MD: Rowman & Littlefield, 2000).

13. J. Peter Euben, *Platonic Noise* (Princeton, NJ: Princeton University Press, 2003), 95.

14. Plato, *The Republic*, 518*a*.

15. Stanley Fish, *Self-Consuming Artifacts: The Experience of Seventeenth-Century Literature* (Berkeley: University of California Press, 1972), 1.

16. Plato, *Phaedrus*, 239–40.

17. Friedrich Nietzsche, *On the Genealogy of Morals*, trans. Walter Kaufmann and R. J. Hollingdale (New York: Vintage Books, 1989), 117.

18. Thomas L. Kuhn, *The Structure of Scientific Revolutions* (Chicago: University of Chicago Press, 1996).

19. See, for example, Julia Annas, *An Introduction to Plato's Republic* (Oxford: Oxford University Press, 1990).

20. John Evan Seery, *Political Returns: Irony in Politics and Theory from Plato to the Antinuclear Movement* (Boulder, CO: Westview Press, 1990).

21. For a recent revival of the argument for the *Republic* as literal blueprint see George Klosko, *Jacobins and Utopians: The Political Theory of Fundamental Moral Reform* (Notre Dame, IN: University of Notre Dame Press, 2003).

22. Urbanowicz, "Personal and Political," 112.

23. Matthew Arnold, *Culture and Anarchy* (New Haven, CT: Yale University Press, 1994); Martha Nussbaum, *Poetic Justice: The Literary Imagination and Public Life* (Boston: Beacon Press, 1995).

24. Plato, *Phaedrus*, 275.

25. Thucydides, *History of the Peloponnesian War* (New York: Penguin Books, 1972).

26. John Rawls, *A Theory of Justice* (Cambridge, MA: Harvard University Press, 1971).

27. Fredric Jameson, "The Politics of Utopia." *New Left Review* 25 (Jan./Feb. 2004), 50.

28. Jameson, "Politics of Utopia," 50.

29. Euben, *Platonic Noise*, 41.

WORKS CITED

Annas, Julia. *An Introduction to Plato's Republic.* Oxford: Oxford University Press, 1990.

Arnold, Matthew. *Culture and Anarchy.* New Haven, CT: Yale University Press, 1994.

Bacon, Francis. *The Advancement of Learning.*

Chidester, David, and Edward T. Linenthal. "Introduction." Pp. 2–42 in *American Sacred Space*, ed. David Chidester and Edward T. Linenthal. Bloomington: Indiana University Press, 1995.

Deneen, Patrick J. *The Odyssey of Political Theory: The Politics of Departure and Return.* Lanham, MD: Rowman & Littlefield, 2000.

Euben, J. Peter. *Platonic Noise.* Princeton, NJ: Princeton University Press, 2003.

Fish, Stanley. *Self-Consuming Artifacts: The Experience of Seventeenth-Century Literature.* Berkeley: University of California Press, 1972.

Gussow, Mel. "Atwood's Dystopian Warning: Hand-Wringer's Tale of Tomorrow." *New York Times,* Tuesday 24 June 2003, B1–B5.

Jameson, Fredric. "The Politics of Utopia." *New Left Review* 25 (Jan./Feb. 2004): 35–54.

Klosko, George. *Jacobins and Utopians: The Political Theory of Fundamental Moral Reform.* Notre Dame, IN: University of Notre Dame Press, 2003.

Kuhn, Thomas L. *The Structure of Scientific Revolutions.* Chicago: University of Chicago Press, 1996.

Le Guin, Ursula K. *The Dispossessed: An Ambiguous Utopia.* New York: Eos, HarperCollins, 2001 (1974).

———. *The Wind's Twelve Quarters.* New York: Harper & Row, 1975.

Nietzsche, Friedrich. *On the Genealogy of Morals.* Trans. Walter Kaufmann and R. J. Hollingdale. New York: Vintage Books, 1989.

Nussbaum, Martha. *Poetic Justice: The Literary Imagination and Public Life.* Boston: Beacon Press, 1995.

Plato. *Phaedrus.*

———. *The Republic.*

Rawls, John. *A Theory of Justice.* Cambridge, MA: Harvard University Press, 1971.

Roth, Philip. *Reading Myself and Others.* New York: Vintage, 2001.

Seery, John Evan. *Political Returns: Irony in Politics and Theory from Plato to the Antinuclear Movement.* Boulder, CO: Westview Press, 1990.

Thucydides. *History of the Peloponnesian War.* New York: Penguin Books, 1972.

Urbanowicz, Victor. "Personal and Political in *The Dispossessed*." *Science-Fiction Studies* 5, no. 2 (July 1978): 110–17.

Winkler, John J., and Froma I. Zeitlin. *Nothing to Do with Dionysos?: Athenian Drama in Its Social Context*. Princeton, NJ: Princeton University Press, 1990.

Wittgenstein, Ludwig. *Philosophical Investigations*. Englewood Cliffs, NJ: Prentice Hall, 1958.

Wolin, Sheldon. *Hobbes and the Epic Tradition of Political Theory*. Los Angeles: William Andrews Clark Memorial Library, 1970.

II

POST-CONSUMERIST POLITICS

• 3 •

The Dispossessed as
Ecological Political Theory

Peter G. Stillman

$\mathscr{T}$*he Dispossessed* was published about four years after the first Earth Day in the United States and the European Year of the Protection of Nature, the beginnings of the contemporary environmental movement.[1] Like many utopias since then, it is attentive to ecological issues. The natural environment of Anarres is so striking as to lead the reader to expect ecological concerns and insights. In this chapter, I shall examine *The Dispossessed* from the point of view of environmental and ecological concerns.[2] Although I am interested in the contributions the book may offer to ecological thought, my primary concern is the insights into *The Dispossessed* we may gain by using the perspectives of environmental issues.

ANARCHY AND THE PROBLEM OF SCARCITY

Environmental issues matter in Le Guin's *The Dispossessed* in one way central to its presentation of anarchy as a realistic possible construction of human social life: as against critics of anarchism who might argue that successful anarchy requires an economy of relative plenty in order to minimize conflict over scarce goods and services,[3] Le Guin shows an ongoing anarchist society on Anarres that has existed for seven generations on a barren, dry, windy planet where there is little margin for error (6: 186) and that continues in the face of an extensive, four-year drought leading to pervasive shortages during Shevek's life. She provides a "thought-experiment" or an "imagined" truth[4] of how an anarchist society can—in a realistic manner, with recognizably human actors—confront scarcities in a sustainable manner.

Anarres employs a variety of strategies to enable human life in an "inimical" environment (4: 118) with limited water, food, forests, and animal life. The Anarresti have made choices among major transportation technologies: they use airships, trains, and bikes to travel, rejecting fuel-guzzling planes and automobiles. They have made choices about housing: because single-family houses are wasteful of building materials, space, and energy, they build dormitory blocks, with common rooms and shared eating areas—one story high because of the earthquake danger.

They are frugal with necessities such as water, introducing faucets that turn themselves off and purifying toilet water in "manure plants" that filter out the waste for agricultural use. They use solar energy and wind turbines; and, to save electricity, lights cannot be turned on until the sun has set low enough to require them. They recycle: Shevek is incredulous when on the spaceship going to Urras his clothes are returned to him, sterilized and wrapped in paper, and the paper is not recycled but disposed of by being burned or ejected from the spaceship, and equally surprised when his "disposable" pajamas are placed in the trash.[5]

When a particularly intense drought hits Anarres, the citizens respond. They accept Divlab postings to jobs that the emergency requires be done, even if the posting entails inconvenience. They accede to a cut in rations (which excepts those engaged in hard physical labor, who need the calories to be able to work, and pregnant women). In general, because all are treated fairly—no one has luxuries while another starves, everyone (except for a few free riders) works—Anarresti are willing to suffer lowered rations and other hardships equally. So Anarres's environmental successes do not derive from unrealistically plentiful resources or from fancifully altruistic, kind, or idealistic people. Rather, the example of Anarres shows that anarchy is ecologically sound because anarchists can use scarce resources efficiently and sustainably over generations, even when debilitating drought occurs.

Because the anarchist society of Anarres can respond effectively to scarcity, it can resolve the problem that Hobbes thought would lead to a state of war of all against all and require a central authority with enough coercive power to establish law and order, determine the distribution of "mine and thine," and maintain the peace. Even Hobbes's liberal respondents, such as Locke, Smith, and *The Federalist Papers*, worry that in conditions of scarcity the poor could be disruptive and so the state needs to be strong. Sharing their concerns about scarcity and conflict, Marx thought that any attempt to replace capitalism, liberalism, and possessive individualism with a free, egalitarian, communist society would fail unless the unprecedented productive powers that capitalism had brought into existence could be maintained and expanded.[6] What liberal capitalism and Marxism cannot do, Le Guin's anarchy, as practiced on Anarres, can: establish and maintain a society of liberty, equality, and community despite severe shortages of resources.

But Le Guin's portrayal of Anarres can lead the reader to a series of questions. From the perspective of environmental and ecological issues, three are perhaps salient. Anarchy on Anarres allows for the resolution of important environmental issues of resource use and disposal, but is anarchy the only social arrangement that can resolve these issues? What about environmental and ecological issues that go beyond resource use and pollution, such as how human beings relate psychologically or spiritually to what surrounds us, how the human species maintains and reproduces itself, and how human beings relate to and fit in with the ecosystem as a whole? Finally, although *The Dispossessed* presents an imagined anarchist society that continues on Anarres under conditions of scarcity, is anarchy possible under conditions of relative plenty? Looked at within the confines of the written text: is anarchy possible on A-Io with its relative plenty? Beyond the written text: is anarchy a possible answer for the high consumption Western world of 1974 or now, and if so how can contemporary industrial-capitalist countries move toward the environmental practices and the human freedom of Anarres? In other words, what is the relevance of *The Dispossessed* to the world in which Le Guin wrote it and in which it continues to be printed and read?

RESOURCES USE AND DISPOSAL

Le Guin gives a direct answer to the first question: anarchy is not the only practical response to scarcity. Although substantially richer in resources than Anarres, Urras's inegalitarian distribution of wealth means that many Urrasti suffer a shortage of resources, as Efor makes clear when he talks about his family's life history. Like other Urrasti countries, A-Io does limit resource consumption. Like a typical state, it has passed laws—it has a set of class-biased regulations and taxes—so that resource-intensive or polluting uses are very limited in number, expensive, and thus available only to the rich or powerful. For instance, A-Io's regulations limit automobile use: only the rich can afford private automobiles, whose pollution would be overwhelming if everyone owned a car. Fur-bearing animals are protected. Shevek's Iotian guides are proud: A-Io "had led the world for centuries, they said, in ecological control and the husbanding of natural resources" (3: 82) brought about in response to serious over-mining (3: 94). What the United States and other industrial-capitalist countries were just beginning to do when *The Dispossessed* was published, A-Io has been doing for centuries.

So, at the level of consumption and pollution, Anarres and Urras present differing answers. Anarchy is not the only form of social or political interaction that can resolve with relative stability and longevity the environmental issues of consumption and pollution. Or, to change perspective, different political systems can resolve resource use and pollution, and so the environmental issues of resource use and pollution cannot determine the one political system that works best, or is most satisfactory.

Consumption and pollution are important dimensions of environmental activity. For instance, the chief United States legislative achievements at the beginnings of the contemporary environmental movement were the Clean Air Act of 1970 and the Clean Water Act of 1972. But environmentalism also involves how human beings relate to nature.

PSYCHOLOGICAL AND SPIRITUAL DIMENSIONS OF NATURE

Some environmental thinkers see nature as a source of inspiration for human beings or see some part of nature as the symbolic locus of a mystical connection between human beings and nature. They stress the aesthetic dimension of nature,
especially natural beauty, and the human response to nature and to beauty. Le
Guin addresses the theme of beauty throughout *The Dispossessed*. From the first,
Shevek is aware of A-Io's natural abundance: trees in profusion, animals (lacking
on Anarres), birds' songs, and live grass underfoot. Looking out the window of his
quarters "was the most beautiful view Shevek had ever seen" (3: 65), a complex
landscape combining nature and art, greenery and buildings, the organic and the
rectilinear.[7] Touring, he sees farms that reflect tidiness and order, soaring handsome architecture, and old buildings exuding tradition. His room's proportions
are graceful, its furnishings "beautifully carved" (3: 64), and the men's and
women's clothes "gorgeous" (3: 83). At first sight Urras appears to Shevek as a
paradise (5: 126, 129).

Shevek knows how much he and other Anarresti could benefit from the
bountiful and polysemous environments of A-Io. He immediately feels at home in
such a handsome world (3: 77). Some experiences, like the singing of birds or the
colors of forests in autumn, provide a context for human enjoyment lacking on
silent and monochromatic Anarres, just as the soaring architecture lifts the spirits
above the functional, plain, and well-proportioned one-story Anarresti buildings.
The past still exists in the present in A-Io: Shevek visits Odo's prison and lives in
rooms inhabited by many previous generations. The existence of mammals of all
sizes serves to connect human animals to nature, other species, and each other (as
Shevek learns when he plays at length with Oiee's son and his otter).

Nonetheless, as he stays in A-Io, Shevek comes to see the limitations of its
rich beauty for the Iotians. The students, pampered in their munificent surroundings, lack initiative and imagination. The professors at the university, intelligent and productive, nonetheless seem driven and tense; not until Shevek goes
to Oiee's home does he see him relaxed and at ease. Shevek's man-servant at the
university, Efor, gains little benefit from the beauty that the professors and students could enjoy: a servant, he has learned to walk with bowed head and lowered
eyes, attentive to the commands of those for whom he works, not to the songs of
the birds or the beauties of the architecture. In the vast profusion of consumer
goods Shevek sees a propertarian perversion of aesthetics, where ownership, fashion, and public display trump other possibilities and render capitalist activity fre-
netic and banal (5: 131).[8] Food and drink are plentiful and various, but cocktail
party conversation is vapid. From Shevek's perspective, Urras's beauty, which
could lead to increased knowledge and aesthetic enjoyment on Anarres, is by and
large wasted on—or even counterproductive for—the inhabitants of A-Io, whose
rich revel in their luxuries while others, like Efor, suffer in poverty.

Whereas Urras has abundant natural beauty, nature on Anarres presents many desolate landscapes punctuated by areas devoted to functionality, where food can grow or people can live. References to physical beauty on Anarres are few. Inhabitants of villages like the display of simple jewelry, a fashion rare in Abbenay, whose inhabitants worry about the connection between "the aesthetic and the acquisitive" (10: 324). Many in Abennay, however, participate in arts and crafts and attend concerts. One place devoted to natural beauty is a small park planted with trees imported from Urras in the Abennay, a park where Shevek occasionally finds peace—but which some Anarresti dislike for its excess and Urrasti connections.

Odo had asserted that "excess is excrement," and many on Anarres have adopted and reified that saying into a kind of functionalism where, if an activity is not directly useful for survival, it is excess, hence "excremental" and to be abandoned. In a light-hearted spoof of such functionalism, Bedap proposes eliminating the color orange because "it serves no vital function in the social organism" (6: 162). More seriously and sarcastically, Bedap notes, in response to a composer who has been assigned a job digging ditches, "music isn't useful. Canal digging is important, you know; music is mere decoration" (6: 175).

Just as many on Anarres respond to natural aesthetic possibilities with a concern about excess and an eye to functionalism, many among the rich in A-Io ignore the aesthetic dimensions of life in "economic and competitive compulsions" manifested in "a kind of mechanical lavishness" (5: 146). But there are some who can free themselves of the dominant ideologies of functional Anarres or luxurious A-Io and respond to nature's aesthetic. Oiee and his wife live in a house characterized by "grace, achieved by restraint" (5: 146). Shevek himself likes the small park in Abbenay and appreciates nature's plenty on Urras: "this is what the world is meant to look like, Shevek thought" as he looked over a Urrasti landscape (3: 65). Takver, a fish biologist, has a real "love of nature" in its complexity, variety, and fascination, and she is conscious of her own body as an integral part of ongoing natural processes, content or even pleased that she will die, rot, and turn into humus (6: 184–86). She also appreciates geometrical nature, representing it with a series of delicate, graceful mobiles with which she decorates their living quarters. As she explains her work with fish to Shevek, he becomes impressed with the "exuberance" of nature (6: 185). Nature can inspire, on Urras or Anarres, but it can only inspire those who, like Oiee and his wife or Shevek and Takver, are open to its inspiration.

Sometimes nature inspires with a sense of nature's full range of possibilities and limits. An earthquake on Anarres demonstrates that "the earth itself was uncertain, unreliable" (10: 314). Where Shevek and Takver find reliability, then, is not from nature but from each other, as they stand "holding each other on the unreliable earth" (10: 315). Nature does not always give beneficence, beauty, or order; so a full appreciation of nature includes awareness of its polyvalence.

ECOLOGICAL ISSUES: SPECIES SURVIVAL

Ecological concerns focus on how human beings as a species relate to one another and to other species—how they endanger or facilitate the maintenance of the community and the species, and act within and effect the larger ecosystem on which their life, their species's life, and all life depends. So ecological political thought looks at human beings as physical beings, as organisms in the earth's ecosystem who must defend and reproduce themselves.

Just as violence and self-defense are central to all species, conflict and violence are integral to life on Anarres. On Anarres individuals are not subjected to social practices (such as states) that generate violence, institutionalize it, and encourage its continual recurrence. Whereas on Urras the police and military are organizations whose established and legal task is the application of coercion and physical force internally and externally, part of what makes Anarres utopian is that violence, which does occur, has been disconnected from institutionalized human structures and is limited, transitory, and specific to a single issue.

Le Guin presents an example of Anarresti violence. A man named Shevet, while working with Shevek, gets annoyed at the similarities of their names; he challenges Shevek to a fight, beats him up, and goes his own way (2: 50–51). Because it is a straightforward fist fight, no one intervenes or even pays much attention. The violence is issue-specific, brief, without (life-threatening) technological instruments, and not linked to any established organization or interest. It is also an important experience in Shevek's growing up. Having learned to use words in kindergarten, Shevek learns a limit to open verbal communication. He also is both reminded of his body and freed from the fear of fighting, for he has learned that he can survive a fight.

The fight between Shevek and Shevet does not threaten human survival on Anarres because it is limited and transitory. Two other types of violence, though rare, are more problematic. When Shevek claims his right as a free agent to depart for Urras and then to return, some Anarresti disagree. Having lived all their lives within their wall, they argue that the original "Terms of Settlement" prohibit all entry, including reentry, and so establish a self-segregation necessary to protect Anarresti principles and identity (or perhaps to enforce their fear of change). Strong feelings and vigorous arguments erupt at the PDC, and one member threatens violence (12: 358). When Shevek talks to a student group, violence erupts (12: 375). Later, some individuals turn from arguments to bricks to prevent Shevek from leaving (1: 4). Consequently, Shevek does not know (nor does the reader find out) how he will be greeted on his return to Anarres, especially because he is bringing Ketho, from the peaceful Hainish civilization. In short, some Anarresti use the threat (and then the practice) of physical force to try to impose their ideas of the right and the proper on their fellows, and in so doing curb open communication and the compulsion of the better argument.

Natural disasters can also result in violence. When the drought on Anarres in places becomes so harsh that people are close to starvation, violence becomes an ever-present possibility.[9] A train carrying 450 people, with no food, stalls in a town that only has enough food for themselves until replenishment comes in a few days (8: 255–56). A crowd in a town with no food blocks a food train bound for another town equally lacking in food (10: 311). With sharp enough scarcity, "then force entered in; might making right; power, and its tool, violence, and its most devoted ally, the averted eye" (8: 256).

Not engaged in systematic organized violence against each other, the Anarresti are also not engaged in violence against or attempts to dominate nature. Words and metaphors of violence do not enter their relations to nature; nor do they engage nature by combat, domination, or violence. Moreover, the lack of war on Anarres means that nature is not polluted, transformed, or destroyed by human beings fighting each other.

On the other hand, the institutionalized violence on Urras means that A-Io and Thu fight out their ideological disagreements in Third World lands, and in A-Io rebellion is suppressed by sudden violence, martial law, and killing. The human species is less likely to destroy itself through violence—through war, ethnic cleansing, or nuclear holocaust—on Anarres than in most societies. The practices of Anarres seem much more conducive to species survival than do those on Urras.

Like violence, reproduction and sexual activity generally on Anarres have been uncoupled from the institutionalized practices that on other societies channel, limit, and repress sexual activity, subordinate it to the goals of reproduction, the maintenance of patriarchal power, the family name, or the state's population, and place it within a context of gender inequality and social power.

On Anarres, sexual activity has been freed from the goal of reproduction, and so no structural constraints or circumstances drive people to have children. Children will not make one richer or more powerful (or give someone who feels neglected an identity or sense of importance), nor provide better for one's old age, nor be necessary to silence one's parents or parents-in-law, who if they want to be with young children can ask for and accept postings in the daycare centers. Like partnership or any promise (8: 244–45), having children is a self-imposed limitation and so not undertaken lightly or blindly (3: 55). Consequently, the ecological issue of population growth seems not to be a problem, although Le Guin does not stress it as a theme.[10] Anarres in drought may not be able to support the current population, but Anarres's population seems to have been set more by the agreement ending Odo's revolution than by any population explosion since then.

Freeing sex from reproduction (and from Urrasti marriage's status and class concerns [5: 151]) opens many possibilities for sexual activity on Anarres: sexual behavior is not limited by laws, norms, or practices except for a mild norm for privacy and norms of equality and nonviolence (8: 245). Experimentation and intercourse occur from adolescence on: "like all children of Anarres [Shevek] had had sexual experience freely with both girls and boys" (2: 51). As children become older, sexual experimentation may start to include commitments to celibacy, limited sex, and long-term partnership. Just as experiencing physical violence is a part of growing up, so too is experimenting with varieties of sexual interactions.

Sexual desire and any subsequent relations on Anarres involve generally the parties treating each other openly and with respect for each other's feelings. As he is growing up, Shevek, like others, learns. "A rejection is a rejection" (2: 50). Beshun takes Shevek out on the plains at night, and Shevek, his lip still split from Shevet's fist, experiences another gift of physical awareness, connection in sex with Beshun—their two bodies joining "annihilate the moment . . . , and transcend the self, and transcend time" in their "freedom of the flesh" (2: 51). The pleasures of sexual intercourse are their own pleasures, but can eventually result in a kind of frustratingly recurring cyclicality: as Takver says, "it got unsatisfying. I didn't want pleasure. Not just pleasure, I mean" (6: 179). The long relation between Takver and Shevek begins with a mutual consent and is sealed with a mutual promise. Possession or "having" seems not a part of sexual relations, nor are they seen as something one party does to another (2: 52–54).

Sexual relations on Anarres, to be open and free, require an equality between partners in which men and women are seen as equal and homosexuality not stigmatized. Good sexual relations require equalities of gender and sexual preferences. There is no heteronormativity: Shevek and Bedap live together for a week; and no one thinks less (or more) of Bedap because he prefers men. There is also much variety. An adolescent usually tries sex with him- or herself, with the opposite sex, and with the same sex—and sometimes even tries celibacy.

In terms of men and women, A-Io serves as a contrast to Anarres. On Urras, sex roles are clearly defined and hierarchical: men live in the public sphere, attending university, holding jobs, doing physics; women decorate parties with their beautiful clothes, pleasantly flirting conversations, and sexy demeanors, but are untouchable except by their husbands, and eventually they raise the children. Having created a masculine public sphere where the feminine is excluded and repressed, the Urrasti unconsciously put "a woman in every table top," so smooth, delicate, and curved was the wood (1: 19). Knowing no relation but that of possession, the Urrasti men are possessed, unable to imagine women as competent or independent: "apparently they, like the tables on the ship, contained a woman, a suppressed, silenced, bestialized woman, a fury in a cage" (3: 74–75). In the private sphere the women themselves are constructed: "she [Vea] was so elaborately and ostentatiously a female body that she seemed scarcely to be a human being" (7: 213). Vea, whose social status gives her more space than other women, rages against this inequality and seeks freedom. But she has been extraordinarily constructed and constrained by her society. So, not surprisingly, in a reciprocal response to a world where power, freedom, and gender are interwoven, she wants power and she wants freedom. But the freedom Vea desires is the freedom and power to do whatever she wants, regardless of its impact on others (7: 220), not the freedom of Anarres, where one is responsible for one's choices and their consequences.

ECOLOGICAL ISSUES: TIME

Sex and violence occur over time, and involve both changes in individuals and in society; and, of course, ecosystem stability or sustainability can only be determined over time. Whereas a free-market economist can sleep peacefully every night knowing that, at the closing bell, the markets have cleared, and supply balanced with demand, the ecologist worries about long-term species survival and ecosystem sustainability.

Like many ecological thinkers, Le Guin has a keen eye to evolution and change: human beings and other species change as they interact over time. As Shevek says, "'We follow one law, only one, the law of human evolution'" (7: 220). But it is evolution that derives from human choice, not a natural selection: for human beings, "change is freedom, change is life" (6: 166), and so "you could go in a promising direction or you could go wrong, but you did not set out with the expectation of ever stopping anywhere" (10: 334). Only when individuals act and change "will the society live, and change, and adapt, and survive. We are not subjects of a State founded upon law, but members of a society founded upon revolution. Revolution is our obligation: our hope of evolution" (12: 359). Attempts to stop change—attempts by some Anarresti to keep the wall and the status quo by rejecting all contact with Urras, which is their past and their defining opposite; attempts by those on A-Io to maintain their hierarchy, their property, and their ignorance of Anarres—end up being self-narrowing and self-limiting. The novel itself ends with the promise of future change: in the last pages, Shevek says to Ketho, "Whatever happens, I am coming home. But you are leaving home" (13: 386), starting a new journey, a new exploration in time, with the likelihood of more changes and more evolving for Ketho and the societies involved.

Le Guin's complex treatment of time includes more than evolution. From the point of view of ecological thinking, there are two further central aspects, inherent in Shevek's comprehensive theory of time: time as a sequence or an arrow and time as a circle or a cycle. As a sequence, time involves change and the possibility of creation; as a cycle, time involves transforming chaos into patterns that can give meaning (7: 222–24). But either aspect of time by itself can lead to "the incoherence of time," where events occur and recur with neither novelty nor meaning. Shevek experiences such incoherence frequently; he feels alienated and purposeless on Anarres when he is frustrated in his work with Sabul and lack of interactions with others (4: 106–25) and on Urras when he cannot work on physics or social change (5: 126–45).

For Le Guin, human promising and human action are necessary interventions into the meaningless passage or incoherence of time. To promise is to unify time into meaning. "To break a promise is to deny the reality of the past; therefore it is to deny the hope of a real future" (7: 225). Against the "unreliable" earth, Le Guin juxtaposes "the enduring, the reliable": "a promise made by the human mind" (10: 314). Human promising keeps the past alive in the present, and asserts the hope for a future in which the promise will be redeemed. "Unless the past and the future were made part of the present by memory and intention, there was, in human terms, no road, nowhere to go" (6: 183–84). On Anarres, promises are not mere social niceties; they are, like social contracts in political philosophy or religious covenants in the Bible, ways of structuring one's relations with others (and with oneself) over time to give coherence, order, and purpose to life.

To act in time is to bring new things into being, to insert one's will into the ongoing process of life: if no choice is made, no direction taken, then it is "exactly as if one were in a jail, [even if it is] a jail of one's own building" (8: 245); "only the individual, the person, had the power of moral choice, the power of change, the essential function of life" (10: 333). One theme of the novel is Shevek's learning to act in order to overcome his own internalized Sabul (10: 332), assert his own Odonian self, and change Anarres's path from its slow movement away from utopian anarchy back to consciously chosen action. To act is not to control or conquer the future[11] but rather to generate change or novelty, resulting in a course that is as open-ended as the last chapter of *The Dispossessed*, when both Shevek and Ketho will step out of the spaceship onto Anarres and into an uncharted future.

To some extent, Le Guin proposes a kind of temporal or time ethic similar to Aldo Leopold's "land ethic," which "changes the role of *Homo sapiens* from conqueror of the land community to plain member and citizen of it."[12] Unable to conquer the future, human beings can act in the present in ways that will affect the future by making moral choices for which they need to accept responsibility. Not acting in the present is also a choice, in which case one can find oneself in a jail of one's own making. Like Leopold on nature, where human beings need knowledge to intervene wisely, where there are not abstract philosophical or scientific rules to serve as blueprints, and where particularities are important, Le Guin sees acting in time as requiring intelligent assessment of possibilities and choice of alternatives. Particularities matter, too; just as nature presents many different faces, so too does time and the individuals who act in time.

The goal of knowledgeable and sensitive action, for Leopold and Le Guin, is not controlling nature or time but "working with it, not against it" (10: 311). The reforestation program is a kind of Leopoldian working with nature (2: 46), trying to restore what nature once supported. Individuals work with time in similar ways. For instance, by changing their sexual behaviors and attitudes toward partnership, by trying to live within the temporal changes they are undergoing, Shevek and Takver in their many discussions and actions (and her mobiles) try to come to terms with ever-changing time. Bedap feels out of touch with time in his sadness about his failure to connect by age thirty-nine when he sees Shevek and Takver together; he feels as though he has let time pass by, rather than working with it (12: 370–71). (Bedap's questioning does raise the hope that his thinking about present and future can help him better to understand his present and act in it to bring about a future he truly wishes.) Human beings live in a landscape of time created by their own imaginations and changed by their own actions, so that, like Leopold's land ethic, "chronosophy does involve ethics" (7: 225).

Some ecological thinkers may object, perhaps, that Le Guin's treatment of time is anti-ecological because it rejects nature as a guide and establishes purely human criteria—action and promising—as the source of meaning and coherence. Certainly, if one sees "nature" as only physical nature, then nature seems unimportant to Le Guin's treatment of time. But I think that Le Guin seeks to recognize that time is an aspect of nature, or, perhaps more precisely, of ecology or the full system of human life; human beings must be conscious of and come to grips with time as integral to our natural world. One lesson of Darwin's theory of evolution is that time is fundamental to modern biology—and Einstein's theory of relativity shows that time is indispensable to modern physics. Just as human beings are physical beings living in a natural landscape, so too they are the "children of time" (13: 385) who must live in a "landscape of time" (10: 335).

ECOLOGICAL ISSUES: PLACE

Many ecological political theorists pay attention to place and to the way that human beings can orient themselves in the world through place and can locate their sense of nature and of wonder by placing themselves. Le Guin, however, de-emphasizes place. Shevek's goal is to break down walls that set off an area as a "place" and which make it different from other areas; and in the end the technological result of his theory of time—the ansible—lessens geographical isolation.

In her conversation with Shevek, Keng's arguments expose the danger of over-emphasizing place. For Keng, place determines the success of a society: a place of plenty is a paradise, a place of scarcity a desert. Urras is a paradise because its abundant resources offer material promise even though its social structures generate inequality and suffering; reciprocally, Anarres is a ruin, despite its utopic social organization, because its material scarcity keeps life at the level of survival. For Keng, suffering comes from material impoverishment; so for her a society's place—its geography as it determines its material wealth—determines the society's success. Paradise, which has a location, trumps utopia, which is not tied to a place. But since suffering is "real," "the condition in which we live" (2: 60), Keng's attempt to palliate it by material goods is misdirected; rather, what is needed is a sympathetic community of human beings, which Anarres can offer, but not in any given geographical place. On Anarres, people move around, friends are found wherever one is, and so the alleviation of pain is a movable feast. For assuaging pain, it is not the place, but the people; and, as Anarres shows, the people need not be connected to any particular place.

Place has another drawback for Le Guin, one apparent on Urras. Attachment to place as place, to an area within geographic boundaries like A-Io or Thu, leads people to defend their places against other people, either in a hierarchical army that defends a state or in guerilla warfare that "only works when the people think they're fighting for something of their own—you know, their homes, or some notion or other" (9: 305). Tied to a geographical place, their ideals and practices are dictated by their geography. As with the Cold War, when Le Guin was writing, the identity of geographic place and sociopolitical content is dangerous and destructive: it segments human solidarity and fragments humans' ability to share pain.

So Le Guin is wary of a paradise that, located at a place, promises material well-being; and she is wary of walls that demarcate areas into places like states, because such imagined communities segment and separate.[13] As with time, some ecological thinkers might question Le Guin's skepticism about the value of place. But Le Guin is not rejecting direct sensuous experience or the appreciation of the variegated details of nature. Rather, she is rejecting the walls or boundaries that separate people and make possible seeing others as an opponent or enemy. Just as Shevek sees the connectedness of time, he wants to tear down walls that break the connectedness of space.

THE DISPOSSESSED, ECOLOGICAL POLITICAL THOUGHT, AND INDUSTRIAL-CAPITALIST COUNTRIES

Like some ecological political theorists, Le Guin does not find a natural or automatic connection between effective environmental policy and political systems: both A-Io and Anarres can regulate resource use and pollution. Because both regulate satisfactorily, anyone wishing to compare the two societies must look to criteria beyond clean air and water. On other issues, however, *The Dispossessed* presents significant and uncommon ideas. Because Anarres decouples violence and sex from institutionalized practices, violence is infrequent and limited; sex is open, free, and egalitarian for the participants; and the survival of the human species and their planet is more likely. Le Guin's treatment of place reflects a kind of skepticism about too much emphasis on location. Her treatment of time insists that ecological thought place nature into a complete system including time.

One final question remains to be considered: is anarchy possible in a society of (relative) plenty like A-Io? Odo thought so. She wrote and acted to transform "the generous ground of Urras" (4: 95). She did not plan on the revolution's leading to founding a society on Anarres. In the novel's present, some Odonians hope to bring about anarchy, or something similar (9: 298), on A-Io in its rich present. On the other hand, some commentators on *The Dispossessed* suggest the "inseparability of utopia and scarcity,"[14] in Jameson's words. Or, as Peter Brigg states: "It can be debated whether the Odonian system has worked because there is little to possess and time for the kind of contemplation required to maintain a high moral standard, or whether only Odo's system could make survival possible on Anarres; in either case, the system and the ecology are inexorably intertwined."[15]

The question whether anarchy is possible in a society of relative plenty has a direct bearing on the relation between *The Dispossessed* and industrial-capitalist countries of 1974 or today.[16] Le Guin's Urras closely resembles our earth in 1974: a consumer capitalist society, A-Io, opposed to a state communist society, Thu, fighting ideological wars on Third World countries like Benbili. The parallels to the United States, the Soviet Union, and Vietnam are clear; and A-Io's inegalitarian consumer capitalism resonates with similarities to G7 countries in 1974 and now. Thus, many of the criticisms of A-Io are likely to be applicable to the United States and other capitalist countries. *The Dispossessed* is a critique of modern accumulation and modern consumer society, as seen extensively in A-Io. In A-Io the sense of freedom is narrow: free to choose (if you have the cash) from a cornucopia of consumer items, one lives within a society highly structured by class, status, and gender, where inequalities dull or pervert the senses and lead to psychological frustration. Your choices are both autonomous and trivial: as long as it is legal, you can choose whatever you want, without worrying about your responsibility to your fellows, your community, your environment, or your future. Like many 1974 and contemporary industrial-capitalist countries, especially the United States, A-Io is an inegalitarian consumer society in which public services like health care suffer while private consumption flourishes, given ideological justification as freedom of choice.[17]

Le Guin's critique also indicates why internally generated change is difficult. Her portrayal of the upper classes on A-Io shows how modern consumer society makes wishing for an alternative difficult because no other society allows many of its members as much physical comfort and so many goods and services; and it makes taking responsibility for one's choices difficult, because society on A-Io is so complex, interlocked, and mutually implicated that finding the results of one's action—discovering one's footprint on society—is almost impossible. Indeed, Shevek concludes, "there is no way to act rightly, with a clear heart, on Urras. There is nothing you can do that profit does not enter into, and fear of loss, and the wish for power" (11: 346). Nor does Shevek's arrival from the outside help: his trip fails to convince the politically powerful or the upper classes in A-Io of the values of Anarresti anarchy. He hoped to be a living example, a person whom Iotians could ask about Anarres. Then he hoped to persuade through rational argument (though at Vea's party his arguments may not have been as rational as he thought). Turning to the working classes, he helped them revolt; but the revolution was crushed. So there seems no assurance that A-Io—or the United States, or Western Europe—will produce a spontaneous and successful anarchist revolution, and it is difficult even to generate good critiques that show where and how individuals are responsible for social problems.

In the face of those difficulties, *The Dispossessed* gives readers a warning: if you simply allow the playing out of the tendencies of consumer capitalist society, then the contemporary world may end up like Keng's Terra: "My world, my Earth, is a ruin. A planet spoiled by the human species. We multiplied and gobbled and fought until there was nothing left, and then we died. We controlled neither appetite nor violence; we did not adapt. . . . We Terrans made a desert," a desert now governed by "total centralization" and "absolute regimentation" (11: 347–48). For Shevek, Urras at present may be a hell, but Terra is substantially worse.

In addition to the critique and warning, Le Guin holds out hope. The hope is, however, not in a utopia as a blueprint or model for her readers to copy. As a utopia Anarres is too "ambiguous" to be copied. Anarres's natural environment is bleak and inimical, and its social and political life has difficulties: public opinion can become too dominant, acceptance of bureaucratic decisions too prevalent, and individuals seeking power too successful. "Copying" an anarchic society also seems incongruous or self-contradictory, because each individual, in copying, would have to give up his "'cellular function,' . . . the individual's individuality" (10: 333) and "parrot Odo's words [and Anarres's practices] as if they were *laws*—the ultimate blasphemy" (6: 168). For Odonian anarchy, the goal is not to copy or follow another but to live independently and freely.

The hopeful future lies in the knowledge that Anarres exists as an ongoing and feasible attempt to create and live a better world, a continuing process or seeking of freedom and mutuality. As the Plenipotentiary responds to a skeptical monarch in a short story Le Guin wrote shortly before she composed *The Dispossessed*: "'No harmony endures,' said the young king. 'None has ever been achieved,' said the Plenipotentiary. 'The pleasure is in the trying.'"[18] Such undertakings occur on Anarres as individuals, knowing that Anarres is flawed but changeable, try to make it a better place: Tirin's play, Bedap's critiques, Takver's work with fish, and Shevek's voyages that begin and end the novel all endeavor to improve Anarres. In the moral decisions of the individual, in working with others to produce change, in action, and in setting out on a new voyage: these activities are where both hope and realism exist, the hope of bringing a new future into the present as a real possibility.

For the Urrasti as well as for Keng and other Terrans, "you will not achieve or even understand Urras unless you accept the reality, the enduring reality, of Anarres" (11: 349), with its promise of "freedom, of change, of human solidarity" (11: 345) and with its opposition to power and domination (11: 342). The same, by extension, holds for the United States and other capitalist countries: Anarres represents the real hopes of some inhabitants of those countries and the fulfillment of some of their cherished national ideals; so understanding the United

States or Western European capitalist countries requires accepting the Anarresti ideals present (if submerged) in the United States and Western Europe. Many possible futures are open for advanced capitalist societies. Terra and Anarres are both possible futures for Urras—and for the United States and the states of Western Europe. Unlike Terra, Anarres is a hopeful future.

Anarres also displays some kinds of insights important for change on Urras (and in contemporary capitalist societies) but not easily available in the complex bustle of everyday life. With its scarcity, Anarres allows the Anarresti—and Le Guin's readers—to see with clarity the effects of their actions on the ecosystem and on other human beings. When Shevek travels to Urras and back to Anarres, he goes with empty hands (13: 387): he does not take with him concerns about his social status, economic class, political power, or patriarchal privilege, and so he is free to discover, act from, and express his own individuality. As Shevek learns on Urras, concern with status, wealth, and power can possess individuals, dominating their lives and limiting their freedom. Even if they live in countries like A-Io, Le Guin's readers need to keep Anarres in mind as a model for analysis and action. What Pae, one of Shevek's hosts on A-Io, rejected, Le Guin's readers should accept: Shevek's offer to engage in direct and egalitarian, rather than roundabout and deferential, interaction and conversation: "I thought you might be glad to be free of the unnecessary" (3: 81).

Those possessed by the norms, institutions, and practices of consumer capitalism—the men and women of Urras—are not conscious of their own possession and so are not capable of understanding themselves on their own. Anarres, however, shows what it is to be dispossessed, and suggests how to think about dispossession: Takver distinguishes wants and needs; Shevek sees that action in time is moral action that produces changes for which the actor is responsible; and they, with Bedap and others, frequently examine and evaluate the issue of how best to lead a fulfilling human life. What is true at an individual level is also true at a social level: the Anarresti need to question self-reflexively what they are doing and how best to pursue a society of free and responsible individuals. Anarres's ambiguities as a utopia flow from the unwillingness of most Anarresti to address thoughtfully music or critical theater as a need (instead of a nonfunctional decoration), to consider how staying within the walls of the status quo affects thought, novelty, and the possibility of change, and to ask whether, in clinging like Keng to the past, they are thereby abandoning the future. In the novel, Anarres is a real society that is undergoing changes, attempting to produce reciprocal harmony between individual and society, and manifesting some flaws that can be counteracted; so Anarres can serve as an existing goal toward which Urras can move because Anarres clarifies issues that are difficult for Urrasti to see when they look only at their own society. For readers of the novel in 1974 or today, Anarres is a fictional society described in enough detail to appear as (analogously) a realistic possibility, a realistic fictional society, a utopia, and a better (though still flawed) future toward which the advanced capitalist countries might move.

Near the end of his stay on Urras Shevek finally realizes (11: 349–50) that Anarres cannot come to Urras. Urras, and by analogy the capitalist nations of the contemporary western world, must come to Anarres. Can anarchy exist in a land of relative plenty? We will know only when we start the journey, act, and make the attempt.

NOTES

My thanks to Laurence Davis, who made extensive, thoughtful, and very helpful remarks on an earlier draft of this chapter. He saved me from numerous infelicities and set me on some promising paths.

1. Ursula K. Le Guin, *The Dispossessed: An Ambiguous Utopia* (New York: Harper & Row, 1974), cited in the text by chapter and page to the 387-page Eos HarperCollins edition of 2001.

2. By "environmental" I mean all that surrounds us; so that environmental thought involves the relation of human beings to our surroundings, including "nonhuman" nature and other organisms. By "ecological" I mean the relatedness of all organisms (including human beings) and all species within their environments, that is, the ecosystem as a whole. The distinction between "environmental" and "ecological," important in some research, is of minor import in this chapter because no argument or thesis depends on it.

3. The terms "scarcity" and "plenty" (or "relative plenty") are of course always relative to needs, resources, and other factors. In *The Dispossessed*, Anarres is a world of scarcity because even basic human nutritional needs may not be met during the drought and people need be attentive at all times to survive at a minimal level of comfort and nutrition. (Terra too is a world of scarcity, made into a desert by human action.) A-Io by contrast is a world of relative plenty (as are the United States and other advanced industrial-capitalist countries of 1974 or today) because some have enough to be extravagant—for example, by using resources for fancy clothes, elegant dinner parties, handsome buildings, and speedy personal transportation—and (almost) everyone has enough to survive, although the uneven distribution of wealth means that some survive at a crude level. (I wish to avoid the economistic argument that unless *all* needs are met, we live in a society of scarcity, because that approach forecloses distinctions between relative scarcity and relative nonscarcity or plenty—distinctions that are present and operative in *The Dispossessed*.)

In discussing Anarres as an anarchist society with scarcity, I am addressing questions that outsiders would make about anarchy. Within anarchist theory there exists an ongoing and spirited debate about the compatibility of anarchy and various levels of industrial growth and wealth: see, for instance, Murray Bookchin, *The Murray Bookchin Reader*, ed. Janet Biehl (London and Washington: Cassell, 1997); André Gorz, *Capitalism, Socialism, Ecology*, trans. Chris Turner (London and New York: Verso, 1994); David Miller, *Anarchism* (London: J. M. Dent, 1984); and J. Roland Pennock and John W. Chapman, eds., *Anarchism: Nomos XIX* (New York: New York University Press, 1978). For Le Guin's general approach to this debate (albeit without directly mentioning it), see the last section of this chapter.

4. As Le Guin states in her (unpaginated) 1976 Introduction to her *The Left Hand of Darkness* (New York: Avon, 1976 [1969]).

5. Anarres's environmental policies are quite similar to Herman Daly's "low through-put" model in Herman E. Daly, *Toward a Steady-State Economy* (San Francisco: W. H. Freeman, 1973). Self-closing faucets were rare in the United States in 1974, and continue to be uncommon in private homes.

6. For concern that the poor might act to overthrow the propertied and their property rights, see *The Federalist Papers* (no. 10): "the most common and durable source of factions has been the various and unequal distribution of property. Those who hold and those who are without property have ever formed distinct interests in society." See also Adam Smith, *The Wealth of Nations*, Bk. V, Pt. III, Arts. II and III. Karl Marx in the *Communist Manifesto* expects the proletariat after the revolution "to increase the total of productive forces as rapidly as possible" (sec. II).

7. Unlike some who would distinguish between nature and art (or culture or civilization), Le Guin seems not to: except for Anarres before the Odonians arrived, she describes both planets in terms of a nature shaped by human beings. So, for instance, Shevek's "most beautiful view" contains both "natural" and "constructed" elements without aesthetic or ethical differentiation between them.

8. Le Guin has a sense that in capitalism, "where greed, laziness, and envy were assumed to move all men's acts, even the terrible became banal" (5: 130–31)—a kind of "banality of evil" that reminds a reader of Hannah Arendt's meditations in her *Eichmann in Jerusalem: A Study in the Banality of Evil* (New York: Penguin, 1977).

9. Except for cases when resources are so meager that some must starve, cooperation and mutual aid are likely to be more successful strategies for mutual survival than violence, as Shevek argues against Vea (7: 220). He makes a similar assertion to Chifoilisk (5: 135).

10. The text implies birth control, because children are generally not the result of the frequent and spontaneous adolescent sex or of the recurring partnership sex; it does not mention abortion, for which see Le Guin's "The Princess" (1982), in her *Dancing at the Edge of the World: Thoughts on Words, Women, Places* (New York: Harper & Row, 1990). In addition to population restraint on Anarres, A-Io does have birth control (Vea's has lapsed, she mentions [7: 230]); and Keng, talking about Terra's ecological disaster, specifically mentions overpopulation—"we multiplied"—as one unrestrained activity (consuming and fighting are the other two) that led to mass death on Terra (11: 347), with the result that the current government of strict regimentation insists on birth control (11: 348).

11. As Le Guin argues in "Science Fiction and the Future" (1985), in her *Dancing at the Edge of the World*, 142–43.

12. Aldo Leopold, *A Sand County Almanac* (Oxford: Oxford University Press, 1966), 239–40.

13. As Kenneth Roemer pointed out to me on October 10, 2004, at the Annual Meeting of the Society for Utopian Studies, Toronto, in many of her other works Le Guin sees place as important and accords it positive value.

14. Fredric Jameson, "World Reduction in Le Guin: The Emergence of Utopian Narrative," *Science-Fiction Studies* 2, no. 3 (Nov. 1975): 228. See also Judah Bierman, "Ambiguity in Utopia: *The Dispossessed*," *Science-Fiction Studies* 2, no. 3 (Nov. 1975): 250.

15. Peter Brigg, "The Archetype of the Journey in Ursula K. Le Guin's Fiction," in *Ursula K. Le Guin*, ed. Joseph D. Olander and Martin Harry Greenberg (New York: Taplinger, 1979), 60.

16. Anarchist theorists actively debate the possibilities for anarchy in a complex industrial society of plenty: see note 3 above. As the remainder of this chapter suggests, Le Guin's striking contribution to this debate is that *The Dispossessed* addresses the issue by utilizing a utopian method. Terra is a warning to A-Io (and to contemporary industrial-capitalist countries) and Anarres serves as a locus for the critique of A-Io and for the clarification of issues of responsibility, community, and freedom, a critique and clarification obfuscated by the complexity, opacity, and ideologies of A-Io. Anarres in its reality also shows that a better society is possible, hope for the future is realistic, and practical activity (informed by the Anarresti experience) holds promise.

17. John K. Galbraith's *The New Industrial State* (Boston: Houghton Mifflin, 1967) depicts a United States with many similarities to A-Io.

18. Ursula K. Le Guin, "Winter's King" (1969), in her *The Wind's Twelve Quarters* (New York: Harper Paperback, 1991 [1975]), 134. Le Guin's *The Left Hand of Darkness*, also set in Winter, focuses on the attempts to establish trust, cooperation, and friendship between individuals and between political entities. The novel is about the process, not the final result, whose details are left for the future beyond the end of the novel.

WORKS CITED

Arendt, Hannah. *Eichmann in Jerusalem: A Study in the Banality of Evil*. New York: Penguin, 1977.

Bierman, Judah. "Ambiguity in Utopia: *The Dispossessed*." *Science-Fiction Studies* 2, no. 3 (Nov. 1975): 249–55.

Bookchin, Murray. *The Murray Bookchin Reader*, ed. Janet Biehl. London and Washington: Cassell, 1997.

Brigg, Peter. "The Archetype of the Journey in Ursula K. Le Guin's Fiction." Pp. 36–63 in *Ursula K. Le Guin*, ed. Joseph D. Olander and Martin Harry Greenberg. New York: Taplinger, 1979.

Daly, Herman E. *Toward a Steady-State Economy*. San Francisco: W. H. Freeman, 1973.

Galbraith, John K. *The New Industrial State*. Boston: Houghton Mifflin, 1967.

Gorz, André. *Capitalism, Socialism, Ecology*, trans. Chris Turner. London and New York: Verso, 1994.

Hobbes, Thomas. *Leviathan*.

Jameson, Fredric. "World Reduction in Le Guin: The Emergence of Utopian Narrative." *Science-Fiction Studies* 2, no. 3 (Nov. 1975): 221–30.

Le Guin, Ursula K. *The Dispossessed: An Ambiguous Utopia*. New York: Eos, HarperCollins, 2001 (1974).

———. *The Left Hand of Darkness*. New York: Avon, 1976 (1969).

———. "The Princess" (1982). Pp. 75–79 in her *Dancing at the Edge of the World: Thoughts on Words, Women, Places*. New York: Harper & Row, 1990.

———. "Science Fiction and the Future" (1985). Pp. 142–43 in her *Dancing at the Edge of the World: Thoughts on Words, Women, Places*. New York: Harper & Row, 1990.

———. "Winter's King" (1969). Pp. 117–48 in her *The Wind's Twelve Quarters*. New York: Harper Paperback, 1991 (1975).

Leopold, Aldo. *A Sand County Almanac*. Oxford: Oxford University Press, 1966.

Marx, Karl. *The Communist Manifesto.*
Miller, David, *Anarchism.* London: J. M. Dent, 1984.
Pennock, J. Roland, and John W. Chapman, eds. *Anarchism: Nomos XIX.* New York: New York University Press, 1978.
Publius (pseudo.), *The Federalist Papers.*
Roemer, Kenneth. Discussion on October 10, 2004, at the Annual Meeting of the Society for Utopian Studies. Toronto.
Smith, Adam. *The Wealth of Nations.*

4

Ursula K. Le Guin, Herbert Marcuse, and the Fate of Utopia in the Postmodern

Andrew Reynolds

In a recent study of American literature and film from the two decades following World War II, M. Keith Booker argues for the emerging hegemony of a "post-utopian" attitude at that time, claiming that "the American utopian imagination, did, in fact, collapse in the long 1950s (1946–1964)."[1] The provocative concept "post-utopian" describes a dominant feature of American culture, most demonstrable according to Booker in cultural productions such as fiction and film, an ethos that occurs within the historical period that has come to be designated "postmodernity." Booker considers his notion to be roughly synonymous with the latter concept, suggesting that the post-utopian condition designates a cessation or failure of utopian imagination and narrative practice in the same manner that postmodernism, according to Fredric Jameson's influential account, involves a more general "crisis in historicity."[2] Perhaps because the death of utopianism in the contemporary period has become a truism, Booker's discussion of the post-utopian oftentimes passes too quickly over the questions of what utopia was and what the prefix "post-" signifies in these terms. This essay reconsiders these matters by way of another "post-," the economic theory of "post-scarcity," arguing that the transition from modernity to postmodernity may be usefully theorized in relation to the mainstreaming of this ideology in the early-to-mid-twentieth century. Furthermore, the category of utopia—itself certainly a product of modernity—appears to change with the appearance of new material abundance after World War II.[3] A revised notion of the post-utopian can thus be a valuable concept for demarcating and conceptualizing the twentieth-century transformation—rather than demise— of utopian thought and narrative, a type of writing I will analyze in detail via two important "post-" texts, Herbert Marcuse's *Eros and Civilization: A Philosophical Inquiry into Freud* (1955) and Ursula K. Le Guin's *The Dispossessed* (1974).

To understand the possible meanings of the term "post-utopian" and the reasons why it might be apt or useful as a description of postwar American culture, it seems appropriate to begin with the idea of utopia and M. Keith Booker's use of the term. He relies heavily upon the theory of Fredric Jameson throughout his study, saying of utopia: "I use the term in a Marxist sense and, in particular, in the very broad sense that Jameson himself employs throughout his work, that is, in the sense of an ability to imagine a preferable systemic alternative to the status quo, while at the same time imagining a historical process that might lead in the direction of that alternative."[4] Booker extrapolates from this abstract description of utopia his own theory of the post-utopian condition as being marked by "a failure to project viable utopian alternatives to the present social order."[5] The vagueness of these definitions, to which he admits, can perhaps be remedied by examining the historical causes he proposes for the shift from the utopian to the post-utopian during the long 1950s.

Booker's most recurrent and theoretically provocative theme places blame for the abeyance of utopian energy upon:

> the rise to complete dominance in America during this period [the long 1950s] of a consumer culture that, while it offered a limited utopian vision in its association of consumption with happiness, was ultimately anti-utopian, because the desire upon which consumer capitalism is built is, of necessity, a desire that can never be satisfied. Meanwhile the pursuit of this desire does not lead to the transformation of society but merely reinforces the status quo.[6]

In other words, "consumer capitalism" demarcates a historical phase of the capitalist mode of production in which the system develops the capability to short-circuit people's critical thinking and inhibit social change by entrapping consciousness in the never-ending, individualistic pursuit of material goods, an evolution in the manufacture of desire that according to Booker "made true satisfaction impossible."[7] This seems to be a conventional enough proposition, drawn from classic mid-twentieth-century analyses of capitalism.[8] However, it may be worthwhile to interrogate the assumptions made here, to consider exactly how consumerism might impede the progressive "transformation of society" and, more interestingly, why this short-circuit appears precisely at this historical moment and not during earlier phases of capitalism.

One explanation for the short-circuit of utopian consciousness is that the design of capitalist production and consumption changed around this time, allowing the creation of more alluring commodities backed by more sophisticated advertisements and so forth. A version of this thesis appears in Max Horkheimer and Theodor Adorno's meditations on the "culture industry" in *Dialectic of Enlightenment* (1944), in which they state that "movies and radio need no longer pretend to be art,"[9] adding that "amusement under late capitalism is the prolongation of work."[10] Alternately, the postwar shift can be explained as the result of changes in the organization of production and consumption, with new strategies such as market segmentation and product-line diversification allowing for greater penetration of capitalism into every aspect of life. This idea is explored by Jean

Baudrillard's *The System of Objects* (1968), which proposes that the seductive quality of contemporary consumerism resides not in the quality or design of the individual commodity so much as in the capitalist "system of objects" or "code."[11] While these developments in the products and structure of capitalism certainly hinder progressive social change, Lizabeth Cohen's *A Consumer's Republic* (2003) provides reason to believe that such hypotheses, by focusing primarily on the pacification and mystification of the individual, overestimate the ill effects of consumerism. From the consumer movement of the 1930s on through the 1970s, Cohen discovers again and again that "for social groups not otherwise well represented, in particular women and African Americans, identification as consumers offered a new opportunity to make claims on those wielding public and private power in American society."[12]

Is there something more to the phenomenon of consumer capitalism? Instead of involving issues of citizen's rights and identity politics, which are the major focus of Cohen's analysis, does the "transformation of society" turn on the question of the distribution of wealth and thus presume the primacy of class? Perhaps the *quantity* rather than the design or organization of production and consumption was altered during the mid-twentieth century, somehow enervating the utopian imagination. Pointing in this direction, Fredric Jameson claims, "one of the more important clues for tracking the postmodern" may be the "immense dilation of its sphere (the sphere of commodities)."[13]

This hypothesis finds support in James Livingston's account of the creation of an "age of surplus" in his *Pragmatism and the Political Economy of Cultural Revolution, 1850–1940* (1994). In brief, he proposes that consumerism develops when capital improvement becomes a dysfunctional strategy for absorbing the surplus production created by industrial machines, while at the same time automation works to make living labor irrelevant to production, leaving the working class potentially unemployed and unable to earn the wages that fuel demand.[14] Under these new conditions, commodities for the first time in history increase in value faster than fixed capital, giving birth to "a capitalist society in which surplus value had lost its investment function" and must be instead absorbed by the increased production of consumer goods.[15] Relying on Livingston's analysis, I propose that these two economic phenomena—the reversal of the value relation between capital and commodities and the subsequent production of a qualitative surplus of consumer goods—cause monumental cultural changes that undermine the very foundations of both class and utopia as these concepts were traditionally conceived.

When the necessity of work is seemingly eliminated by machines and people become valuable to the economy primarily as consumers of abundance, the entire logic of wealth distribution, entitlement, and earnings falls apart. What results is a crisis in class identity, which can be conveniently traced through the PMC (professional and managerial class). During the long 1950s, the PMC's "socially unnecessary" immaterial labor rose significantly in value and as a percentage of the total labor market, causing a wave of anxieties that were recorded by

David Riesman's *The Lonely Crowd* (1950) and William H. Whyte's *The Organization Man* (1956). Most unsettling to these sociologists was the realization that the creation of material surplus, the automation of repetitive manual labor, and the collapse of the traditional class structure—developments which seem to herald a progressive transformation of society, perhaps even the end of capitalism—only resulted in a deepened dependence upon capitalism to mediate all social relations, the necessity of alienating "other-directed" labor in service of the corporations, and the even more unequal distribution of wealth through mechanisms such as consumer credit and finance capital. Indeed, their contemporaries Horkheimer and Adorno viewed this paradox with deeper pessimism, believing that, for all the modern advances made in technics and productivity, there exists a dialectical countertendency toward irrationality and domination, witnessed foremost in fascism. "The curse of irresistible progress is irresistible regression,"[16] or so they claim, and thus consumer society seemed to have definitively foreclosed the promises of utopia.

The fate of utopia in the postmodern seems clear, yet what was utopia? If utopian practice and thought is fundamentally disrupted or short-circuited by the realization of consumerist material abundance, then the utopian problematic must be retroactively defined in terms of the experiences of scarcity and material inequality, and "utopia" comes to mean the (imagined) resolution of these problems via the political, cultural, and/or economic reorganization of society (for example, through production, technics, law, or education).[17] Only when defined this way does the causal relationship between consumer society, postmodernism, and utopia make sense. However, despite all the evidence in favor of a negative post-utopian "end of History" that M. Keith Booker locates in the long 1950s, the very definition of utopia via reference to scarcity may contain the seeds of hope. Could it be possible to think progressive social change without this reference? Can there be a positive post-utopian imagination, one premised on the prior achievement of capitalist commodity surplus and addressing a new problematic rooted in "post-scarcity"? While the fictional texts Booker examines from the long 1950s suggest not, during the same period Herbert Marcuse constructs the foundations of such a thought.

How did Marcuse, who was affiliated with the neo-Marxist Frankfurt School, come to the point of seemingly abandoning—or at least remarkably subordinating—the economic in his theorizing of social revolution and personal liberation? Like Horkheimer, Adorno, and his other collaborators, Marcuse's thought was profoundly influenced by the rise of totalitarianism and a resulting "crisis of Marxism."[18] Industrialized capitalist society did not develop as orthodox ("scientific") Marxism predicted during the 1920s and 1930s, but instead "regressed" into fascism. At the same time, some on the Left feared that the Soviet communist experiment was no better an alternative, that each totalitarian system was premised upon a similar diminution of the free individual in the name of a dysfunctional, irrational mode of production and consumption.

Rather than abandon philosophy and radical thought, the critical theorists developed their interdisciplinary mode of social analysis as a way to stay true to the Marxian concepts of dialectics, negation, and revolution. In the mid-1950s, with European fascism defeated, Marcuse turned their methodology to the task of exploring new post-utopian values in the age of the consumer society, unleashing Freudian psychology upon the popular ideology of abundance in his *Eros and Civilization: A Philosophical Inquiry into Freud.*

Marcuse's work, as the subtitle hints, offers a radical rethinking of Freud's "metapsychology,"[19] the anthropological, biological, and philosophical counterpart to his practical, clinical psychology. In *Beyond the Pleasure Principle* (1920), Freud outlines the final version of his metapsychological theory of instincts, premised on his belief in "the *conservative* nature of living substance" and "the hypothesis that all instincts tend toward the restoration of an earlier state of things."[20] On these grounds he develops his "Nirvana principle," which holds that "the dominating tendency of mental life, and perhaps of nervous life in general, is the effort to reduce, to keep constant or to remove internal tension due to stimuli."[21] Along very similar lines, he rearticulates the "pleasure principle" as "a function whose business it is to free the mental apparatus entirely from excitation or to keep the amount of excitation in it constant or to keep it as low as possible."[22] Instinctual energy is thus organized according to two competing strategies, given the names "Thanatos" and "Eros." The former instincts seek to resolve tension through the most direct path, the death of the organism. The latter, however, seek to achieve satisfaction through the preservation of life, which occurs in two primary ways, through sexual reproduction and by "combin[ing] organic substances into ever larger unities" (that is, social behavior).[23] For Freud and Marcuse as well, instinctual satisfaction remains the ultimate standard by which to judge the quality of human life.

According to Freud's account of the evolution of the psyche, the primordial equilibrium between Eros and Thanatos is upset by the appearance of the ego, which replaces the pleasure principle with a "reality principle."[24] As Marcuse explains, the ego improves the likelihood of instinctual gratification by "observing and testing the reality, taking and preserving a 'true picture' of it, adjusting itself to the reality, and altering the latter in its own interest" (*EC*, 30). The ego changes the structure of the instinctual functions by instituting "repression" and "sublimation," the rational delay, denial, or transformation of instinctual satisfaction in the name of survival and the possibility of future pleasure (*EC*, 206). The reality principle also results in the subordination of Thanatos to Eros, as the destructiveness of the death instinct is channeled into outwardly directed "aggression" in order to increase the organism's possibilities of survival and satisfaction.[25] The advent of the reality principle thus marks the beginning of human civilization. Freud imagines that "civilization is a process in the service of Eros, whose purpose is to combine single human individuals, and after that families, then races, peoples and nations, into one great unity, the unity of mankind."[26] Despite this laudable goal, both Freud and Marcuse find the event to be a mixed blessing nonetheless. As Marcuse explains:

> The scope of man's desires and the instrumentalities for their gratification are thus immeasurably increased, and his ability to alter reality consciously in accordance with "what is useful" seems to promise a gradual removal of extraneous barriers to his gratification. However, neither his desires nor his alteration of reality are henceforth his own: they are now "organized" by his society. And this "organization" represses and transubstantiates his original instinctual needs. If absence from repression is the archetype of freedom, then civilization is the struggle against this freedom. (*EC*, 15)

Marcuse's revision of Freudian metapsychology begins with his historicization of the reality principle. Opposing Freud's program of therapy and adjustment, Marcuse argues that modern societies repress the individual more than they benefit him or her, that capitalism surpasses the reality principle and institutes a new "performance principle" under which "society is stratified according to the competitive economic performances of its members" (*EC*, 44). Through this principle, the processes of rationalization, organization, repression, and sublimation become reified as ends in themselves. Instead of providing more secure, improved pleasure, modern capitalist societies impede instinctual gratification, generating unnecessary "surplus repression" via the alienation of labor, "mass manipulation" during leisure time, and the general "desexualization" of everyday life (*EC*, 47–48, 87). When this condition, which Marcuse terms "domination" (*EC*, 36), comes to determine all social relations—as it does in consumer society—then the equilibrium between Thanatos and Eros reverses: "the perpetual restrictions on Eros ultimately weaken the life instincts and thus strengthen and release the very forces against which they were 'called up'—those of destruction" (*EC*, 44). In this way, Marcuse uses Freud's instinctual categories to provide a psychological explanation for fascism, nihilism, and "the fatal dialectic of civilization" (*EC*, 54).

While the performance principle seems to lead to the regression of civilization and the end of utopian imagination, Marcuse argues to the contrary that it "has perhaps created the preconditions for a qualitatively different, non-repressive reality principle" (*EC*, 129). For the original reality principle developed out of the historical condition of material scarcity and the struggle for existence, "which teaches men that they cannot freely gratify their instinctual impulses, that they cannot live under the pleasure principle" (*EC*, 16–17). Although the performance principle irrationally exacerbates repression to the point of dysfunction, it has the positive effect of stimulating science, technics, and productivity, thereby creating "the material (technical) preconditions" necessary to end scarcity (*EC*, xv).[27] For instance, on the subject of automation Marcuse remarks, "The elimination of human potentialities from the world of (alienated) labor creates the preconditions for the elimination of labor from the world of human potentialities" (*EC*, 105). Again, therefore, Marcuse suggests that some of Freud's most important concepts—

scarcity, repression, labor—must be reconsidered as historical, contingent phenomena, and psychology in his hands shifts from its therapeutic role to become an instrument of individual liberation and social revolution.

Despite Marcuse's unabashed enthusiasm for automation, he does not naively adopt the progressive ideology of material abundance, which would ignore the problem of commodification discussed earlier vis-à-vis consumer society. He remains aware of the social imbalance caused by the overproduction of certain private goods and considers a true end of scarcity as dependant upon a redefinition of the concept, admitting, "The material as well as mental resources of civilization are still so limited that there must be a vastly lower standard of living if social productivity were redirected toward the universal gratification of individual needs" (*EC*, 151). Unlike the very similar argument made by John Kenneth Galbraith in *The Affluent Society* (1958), however, Marcuse's judgment relies on values set by his idealistic psychological theory rather than those of established economic rationality. As Marcuse explains:

> regression to a lower standard of living, which the collapse of the performance principle would bring about, does not militate against progress in freedom. . . . The definition of the standard of living in terms of automobiles, television sets, airplanes, and tractors is that of the performance principle itself. Beyond the rule of this principle, the level of living would be measured by other criteria: the universal gratification of the basic human needs [i.e., instincts], and the freedom from guilt and fear—internalized as well as external, instinctual as well as "rational." (*EC*, 153)

Marcuse later clarifies his radical understanding of the economic category of "needs," arguing that "All human needs, including sexuality, lie beyond the animal world. They are historically determined and historically mutable,"[28] as opposed to the permanent biological instincts—a distinction which will shape his entire theory. In these passages, Marcuse displays a consciousness of post-scarcity, defined as skepticism toward economic progressivism and the ideology of abundance, as the crucial insight emerging from postmodern consumer society. Building on this idea, post-utopianism can be understood as the positive imagination of a resolution to the postmodern problematic without recourse to either production or consumption as the ultimately determining factors of human experience. Marcuse's theory of an erotic civilization is one such vision.

In Marcuse's attempt to imagine the liberation of Eros from the performance principle, he distinguishes between a destructive "explosion of libido" that continues to bear the mark of repression—as witnessed in the phenomenon of fascism—and his preferred alternative, the more instinctually rewarding "eroticization of the entire personality" and "spread [of libido] over private and societal relations" (*EC*, 201). Eros can be truly liberated only when "the primacy of the genital function is broken" (*EC*, 205), and Marcuse accordingly stresses the importance of "a resurgence of pregenital polymorphous sexuality" (*EC*, 201), which would extend libido to previously tabooed areas of the body and domains of life. While the experience of sex remains one of the most important and most obvious sites of the transformation of libido, Marcuse's psychological theory surprisingly says very little about the rehabilitation of the act itself. Although he frequently mentions polymorphous perversity, he never articulates exactly how sexual behavior would occur beyond the production principle or how practices such as monogamy and marriage might be affected.

Rather than discuss the immediate satisfaction of the sexual instinct, Marcuse continually emphasizes that sex must undergo "non-repressive sublimation," which describes the function of libido under a new, post-performance reality principle. He claims that through such sublimation, "instinct is not 'deflected' from its aim; it is gratified in activities and relations that are not sexual in the sense of 'organized' genital sexuality and yet are libidinal and erotic" (*EC*, 208). Recall that the "aim" of Eros is the preservation of the organism through sexual reproduction as well as through the creation of "larger unities." Thus, he is arguing (against Freud) that the life instincts can be fulfilled while being pressed into the service of civilization[29]: "The culture-building power of Eros *is* non-repressive sublimation: sexuality is neither deflected from nor blocked in its objective; rather, in attaining its objective, it transcends it to others, searching for fuller gratification" (*EC*, 211). In other words, the individual liberation of sexuality demands social revolution as well: "Non-repressive order is possible only if the sex instincts can, by virtue of their own dynamic and under changed existential and societal conditions, generate lasting erotic relations among mature individuals" (*EC*, 199). The structure of these new libidinal relations, which he terms "community" (*EC*, 224), nonetheless remains as vague as the arrangement of sex.

Work is perhaps the most important domain to undergo revision, considering its preeminent role under the performance principle and its intimate relationship with scarcity and abundance. Through the new technology of automation, the devaluation of productivity, and the revaluation of instinctual gratification, Marcuse believes "toil" and enforced labor can be forsaken, allowing work to become a revived source of libidinous pleasure. He predicts, "if work were accompanied by a reactivation of pregenital polymorphous eroticism, it would tend to become gratifying in itself without losing its *work* content. . . . The altered societal conditions would therefore create an instinctual basis for the transformation of work into play" (*EC*, 215). Play defines the individual's interaction with the world of objects in a new, rehabilitated way that satisfies the life instincts. Whereas work signified a form of conflict with the external world, undertaken in the name of self-preservation and/or artificial compulsion (that is, the ideologies of performance and needs), "play expresses objectless autoeroticism" and the freedom of the individual (*EC*, 214). Like sex-become-libidinal community, work-become-play is a definitive instance of Marcusean nonrepressive sublimation, though again the theory is wanting in practical details, such as how the apparatus of production would be nonrepressively organized and coordinated. Marcuse sidesteps such concerns, declaring for instance, "Work as free play cannot be subject to administration; only alienated labor can be organized and administered by rational routine" (*EC*, 218). These evasions are not accidental or the result of a lack of imagination, I argue, but instead reveal the implicit social minimalism of Marcuse's theory.

Once scarcity can be circumvented and labor dispensed with, why should the individual continue to submit to any reality principle, even a nonrepressive one? Why not revert to the pleasure principle? Why maintain civilization? Following Marcuse's revision of Freud, we can imagine three such reasons. Continued freedom from material scarcity is certainly a logical reason for people to maintain the automated apparatus of production that Marcuse envisions. As discussed earlier, though, he gives no hint as to how much—or even if—work/play would be required for this task and thus no indication that his nonrepressive mode of production would necessarily require human socialization, however far fetched the idea of total automation may be. Likewise, the satisfaction of socially contingent desires cannot justify civilization or the reality principle. If Marcuse's goal is nonrepressive existence and the satisfaction of biologically based instinct, then, in order to protect the autonomy of desire from its "organization" or overdetermination by society, he can allow no socially contingent desires or "needs" to remain. All instinctual desire must be amenable to surrogate, autonomous satisfaction—hence his emphasis on the nonrepressive sublimation of sexuality into community and the "objectless autoeroticism" of play, for sex makes the individual dependent upon another for gratification and (oddly) contradicts his program of liberation. Indeed, his "eroticized" society often sounds no more directly sexual than the culture of performance and domination, and we will see that Marcuse continually rehabilitates pleasure in ways that seem to intentionally minimize interpersonal dependence and the necessity of interaction.

The security of instinctual gratification is the only remaining justification for civilization, and it continues to validate Marcuse's new reality principle. However, under a nonrepressive principle in which the autonomy of individual pleasure is preserved, libidinal security cannot be coercive and the organizational aspect of society must fall away. This perhaps explains why Marcuse refuses to theorize or endorse any substantial form of post-utopian social organization, whether in the form of a state, bureaucracy, collectivity, work group, or sexual partnership. Instead, he puts forward the concept of libidinal "community," which I believe can be fairly interpreted to signify a group of free individuals held together by a weak bond of mutual commitment to noninterference in their independent pursuit of instinctual satisfactions. Indeed, we might consider community as the social analogue to economic automation. It only makes sense, then, for this "negative" community itself to be the object of sublimated sexual desire as Marcuse argues, since despite its intimation of collective existence, such a community is really another—perhaps the highest—expression of individual autonomy.

This reading of *Eros and Civilization* finds support in one of the most interesting elements of Marcuse's post-utopian thought, the bracketing of the object that occurs as part of his radical rethinking of material needs. Instead of considering the different possible functions of material wealth,[30] Marcuse veers away from any positive discussion of goods, preferring instead to focus on the transformation of subjective experience under the new reality principle. By his account, "The realm of freedom is envisioned as lying *beyond* the realm of necessity: freedom is not within but outside the 'struggle for existence.' Possession and procurement of the necessities of life are the prerequisite, rather than the content, of a free society" (*EC*, 195). Any mention of goods occurs in this minimalist manner; things are to be provided via automated labor and seemingly held separate from the truly pleasurable immaterial experiences, which do not appear to include production or consumption.[31] When Marcuse says that "play is *unproductive* and *useless*" and that it "expresses objectless autoeroticism" (*EC*, 195, 214), he certainly could mean that play has no economic value or motivation, but these statements also suggest that the object of play may itself be fundamentally irrelevant to instinctual satisfaction, that play is an intellectual pursuit beyond the material sphere.

Such conclusions are upheld by Marcuse's theorization of the "aesthetic dimension," an aspect of his philosophy that bears much of the weight of explaining the renewed libidinous interaction of the individual with the environment. Art could seemingly provide a logical context for the rehabilitation of the object, liberating it from its commodified form, yet he does not consider this possibility. Instead, he returns to the idealism of Kant and Schiller, tracing a common etymology of "sense" and "sensuousness" in order to argue for the instinctual liberation of our everyday perception of the world through the abstract, mental experience of "beauty" (*EC*, 183). Parallel to his ideas of libidinal community and play, therefore, Marcuse proposes a libidinal aesthetics that makes instinctual pleasure a function of the free individual rather than the object, its composition or consumption. He writes, "aesthetic perception is accompanied by pleasure. This pleasure derives from the perception of the pure *form* of an object, regardless of its 'matter' and of its (internal or external) 'purpose.' An object represented in its pure form is 'beautiful.' Such representation is the work (or rather the play) of *imagination*" (*EC*, 177). Marcuse's rehabilitation of everyday life as abstract aesthetic experience further demonstrates his generalized resistance toward recognizing any dependence on the world of objects or other subjects for the free satisfaction of instinct.[32]

Eros and Civilization represents one version of post-utopianism, in which a theory of instinctual pleasure promises to reshape economics, sex, social organization, and even perception. Perhaps revealing his affinity with Adorno, Marcuse imagines a rarefied, contemplative mode of experience that resonates with the categories of traditional European high culture. Instinct is consistently shunted away from the satisfactions that are bound to bodies or objects, leaving intellectual community as possibly the ultimate pleasure. The utopian problems of scarcity and material inequality can thus be bypassed; it remains unstated how wealthy or poor a nonrepressive society would be, since this condition has little impact on free instinctual satisfaction. Marcuse's vision of social and material minimalism, coherent on its own terms and based on a genuine fear of commodified domination, can nevertheless be criticized. Through his optimistic reliance on the technology of automation as a way to bracket the economic, he avoids some of the most difficult problems for turning post-utopian theory into practice. Can individual freedom and psychological satisfaction be preserved within a civilization premised on economic and social interdependence rather than independence? Can body and object relations be rethought so that the dependency implicit in sex and the utility implicit in labor would be reconciled with individual freedom? Can post-scarcity consciousness survive the experience of hunger? These are a few of the significant questions that Ursula K. Le Guin's novel *The Dispossessed* addresses.

The Dispossessed and *Eros and Civilization* have many affinities, the most significant being their post-utopian approach to the problems posed by postmodern consumer society. While their imagined rehabilitations of some everyday experiences such as work and sex are surprisingly complementary, their philosophical premises remain distinct. Marcuse values individual freedom only as a correlative of his theory of biological instincts, their structure and gratification; the Nirvana and pleasure principles are his foundational assumptions. For Le Guin, however, freedom itself ultimately comes to stand as the sole reference point for judging the value of human life. Rather than presenting a psychological theory of pleasure, *The Dispossessed* represents and analyzes the politics of freedom, which for her means anarchism—"the most idealistic, and to me most interesting, of all political theories."[33]

The fountainhead of the anarchist movement in the novel is Odo, a woman who lived and died on the planet Urras several generations before the action of the novel takes place. In writings such as *The Social Organism* and *Analogy*, Odo developed the political philosophy that eventually sparked a great social revolution on Urras after her death. From the fragments of "Odonianism" sprinkled throughout *The Dispossessed*, it appears that she—like Marcuse—comes at the problem of rethinking human society by way of reference to biological theory rather than economics. Her critique of the "propertarian" societies on Urras thus takes the form of a functionalist and organicist analysis. For instance, one Odonian maxim states that "excess is excrement"[34] (4: 98) which by analogy allows her to argue against material luxury in the social body.

Following out the metaphor, the individual is conceived of as a cell, yet Odo seems to assume each cell must be free to find its own function. In an important passage, the protagonist Shevek considers the work he wants to do

> in Odonian terms, as his "cellular function," the analogic term for the individual's individuality, the work he can do best, therefore his best contribution to his society. A healthy society would let him exercise that optimum function

freely, in the coordination of all such functions finding its adaptability and strength. That was a central idea of Odo's *Analogy*. (10: 333)

Certainly danger lies in such thinking; radical freedom at the cellular level, if interpreted as cancer, could just as easily provide validation for authoritarianism. Many of Odo's metaphorical theories contain such interpretive pitfalls: for example, "function" can become simply another way to express the idea of utility, and thus a means to induce conformity to an economic production ethos—as Shevek encounters when Sabul, the "expert" member of his syndicate, disallows his work in theoretical physics in the name of "organic function" and "practicality" (8: 264–65). The fact that Le Guin's text itself addresses these concerns suggests that Odonianism represents a classical or "scientific" stage of anarchism, which I argue her novel attempts to think beyond, refining out a principle of radical freedom through the experiences of Shevek.[35]

Odo's anarchism, like Marcuse's critical theory, remains "the product of a very high civilization, of a complex diversified culture, of a stable economy and a highly industrialized technology" (4: 95). However, the viability of her philosophy is tested not on Urras but Anarres, its twin world, arid and lacking in material resources where the former is lush and rich. Much has been made of this significant choice of setting. According to Fredric Jameson, Le Guin's ground for her anarchist civilization ultimately reveals "a sociopolitical hypothesis about the inseparability of utopia and scarcity."[36] Whether this hypothesis is based on a belief in the insidiousness of consumerism and the insurmountable psychological effects of wealth (a "puritanical" notion that may have affinities with Marcuse's critical theory) or instead reflects back on the limits of our Earth's resources in the face of global poverty, Jameson does not decisively say. Overlooked here are the radical possibilities of post-scarcity and post-utopia, namely the idea that revolutionary political values can be conceived independently of material conditions and materialist ideologies. As Shevek's friend Bedap, an anarchist among anarchists, remarks, "even on Urras, where food falls out of the trees, even there Odo said that human solidarity is our one hope" (6: 167). Anarres's lack of material resources therefore serves as a test of the separability of post-utopia and scarcity, or, in Odonian terms, a test of the axiom "the means are the end" (5: 144). By imagining how post-scarcity consciousness would fare against seemingly incontrovertible experiences such as hunger, Le Guin addresses some of the potential shortcomings of both Odo's and Marcuse's theories, thereby enriching the concept of post-utopia that all seem to move toward.

Life on Anarres is Spartan in many respects. What little the anarchists have in the way of material goods is held in common, and individuals do not retain many personal effects, perhaps some jewelry or a sentimental item. Housing is similarly arranged because "the economy of Anarres would not support the building, maintenance, heating, lighting of individual houses and apartments" (4: 110). Their economy and environment require a significant amount of human labor in order to provide this meager standard of living, furthermore, for they lack the automated industry that Marcuse thought necessary for liberation. Nonetheless, their society is not organized in an attempt to surmount these conditions but rather to incorporate them—if and when necessary—into the experiences of freedom and solidarity. For instance, there exist no formal means of prohibiting the accumulation of personal wealth; "if you want things you take them from the depository" (5: 149). The reason that people typically do not take more than the society can afford is obvious: those immediately around them would suffer. Thus, "community" in *The Dispossessed* comes to have an organic, spatial materiality that is lacking in Marcuse's work—despite or perhaps because of poverty.

Similarly, the rationale behind people's eagerness to work, even at disagreeable or dangerous jobs, lies in the value anarchism places on free choice. Although the socially necessary work assignments are generated by the "PDC (Production and Distribution Coordination)" (3: 76), individuals decide what jobs to undertake or even if they will work. The connection between labor, remuneration, and coercion is thus broken, allowing unalienated work and social obligations to emerge. As Shevek explains to some incredulous Urrasti, "work is done for work's sake. It is the lasting pleasure of life. The private conscience knows that. And also the social conscience, the opinion of one's neighbors. There is no other reward, on Anarres, no other law" (5: 150). Indeed, Le Guin's depiction of work closely mirrors Marcuse's: the anarchist language "Pravic" has only one word encompassing both work and play (8: 269). A separate word for drudgery does exist, however, referring to tasks that are simply "boring" rather than difficult or displeasing (4: 92).[37] Posing a semantic distinction between these active and passive modes rather than one based on either pleasure or utility is ideologically significant, for the Odonians attempt not only to rehabilitate work in Marcusian fashion but also to demonstrate that "non-repressive" work can be socially useful as well, as opposed to the "objectless," "unproductive and useless" activity envisioned by Marcuse. In other words, the Anarresti attempt to achieve freedom and solidarity in their own lives, in the present moment, under whatever conditions, rather than idealistically bracketing the economic in the hopes of a technologically-provided liberation.

The real test of post-scarcity consciousness, though, comes with the experiences of pain, hunger, and death, for these seem to resist redefinition or any similar strategy. In the course of the novel, several severe droughts occur, which lead to the PDC system impinging on everyday freedoms in the name of the society's survival. During one drought, "Rationing was strict; labor drafts were imperative" (8: 246). Surprisingly, the population becomes even more enthusiastic about the struggle for survival: "There was an undercurrent of joy . . . a lightheartedness at work however hard the work, a readiness to drop all care as soon as what could be done had been done" (8: 247). Le Guin's suggestion is that, so long as anarchism allows people to differentiate between natural and social compulsion, between adversity and injustice, if suffering is freely shared like everything else, then even the most extreme hardship may be chosen and made part of one's freedom. In what is for me the most shocking moment of *The Dispossessed*, it appears that during another drought some mill workers on an emergency posting simply "died of hunger on the job. Just went a little out of the way and lay down and died" (10: 311)—a choice made in the name of freedom rather than personal pleasure or survival. Indeed, one of Marcuse's weakest moments comes when he attempts to reconcile his vision of instinctual gratification with the inevitability of death (*EC*, 222–37). Post-scarcity anarchism on the other hand not only destabilizes the ideology of needs but also deconstructs the inflexible, conservative standards of the Nirvana and pleasure principles. A psychology of freedom and solidarity, the novel suggests, can potentially be more powerful than "biological instincts," as demonstrated by the different responses of two groups of hungry people facing similar opportunities to satisfy themselves at the expense of the larger society. While one breaks out into mob violence, attacking a supply train (10: 313), the other debates such action but manages to restrain themselves (8: 256). As I read it, *The Dispossessed* is equally the product of anarchism and Nietzschean postmodernism: Le Guin responds to the impossibility of setting an objective standard to human "needs"—or "pleasure" for that matter—and attempts to transform that relativity of value into the precondition to a philosophy of liberation.

Of course, the post-utopian principle of freedom is not adopted on Anarres as thoroughly as the above scenarios might suggest. The drama of the novel builds around the imminent clash between two factions, on the one side people such as Sabul who adopt the Odonian language of functionalism to strengthen the influence of the PDC and the established syndicates, and on the other Shevek and his unpopular Syndicate of Initiative who adhere to the ideal of radical freedom behind Odo's analogies and metaphors. Through their conflict, the novel reflects on the flaws of Odonian anarchism, most importantly the reemergence of coercive social power. As Shevek comes to realize, "We don't cooperate—we *obey*. We fear being outcast, being called lazy, dysfunctional, egoizing. We fear our neighbor's opinion more than we respect our own freedom of choice" (10: 330). A related exploration of the Anarresti shortcomings occurs via comparison with the Urrasti capitalist society of A-Io. After Shevek's interplanetary voyage, he discovers what his homeworld lacks: luxury, leisure, the unhindered pursuit of cultural and intellectual excellence—all privileges afforded the elite of A-Io. These two strands of (self-)criticism, I argue, address somewhat tangential deformations of anarchism stemming from the extreme conditions under which Le Guin's "most idealistic" politics has to prove itself.[38] That post-scarcity anarchism can potentially overcome even the instinct for survival does not mean this should be its regular function, after all. Rather than belaboring Anarres's failings on these counts, I turn to what John Fekete rightly sees as "The more interesting range of speculative questions, having to do with permanent revolution and the forms of freedom in a libertarian post-scarcity society,"[39] especially the problems that might arise under even the best conditions.

The fetishization of hardship and hardness is obviously a danger on Anarres, and, while the anarchists' masochistic expressions of solidarity can be taken as simply a product of their environment, the ubiquity of this attitude suggests that perhaps the principle of freedom is to blame as well, at least indirectly. The deeper problem of which masochism is symptomatic materializes in a gesture that Le Guin utilizes repeatedly, the empty hand, which comes to symbolize the essence of anarchy in Shevek's speech to the Urrasti strikers and demonstrators (9: 300–301). As Fekete interprets it, "the empty hand image thus does double duty for Le Guin: it signifies both the valued social absence of private property and the valued social presence of an environmentally coerced interdependence of the propertyless for survival."[40] To these we can add yet another layer of meaning: freedom, the gesture indicates, is itself an empty ideal. For freedom has no fixed referent or logic, unlike Marcuse's pleasure principle, a quality that potentially makes it a progressive concept in contrast to the "conservative nature" of the instincts. Yet seemingly any end—including this debilitating masochism—can be followed under its banner. Is freedom's intrinsic openness both its greatest strength and its fatal weakness?

Le Guin addresses this concern early in the novel through Shevek's youthful experience of relative luxury as a student in the central city of Abbenay prior to the droughts. Shevek enjoys many privileges compared to other Anarresti: he is provided "his own room" rather than a dormitory (4: 103), has dessert served to him every night (4: 111), and most importantly maintains "total independence" (4: 106). Free to pursue his education in theoretical physics, he opts out of almost all social relationships, doing only the minimum amount of rotational labor (4: 107). Despite these seemingly ideal conditions, he nevertheless becomes physically ill and depressed, believing that "nothing he did was meaningful. He was fulfilling no necessary function, personal or social. In fact—it was not an uncommon phenomenon—he had burnt out at twenty. He would achieve nothing further. He had come up against the wall for good" (6: 161). Why does the relatively carefree life of the student lead to thoughts of suicide (6: 164), whereas later Shevek manages to be a brilliant and healthy scientist while also being a partner, a parent, an emergency laborer, a revolutionary, and many other things besides?

The answer lies in the distinction to be made between two kinds of freedom, the negative type young Shevek experiences and a positive form best captured in his mature partnership with Takver. Le Guin's contention is that freedom does not exist in the abstract, as achieved through renunciation or isolation, what she refers to metaphorically as "wall building." Both Shevek and his society are guilty of this practice in different ways, he for engaging in the narcissistic intellectualism that Marcuse's philosophy tends toward, the anarchists for failing to recognize their ethical obligation to the revolution and the people of Urras, for masochistically embracing their situation of self-exile. As Le Guin suggests, "to deny is not to achieve" (3: 89). Positive freedom on the other hand abides in the choice made, in commitment and obligation, and most basically in communication, an idea beautifully articulated in *The Dispossessed* by partnership and promise.

Although partnership can be viewed as an anomalous holdover from the propertarian, sexist societies of Urras, Shevek comes to understand the value of pair bonding as an alternate way to resolve the problem Marcuse addressed through his recovery of the pleasure principle in a nonrepressive reality principle, namely: how can one not be traumatized by the consciousness of the separation between the self and the world? Necessity, contingency, risk, and lack are insurmountable features of human existence—as Shevek says, "we can't prevent suffering. This pain and that pain, yes, but not Pain. A society can only relieve social suffering, unnecessary suffering" (2: 60). Le Guin, much more so than Marcuse, remains skeptical of attempts to mitigate these, to discover or recover some pleasurable reconciliation with the world. If Marcuse replaces abundance with the satisfaction of the individual libido, what then does Le Guin's anarchist theory of freedom offer besides a choice of hardships? The only hope of averting an existential crisis resides in the idea of the promise as a way of "getting time on your side. Working with it, not against it" (10: 311). Partnering exemplifies this by putting the individual into time, binding one to it in a positive, even libidinal fashion through the other person. Instead of trying in vain to escape time's flow, promise allows choice to consciously extend into the future and return back to the past. What seems like restriction becomes the precondition for authentic freedom. After pairing with Takver, Shevek comes to realize this point, recognizing that regret is meaningless, that he cannot begrudge his former ignorance of her or his hard times in Abbenay because these experiences "had all been part of his present great happiness, because they had led up to it, prepared him for it. Everything that had happened to him was part of what was happening to him now" (6: 183). By revealing temporal and intersubjective connections, the promise makes separation and pain bearable, it makes meaning arise, and it transforms the emptiness of freedom into plenitude. Le Guin's ultimate expression of post-utopian anarchism thus comes when Shevek "promised himself that he would never act again but by his own free choice" (1: 8)—bonding and liberation circling each other in harmony.

The Dispossessed represents another version of post-utopia, a celebration of freedom and the redemption of hardship, suffering, and "dispossession" in all its ambiguity—if not material then certainly existential. Shevek strips Odonian anarchism bare, revealing the emptiness of freedom as the source of joy, meaning, and true solidarity if rightly approached through the notions of promise and partnership. Of course, even these experiences maintain a dialectical relationship to suffering; as the narrator remarks, "there is exhilaration in finding the bond is stronger, after all, than all that tries the bond" (8: 247). There remains something valid, after all, to the accusation one person makes to Shevek: "You're making a cult of pain" (2: 61)—not in the sense of actively seeking it perhaps, but by making pain a foundational premise for thinking. In doing so, *The Dispossessed* offers a significant contrast to the philosophy of pleasure elaborated in *Eros and Civilization*, thereby presenting us with two possible strands of what remains one coherent practice: the post-utopia.

In their common response to postmodern consumer society and the crisis of utopia it elicits, both Le Guin and Marcuse envision similar reconstitutions of work, and both recognize sexuality—thought in very different ways—as a key to overcoming authoritarian society. More problematically, they share an implicit distrust or disdain toward material goods as part of a program of liberation and revolution. Indeed, the commodity form might be understood on Le Guin's terms as a sort of "bad promise," an unconscious, unwilled binding of the individual to the system of production that occurs through the tacit acceptance of the invisible social relations embedded in the object. Le Guin's preference, as John Fekete notices, is for "total transparency" in social relations.[41] The "ansible," her most provocative *novum* in the novel, represents this dream on the cosmic scale, just as partnership seems to do in microcosm.[42] Nonetheless, the ansible remains, like Marcuse's automated labor process, a muted note of hope in technology within a symphony dedicated to immaterialism. The future of the post-utopian imagination might lie in a less antagonistic stance toward the world of objects, the goal being neither to unrealistically bracket economic life nor to pose the problem of liberation within the context of the struggle for survival. Surprisingly, postmodern consumer society may provide an important means or model for such thinking. After all, consumerism, which entails the subjection of every aspect of life to the abstractions of commodity and exchange relations, might have allowed the very idea of post-scarcity and the radical relativity of "needs" to come to consciousness in the first place. If such is the case, the task for the future may be to uncover other seeds of liberation and revolution planted within the postmodern.

NOTES

My sincere thanks to Candi Churchill, Ariel Gunn, Jessica Livingston, and Aaron Shaheen for their support, encouragement, and suggestions.

1. M. Keith Booker, *The Post-Utopian Imagination: American Culture in the Long 1950s* (Westport, CT: Greenwood Press, 2002), 1.

2. Fredric Jameson, *Postmodernism, or, The Cultural Logic of Late Capitalism* (Durham, NC: Duke University Press, 1991), 25.

3. On the modernity of utopia, see Phillip E. Wegner, *Imaginary Communities: Utopia, the Nation, and the Spatial Histories of Modernity* (Berkeley: University of California Press, 2002), 1–61.

4. Booker, *Post-Utopian*, 5.

5. Booker, *Post-Utopian*, 4.

6. Booker, *Post-Utopian*, 4.

7. Booker, *Post-Utopian*, 2.

8. See for instance Vance Packard, *The Hidden Persuaders* (New York: D. McKay Co., 1957), Ernest Dichter, *The Strategy of Desire* (New Brunswick, NJ: Transaction, 2002), and John Kenneth Galbraith, *The Affluent Society* (New York: New American Library, 1958).

9. Max Horkheimer and Theodor W. Adorno, *Dialectic of Enlightenment*, trans. John Cumming (New York: Continuum, 1996), 121.

10. Horkheimer and Adorno, *Dialectic*, 137.

11. Jean Baudrillard, *The System of Objects*, trans. James Benedict (London: Verso, 1996), 25.

12. Lizabeth Cohen, *A Consumer's Republic: The Politics of Mass Consumption in Postwar America* (New York: Knopf, 2003), 32.

13. Jameson, *Postmodernism*, x.

14. James Livingston, *Pragmatism and the Political Economy of Cultural Revolution, 1850–1940* (Chapel Hill: University of North Carolina Press, 1994), 7–19.

15. Livingston, *Pragmatism*, 19.

16. Horkheimer and Adorno, *Dialectic*, 36.

17. My definition here may appear overly reductive, especially considering the "utopias of sensual gratification or body utopias" that Lyman Tower Sargent identifies as comprising one side of the genre—the other pole being "the utopia of human contrivance or the city utopia" of which I seem to have been speaking ("The Three Faces of Utopianism Revisited," *Utopian Studies* 5, no. 1 [1994]: 10–11). Yet the body utopia can be dismissed rather summarily as offering no significant challenge to postmodern consumer society for reasons touched on earlier (for example, the culture industry). The critical question Sargent's category raises, though, is whether the preexistence of this alternative utopianism invalidates the hypothesis of a positive post-utopia. Indeed, the body utopia anticipates Marcuse's vision of libidinal liberation in important ways. However, as *The Dispossessed* demonstrates, post-utopianism can ultimately encompass a wider range of noneconomic strategies than sensualism. Most importantly, the post-utopian imagination—necessarily founded on the idea of post-scarcity as I will argue—remains conscious of the hazards of economic thinking in ways the traditional body utopia simply could not yet be.

18. See Douglas Kellner, *Herbert Marcuse and the Crisis of Marxism* (Berkeley: University of California Press, 1984), 115–29.

19. Herbert Marcuse, *Eros and Civilization: A Philosophical Inquiry into Freud* (Boston: Beacon, 1966), 6. All further references are cited in the text as *EC*.

20. Sigmund Freud, *Beyond the Pleasure Principle*, trans. and ed. James Strachey (New York: Norton, 1961), 30–31.

21. Freud, *Pleasure Principle*, 49–50.

22. Freud, *Pleasure Principle*, 56.

23. Freud, *Pleasure Principle*, 36.

24. Freud, *Pleasure Principle*, 4.

25. Sigmund Freud, *Civilization and Its Discontents*, trans. and ed. James Strachey (New York: Norton, 1961), 60–61.

26. Freud, *Civilization*, 69.

27. For this reason, Marcuse did not consider his theory utopian, arguing: "Utopia is a historical concept. It refers to projects for social change that are considered impossible," and because "the material and intellectual forces for the transformation [of society] are technically at hand . . . I believe, we can today actually speak of an end of utopia" (*Five Lectures: Psychoanalysis, Politics, and Utopia* [Boston: Beacon, 1970], 63–64).

28. Marcuse, *Five Lectures*, 65.

29. See Freud, *Civilization*, 56.

30. For an example, see John Kenneth Galbraith, *The Affluent Society* (New York: New American Library, 1958), 101–31.

31. Douglas Kellner suggests that "One major flaw of many neo-Marxist theories of consumer society, evident sometimes, but not always, in Critical Theory, is a totalizing view and denunciation of the commodity, consumer needs and consumption," which he goes on to characterize as "puritanical" (*Critical Theory, Marxism and Modernity* [Baltimore: Johns Hopkins University Press, 1989], 158).

32. Marcuse's aestheticized concept of instinctual autonomy has an unlikely affinity with the consumerist capitalism he targets, as Regenia Gagnier's recent work indirectly demonstrates. Following the paradigm shift from production to consumption, Gagnier argues that "Knowledge and freedom in market society may be reducible to a single dominant narrative about the total actualization of individual pleasure" (*The Insatiability of Human Wants: Economics and Aesthetics in Market Society* [Chicago: University of Chicago Press, 2000], 1).

33. Ursula K. Le Guin, *The Wind's Twelve Quarters* (New York: Harper & Row, 1975), 285.

34. Ursula K. Le Guin, *The Dispossessed: An Ambiguous Utopia* (New York: Harper & Row, 1974), cited in the text by chapter and page to the 387-page Eos HarperCollins edition of 2001.

35. This reading differs from that of John Moore, who argues that Le Guin's entire novel remains at this stage: "The anarchism projected in *The Dispossessed* is an extension of the nineteenth-century Western faith in secularism and scientific progress . . . like the classical anarchist sources from which it derives inspiration" ("An Archaeology of the Future: Ursula Le Guin and Anarcho-Primitivism," *Foundation: The Review of Science Fiction* 63 [Spring 1995]: 33).

36. Fredric Jameson, "World-Reduction in Le Guin: The Emergence of Utopian Narrative," in *Ursula K. Le Guin*, ed. Harold Bloom (New York: Chelsea House, 1986), 68.

37. I am indebted to Peter Stillman for calling my attention to this point and for his many helpful comments regarding this chapter.

38. For an excellent discussion of this point in more detail, see John Fekete, "*The Dispossessed* and *Triton*: Act and System in Utopian Science Fiction," *Science-Fiction Studies* 6, no. 2 (July 1979), 134–35.

39. Fekete, "Act and System," 135.

40. Fekete, "Act and System," 133.

41. Fekete, "Act and System," 133.

42. For a critique of the technology and politics of transparency, see Jean Baudrillard, *The Ecstasy of Communication*, trans. Bernard Schutze and Caroline Schutze, ed. Sylvère Lotringer (New York: Semiotext(e), 1988).

WORKS CITED

Baudrillard, Jean. *The Ecstasy of Communication*. Trans. Bernard Schutze and Caroline Schutze. Ed. Sylvère Lotringer. New York: Semiotext(e), 1988.

———. *The System of Objects*. Trans. by James Benedict. London: Verso, 1996.

Booker, M. Keith. *The Post-Utopian Imagination: American Culture in the Long 1950s.* Westport, CT: Greenwood Press, 2002.

Cohen, Lizabeth. *A Consumer's Republic: The Politics of Mass Consumption in Postwar America.* New York: Knopf, 2003.

Fekete, John. "*The Dispossessed* and *Triton*: Act and System in Utopian Science Fiction." *Science-Fiction Studies* 6, no. 2 (July 1979): 129–42.

Freud, Sigmund. *Beyond the Pleasure Principle.* Trans. and ed. James Strachey. New York: Norton, 1961.

———. *Civilization and Its Discontents.* Trans. and ed. James Strachey. New York: Norton, 1961.

Gagnier, Regenia. *The Insatiability of Human Wants: Economics and Aesthetics in Market Society.* Chicago: University of Chicago Press, 2000.

Galbraith, John Kenneth. *The Affluent Society.* New York: New American Library, 1958.

Horkheimer, Max, and Theodor W. Adorno. *Dialectic of Enlightenment.* Trans. John Cumming. New York: Continuum, 1996.

Jameson, Fredric. *Postmodernism, or, The Cultural Logic of Late Capitalism.* Durham, NC: Duke University Press, 1991.

———. "World-Reduction in Le Guin: The Emergence of Utopian Narrative." Pp. 57–83 in *Ursula K. Le Guin,* ed. Harold Bloom. New York: Chelsea House, 1986.

Kellner, Douglas. *Critical Theory, Marxism and Modernity.* Baltimore: Johns Hopkins University Press, 1989.

———. *Herbert Marcuse and the Crisis of Marxism.* Berkeley: University of California Press, 1984.

Le Guin, Ursula K. *The Dispossessed: An Ambiguous Utopia.* New York: Eos, HarperCollins, 2001 (1974).

———. *The Wind's Twelve Quarters.* New York: Harper & Row, 1975.

Livingston, James. *Pragmatism and the Political Economy of Cultural Revolution, 1850–1940.* Chapel Hill: University of North Carolina Press, 1994.

Marcuse, Herbert. *Eros and Civilization: A Philosophical Inquiry into Freud.* Boston: Beacon, 1966.

———. *Five Lectures: Psychoanalysis, Politics, and Utopia.* Boston: Beacon, 1970.

Moore, John. "An Archaeology of the Future: Ursula Le Guin and Anarcho-Primitivism." *Foundation: The Review of Science Fiction* 63 (Spring 1995): 32–39.

Sargent, Lyman Tower. "The Three Faces of Utopianism Revisited." *Utopian Studies* 5, no. 1 (1994): 1–37.

Wegner, Phillip E. *Imaginary Communities: Utopia, the Nation, and the Spatial Histories of Modernity.* Berkeley: University of California Press, 2002.

5

The Alien Comes Home: Getting Past the Twin Planets of Possession and Austerity in Le Guin's *The Dispossessed*

Douglas Spencer

INTRODUCTION

The Dispossessed is an "ambiguous Utopia" with an ambiguous title.[1] Its ambiguity hinges around *possession* as ownership and *dispossession* as deprivation, on the one hand, and *possession* as bewitchment and *dispossession* as liberation on the other. In terms of political philosophy, the novel's title suggests an engagement with the Marxian themes and theories of commodity fetishism and alienation. In more contemporary terms it suggests a kinship with critical accounts of consumerism from Lefebvre[2] and Debord[3] in the 1960s to Klein's *No Logo*[4] and the anticonsumerist movement of today; a critique whose essence is captured in aphoristic form by *Fight Club*'s Tyler Durden: "The things you own, end up owning you."

Le Guin's novel articulates these themes by shuttling back and forth between the novel's two worlds—the "possessed" Urras and the "dispossessed" Anarres—and weaving a network that both articulates and calls into question the apparent dualisms of possession and dispossession. From Urras the Anarresti appear as impoverished Utopians self-exiled on a barren world, while from the anarchist planet its nonidentical twin appears rich in material resources inequitably distributed and squandered on frivolous display. Critically, the novel's protagonist, Shevek, experiences these ambivalences and oppositions not so much through "raw" political philosophy or ideological discourse, but in his material and experiential encounters with objects, architectures, design, and aesthetics—the "glass and steel" buildings of Urras, the "erotic" furniture of the spaceship, the shop windows on the "street of nightmares," Vea's clothing, and Takver's mobiles. This is more than a tangent to the novel's politics, though; the concern with how objects and architectures are designed, manufactured, distributed, and experienced is a recurrent feature of radical and Utopian thought and social practice.

The English socialist and pioneer of "design reform," William Morris, drew upon a romanticized interpretation of the medieval period, and the writings of Marx, to develop a critique of nineteenth-century industrialization and the design standards of its products. In response Morris not only produced his own work of Utopian fiction—*News from Nowhere*[5]—but his own designs for furniture, buildings, wallpaper, and typography as a largely rhetorical counterdiscourse to the practice of the division of labor and the aesthetic aberrations of the Victorian era.

The conditions in the newly-formed USSR generated a similar confluence of Utopian thought and radical design practice. In the midst of the political and economic crises of the 1920s, the Bolshevik leadership actively supported the establishment of new design schools operating along avant-garde lines, and within this fertile environment figures such as Moisei Ginzburg and Alexander Rodchenko produced architectures and objects intended not merely to represent the values of a communist Utopia, but to generate the conditions in which it could be actively realized.

Contemporary to the publication of *The Dispossessed* was the work of 1960s and 1970s radical design groups such as Utopie in France and Superstudio in Italy. These groups were politically informed by a revived reading of the early Marx and the theories of alienation and commodity-fetishism, ideas which had assumed increasing relevance in postwar "consumer society." Seeking a historical path from this "consumer society," and acknowledging the culpability of their own profession in its creation, these groups developed Utopian architectural and design projects in which alienation could be transcended through a reshaping of the material world.

This nexus of Utopian thought and critical design practice also encompasses another feature of Le Guin's novel: the mobilization of science-fiction discourse as radical imagining of future possibility. In Soviet Constructivism, for example, rhetorically "modern" materials—steel, concrete, and plate glass—were employed to suggest transport to the new socialist Utopia of the future and departure from the old feudal and preindustrial world of Tsarist Russia. The geometries of circles, squares, triangles, and helixes into which these materials were formed also suggested a futuristic and cosmic dimension: in *Of Two Squares* the Constructivist El Lissitzky used prototypically modernist graphic design to narrate the arrival of the "pure" geometry of the square to earth from space and its transformation of the terrestrial world.

Radical design groups of the 1960s and 1970s also recruited the imagery and language of science fiction to their projects. The inflatable structures of the Utopie group suggested some escape from the pull of the Earth's gravity and the weight of its "materialism," while the English Archigram and Italian Superstudio groups appropriated science fiction comic imagery and photos of manned space flight in their graphics and manifesto-like publications to promote their futuristic and Utopian connotations. Meanwhile, in France, the Situationists "detourned" Barbarella-like comic strips so that its heroes and villains spouted revolutionary critique from their speech bubbles.

So *The Dispossessed* can be situated in the context of a social, political, and cultural "moment" in which the themes and concerns of alienation, consumerism, and science fiction converged in a critical fashion. In particular, Le Guin's exploration of the role and place of aesthetics in Utopian discourse, and the possibilities this suggests for transcending the often ascetic and austere positions of these alternatives to consumerism, are worth considering.

ALIEN(ATED) ENCOUNTERS

Shevek first experiences Urrasti civilization on the spaceship that carries him from his home world, Anarres, to theirs. On the journey he is struck by the "strange" objects of the Urrasti—the "caressing suppleness" of the mattress, the "decidedly erotic" "hot-air-nozzle-towel"—and speculates on the sublimation that might drive their design:

> the smooth plastic curves into which stubborn wood and steel had been forced, the smoothness and delicacy of surfaces and textures: were these not also faintly, pervasively erotic. . . . Were Urrasti cabinetmakers all celibate? (1: 18–19)

A similarly alienating encounter with a new material world also happens on Earth beginning sometime around the 1950s. Consumer goods, TVs, hi-fis, cars, and fridges begin to occupy a central role in everyday life in Northern America and Western Europe. This terrestrial encounter with a new material world, and the estrangement it implied, was met by a critique that took on the new conditions of consumerism and its implications for everyday life. Central to this critique and its origins was the work of the French philosopher, urbanist, and theorist of the quotidian, Henri Lefebvre.

Lefebvre had argued against the orthodoxy of the French Communist Party (PCF)—from which he was expelled in the mid 1950s—that the key to understanding the most urgent needs of contemporary humanity was Marx's account of alienation. This account, rediscovered and reevaluated by Lefebvre in Marx's *1844 Philosophical Manuscripts*, emphasized the necessity of the "total man" as the goal and expression of human liberation. Whereas in capitalism all human relations were mediated by the mercantile economy, its social hierarchies, and the commodities it produced as its material expression, Marx's "humanist" socialism sought to establish a realm in which the "total man" could express himself and fulfill his essential "nature" in a direct and nonalienated fashion. This position was in sharp contrast to the orthodox Marxism of the PCF, which concerned itself with overcoming "exploitation" in its narrow and purely economic definition.

Already there are resonances here with the politics of Le Guin's novel. In common with the various expressions of nonauthoritarian, far-left communism and libertarian socialism, of which Lefebvre along with the Hungarian Georg Lukács was a vital influence, *The Dispossessed* suggests that even the *de facto* beneficiaries of an exploitative society are enslaved to its narrowly economic dimensions; even the socially privileged Urrasti with whom Shevek spends most of his time on Urras are alienated by the logic of "possession":

> you the possessors are the possessed. You are all in jail. Each alone, solitary, with a heap of what he owns. You live in prison, die in prison. It is all I can see in your eyes—the wall, the wall! (7: 229)

The spatial terms in which the condition of "possession" is put by Le Guin also parallels Lefebvre's thinking. As Rob Shields has noted: "Lefebvre's 'alienation' is a spatial concept referring to displacement and distance" and "Alienation is defined by Lefebvre as the 'single yet dual movement of objectification and externalization–or realization and de-realization.'"[6] The inner life and passion of the Urrasti has likewise become externalized and alienated into the material of their objects and their design:

> Everyone was very polite and talked a great deal, but not about anything interesting; and they smiled so much they looked anxious. But their clothes were gorgeous, indeed they seemed to put all their light-heartedness into their clothes, and their food, and all the different things they drank, and the lavish furnishings and ornaments of the rooms in the palaces where the receptions were held. (3: 83)

The motifs of walls, containment, and packaging that run throughout *The Dispossessed*, contrasted with those of mobility and communication as freedom, suggest a spatialization of politics that is part of a larger "spatial turn" in critical theory, a movement for which Lefebvre, particularly in his *The Production of Space*,[7] was chiefly responsible.

But this turn to alienation and a spatialized understanding of the social itself needs to be understood in historical and social terms. Lefebvre's thinking was largely a response to the rapid changes in French culture that occurred after World War II. The flooding of a new and relatively affluent market with consumer goods, alongside the growth in mass tourism, organized sport, and the spread of advertising, marked a full-scale change in the experience and nature of everyday life. Not only were people economically exploited at work, but their "free time" and space had been colonized by the new consumer culture too. As the wholesale commodification of lived material culture took place, the entrenched subjects of this critique had to fight against their total "possession" by things. As one example of May 1968 graffiti in Paris declared, "cache-toi, objet!" (hide yourself, object!).

In his own account of the object, *The System of Objects*, Lefebvre's student and assistant, Jean Baudrillard, tried to show how the object had escaped its utilitarian servitude and now occupied an autonomous position in the center of the new consumerist world. Here we find Baudrillard not only following Lefebvre's lead, arguing against a world in which human nature has been externalized and alienated into the sphere of objects, but also chiming with the presence of these themes in *The Dispossessed*:

> Indeed, a genuine revolution has taken place on the everyday plane: *objects have now become more complex than human behaviour relative to them.* Objects are more and more highly differentiated—our gestures less and less so. To put it another way: objects are no longer surrounded by the theatre of gesture in which they used to be simply the various roles; instead their emphatic goal-directedness has very nearly turned them into the actors in a global process in which *man* is merely the role, or the spectator.[8]

In this early work Baudrillard produced a perceptive account of the material experience of everyday life and its symbolic dimensions. In the consumer society the object had moved beyond its utensile servitude, its status as "tool," into an autonomous zone where it stood alone and apart as a fetish of consumption itself: an image of the reified system of advanced capitalism where all human relations and communications were relayed through commodities and their possession. Baudrillard's approach here is resonant with Le Guin's recurrent themes of containment and packaging. On Urras Shevek observes how objects are held apart from one another, and from people; isolated and self-contained: "Even packets of paper," he notes, "were wrapped in several layers of papers. Nothing was to touch anything else" (7: 199).

These practices of packaging and isolation also extend to the urban and architectural scale where they evoke the experience of the tangible emptiness of everyday life at the heart of this "consumer society":

> He came to Saemtenevia Street and crossed it hurriedly, not wanting a repetition of the daylight nightmare. Now he was in the commercial district. Banks, office buildings, government buildings. Was all Nio Esseia this? Huge shining boxes of stone and glass, immense, ornate, enormous packages, empty, empty. (7: 209)

In the France of the 1960s Baudrillard observed the same operative motivation in the use of glass as the default material of consumer society:

> A shop window is at once magical and frustrating—the strategy of advertising in epitome. The transparency of jars containing food products implies a formal satisfaction, a kind of visual collusion, yet basically the relationship is one of exclusion. Glass works exactly like atmosphere in that it allows nothing but the *sign* of its content to emerge.[9]

Like Le Guin's protagonist Shevek, Baudrillard is alert to the perversion at work in this "system of objects," where beings are dispossessed of their sexuality and objects themselves assume an erotic character. Where Shevek becomes aware of the eroticism of the furnishings on the spaceship, and speculates on the celibacy of the Urrasti cabinetmakers, Baudrillard observes how design shapes the object world into eroticized forms advertised and consumed as fetishized "woman-objects." Both are also alert to the gender politics of this sublimation. In a perhaps direct reference to the sculpture of British Pop artist Allen Jones, Le Guin makes several mentions of "the woman in the table" as an image of the Urrasti's displaced and objectified sexuality, an operation where objects not only take on the functions of the erotic, but beings, particularly female ones, have to objectify themselves in order to express sexuality.

> To look at her, Vea was the body profiteer to end them all. Shoes, clothes, cosmetics, jewels, gestures, everything about her asserted provocation. She was so elaborately and ostentatiously a female body that she seemed scarcely to be a human being. She incarnated all the sexuality the Ioti repressed into their dreams, their novels and poetry, their endless paintings of female nudes, their music, their architecture with its curves and domes, their candies, their baths, their mattresses. She was the woman in the table. (7: 213)

In strikingly similar terms, Baudrillard notes the perversion of this objectified sexuality and its fracturing of the "total person" as an expression of the alienation produced in the "system of objects":

> If perversion as it concerns objects is most clearly discernable in the crystallized form of fetishism, we are precisely justified in noting how throughout the system . . . the possession of objects and the passion for them is, shall we say, a tempered mode of sexual perversion. Indeed, just as possession depends on the discontinuity of the series . . . sexual perversion is founded on the inability to apprehend the other qua object of desire in his or her unique totality as a person, to grasp the other in any but a discontinuous way.[10]

In *Mythologies* Roland Barthes used a similar semiotic methodology to Baudrillard's to account for the profuse invasion of consumer objects, advertising, and the leisure industry into French everyday life in the postwar period. Dealing with topics as diverse as detergents, film stars, Michelin guides, and cars, Barthes sought to reveal the bewitching power of these cultural manifestations by reference to their mythmaking, and the role of these myths within a larger ideological system. A vital source of these objects' mythological power was their tendency to appear as what Barthes termed "pure signs," autonomous images severed from any connection to their original production and construction, and hence free to float as signs that could refer to more abstract myths—the "good life," purity, nationalism, and so forth. Writing about the Citroën DS in "The New Citroën" Barthes commented:

It is obvious that the new Citroën has fallen from the sky inasmuch as it appears at first sight as a superlative object. We must not forget that an object is the best messenger of a world above that of nature: one can easily see in an object at once a perfection and an absence of origin, a closure and a brilliance, a transformation of life into matter (matter is much more magical than life), and in a word a silence which belongs to the realm of fairy-tales.[11]

This abstraction of the object from its conditions of production and its miraculous capacity to appear "as if from nowhere" also occupies Shevek during his visit to the shops of Nio Esseia's *Saemtenevia Street*, the "street of nightmares":

And the strangest thing about the street was that none of the millions of things for sale was made there. Where were the workshops, the factories . . . ? Out of sight, somewhere else. Behind walls. All the people in all the shops were either buyers or sellers. They had no relation to the things but that of possession. (5: 132)

So Le Guin's novel strikes a significant chord with near contemporaneous accounts of consumerism and the centrality of a system of fetishized and mythified objects at a critical moment in advanced capitalism. Much as Shevek encounters the world of Urras as both alien and alienating, philosophers, theorists, and others experienced the rapid transformation of the West into a "consumer society" as an ominous herald of a new world governed by a generalized alienation.

While these critiques focused their attention on the object, the possibility of some escape from alienation was also explored through a dialectical reversal in which objects, differently designed, strategically "hidden," and alternatively deployed might play a significant part. And again these developments find their parallel in Le Guin's fictive exploration of design and aesthetics.

THE RHETORIC OF THE OBJECT

There are critical moments when the invention of Utopias appears either as urgent necessity—Morris's industrial England or the consumer society of postwar Europe—or an immanent possibility—as in the Soviet Union of the 1920s. At these points the arguments for radical social transformation frequently assume material form in the shape of new aesthetic paradigms and rhetorical objects; a coalescence of technologies, material formations, and avant-garde designs mobilized in a Utopian discourse that announces the possibility and necessity of transcending existing social conditions and experience.

A prime and prototypical example is, of course, the Arts and Crafts movement's employment of vernacular materials, ornament, and production methods as an argument against the industrial division of labor in an increasingly urbanized modernity. But closer to the futurism of much 1960s design, and of a more direct lineage, would be the work of the Russian Constructivists of the 1920s. Due to the material and economic conditions of the new Soviet society, the grander designs of this avant-garde were typically unrealizable in all but model form. Vladimir Tatlin's towering *Monument to the Third International*, conceived as a rival to the skyscrapers of the capitalist world, remained unrealized at its intended scale. Rhetorically, though, its formal and technological qualities signaled the ambitions of the USSR. Its rotating inner volumes and helical outer structure signified revolutionary mobility and dynamism, while the technology and engineering, which was supposed to drive its mechanisms and project Soviet slogans into the skies, suggested a promethean transcendence of nature and the conquest of space. Circles, spirals, and helixes became favored geometrical tropes at this time, figures whose inherent mobility and self-transformation stood analogically for the goals and direction of the new society. Alexander Rodchenko's mobiles often employed these geometries in structural and tectonic experiments in materials, form and movement, and there is a suggestive parallel here with Takver's mobiles in *The Dispossessed*:

> she went to her old dormitory, once for her clothes and papers, and again, with Shevek, to bring a number of curious objects: complex concentric shapes made of wire, which moved and changed slowly and inwardly when suspended from the ceiling. She had made these with scrap wire and tools from the craft supply-depot, and called them Occupations in Uninhabited Space. (6: 182–83)

In the fictive worlds of *The Dispossessed* kinesis is discursively privileged over immobility much as it was Soviet Russia in the 1920s. And there are further parallels. The briefly fertile moment of the avant-garde in which experiments such as Rodchenko's could receive official state approval and sponsorship had ended by 1930 with the ascendancy of Stalinism, and its intolerant and utilitarian orthodoxy. Similarly the character Bedap complains that the initial revolutionary ferment of life on Anarres has congealed into a sterile and intolerant utilitarianism:

> Bedap spoke more gravely: "They can justify it because music isn't useful. Canal digging is important, you know; music's mere decoration. The circle has come right back around to the most vile kind of profiteering utilitarianism. The complexity, the vitality, the freedom of invention and initiative that was the center of the Odonian ideal, we've thrown it all away. We've gone right back to barbarism. If it's new, run away from it; if you can't eat it, throw it away!" (6: 175–76)

Here Le Guin points to the ambiguities of life on Anarres and the tendency of Utopian thought to ossify into a rigid dogmatism. On Anarres, as in Soviet Russia, ideas had become abstracted into an autonomous ideology unresponsive to the lived, spontaneous nature of everyday life.

The avant-garde groups of the 1960s were inspired by their predecessors of the early twentieth century but typically addressed a new set of conditions and possibilities. For Utopie in France and Superstudio in Italy, the degrading of everyday life through a generalized consumerism and its attendant alienating consequences were the most pressing concerns for design. Through new materials, buildings, and landscapes they sought to transform human relations with objects and spaces into nonalienated and enabling scenarios.

Inspired by the thought of Lefebvre, Utopie was formed in 1967 as a grouping of the architects Jean Aubert, Jean-Paul Jungmann, and Antoine Stinco and a more theoretical arm including Jean Baudrillard, Hubert Tonka, and Isabelle Auricoste. In their collaborative constitution this group attempted to give radical critique an expression in material form and an operative dimension in everyday life. In the work of its designers Utopia took the shape of various *structures gonflables* (inflatable structures). Further radicalized by the events of May 1968, Utopie saw in the inflatable structure a pure and transcendent space for a post-consumerist existence. As Marc Dessauce comments:

> In any case, if the word "alienation" had become the chief cant phrase of our time, and the struggle against it a central mot d'ordre of the student protest, a representation of the corresponding remedy—the asylum—would assume equal popularity. Operating a synthesis between the grotto and the airship, pneumatic structures seem designed to epitomize this type of asylum, with its dialectic of confinement and cure, of fusion and evasion—thus, the alternative use of inflatable domes for group experience and meditative isolation.[12]

The inflatable structures of the group promised insulation from the environmental bombardment of objects and advertising. The taut skins of the structures offered protection from the hostile atmosphere of consumerism and the provision of an object-free interior world where alternative social relations might emerge. The composition of these structures also suggested ethereal qualities opposed to the materialism of the times: their thin transparent membranes, given volume only by air itself, produced a near immaterial essence, and the ephemerality and disposability of these designs mitigated against their fetishization as "consumer goods" and against the possession of the subject by the object.

Similar ends were pursued by Superstudio in Italy at this time. The major part of their work was given over to the search for a "degree zero" in design, architecture, and aesthetics, and their resultant *Continuous Monument* project proposed a stripped down, homogenous tectonic grid as the "once and for all" solution to the architecture of the human environment. The barest and most semiotically neutral aesthetic would suffice to generate the minimal surfaces for human inhabitation. In a series of collages and staged scenarios Superstudio envisioned a future in which the neutral monochrome grid of the *Continuous Monument* formed a mute support for a nomadic Utopia. In this liberated environment human figures wandered, played, dined, and slept in direct unmediated relationship to one another.

As was the case for Utopie in France, and the lead they had taken from Lefebvre and Baudrillard, Superstudio saw the rise in consumerism as a new stage in capitalist development in which there was even more at stake than the economic exploitation of one class by another. Group member Adolofo Natalini observed in 1971:

> if design is merely an inducement to consume, then we must reject design; if architecture is merely the codifying of the bourgeois models of ownership and society, then we must reject architecture; if architecture and town planning is merely the formalization of present unjust social divisions, then we must reject town planning and cities . . . until all design activities are aimed towards meeting primary needs. Until then, design must disappear. We can live without architecture.[13]

Superstudio also shared Utopie's broader strategic response to consumerism; a distinct asceticism in their treatment of objects, design, and aesthetics. Any aesthetic stimulus toward pleasure in objects themselves is eschewed as a refusal of patterns of consumption and possession. Objects and spaces are designed only to provide the minimal and pure conditions that would support direct and non-alienated social relations free of their mediation through the object.

This fear of ornament has a special significance in modernist and Utopian discourse and is also voiced in *The Dispossessed*. But here it is bracketed within the rhetoric of the Odonian orthodoxy that reigns on Anarres and subjected to a more demanding critique.

BEYOND EXCREMENT

For the Austrian architect and theorist, Adolf Loos, ornament was crime; on Le Guin's Anarres "Excess is excrement" (4: 98). Throughout the novel Shevek observes the "excremental" waste of the Urrasti, their excess of ornament and decoration, as symptomatic of their inner poverty. Like their fellow consumers on Earth they know "no relationship but possession." By contrast the citizens of Anarres are materially impoverished but rich in humanity. The austerity and asceticism of Anarres is a material necessity, but one given a virtuous moral gloss in this opposition. Again this echoes the austere and purifying practices of groups such as Utopie and Superstudio.

But Le Guin introduces a third position to upset this apparently reasonable equation:

> People in the small towns wore a good deal of jewelry. In sophisticated Abbenay there was more sense of the tension between the principle of nonowner-ship and the impulse to self-adornment, and there a ring or pin was the limit

of good taste. But elsewhere the deep connection between the aesthetic and the acquisitive was simply not worried about; people bedecked themselves unabashedly. (10: 324)

Le Guin suggests that in the first instance it is only the conditions of material scarcity on Anarres that produce a corresponding ethical and aesthetic opposition to waste and excess. But there is nothing either "natural" or necessarily superior about these positions. On the contrary Shevek has to learn to curb the instinctive "propertarian" drives that come before he is taught Odonian communitarian ethics. In the quotation above, and elsewhere, the desire to possess appears to be a natural consequence of aesthetic stimulation. At Oiie's home we find Shevek approving of his host's taste:

> A relative absence of furniture pleased Shevek's eye at once: the rooms looked austere, spacious, with their expanses of deeply polished floor. He had always felt uneasy amidst the extravagant decorations and conveniences of the public buildings in which the receptions, dedications, and so forth were held. The Urrasti had taste, but it seemed often to be in conflict with an impulse towards display—conspicuous expense. The natural, aesthetic origin of the desire to own things was concealed and perverted by economic and competitive compulsions, which in turn told on the quality of the things: all they achieved was a kind of mechanical lavishness. Here, instead, was grace, achieved through restraint. (5: 145–46)

Certainly Shevek enjoys the restraint of his host's taste, but what is striking in this passage is the suggestion that the desire to own things might be "natural." This statement is at odds with the equation of possession with alienation and a provocation that upsets the notion of renunciation as liberation; it is a seemingly audacious claim that could not have been reasonably made within the broadly Marxian framework of anticonsumerist discourse or radical design theory. Yet placed within the discourse of science-fiction on a distant planet it enables a reframing of Utopian approaches to objects and aesthetics.

The reframing of Utopian discourse suggests that the Utopia of Anarres is not an unambiguous alternative to consumerism or a viable model for a future society in itself. Whereas Utopie or Superstudio could renounce the need for objects through choice and Lefebvre, like Morris before him, could look back nostalgically at apparently nonalienated historical moments, on Anarres scarcity is a precondition, and, moreover, a precondition that inhibits the ability of the Anarresti to achieve total self-realization. Instead, they are frequently reduced to the same narrowly economic dimensions of existence as the Urrasti: one is enslaved by scarcity, the other by luxury.

In this way Le Guin's novel points to a critique of the strategies of the groups and individuals discussed here. Whereas the ascetic tenor and an anticonsumerist austerity of these equates renunciation with salvation and freedom, some of Le Guin's characters achieve real aesthetic pleasure, satisfaction, and self-realization through their relationship to objects, even their possession, and against the dogma that would label them "propertarian." Others, significantly, such as the composer Salas, have their aesthetic experiments thwarted in the name of functionalist orthodoxy.

Again the thematics of containment versus mobility come into play here, between utopian fiction and utopian design, because, while both Anarres and Urras are trapped in their circumstances and unwilling to change or develop, this same dynamic lack and the inability to account for kinesis mark the projects and thinking of radical design in the 1960s and 1970s. The new spaces they proposed for human inhabitation were as free of objects and as aesthetically muted as possible, as if this might provide a pristine environment in which subjects could realize their essentially nonalienated and unmediated individual and social being. But this was only a polarized reversal of the late capitalist condition in which people could only find their identities and relate to the social *through* objects. You are either alienated by objects or liberated by their absence. Both Urrasti capitalism, where objects are the source of human identity and sociability, and Anarresti anarchism, where objects alienate and their absence allows for identity and sociability, represent polar positions; Le Guin brings the two worlds, and by implication the two positions, into a proximity that starts to undermine the stability of both. The "propertarians" of Urras are capable of simple and refined aesthetic taste and the anarchists of Anarres are capable of turning ethical principles into a dogmatic and repressive orthodoxy. Their relationships to objects are not parceled neatly into the categories of "alienated by" or "liberated from." Challenging this binary logic some of the novel's characters relate intimately to objects without succumbing to their powers of alienation; on the contrary their subjectivity engages with the social through the world of objects as an extension of their individual agency. The mobiles that Takver constructs, for instance, suggest a tactile and haptic relation to the material world and its potential to be worked into meaningful and empathetic forms: their embodiment of kinesis in space makes concrete the abstract theorizing of Shevek for the novel's world. In contrast to the drift toward a purely semiotic epistemology, initiated by Baudrillard and Barthes, or the drive to eviscerate the object that takes place in Utopie or Superstudio, Le Guin's novel, anticipating much contemporary critical thought,[14] suggests the mimetic potential of our relationship to the world of things and points toward the mutually enabling and transformative mediation between people, objects, technologies, and ideas. As such it remains a significant parable for our consumerist planet.

NOTES

The author would like to acknowledge the volume's editors, whose comments and criticisms played a significant role in developing this chapter from its initial draft to its present form.

1. Ursula K. Le Guin, *The Dispossessed: An Ambiguous Utopia* (New York: Harper & Row, 1974), cited in the text by chapter and page to the 387-page Eos HarperCollins edition of 2001.

2. Henri Lefebvre, *Critique of Everyday Life, Volume One*, trans. J. Moore (London and New York: Verso, 1991), 66.

3. Guy Debord, *Society of the Spectacle* (London: Rebel Press/Dark Star, 1977).

4. Naomi Klein, *No Logo* (London: Flamingo, 2001).

5. William Morris, *News from Nowhere* (London: Penguin, 1993).

6. Rob Shields, *Lefebvre, Love and Struggle: Spatial Dialectics* (London and New York: Routledge, 1999), 40–41.

7. Henri Lefebvre, *The Production of Space*, trans. D. Nicholson-Smith (Oxford: Blackwell, 2000).

8. Jean Baudrillard, *The System of Objects*, trans. J. Benedict (London and New York: Verso, 1996), 56.

9. Baudrillard, *System of Objects*, 42.

10. Baudrillard, *System of Objects*, 99.

11. Roland Barthes, *Mythologies*, trans. A. Lavers (London: Paladin, 1985), 88.

12. Marc Dessauce, "On Pneumatic Apparitions," in *The Inflatable Moment: Pneumatics and Protest in May '68*, ed. Marc Dessauce (New York: The Architectural League of New York, 1999), 14–15.

13. Cited in Peter Lang and William Menking, "Only Architecture Will Be Our Lives," in *Superstudio: Life Without Objects*, ed. Peter Lang and William Menking (Milan: Skira, 2003), 20–21.

14. On "mimesis" see Mark Hansen, *Embodying Technesis: Technology Beyond Writing* (Ann Arbor: University of Michigan, 2000), especially chapter 9; Susan Buck-Morss, *The Dialectics of Seeing* (Cambridge, MA: MIT Press, 1989); and Michael Taussig, *Mimesis and Alterity: A Particular Study of the Senses* (London: Routledge, 1992); on the critique of modernity's purifying operations see Bruno Latour, *We Have Never Been Modern* (Cambridge, MA: Harvard University Press, 1993); and for his critical account of Latour see Scott Lash, *Another Modernity: A Different Rationality* (Oxford: Blackwell, 1999).

WORKS CITED

Barthes, Roland. *Mythologies*. Trans. A. Lavers. London: Paladin, 1985.

Baudrillard, Jean. *The System of Objects*. Trans. J. Benedict. London and New York: Verso, 1996.

Buck-Morss, Susan. *The Dialectics of Seeing*. Cambridge, MA: MIT Press, 1989.

Debord, Guy. *Society of the Spectacle*. Translation unaccredited. London: Rebel Press/Dark Star, 1977.

Dessauce, Marc. "On Pneumatic Apparitions." Pp. 13–25 in *The Inflatable Moment: Pneumatics and Protest in '68*, ed. Marc Dessauce. New York: The Architectural League of New York, 1999.

Hansen, Mark. *Embodying Technesis: Technology Beyond Writing*. Ann Arbor: University of Michigan, 2000.

Klein, Naomi. *No Logo*. London: Flamingo, 2001.

Lang, Peter, and Menking, William, eds. *Superstudio: Life Without Objects*. Milan: Skira, 2003.

Lash, Scott. *Another Modernity: A Different Rationality*. Oxford: Blackwell, 1999.

Latour, Bruno. *We Have Never Been Modern*. Trans. Catherine Porter. Cambridge, MA: Harvard University Press, 1993.

Lefebvre, Henri. *Critique of Everyday Life, Volume One*. Trans. J. Moore. London and New York: Verso, 1991.

———. *The Production of Space*. Trans. Donald Nicholson-Smith. Oxford: Blackwell, 2000.

Le Guin, Ursula K. *The Dispossessed: An Ambiguous Utopia*. New York: Eos, HarperCollins, 2001 (1974).

Morris, William. *News from Nowhere*. London: Penguin, 1993.

Shields, R. *Lefebvre, Love and Struggle: Spatial Dialectics*. London and New York: Routledge, 1999.

Taussig, Michael. *Mimesis and Alterity: A Particular Study of the Senses*. London: Routledge, 1992.

III

ANARCHIST POLITICS

6

Individual and Community in Le Guin's *The Dispossessed*

Dan Sabia*

*W*hen political theory turns to political literature for instruction or inspiration, there are bound to be potential dangers as well as potential rewards; but the latter, I think, far outweigh the former. Political theory tends to be abstract, political literature concrete. Theory focuses on suppositions and arguments, literature on characters, relationships, and situations. Theory tries to explain and expound, literature to describe, evoke, suggest. Theory tends to analyze, literature to imagine. The differences point to the possibility that a careless theorist might be misled by the particularity or lack of rigor characteristic of political stories; but they point also to the possibility that political literature might help thoughtful theorists see what they may have missed, or illuminate what they may have seen only dimly. This is the case, I believe, with Ursula Le Guin's *The Dispossessed*.

The illumination I have in mind concerns our understanding of anarchist communism in general, and of the plausibility of that theory's claim to be able to reconcile individuality and community in particular. This is because *The Dispossessed* depicts and interrogates, in an informed and provocative fashion, an imaginary "experiment in nonauthoritarian [i.e., anarchist] communism . . . that has survived for a hundred and seventy years" in an imaginary place called Anarres in an imaginary future (11: 342). Despite this focus, and despite many discussions of this famous text, the number of theoretically informed, intensive analyses of the version of anarchist communism evoked in and by the novel is slim.[1] I hope in what follows to demonstrate how undeserved this relative silence has been.

Le Guin has several times made clear that *The Dispossessed* reflects her considerable knowledge of anarchism, as well as her strong sympathy for the central ideas and ideals of the communist or communal versions of anarchism that one finds in thinkers like Proudhon and (much of) Marx, in Bakunin and Malatesta

---

*This essay elaborates and develops arguments first articulated in the article "Utopia as Critique," which appeared in the journal *Peace Review* 14 (2002): 191–97.

and Morris, and especially in Kropotkin, Goldman, and Goodman.[2] One year after the publication of the novel, Le Guin explained that she wrote the story because she found anarchist communism, of the sort "prefigured in early Taoist
thought, and expounded by Shelly and Kropotkin, Goldman and Goodman . . .
[to be] the most idealistic, and to me the most interesting, of all political theories."[3] Years later, Le Guin again explained that she had "formulated" the novel's
"political theory" only after considerable study of "Kropotkin and Emma Goldman and the rest," and she repeated her commitment to it: anarchism, she said, is
rather "like Christianity; it's never really been practiced . . . [but] it is a necessary
idea."[4]

The attractions of anarchist communism, its desirability or practical necessity, are many, and Le Guin's novel does a fine job identifying and describing virtually all of them. The novel offers an imaginative reconstruction and defense of
the foundational assumptions and principles, aspirations and ideals, and key institutions and practices, characteristic of anarcho-communist ideology. But it is
not for this reason alone, or even primarily, that the novel deserves our attention.
A key attraction of the ideology has always been its stress on the equal and paramount value of both individualism and community, personal autonomy and social
solidarity, individual freedom and responsibility to others, together with a history
of theoretical argument, and practical experimentation, aimed at showing why
and how self and society, or individuality and community, can be reconciled or
harmonized.[5] What *The Dispossessed* offers, beyond its informed and sympathetic
portrayal of anarchist communism in general, is a stimulating and highly suggestive account of how this promise of reconciliation might in fact be approximated,
and an equally suggestive account of why that promise can never be wholly satisfied. It even explains why this inadequacy serves, paradoxically, to recommend the
theory.

As an artist keenly interested in the connections and conflicts between individuals and their cultures, it is surely this aspect of anarchist communism that Le
Guin had most in mind when she referred to it as the "most interesting" of all political theories.[6] I intend in what follows to pursue the same interest by turning
attention to, and by drawing on, her novel. In the first section, I identify the key
theoretical claims and arguments, and describe some of the practices and institutions, that help explain why the ideal of reconciliation is so attractive and how it
can be approximated; in the second section, I explore some of the key reasons why
complete reconciliation is neither possible nor desirable.

I

The term "anarchist communism" was coined by Kropotkin. In 1880, he urged the
members of an international anarchist congress in Switzerland to adopt the label,

believing, as Novack has nicely put it, "that it conveyed the idea of unity or harmony between individual freedom and a 'well-ordered' society. Anarchist communism views the individual as essentially a social being who can achieve full development only in society, while society can benefit only when its members are free."[7] Kropotkin famously believed that both evolutionary theory and human history vouched for the truth of this leading idea. Individuals need the nourishment and protection that only a humane social order can provide, while societies need the intelligence and cooperation of free individuals if they are to remain viable in a constantly changing world. The survival and progressive development of humanity in general, and of societies and civilizations in particular, Kropotkin believed, depend on the voluntary cooperation of autonomous, ethical, beings.[8]

The interdependence of individual and society in a constantly changing natural and human environment is also a central tenet of Anarresti anarchist communism. The knowledge that change is a permanent feature of the world, that one cannot "go down twice to the same river," means that survival, whether of the individual or the community, requires a willingness and capacity to change and adapt (2: 54). But the source of willed, intelligent, and potentially ethical or progressive change and adaptation lies within individuals. "Society" is ultimately an abstraction; "only the individual, the person, had the power of moral choice—the power of change" (10: 333). Hence, social survival and well-being require the nourishment and protection of individuals; any viable social order must enable and protect the autonomy and liberty of each and every person, so that individuals will be willing and able to contribute to society, to initiate needed action, to innovate and take risks when opportunities and dangers appear.

Unfortunately, self-governing individuals can deploy their freedom in irresponsible ways, and societies, and the myriad social relationships, groups, and associations within any social order, can easily become oppressive. As we will see, precisely this is happening in Anarres: *The Dispossessed* describes a flawed, not a perfect, utopia. Theoretically, the essential problem may be described as finding ways of maximizing individual autonomy and liberty and a humane social order without inviting either widespread forms of individual irresponsibility or of social oppression or stagnation. Put another way, the problem is how to reconcile individual autonomy and agency with both the inevitable rules and demands of social units, and the inevitable duties and responsibilities individuals incur as social beings. Because individuals are both uniquely particular *and* social beings, they must find a way of harmonizing within themselves their self and social interests and duties; similarly, the social order they help construct and sustain must find a way of harmonizing practices that develop and respect the independence, autonomy and agency of individuals with those that develop and respect their interdependence and social needs and bonds.[9]

There is no question but that the hero and central character of *The Dispossessed*, Shevek, embraces precisely this ideal goal of harmony, even while acknowledging the imperfections of his society. He contends that the fact that "Anarres had fallen short of the ideal" does not undermine the appeal or validity of the theory. Given the right understanding, the right ethics, and the right institutions and practices, "true community," he says, can be achieved (10: 333). "True community" is of course shorthand for the reconciliation of self and society, freedom and sociality. The phrase is reminiscent of Emma Goldman, who once remarked that community "in the true sense" is rather like a living organism, the character and vitality of which is made possible only by the "mutual cooperation" of the "cells" which, in turn, are able to "attain [their] highest form of development" only within the organism.[10] Similarly, Shevek and others on Anarres contend that "true community" models itself after the cell/organism analogy emphasized by Anarres' anarcho-communist ideology, according to which the individual and society nourish and serve one another through voluntary cooperation and mutuality (10: 333). Such a community achieves social unity on the basis of diversity and freedom rather than on the basis of uniformity and conformity (1: 4; 3: 81). But how, exactly, does it do so?

True community "begins in shared pain." Actually, it is "brotherhood" which is said to "begin in shared pain," a claim repeated throughout the novel (for example, 2: 60; 4: 124; 9: 300). The suggestion is that recognition of the individual's weaknesses and vulnerability is most starkly felt when one suffers, or sees others suffering. On those occasions, human beings instinctively reach for aid or comfort, or try to provide it, and in that moment the need for others, and hence for brotherhood or solidarity, becomes particularly clear. This cognitive recognition helps explain, and more importantly affirms the existence of, the "impulse to mutual aid" or "solidarity instinct" implanted in human beings by nature (e.g., 6: 68). Explicable (as Kropotkin emphasized) in terms of evolutionary processes, this instinct, or innate tendency, serves as the foundation for what might be termed an ethic of "mutual aid and solidarity" (e.g., 4: 117). In turn, both the propensity for solidarity, and the ethic, facilitate social cooperation, which is the key to social and individual survival and well-being. "The law of evolution is that the strongest survives!" asserts a minor character in the novel, to which Shevek replies, "Yes, and the strongest, in the existence of any social animal, are those who are most social. In human terms, the most ethical" (7: 220).[11]

Before describing this ethic of mutual aid and solidarity, I need to elaborate the important claim that individuals gain from social solidarity and cooperation. Individuals are on the account of the anarcho-communists radically social. They need one another not only when they are in pain, or in trouble. Rather, there is little the individual can do or be, little he or she can become or achieve, without the help and cooperation of others: "*To be whole is to be part*," reads the tombstone of the revolutionary founder of Anarres (3: 84). True in all societies, the need for others as a condition of self-development and well-being is especially true in an anarcho-communist society, because there the absence of a state, or of centralized authority, entails that the viability of all social institutions and practices depends, entirely, on voluntary cooperation and sharing. Hence individual welfare and community well-being are intimately connected; there is no third party on which individuals can rely to advance their interests or welfare. They must create the conditions and practices of their liberation through their cooperation.

Now, one very important implication of the social character of human being and living is that the concept of individual freedom has to be carefully constructed. The notion that freedom can be defined negatively must be rejected, and the idea that it must be used responsibly, because its exercise involves the welfare of others, must be emphasized. The novel suggests that it is in a sense possible for people of privilege to "enjoy" negative freedom, but they can do so only by isolating themselves "from want, distraction, and cares. What they were free to do, however, was another question. It appeared to Shevek that their freedom from obligation was in exact proportion to their lack of freedom of initiative" (5: 127). By contrast, Shevek really was a free man: "Since those [youthful] years his social and personal life had got more and more complicated and demanding. He had been not only a physicist but also a partner, a father, an Odonian [that is, a responsible member of his community], and finally a social reformer. As such . . . [he] had not been free from anything, only free to do anything" (5: 29).[12]

Shevek's freedom to do what he wants to do sets him on a variety of paths where he voluntarily incurs obligations to others. That the obligations are self-incurred (and can be terminated at the initiative of the individual), and that those obligations reflect and serve the (hopefully autonomous) decisions, interests, and goals of the individual, is what makes Shevek's society anarchic. The individual is sovereign; the only final authority Shevek recognizes is his own conscience (1: 8; 3: 76). But that the exercise of liberty almost always affects other human beings, and that it almost always requires interacting, cooperating, and often sharing with others, mean that free actions do impose general and particular obligations on the individual, and this is what makes Shevek's society an ethical community.[13]

A proper social morality, or an ethic of "mutual aid and solidarity," would accordingly stress a relatively small number of basic principles or ideals. Always value the particularity and autonomy, and respect the freedom, of individuals. Understand that all persons are moral equals, indeed brothers, deserving of equal respect and concern.[14] Help those in need. Never intentionally harm or take advantage of another.[15] And contribute to society by doing "the work [you] can do best," and by cooperating—fairly—when it is mutually beneficial to do so (10: 333). Assuming such an ethic were actually practiced, one important result would be that individuals would tend to assume, as Shevek does, that other "people would be helpful [and could be] trusted" (7: 204). Trusting others is the basis of mutual aid—of reciprocity and collective action.

Although mutual trust is presupposed in an anarcho-communist society, the presupposition is not unconditional. It is instead subject to experiential confirmation. The trust initially extended by someone like Shevek to others will be withdrawn if their conduct proves irresponsible. People who fail to reciprocate or to cooperate in a fair and reasonable manner, who are unwilling to contribute to society through work, or who shirk their social obligations and responsibilities or engage in exploitative behavior—such people will not be trusted. Widespread conduct of this sort accordingly spells the collapse of trust and therefore of (voluntary) cooperation. And since, to repeat, mutual trust is the basis of social cooperation, and social cooperation is the basis of both individual and social well-being, insuring responsible conduct must be the central goal of (ethical) education.

But education is not enough, in part because "the will to domination is as central in human beings as the impulse to mutual aid is" (6: 168). The will to power or domination, or more generally egoism or selfishness, is a deep-rooted characteristic of human beings not likely to be extinguished by an education in the ethics of mutuality and solidarity, even an education that seeks to suppress egoistic tendencies as Anarresti education does (a point to which I shall return in section II). Instead, a whole panoply of social institutions, conventions, and practices are needed to embody, encourage, and reinforce the ethic of solidarity and thereby insure the responsible exercise of freedom by individuals.

A very brief identification of particularly important institutions and practices should begin with the economy. The anarchist communism of the Anarresti rejects not only capitalism but also materialism (excessive and unnecessary wealth is "excrement"). The private ownership of property (and people), the profit motive, money, and most of the other trappings of capitalism, are all absent in Anarresti society, as is the belief that material possessions or personal wealth is essential to one's happiness or welfare (the view, instead, is that possessions corrupt). As a result, individuals do not and cannot compete for, nor can they seek to accumulate, property or wealth and the forms of power and status based on property and wealth as is common in both traditional and capitalistic societies. People are instead economically equal in the sense that economic distribution (in the form of goods and services) is according to need (within the constraints of local availability, people take what they need from, for instance, storehouses, common dining halls, and school curricula). They are also relatively poor; Anarres is a barren planet (actually a moon), a fact that may well reinforce both the rejection of materialism and recognition of the need for solidarity.[16]

The economy, like the organization of social life in general, is more or less decentralized and democratically governed, although economic, social, and geographic units are federated to permit the coordination of economic relations and social activities between the typically small, always self-governing, local units. Decentralization and small size are essential to insuring responsible behavior, and not just because "power inheres in a center" (2: 58). Groups that operate on (or approximate operating on) a face-to-face basis facilitate personal responsibility and the maintenance of mutual trust and therefore cooperation. This is because small groups, generally speaking, increase the ease with which differences of opinion can be resolved or accommodated, reduce the incentives for shirking, and increase the ease with which shirking and other forms of irresponsible, trust-destroying behavior can be identified and sanctioned (for instance, by criticism, ostracism, or even exclusion). Because, moreover, economic and social life is decentralized, the norms and habits of solidarity—the willingness to cooperate, to pitch in, to play fair, even to sanction the irresponsible—are more likely to be carried over into forms of participation in larger, more anonymous contexts. When, for example, a planet-wide drought presents a society-wide crisis, a "labor draft" is instituted and the vast majority of Anarresti willingly, even eagerly, respond (8: 247).[17]

Other institutions and practices also encourage mutual trust and responsible behavior, or reduce the incentives or occasions for irresponsible conduct, or both. The practice of rotating leadership (and other) positions within organizations, for instance within economic and educational units, is one; it is difficult to be corrupted by power, and to misuse it, if one doesn't have (very much of) it for very long. Of course, the absence of a state removes a host of related temptations, including the training of experts in the use of organized coercion, perhaps the most potent source of human corruption and social injustice and conflict. The elimination of marriage and the nuclear family is likewise conceived, in part, as removing opportunities for domination and exploitation, and as encouraging more libertarian and egalitarian social relationships and habits (sexual relations and partnerships, for example, are as varied, and as temporary or permanent, as individuals wish them to be). The elimination of these institutions also serves to integrate people into community life. In general, people live a very public or communal existence on Anarres. Privacy is respected to a degree, but it is difficult to avoid social contact and communal living given the (largely) communal rearing of children, public housing and transportation, public schooling, communal dining, ongoing democratic governance, public service days (every tenth day, local communities organize, and people volunteer for, jobs such as garbage collection and grave digging), and the like that mark everyday life. Communal living does not only embody communal practices, norms, and values, it normalizes and promotes them. Individuals come to regard as quite ordinary and desirable reciprocal and cooperative arrangements, egalitarian practices and forms of sharing, the suppression of egoistic behaviors and attitudes, volunteering for social activities, and working as effectively as one can for the good of the social whole as well as for the benefit of self. The ethic of solidarity and mutual aid must be practiced to be efficacious, and on Anarres, generally speaking, it is.[18]

This ethic, recall, includes the values of individual autonomy and freedom. If social practices neglect or discount individuality, the result may be a community of sorts, but it will not be the "true community" in which self and community, liberty and solidarity, are reconciled or harmonized. Now, one central way to protect, and to some degree promote, individual liberty is to make it difficult for individuals and groups to gain power over one another. Thus, most of the institutions and practices mentioned above promote or protect freedom as much as they do solidarity and community: the absence of concentrations of economic and political power, the decentralized self-government of economic and social life, the rotation of positions of leadership within organizations, and so on. But there are other protective and reinforcing practices as well.

The educational system, for example, is supposed to promote autonomy and self-confidence as well as fraternal sentiments and habits of cooperation, and it is designed to encourage students to explore and develop skills and talents which best suit their character or which seem to them most appealing or challenging. Though the system is in Anarresti practice less than perfect (as described below), Shevek is evidence that the system has value and is relatively successful. While it is true that Shevek must throughout the novel struggle for personal and political success, he nonetheless develops an autonomous, reflective self, he is able to practice the work he wants to do, he is able to follow this work to a successful conclusion, and he is both confident and free enough to become a successful reformer or "revolutionary" (6: 176).[19]

Job posting is also a key social practice that embodies respect for individuals and liberty. A centralized computer system maintains constantly updated records of job openings throughout Anarres, and is geared to match positions to personal skills and needs, subject to availability. Even in times of social crisis, when people are "drafted" to serve in socially essential positions, there is an effort to match people with jobs and locales they prefer, and people are free to decline the draft if, as is often the case in times of crisis, no match is available. This (conventional, not of course legal) right of refusal symbolizes and protects the liberty and empowerment of the individual, as does the related right of exit. As earlier indicated, no Anarresti can be forced to do anything against his or her will or conscience; hence, except for young children, people are generally speaking free to come and go as they wish. It is even possible to wholly remove oneself from the community and its expectations and obligations by playing the role of hermit. People who do so are called "nuchnibi." Although nuchnibi hardly integrate themselves into the social order, the right to withdraw symbolizes the commitment of the community to individual sovereignty. On Anarres, "there were a good many solitaries and hermits on the fringes of the older . . . communities, pretending that they were not members of a social species" (4: 110–11). Sometimes, to be sure, the pretense is a screen for free riding, in which case the nuchnibi are not treated well by their neighbors. "They make fun of him, or they get rough with him, beat him up; in a small community they might agree to take his name off the meals listing, so he has to cook and eat all by himself; that is humiliating" (5: 150). Just as one cannot and should not expect coworkers to tolerate shirking, so too one can not expect the neighbors to take kindly to parasitism. But though shirking is wrong, exit is not; and though parasitism will not be tolerated, withdrawal will be.

One final example concerns what might be called the right of initiative, which is a more positive and striking encouragement of individual freedom. In Anarresti society, individuals are free to start new groups and organizations and, within the constraints of availability, draw on local or even more distant resources to make a go of their projects. In the context of the economy, for instance, workers can start a new production syndicate and can request and expect to receive needed resources (say, tools or other forms of equipment) from established producers. In the context of education, students have the right to request, and teachers to offer, courses and classes pretty much at will. Shevek begins a printing syndicate, termed the Syndicate of the Initiative, in order to pursue his scientific work and the work of political reform. Thus, as one would expect in an anarchist community, consenting adults can pretty much do what they want when they want, subject to the constraints of nature and the feelings (and resources) of the neighbors.

The institutions and practices of Anarresti culture are clearly intended, then, to stimulate, cultivate, reinforce, and protect both individuality and community, both the ideals of individual autonomy and freedom on the one hand, and the norms and habits of social solidarity and cooperation on the other. But the degree to which those social practices succeed in reconciling these values is another, related but different, question. I have already indicated that success on Anarres has been limited—this gives Shevek his political mission and the novel much of its drama—and I shall offer some explanations for this shortly, in section II. As a preliminary to that, I want to suggest that the possibility of reconciliation can be viewed as being dependent, in the final analysis, on the recognition by individuals of their mutual or shared interest in supporting precisely the institutions and practices that define anarchist communism. Because of their weaknesses and vulnerabilities, individuals must come to understand that it is in their general, long-run interest to participate in and support the kind of community that provides them with the intellectual, emotional, and material resources, the security and protections, and the opportunities for the exercise of freedom, that they need in order to achieve a meaningful and fulfilling life. An anarcho-communist society is in the self-interest of each and all; enlightened self-interest lies at the bottom of this political theory and its promise of reconciliation.

The Dispossessed seems to confirm this suggestion and Le Guin, I think, intends to make this point, by what she says about altruism. Superficially, anarchist communism may seem to rely on altruism defined as conduct motivated, exclusively or primarily, by concern for the welfare of others. Were a reader of the novel to make this assumption, he or she would be surprised to discover that the word is rarely used by Le Guin, and much more surprised by what is said about it when it is used. Altruistic motivation is ascribed only to special categories of people, and it is explicitly denied a significant role in Anarresti social life and political thinking. Specifically, "youthful" Anarresti are often eager to serve others, and some of the Anarresti practitioners of "the medical arts" behave altruistically (3: 93; 4: 121). But altruistic motivation and conduct is explicitly said *not* to be "an Odonian [anarcho-communist] virtue" (8: 226). Most strikingly, Shevek explicitly exclaims at one point that he is "no altruist!" (11: 350). Near the end of the novel, Le Guin describes another race of people, the Hainish (a people who appear in a number of her early novels), who *are* altruists. They are, as well, a very old race, and one "moved . . . by guilt" (11: 348). Perhaps this means that altruism is the fruit of a very long evolution, or perhaps that it is only a bad conscience which can sustain such a demanding and self-abnegating disposition. In either case, the Anarresti, in contrast to the Hainish, are not moved by altruism. But, of course, neither are they (supposed to be) moved by egoism. Between altruism and self-ishness lies a proper or enlightened sense of self-interest, the kind of human motive that, just perhaps, can serve as the basis for reconciling individual and community.

II

But even with enlightenment, reconciliation is not easily achieved, and it is virtually certain that anything like a complete reconciliation—a state of affairs marked by the absence of tensions, conflicts, discordant relationships, irresponsible conduct on the part of individuals, oppressive practices, and the like—is an impossibility. The novel offers and suggests a number of reasons for this, but I intend to focus only on those reasons that seem to me to be particularly intractable, in part because these sources of disharmony are also sources of harmony. This duality or ambiguity explains, I think, why Le Guin's novel is subtitled *An Ambiguous Utopia*.

These ambiguous sources of harmony and disharmony are underlying features of the human condition which give rise to both the promise and the corruptions of individuality and community—that is, the ineradicable vulnerability, and the inherent particularity, of human beings. We have seen how the vulnerability and weaknesses of the isolated individual lie at the root of his or her (enlightened) self-interest in maintaining a humane, anarcho-communist social order and, therefore, in maintaining a commitment to the communal values of solidarity, equality, and fair play and, relatedly, to the suppression and control of egoism and selfish forms of conduct like shirking and domination. Unfortunately, the need for a social order sufficiently stable, productive, and sophisticated to support this kind of community and the manifold needs of its members requires, it turns out, a good deal of centralization. Centralization, in turn, is the source of a host of problems which undercut the promise of reconciliation.

Le Guin is very clear about this point, a reflection perhaps of the emphasis placed on the importance of decentralization by so many anarchist theorists and activists. In a key passage in the novel, the reader learns that the revolutionary founder of Anarres's version of anarchist communism had intended for decentralization to be "an essential element" of the new, post-revolutionary order on her planet (the planet of which Anarres is the moon). Basically, self-sufficient communities would be loosely "connected by communication and transportation networks . . . but the network was not to be run from the top down. There was to be no controlling center, no capital." However, the founder's plans had not envisioned the barren, arid moon of Anarres.

> On arid Anarres, the communities had to scatter widely in search of resources, and few of them could be self-supporting, no matter how they cut back their notions of what is needed for support. They cut back very hard indeed, but to a minimum beneath which they would not go; they would not regress to pre-urban, pre-technological tribalism. They knew that their anarchism was the product of a very high civilization, of a complex, diversified culture, of a stable economy and a highly industrialized technology that could maintain high production and rapid transportation of goods. (4: 95)

So there had to be a center after all. The administration and coordination of labor, transportation, communications, and distribution were in fact, and by necessity, centralized, and "from the start the Settlers [of Anarres] were aware that that unavoidable centralization was a lasting threat" (4: 96). By the time Shevek is a young man, a century and a half or so later, the center had become "basically an archistic bureaucracy." The need for centralization and coordination unavoidably became the need for bureaucratic "expertise and stability," and hence new sources of power, based on proficiency, knowledge, information, and strategic position, were created. The need for a humane social order, indeed for an anarcho-communist order, seems to *require* something like a state, and this "gives scope to the authoritarian impulse" (6: 167).

Nor is that all. In order for this relatively centralized, bureaucratic system to function well, in order for it to secure economic efficiency and production, and social and economic predictability and stability, it is indeed necessary to promote the virtues of solidarity, of fellow feeling, community spirit, a willingness to get along and go along, to work hard for the good of society, and to take seriously the beliefs and demands of public opinion, keeper of "the social conscience." Apart from the fact that a quasi-state can, and in Anarres does, manipulate public opinion (6: 165), the real problem here is, of course, that the legitimate interest in and demand for solidarity and trust and community spirit and the rest can easily become an interest in and demand for uniformity and conformity. In a society in which "the social conscience, the opinion of others, was the most powerful moral force motivating the behavior of most Anarresti," the lines between cooperation and obedience, persuasion and manipulation, conviction and conformity, tend to blur (4: 112; 6: 167). The problem is in the novel symbolized by the institution of the "Criticism Session," a legitimate "communal activity . . . wherein everybody stood up and complained about defects in the functioning of the community," but ended up attacking "defects in the characters of the neighbors" (6: 176).

Because the anarchist community depends on enlightened self-interest or voluntary acceptance of the ethic of solidarity and mutual aid, the members of the community must fear, and must work to eradicate or at any rate constrain egoism in themselves and their neighbors. Again, egoism threatens social order; its appearance is always associated with suboptimal performance within groups and organizations as well as with immorality and bad faith. Educators and other socializing agents are likely in consequence to view their job as promoting solidarity and disciplining egoism rather than, or more than, enabling the autonomy, the self-confidence and self-assertion, of the individual. Indeed, even the most well-intentioned can have a hard time differentiating self-assertion and self-interest from egoism and selfishness. On Anarres, the not so well-intentioned and the confused have become common in the educational system. "Education . . . has become rigid, moralistic, authoritarian. Kids learn to parrot [rather than critically examine the ideals of anarchist communism]" (6: 168). Very early in the novel the reader witnesses this treatment applied to a young Shevek, whose creative and playful efforts in the classroom are met by disapproval and discipline from his teacher (2: 29).

Another manifestation of this perhaps inevitable corruption of the ethic and practices of solidarity and mutual aid concerns practices of inclusion and exclusion. We have seen that noncooperators, shirkers for instance, are subject to various kinds of sanctions, the most extreme of which would generally be exclusion (for example, from a syndicate or a local community). Because of the importance of solidarity and cooperation, and the fear of egoism, the practice of exclusion can easily be used to punish and isolate those who threaten or question convention—those who might, for instance, wish to change organizational procedures or goals, or question prevailing notions of fair play, or hard work, or good work. The maintenance of community or organizational solidarity and cooperation at that point becomes indistinguishable from the suppression of individuality, freedom, and difference. Much of the drama of *The Dispossessed* centers precisely on Shevek's exclusion from his society for this kind of reason, a treatment which he learns has become rather common. Shevek discovers the existence in the central city of a large group of "intellectual nuchnibi who had not worked on a regular posting for years," not because they sought, like real nuchnibi, to withdraw from society, but because society withdrew from them, that is, isolated and excluded them because they did not conform sufficiently to prevailing notions of normalcy and morality (6: 173).

If the sources of forms of social oppression and ossification are rooted in the needs for solidarity and for a stable social order (which in turn are rooted ultimately in the vulnerability and weaknesses of the isolated individual), the remedy for these evils is to be found in liberty. As Shevek's political consciousness matures, he comes to understand that the fundamental key to the maintenance of an ideal or just society is "eternal vigilance" and "permanent revolution" (4: 96; 9: 301). The quality of community life, of the structures and processes defining a social order, necessarily depend on individuals who are able to critically reflect on their society, its actual practices as well as its promises, and who are willing to take the kinds of risks and actions that might set things aright (4: 96). Individuals can not "make" a revolutionary society, says Shevek in a rousing speech, they "can only be" such a society (9: 301). So freedom, or the kinds of ethical action freedom makes possible, is the antidote to social injustice, to oppression and conformity and conservatism. But freedom, like solidarity and social order, is also an ambiguous good, and not just because individuals can exercise their freedom in irresponsible ways.

The commitment to individual autonomy and liberty, which defines anarchist communism as much as the commitment to solidarity and cooperation does, guarantees the proliferation of difference—of different characters and personalities, values and attitudes, beliefs and perspectives, interests and ambitions. This is because particularity or uniqueness is a fact of human nature which a properly structured regime of freedom will encourage and allow to blossom and proliferate. But differences often generate disagreement, conflict, disharmony, and too often fear and envy as well. Two common forms of conflict are those due to divergent interests, and those rooted in competing obligations. Divergent interests are particularly problematic in anarchist communism, because its success is so dependent on the mutuality of interests rather than on altruism.

The Dispossessed provides a number of examples of the absence of mutuality in order to dramatize how diversity amidst freedom generates social conflict. The most dramatic examples concern conflicts between the elites who dominate science and politics on Anarres and Shevek and his Syndicate. The Anarresti scientific establishment is invested in and comfortable with orthodox physical theories, and this causes nearly all of the physicists to fear, ignore, and/or criticize Shevek's innovative scientific work. Relatedly, the political establishment, in the form of the power elite in the central city (seat of the quasi-state), aim not simply to retain their power and privileges, but to protect traditional interests and goals, beliefs and values. In particular, the political elite are like most Anarresti committed to the continued isolation of Anarres from the mother planet, Urras, and from all other worlds. This entrenched policy, dating from the founding of the Anarresti community, seems in their view prudent, serving on the one hand to protect Anarres from the superior military might of Urras, and on the other to insulate it from the presumably inferior yet potentially dangerous ideas prevalent on Urras and every other alien world. Shevek and his Syndicate challenge this policy on the basis of contrary beliefs, counter-interests, and different goals, and they thereby threaten established routines, expectations, and stability. They contend that the old policy constitutes a betrayal of the revolution, both because it means giving up on the goal of spreading revolutionary ideas and ideals, and because it denies the revolution's commitment to freedom and change by implicitly presupposing that Anarresti society had achieved utopia, that it no longer needed to evolve, and that exposure to diverse and novel forces and ideas outside (as well as inside) its borders could only contaminate and never contribute to positive change.

The divergence of perspectives and interests in these cases engenders quite serious conflict between the elite/traditionalists and the Syndicate/rebels. Shevek, for instance, is widely regarded as a traitor, he becomes the target of death threats and lethal force, and his family, including his children, suffer social criticism and ostracism. The conflict reaches something of a zenith when the Syndicate formally proposes that Anarres open its borders to outsiders and then declares, when this proposal fails amidst overwhelming opposition, that Shevek will travel to Urras. Shevek undertakes this bold and risky journey for both personal and political reasons. Struggling for years in the inhospitable climate of Anarresti science to complete his revolutionary work in physics, he concludes that possible success requires the "stimulus" of "alien" ideas (and the more elaborate scientific resources) available on cosmopolitan Urras (6: 160–63; 11: 345). Politically, Shevek believes that the journey could serve to spread the revolution's ideals, and that it might end the excessively cautious, smug, voluntary "exile" of the Anarresti (5: 138). Shevek hopes, in other words, that his journey will serve to "keep the Revolution alive— on both sides" (12: 376).

Quite apart from conflict engendered by opposed interests, values, and beliefs is the common problem of divided and conflicting loyalties and obligations, a problem likewise rooted in diversity and freedom. Because the Anarresti are free, and because they live in a complex, modern society, they typically incur responsibilities for and obligations to a multiplicity of people and groups. As a result, individuals often find their loyalties split, their duties in conflict, and reconciliation an impossibility. The practice of partnership in general, and Shevek's specific long-term partnership with a woman, are portrayed at considerable length in the novel to illuminate precisely this problem. For example, during the great drought crisis, which lasts a number of years, Shevek has to choose between doing socially useful work and being with his partner—he cannot do both; later in time he must choose between the effective pursuit of his intellectual and political goals by traveling to Urras with no guarantee of return, or remaining with his partner and children—again, he cannot simultaneously satisfy these conflicting loyalties and duties to self, to others, and to the community.

Given the commitment to autonomy and liberty characteristic of anarcho-communist society, and given the particularity of human beings, some degree of conflict and instability is likely, then, to be both ongoing and inevitable. To their credit, the communal and communist anarchists recognized this fact, although I believe they too often downplayed its significance in order to secure the promised ideal of harmony. Kropotkin, for instance, certainly recognized that there would be "nothing immutable" in an anarchist community established on the basis of "free agreements concluded between [individuals and groups] . . . for the satisfaction of the infinite variety of needs and aspirations of a civilized being;" but he also contended that "harmony would [nonetheless] . . . result from an ever-changing adjustment and readjustment of equilibrium between the multitudes of forces and influences [that would emerge over time]."[20]

Le Guin's emphasis is different. Rather than supposing that harmony is the norm, she implies that it remains an elusive ideal, and that this should be cause for celebration as well as concern. Given the interdependence of self and society, and the individuality and sociality of human beings, the yearning for harmony is natural, and a normative good. But a complete reconciliation of individuality and community, of personal freedom and social responsibilities, would imply the complete satisfaction of individual needs and desires, values and aspirations. As long as individuals, in their manifest particularity, are free, one must expect diversity and innovation, and so, then, different and often conflicting, unsatisfied, and changing needs, desires and aspirations. The ideal of complete harmony implies the death of freedom, and of life: "Change is freedom, change is life—is anything more basic to [anarcho-communist] thought than that?" (6: 166).

In *The Dispossessed*, Shevek's personal and political struggles and journey culminate in a revolutionary advance in physics and, seemingly, a progressive, even revolutionary, change in his society (the promise of this happy ending is clearly present at the conclusion of the novel, although it is hardly guaranteed; for a free people, the future is always open and unpredictable). He appears, accordingly, to symbolize the view that one must embrace liberty, diversity and novelty, and therefore change and even conflict, in order to keep the revolutionary idea alive. Whether in science or in politics, the "idea is like grass. It craves light, likes crowds, thrives on crossbreeding, grows better for being stepped on" (3: 72; see also 11: 345, when Shevek says that Anarres "is also an idea"). Shevek's successes require transgressing customary physical and psychic borders, and disrupting social harmony. Using this ending as a signpost, the message would appear to be that not even anarchist communism can reconcile completely the ideals of individualism and community, and this bad result is, also, good.

NOTES

1. Excluding some of the contributions to this volume, the only exceptions of which I am aware are Philip E. Smith II, "Unbuilding Walls: Human Nature and the Nature of Evolutionary and Political Theory in *The Dispossessed*," and John P. Brennan and Michael C. Downs, "Anarchism and Utopian Tradition in *The Dispossessed*," both in *Ursula K. Le Guin*, ed. Joseph D. Olander and Martin Harry Greenberg (New York: Taplinger, 1979), 77–96 and 116–52; and Victor Urbanowicz, "Personal and Political in *The Dispossessed*," in *Ursula K. Le Guin*, ed. Harold Bloom, (New York: Chelsea House, 1986), 145–54. Ursula K. Le Guin, *The Dispossessed: An Ambiguous Utopia* (New York: Harper & Row, 1974), cited in the text by chapter and page to the 387-page Eos HarperCollins edition of 2001.

2. Smith, "Unbuilding Walls," plausibly argues that it is Kropotkin's ideas which seem most to inform *The Dispossessed*.

3. Ursula K. Le Guin, *The Wind's Twelve Quarters* (New York: Harper & Row, 1975), 285. Le Guin has considerable knowledge of, and sympathy for, Taoism. This is of particular interest in the context of this paper, not because of the anarchist tendencies of Taoist thinkers, but because of the insight central to Taoism to the effect that apparent dualities or oppositions always embody or reflect an underlying, interdependent and dynamic, unity.

In similar spirit, I shall be suggesting that individuality and community, freedom and responsibility, are interdependent and interpenetrating, both supportive and destructive of one another.

4. Ursula K. Le Guin, "An Interview with Ursula K. Le Guin," in Larry McCaffery, *Across the Wounded Galaxies* (Chicago: University of Chicago Press, 1990), 166.

5. Useful accounts of the intellectual history, and to a lesser degree of historical practices, of anarchism in its many guises include those by James Joll, *The Anarchists* (London: Eyre and Spottiswoode, 1964), and David Miller, *Anarchism* (London: J. M. Dent, 1984).

6. Many commentators agree with Elizabeth Cummins, *Understanding Ursula K. Le Guin* (Columbia: University of South Carolina Press, 1990), 21, that two recurring questions in Le Guin's fiction have been how "best to balance individual and human community," and what "trade-offs [are] necessary to attain that balance."

7. D. Novak, "The Sources and Varieties of Anarchism," in *Patterns of Anarchy*, ed. Lawrence I. Krimerman and Lewis Perry (New York: Anchor, 1996), 9–10.

8. See, e.g., Kropotkin's most widely read work, *Mutual Aid* (New York: Harper & Row, 1989).

9. In "Anarchism and Political Philosophy," J. Roland Pennock and John W. Chapman describe as "authentic anarchists" those thinkers who prescribe the intensification and integration of the individuality and sociality of human beings; see their edited work, *Anarchism: Nomos XIX* (New York: New York University Press, 1978), esp. xxiv–xxix.

10. Emma Goldman, *Anarchism and Other Essays* (New York: Dover, 1969), 36.

11. The contention that evolutionary processes instilled in human beings something like a solidarity instinct or innate cooperative tendency, popular with virtually all communal and communist anarchists, has often been disputed and debated. Hence it is worth observing that the "existence of innate cooperative dispositions" is now both "well-documented" and widely accepted in the life sciences, as is the view that these dispositions should be explained in evolutionary terms. For a brief account of the current leading evolutionary explanations, see the authors of this recent statement, John Orbell, Tomonori Morikawa, Jason Hartwig, James Hanley, and Nicholas Allen, "'Machiavellian' Intelligence as a Basis for the Evolution of Cooperative Dispositions," *American Political Science Review* 98, no. 1 (February 2004): 1–15.

12. Compare Paul Goodman: "In my opinion, we must understand freedom in a very positive sense: it is *the condition of initiating activity*. Apart from this pregnant meaning, mere freedom from interference is both trivial and *in fact cannot be substantially protected*" (*Patterns of Anarchy*, ed. L. I. Krimerman and L. Perry, 55).

13. Hence it seems to me that the argument of Crowder is inapplicable to Le Guin. He argues that "classical anarchists" like Bakunin and Kropotkin embrace a positive conception of freedom according to which conformity to objective moral laws is the essence of freedom. In Le Guin, it seems, freedom consists in conformity to one's will, including one's willed obligations. See George Crowder, *Classical Anarchism* (Oxford: Clarendon Press, 1991), esp. chaps. 1 and 4.

14. Something like the principle of moral equality, and therefore of equal respect and concern, is one of the first ethical notions broached in the novel, specifically, and somewhat humorously, in the context of Shevek's encounter with a representative of a sexist society (in the person of a doctor named Kimoe): "The matter of superiority and inferiority," Shevek reflects, "must be a central one in [their] social life. If to respect himself Kimoe had to consider half the human race as inferior to him, how then did women manage to respect

themselves—did they consider men inferior?" (1: 18). Notice here the presupposed relation between self and social respect. Note too that these egalitarian ideals are both presupposed by, and help reinforce, the ideal of solidarity or fraternity.

15. A major crisis in Shevek's life involves his knowing submission to being exploited by another physicist, the corrupt but strategically powerful Sabul. "Obviously an ethically intolerable situation," that Shevek nonetheless could neither "denounce [nor] relinquish" because "he needed Sabul." The best Shevek can do is bargain with Sabul; they bargain "like profiteers," where each treats the other as a means to wholly self-centered ends. "Not a relationship of mutual aid and solidarity, but an exploitative relationship" (4: 117).

16. In a 1990 interview, Le Guin was surprisingly vague on the political utility of austerity or relative poverty; see McCaffery, "An Interview," 166–67.

17. Le Guin is aware of some of the key problems posed for voluntary cooperation by large size, including the facts that large size increases anonymity and decreases the significance of individual effort, thereby increasing the likelihood of shirking, free riding, apathy, and other forms of egoistic conduct; see in particular 4: 107. For a more detailed discussion of these issues, see especially Michael Taylor, *Community, Anarchy and Liberty* (New York: Cambridge University Press, 1982), and his *The Possibility of Cooperation* (New York: Cambridge University Press, 1987); also Dan Sabia, "Rationality, Collective Action, and Karl Marx," *American Journal of Political Science* 32, no. 1 (Feb. 1988): 50–71.

18. Taking a cue from thinkers like Kropotkin, Taylor, in *The Possibility of Cooperation*, 168–69, argues that the presence of a state, especially the modern state, serves to undercut the capacity of individuals to resolve collective problems through voluntary cooperation precisely because the state performs social functions that they could do, and often used to do, themselves; "altruism and voluntary cooperation *atrophy* in the presence of the state and *grow* in its absence." The same point is made in the novel; as just noted, the Anarresti are pretty good at social cooperation because, in the absence of a state, they have had to develop practices and associated habits that facilitate just that; on the other hand, as we will briefly see in section II, the growth of a quasi-state on Anarres has begun to undermine individual initiative and the capacity to build novel cooperative efforts for a changing environment.

19. This is a central theme of the very fine piece by Urbanowicz, "Personal and Political."

20. Kropotkin, "Anarchism," *Encyclopaedia Britannica* (1910), first paragraph, at http://recollectionbooks.com/siml/library/anarchismEncyBrit.html.

WORKS CITED

Brennan, John P., and Michael C. Downs. "Anarchism and Utopian Tradition in *The Dispossessed*." Pp. 116–52 in *Ursula K. Le Guin*, ed. Joseph D. Olander and Martin Harry Greenberg. New York: Taplinger, 1979.

Crowder, George. *Classical Anarchism*. Oxford: Clarendon Press, 1991.

Cummins, Elizabeth. *Understanding Ursula Le Guin*. Columbia: University of South Carolina Press, 1990.

Goldman, Emma. *Anarchism and Other Essays*. New York: Dover, 1969.

Goodman, Paul. "Is Anarchism Distinct from Liberalism?" Pp. 53–56 in *Patterns of Anarchy*, ed. Leonard I. Krimerman and Lewis Perry. New York: Anchor, 1966.

Joll, James. *The Anarchists*. London: Eyre and Spottiswoode, 1964.

Kropotkin, Peter. "Anarchism." In *The Encyclopaedia Britannica*. At http://recollectionbooks.com/siml/library/anarchismEncyBrit.htm. 1910.

———. *Mutual Aid*. New York: Harper & Row, 1989.

Le Guin, Ursula K. *The Dispossessed: An Ambiguous Utopia*. New York: Eos, HarperCollins, 2001 (1974).

———. "An Interview with Ursula K. Le Guin." Pp. 151–75 in *Across the Wounded Galaxies*, by Larry McCaffery. Chicago: University of Illinois Press, 1990.

———. *The Wind's Twelve Quarters*. New York: Harper & Row, 1975.

Miller, David. *Anarchism*. London: J. M. Dent, 1984.

Novak, D. "The Sources and Varieties of Anarchism." Pp. 5–15 in *Patterns of Anarchy*, ed. Lawrence I. Krimerman and Lewis Perry. New York: Anchor, 1966.

Orbell, John, Tomonori Morikawa, Jason Hartwig, James Hanley, and Nicholas Allen. "'Machiavellian' Intelligence as a Basis for the Evolution of Cooperative Dispositions." *American Political Science Review* 98, no. 1 (Feb. 2004): 1–15.

Pennock, J. Roland, and John W. Chapman. "Anarchism and Political Philosophy." Pp. xvii–xlv in *Anarchism: Nomos XIX*, edited by Pennock and Chapman. New York: New York University Press, 1978.

Sabia, Dan. "Rationality, Collective Action, and Karl Marx." *American Journal of Political Science* 32, no. 1 (Feb. 1988): 50–71.

Smith, Phillip E., II. "Unbuilding Walls: Human Nature and the Nature of Evolutionary and Political Theory in *The Dispossessed*." Pp. 77–96 in *Ursula K. Le Guin*, edited by Joseph D. Olander and Martin Harry Greenberg, New York: Taplinger, 1979.

Taylor, Michael. *Community, Anarchy and Liberty*. New York: Cambridge University Press, 1982.

———. *The Possibility of Cooperation*. New York: Cambridge University Press, 1987.

Urbanowicz, Victor. "Personal and Political in *The Dispossessed*." Pp. 145–54 in *Ursula K. Le Guin*, ed. Harold Bloom. New York: Chelsea House, 1986.

· 7 ·

The Need for Walls: Privacy, Community, and Freedom in *The Dispossessed*

Mark Tunick

INTRODUCTION

$\mathcal{U}$rsula K. Le Guin has been criticized for not being sufficiently utopian or radical in her book *The Dispossessed*.[1] Tom Moylan, who casts Le Guin as an anarcho-communist libertarian with an affinity for Taoist mysticism, sees her purpose as getting us to break down walls. On his view, Anarres, with its absence of walls and possessiveness, comes close to Le Guin's ideal. But, he argues, despite Le Guin's valiant efforts to depict an anarchist-communist world without privacy protecting walls, she reveals, in her implicit criticism of Anarres—of its barrenness in contrast to the beauty of Urras, and of its rejection of the nuclear family—both her conservatism and the limits of her utopian radical thought. Moylan adds that activists in the novel are displaced to the margins, which for him is a signal of Le Guin's inability to imagine a truly revolutionary, emancipatory politics.[2] Nadia Khouri is critical of Le Guin's alleged failure to envision a utopia that could emerge once we recognize the "internal and external contradictions" of both Anarres and Urras. To Khouri, Le Guin falls back on a "psychologizing individualism": she converts a political crisis into a crisis of consciousness, and is "stuck in her own aesthetic project," failing to face the objective world and the real changes needed to transform it.[3] In effect, Khouri says of Le Guin what Marx and the Left Hegelians said of Hegel and the German idealists: they are content with merely a new consciousness of the world, but we need to get our hands dirty and change it.[4]

I interpret Le Guin's project as Hegelian rather than either Marxian or utopian.[5] As a utopia, or a vision of a society to which we ought to aspire, Anarres leaves much to be desired. Its faults have been apparent to others, some of whom have tried to explain its ambiguities as a utopia by suggesting that Le Guin was too timid to imagine how its limitations could be overcome in practice. I shall not have much to say about what Le Guin's intentions actually were. I approach her work as a political theorist intrigued by the ways in which it invites us to think about important political concepts. I take *The Dispossessed*, though subtitled "An Ambiguous Utopia," as an unambiguous treatment of the tensions between one anarchist ideal, of freedom without law and authority, and another ideal central to some anarchists, such as Kropotkin, of community (as distinguished from "collectivity" [1: 4]).[6] *The Dispossessed* is not a failure in imaginative political theory, but a rich and critical examination of the anarchist ideal of tearing down walls for the sake of freedom. *The Dispossessed* explores the relationships between walls, privacy, freedom, and community. Anarres has but one boundary wall, and little privacy, in contrast to Urras, with its "massive walls of stone and glass," prisons, private possessions, and possessiveness. Shevek wants to unbuild walls. But, as Takver notes, without walls "it may get pretty drafty" (10: 333). Certain walls may be needed to preserve privacy and individuality; but too many walls may undermine the sense of community valued on Anarres. The freedom Shevek seeks requires community, but community itself may require the preservation of individual autonomy and the building of some walls without creating a state of possessive individualism as exists on Urras.

FREEDOM

In discussing the connection between privacy, community, and freedom, I draw on a conception of freedom that must be distinguished from the classical liberal understanding of freedom as the ability to do as one pleases absent unjustified constraints.[7] The conception of freedom I shall invoke was developed by G. W. F. Hegel, for whom true freedom is not merely the unrestricted ability to do as one pleases, or "negative freedom," though that is an essential aspect of freedom. Rather, for Hegel true freedom involves experiencing a deep sense of fulfillment or satisfaction—the German word Hegel uses is *Befriedigung*—and of being "at home" in one's world.[8] On Hegel's view, the limitations on our desires imposed by laws and the obligations and duties we have as members of the state and its subordinate institutions, including family and the institutions of civil society, are not to be understood as restrictions on our freedom if we are "at home" in our state and its institutions, and so long as we freely choose them. For Hegel, "the limitation of impulse, desire, passion . . . [and] of caprice and willfulness, is [wrongly] taken as a limitation of freedom. On the contrary, such limitation is the very condition leading to liberation, and society and the state are the very conditions in which freedom is realized."[9] Freedom is not freedom from, merely, but is also freedom in.[10] This idea is not foreign to the founder of Anarres, Odo, who came to see that promises, which restrict negative freedom, in fact promote freedom as they promote the idea of fidelity, which is essential "in the complexity of freedom" (8: 245); nor is it foreign to Shevek, who connects freedom with the idea of being responsible to one another (2: 45) and with the principle of mutual aid between individuals (9: 300).

The Dispossessed centrally addresses the question of the conditions under which we can be truly fulfilled and at home, and this is an important sense of what it is to be free. Shevek, a physicist from the planet Anarres, visits Urras, from which the inhabitants of Anarres originated but which their ancestors left to found a new anarchic society.[11] Shevek has in the past reflected on whether he is fulfilled and at home in his commitments on Anarres. For example, he thinks about his partnership with Takver, which he maintained even after four years of separation, and we learn that "it had not occurred to either of them to escape the suffering by denying the commitment"—"it was joy they were both after—the completeness of being. . . . Pleasure you may get, or pleasures, but you will not be fulfilled. You will not know what it is to come home" (10: 334). Mere pleasures do not provide the sense of fulfillment and of being at home that constitutes freedom.

When Dr. Atro welcomes Shevek to Urras he says "welcome home!"(3: 67) even though Shevek had never before set foot on Urras. When Shevek first breathes its air it is said to be "the air of the world from which his race had come, it was the air of home" (1: 20; cf. 3: 77). Yet after spending time on Urras he has a thought that threatens to break down the gates, flooding him with an "urgent yearning" for Anarres: "To speak Pravic, to speak to friends, to see Takver, Pilun, Sadik, to touch the dust of Anarres" (9: 273). So where is Shevek truly at home? Shevek is driven to leave the barren Anarres where his physics work is hampered and he is parted from his family. He seeks something more universal than the provincial Anarres life. The Anarresti strive for negative freedom without authority as well as a genuine community that, on Hegel's view, is precisely the sort of transcending commitment that we all need to give meaning to our lives and be free. But one is left wondering whether the Anarresti's nearly complete rejection of walls and privacy and, more broadly, of the possessive individualism so valued on Urras, is compatible with achieving a meaningful community in which they can be at home. Yet Shevek doubts that the Urrasti of A-Io are free either, though many of them have material wealth that purchases them physical and intellectual pleasures.

ANARRES

Anarres may commonly be thought of as Le Guin's utopia, but it would be an odd choice in some ways. Life on Anarres is Spartan. The people, wearing their coarse clothing of holum-fiber fabric (1: 13), live in a harsh, arid mining colony with no animals, no lush foliage, and occasional famine-producing droughts (chap. 4). The founder Odo apparently could not take Machiavelli's advice and found a city on fertile soil.[12] Urras, in contrast, has a beauty in its combination of nature and artifice, a beauty arising from "the tenderness and vitality of the colors, the mixture of rectilinear human design and powerful, proliferate natural contours, the variety and harmony of the elements," all of which give "an impression of complex wholeness such as [Shevek] had never seen" (3: 65). It is the forbidding environment on Anarres, Shevek at one point speculates, and not the social structure that "frustrates individual creativity": "This planet wasn't meant to support civilization" and so human solidarity is its only resource (6: 167). Perhaps the desolateness promotes community, focusing attention on people's relations and interactions with each other. There is a spot on Depot Street on Anarres where Urrasti trees are grown, and Shevek wonders whether the extravagant foliage is mere excess, "excrement." They require constant watering, rich soil, much caring (4: 100); by their absence the Anarresti are left to nurture their characters and interpersonal relationships without the distraction of material or natural excess. Yet standing under these dark tree limbs, with their green hands, "awe came into him" (4: 100). Strong evidence that for Shevek there is something sorely missing on Anarres, something found on Urras that the Anarresti feebly replicate. Anarres emphasizes community, in contrast to the more individualist society of A-Io on Urras, yet there is a sense of belonging on Urras, of feeling a part of the whole earth, that its inhabitants share with other animals, a feeling absent on Anarres: "Think of it: everywhere you looked animals, other creatures, sharing the earth and air with you. You'd feel so much more a *part*," says Takver when pondering the abundance and variety of life on "the Old World" (6: 186). In addition to its natural abundance and beauty, Urras is steeped in traditions, symbolized by the buildings Shevek sees which tell him "I have been here for a long time, and I am still here" (3: 89). Edmund Burke argued that traditions are an important tie that binds members of a community, that connects the future with the past, and that gives meaning to our lives, and that they are hard to build from scratch: "Alas! They little know how many a weary step is to be taken before they can form themselves into a mass which has a true politic personality. . . . A nation . . . is an idea of continuity which extends in time as well as in numbers and in space. And this is a choice not of one day or one set of people, not a tumultuary and giddy choice; it is a deliberate election of ages and of generations; it is a constitution made by what is ten thousand times better than choice."[13] One wonders what gives meaning to the Anarresti, who lack a connection either to place or traditions. What is special about belonging to their community that would justify individual sacrifices—sacrifices that can be considerable? Shevek had "given up his book, and his love, and his child. How much can a man be asked to give up?" (8: 258). And for what?

Perhaps what binds them and gives them meaning is not a relation to their natural environment or shared customs and traditions, but a commitment to certain ideals. Anarres is supposedly classless and egalitarian: "there was no rank, no terms of rank, no conventional respectful forms of address" (4: 101). Through their commitment to an ideal of equality understood as the rejection of privilege and hierarchy based on status, even merited status, or in the words of Kropotkin, who would have professors clean hallways, as the ruling out of "privileged labor," the Anarresti avoid the ranking and judging that is so prominent on Urras and that makes solidarity less likely.[14]

Yet Le Guin casts doubt on whether the Anarresti genuinely value equality in this sense. It turns out there are privileges based on status, as Shevek learns when he goes to the Central Institute of the Sciences and gets dessert nightly, rather once or twice a decad (ten days) as at most refectories (4: 111). And doubt is cast also on whether a completely egalitarian society should be their ideal. Shevek is warned about "false egalitarianism," that is, denying that some are better than others. He is told to work with the best physicists (2: 57–58), and he recognizes that in physics "he had had no equals" on Anarres. Only in A-Io, "in the realm of inequity," did he have competent colleagues (3: 71). In A-Io, Shevek is bowed to for the first time in his life, and he observes how "the Urrasti were forever using titles and honorifics" (3: 66). People are categorized as superior and inferior (1: 15). Yet the results are not entirely unhappy: the people are more refined and the students are better. Shevek notes, "they never fell asleep in class because they were tired from having worked on rotational duty the day before"— but he adds, "their freedom from obligation was in exact proportion to their lack of freedom of initiative" (5: 127).

Shevek, here, points to one apparent advantage Anarres has over Urras: the realization of another ideal to which the Anarresti are committed, negative freedom, promoted by a guiding principle: no laws or boundaries. On Anarres there is only "one law" (1: 7)—the law of evolution or change (7: 220; 12: 359)—and one "right": "the right of the Odonian individual to initiate action harmless to others" (12: 357).

Having no laws, the Anarresti have little sense of guilt and do not punish. For a society that strives to regard each as of equal worth, notions of desert and blame may be problematic, and without blame and guilt there is no retribution. Odo, in her *Prison Letters*, implores Odonians: "free your mind of the idea of deserving, the idea of earning, and you will begin to be able to think"(12: 358). When Shevek takes double helpings of food during the famine, he declares "need is right. He was an Odonian, he left guilt to profiteers"(8: 261). Not only is there apparently no internal guilt, there is no visible practice of legal punishment and there are no prisons (2: 34–40). The very notion of a prison can be repulsive to the Anarresti, as Shevek learned when as a child he and his friends, out of curiosity and in play, built a makeshift cell in which they confined Kadagv. Shevek, playing a guard, felt a sense of "secret power" that made him suddenly uncomfortable to the point that he had to lean over a bowl and vomit (2: 39–40).

Even an egalitarian society without a notion of desert could justify punishment as a deterrent. But on Anarres there is little need even for that. For example, there are no sexual violations since "molestation was extremely rare in a society where complete fulfillment was the norm from puberty on" (8: 245). However, there are asylums (6: 170) and sometimes "they make you go away by yourself for a while" (5: 150).

That should give us pause. "Everybody on Anarres is a revolutionary," and no one is supposed to have authority. The only authority is public opinion (3: 76). No one is supposed to be forced or ordered on this anarchic world. Yet sometimes "they make you go away by yourself." It turns out there is considerable social pressure, and this makes us wonder how much of even the classical liberal sense of freedom the Anarresti really enjoy. With no threat of punishment for breaking laws, why do the dirty work? Because, explains Shevek to Oiie, it is done together, in little communities, with others; and there is the challenge: "Where there's no money the real motives are clearer, maybe. People like to do things." Curiously, Shevek adds "people . . . can—egoize, we call it," using a derogatory Anarresti word for showing off (5: 150). Another motivator is "the social conscience, the opinion of one's neighbors. There is no other reward, on Anarres, no other law. One's own pleasure, and the respect of one's fellows" (5: 150). Someone who just won't cooperate is made fun of, others get "rough with him, beat him up." His name might be removed from the meals listing so he has to cook and eat by himself, which is "humiliating," so he either conforms, or becomes a "nuchnibi" (5: 150–51).

No one on Anarres is threatened with legal punishment if they pursue what they want rather than fulfill their social obligations, so long as they do not harm others.[15] Yet there are other forms of coercion besides legal punishment. John Stuart Mill developed his harm principle to demarcate limits on the state's use of coercion, but he also worried about other ways in which liberty is restricted, including public opinion, the power of custom, and expressions of distaste.[16] Such forces prevail on Anarres, imposing great pressure to fulfill one's duties. In a key passage Shevek is talking to Takver and notes how they lie about their freedom: they say they make their own choices, yet in fact they go where PDC posts them and stay till they are reposted, even though it means being apart. Shevek had been told he "could do what he pleased"(8: 269), in contrast to how on Urras he was explicitly called upon to do physics against his will (9: 272). But, Shevek remarks to Takver, on Anarres "we always think [I'm a free man], and say it, but we don't do it. We keep our initiative tucked away safe in our mind," we say "I make my own choices," but then we do what we're told. Indeed, notes Shevek, few Anarresti refuse to accept a posting, because people are ashamed: "the social conscience completely dominates the individual conscience, instead of striking a balance with it. We don't cooperate—we *obey*" (10: 329–30).

Bedap also sees the social conscience as a freedom-stifling "power machine, controlled by bureaucrats" (6: 167), and gives the example of how the physicist Sabul prevents Shevek from publishing his new ideas in physics. "Public opinion! That's the power structure . . . that stifles the individual mind" (6: 165). Replace government and "legal" use of power with "customary," says Bedap, and you have

Sabul and the Syndicate (6: 166). Le Guin presents other examples of how on Anarres social conscience can be as coercive as laws. Shevek's child Sadik is shunned by her dorm mates because Shevek advocates going to Urras (12: 370). Public opinion effectively censors Sala's music (6: 175) and virtually exiles the poet and dramatist Tirin. Tirin "was a free man, and the rest of us, his brothers, drove him insane in punishment for his first free act." Shevek adds, "we force a man outside the sphere of our approval, and then condemn him for it. We've made laws, laws of conventional behavior, built walls all around ourselves, and we can't see them, because they're part of our thinking" (10: 330–31).

So there are walls on Anarres, but they are mostly hidden. There is authority and control, but by virtue of being noninstitutionalized these are harder to point to. Bedap says the real problem on Anarres is the hypocrisy and self-deception: "It's the lies that make you want to kill yourself" (6: 166). One might conclude that the solution is to get rid of the hidden walls and subtle forms of coercion, to better live up to the anarchic ideal. Shevek at one point reflects: "That the Odonian society on Anarres had fallen short of the ideal [of letting the individual exercise his optimum function so as to contribute best to the whole society] did not, in his eyes, lessen his responsibility to it" (10: 333). We have seen that Le Guin's alleged failure to follow through on the project of breaking down walls and constructing an anarchic community has led some commentators to charge her with political timidity and conservatism. Moylan, for example, criticizes Shevek for being a phallocratic male hero too attached to conservative and bourgeois institutions such as family to effectively realize Le Guin's utopia.[17] I follow the text in another direction. We see that there is an essential tension between freedom without authority, and a freely chosen but meaningful community. We come to admit that some privacy and walls are needed, but they should be visible. The Urrasti Vea picks up on the Foucauldian notion that laws and punishment would somehow be more honest and less intrusive than the power of public opinion since at least they can be seen.[18] She notes how the Odonians got rid of law, but instead they have their consciences, so they are still slaves. It is better to have the orders come from outside, from a Queen Teaea (the Queen against whom the Odonians rebelled), for at least then "you could rebel against her" (7: 219). This might seem a troubling recipe, until we recognize that walls and privacy may be necessary for true freedom in a community: so long as the construction of walls does not lead to the extreme of possessive individualism as in A-Io.

A-IO, ON URRAS

In many ways A-Io seems the opposite of Anarres: a consumerist society where people are seen not as members of a community, but as self-interested individuals who use each other in the pursuit of their own pleasures. Shevek experiences the "nightmare street" of Saemtenevia Prospect, in Nio Esseia, a main city in A-Io, with its retail shops selling all sorts of clothes, in hundreds of cuts, for every conceivable purpose, as well as perfumes, clocks, lamps, statues, "acres of luxuries, acres of excrement"; "All the people in all the shops were either buyers or sellers. They had no relation to the things but that of possession" (5: 132). In contrast to the hardworking Anarresti, Urrasti spend their time "lying around naked in the sun with jewels in their navels" (2: 41). The Urrasti use people as objects. They use Shevek with the hope that he will reveal his discoveries in physics: "Nine, ten months we've been feeding the bastard, for nothing!" says Pae to Oiie (7: 232), revealing his ulterior motives for inviting Shevek. There is always a self-interested motive, a using of others for one's own ends.

One result of A-Io's capitalist social structure and its people's consumerist mentality is striking inequality with its horrible costs. In A-Io, while the wealthy have leisure, many live in wretched poverty. Efor, a servant, tells Shevek about the rats, insane asylums, poorhouses, unemployed, dead babies in ditches, and the difference between the hospitals for the rich, and those for the poor, which are "dirty. Like a trashman's ass-hole" (9: 283). Anarres has poverty too, but as Shevek notes, the difference is that on Anarres "nobody goes hungry while another eats" (9: 285). A-Io has gender inequality as well, in contrast to Anarres (1: 16). In A-Io women are objects.[19] Women are thought to be unable to engage in abstract thought (3: 73). They are not permitted at the University and to avoid distraction students are not permitted to marry (5: 129).

The class structure and consumerism contribute to a society without community, without freedom in Hegel's sense, and with many lacking even negative freedom. Our omniscient narrator describes it as a society of "not mutual aid but mutual aggression" (7: 208). People are indifferent. When the rebellion was put down, a man beside him is hurt and although Shevek asks for help to carry him, the people hurry on (9: 304). Yet people on Anarres hardly differ in this respect. During the famine on Anarres, a truck driver runs over people desperate for food. There are "propertarians" and "egoizers" on Anarres, such as Desar (6: 154–55)— something we have already seen when Shevek explains that egoizing is a motivation to work, for some Anarresti (5: 150).

Yet with all its faults, Urras holds many attractions for Shevek, whose attitude toward it is deeply ambivalent and wavers. Shevek comes to see that the Urrasti "were not the gross, cold egoists he had expected them to be: they were as complex and various as their culture, as their landscape; and they were intelligent; and they were kind. . . . And he did feel at home . . . this was home indeed, his race's world; and all its beauty was his birthright" (3: 77). Yet after going to a series of receptions, he thinks that "everyone was very polite and talked a great deal, but not about anything interesting; and they smiled so much they looked anxious. But their clothes were gorgeous" and there was the food, drink, lavish furnishings, and ornaments (3: 83). Shevek was taught of the inequity, iniquity, and waste, but as he travels by car or train through the villages, he sees the people are well dressed, well fed, industrious; they were busy and energetic; "the lure and compulsion of *profit* was evidently a much more effective replacement of the natural initiative than he had been led to believe" (3: 82). However, later in the novel, once he sees its poverty, Shevek is again critical: "There is no way to act rightly, with a clear heart, on Urras. There is nothing you can do that profit does not enter into, and fear of loss, and the wish for power. . . . You cannot act like a brother to other people, you must manipulate them, or command them, or obey them, or trick them. . . . There is no freedom," he says (11: 346–47), meaning freedom in Hegel's sense. But then Keng, Ambassador of Terra, replies with a more favorable view of Urras: yes it is full of evils, but it is also "full of good, of beauty, vitality, achievement. It is what a world should be! It is *alive*," and Shevek nods in agreement (11: 347). This is not an unambiguous nod of approval, as Shevek's subsequent remarks make clear. But it should not be dismissed.

Neither the Anarresti nor the Urrasti are fully free. The societies on each world limit the freedom of the individual in the classical liberal sense of freedom, though in different ways: on Urras, through institutional coercion, on Anarres, through noninstitutional forms of social pressure. One problem is that the people on both worlds are too complex to be constrained by the ideals they articulate and fail to live up to. Measured against their one-sided ideals they are hypocrites. The political solution may be a dialectical mediation between conflicting ideals.

PRIVACY AND COMMUNITY

Anarres makes a claim to classical liberal (or negative) freedom by its absence of laws—though we have seen that coercion finds other ways of seeping in. It makes a claim to freedom in Hegel's sense of "being at home" by attempting to establish a meaningful community, and one way it does this is through its lack of separating boundaries. There is little privacy—apart from the modest privacy accorded to sexual partners (8: 245)—and few apparent walls: "nothing was hidden" (4: 98). "There were no disguises and no advertisements. It was all there, all the work, all the life of the city, open to the eye and to the hand" (4: 99). Private rooms are rare (4: 102–3); the only boundary wall on the world was at the port (1: 2). Letters are public and unsealed (8: 251).[20] This marks a stark contrast with Urras, where people lock their doors (1: 11). Whereas on Anarres private life is virtually nonexistent, on Urras private lives are so guarded from the public sphere that there are literally separate private and public persona. Oiie, of Urras, "was a changed man at home. The secretive look left his face, and he did not drawl when he spoke . . . at home, he suddenly appeared as a simple, brotherly kind of man, a free man" (5: 147).

Shevek thinks freedom requires openness not secrecy (4: 109). He is critical of both the physical and metaphorical walls he finds on Urras. On first arriving on Urras he notes the "massive walls of stone and glass. . . . Stone, steel, glass, electric light. No faces" (1: 21). When he discusses politics with Pae he hits another wall, the wall of "charm, courtesy, indifference" (3: 80). The workers of the retail street Seamtenevia Prospect that overwhelms him are hidden "behind walls" (5: 132). He later notes that he let a "wall be built around him" that kept him from seeing the poor people on Urras (7: 193)—he had been co-opted, with walls of smiles of the rich, and he didn't know how to break them down (7: 193). Yet it turns out that the Anarresti need their own protective walls between the public and the private, to shelter them from the force of public opinion. While on Anarres we would expect open sexual relations, this is one of the few areas to which privacy is accorded.[21] And at the Central Institute there was also privacy, which helped with Shevek's work (4: 111). On my reading, Shevek's original view toward walls comes to be seen as one-sided and inadequate. Freedom lies not in an even more radical commitment to his ideal of openness, but in a recognition of the limits of this ideal, and of the need for some walls.

Connected to the idea of privacy are the notions of possession, possessiveness, and exclusive ownership.[22] Property can promote the same boundaries and isolating individualism that walls create. Urras is so property-oriented that its birds sing "Ree-dee, tee-dee. This is my propertee-tee, this is my territoree-ree-ree, it belongs to mee, mee" (7: 205–6). On Anarres, in contrast, just as privacy is disavowed, there is no private property, no possessiveness, no territoriality. One shares. Odo had written, "To make a thief, make an owner; to create crime, create laws" (5: 139). There is no robbery on Anarres as nobody owns anything to rob: "If you want things you take them from the depository" (5: 149). As Shevek arrives on Urras, he notes that he did not bring much, and certainly not enough food for his visit, and he will rely on their handouts. Shevek explains, "I am an Anarresti, I make the Urrasti behave like Anarresti: to give, not to sell" (1: 13). When asked by Vea if there is anything he is not, Shevek replies, "a salesman" (7: 216). There is no profit motive: people do things for other reasons (5: 150). The difference in Anarresti and Urrasti views toward property leads to an amusing clash of cultures during Shevek's visit to Oiie's home. Shevek does not say thank-you to Oiie's child Ini when he was given a dish of pickles, explaining that he thought Ini was sharing them with him, and on Anarres one does not say thanks for sharing. Ini admits he does not even like pickles, and Shevek notes that makes it very easy to share (5: 147).

Shevek at one point speculates that the people on Urras are not truly free precisely because they have so many walls built between people and are so possessive: "On Anarres nothing is beautiful, nothing but the faces. . . . Here [on Urras] you see the jewels, there [on Anarres] you see the eyes. And in the eyes you see the splendor, the splendor of the human spirit. Because our men and women are free—possessing nothing, they are free. And you the possessors are possessed. You are all in jail. Each alone, solitary, with a heap of what he owns. You live in prison, die in prison. It is all I can see in your eyes—the wall, the wall!" (7:

228–29). Shevek sees possessiveness and the "labyrinths of love/hate" as just so many walls restricting freedom.

It may seem puzzling for an anarchic society to disavow privacy and possessiveness. The Anarresti value negative freedom, and we may think that this sort of freedom requires protective barriers. The very idea of a right to do as one pleases so long as one does not harm others can be seen as requiring the construction of walls around individuals that must not be penetrated. It is less puzzling when we recognize that the Anarresti also strive to obtain freedom in Hegel's sense, or freedom in, though they would reject Hegel's advocacy of the rule of law and institution of property, and instead aim for the anarchist-communist ideal of a genuine community achieved only through the absence of laws and other coercive institutions relied on by states. Building a strong community providing a meaningful commitment is a condition for achieving a sense of belonging, a feeling of being at home, that constitutes freedom in this sense, and we might think walls and possessiveness deter community.

Yet the ideals of dispossession and of sharing with others are not always lived up to on Anarres. The Anarresti, who disavow the pursuit of power and profit, are sometimes hypocrites. In charge of the physics syndicate, Sabul must be bargained with: "bargained like profiteers. It had not been a battle, but a sale. You give me this and I'll give you that. Refuse me and I'll refuse you. Sold? Sold! Shevek's career, like the existence of his society, depended on the continuance of a fundamental, *unadmitted* profit contract. Not a relationship of mutual aid and solidarity, but an exploitative relationship" (4: 117, emphasis added). During the famine, Shevek realizes that it is easy to share when there is enough, just as it was easy for Ini to share what he did not want for himself, but when food is scarce, force enters, and violence; and so the townsfolk hid behind their walls and did not share their food with the passengers on the trains (8: 256). Living in a Spartan environment that eschews materialism and excess, many Anarresti, like Bedap, are functionalists. Bedap, observing a handmade orange blanket in Shevek's room, declares that Shevek lives "like a rotten Urrasti profiteer": "an excremental color. . . . As a functions analyst I must point out that there is no need for orange. Orange serves no vital function" (6: 162). Yet there is some jewelry on Anarres, worn by people in the small towns (10: 325). Even Shevek is possessive of his ideas at first (8: 240), and we learn that possessiveness seems to be innate and must be overcome by socialization.[23] On Urras, Shevek became used to the possessive pronoun "and spoke it without self-consciousness," as in "my rooms" (5: 134).

Shevek ultimately is ambivalent toward privacy. He wants the walls down. He is uncomfortable with the large private room he has on Urras and sees the privacy it affords as "excess, waste" (4: 110). Yet he sees that privacy is as desirable for physics as it was for sex, and even on Anarres they like their sex private (4: 111). Shevek is critical of the possessiveness and materialism on Urras, including the possessiveness evident in monogamous relations. Yet Shevek himself falls in love. The ideal on Anarres of being dispossessed, of lacking privacy and property, has costs: without privacy and without property one risks losing one's individuality. Such a loss has been avoided on Anarres. The Anarresti are unique individuals. They are "members of a community, not elements of a collectivity," as they are not moved by mass feelings (1: 4). But on Anarres individuality has been preserved by hypocrisy, by the emergence of subtle and unacknowledged forms of privacy and possessiveness, just as the need in a community for order has been met on this anarchic world, to an unfortunate and excessive degree, by the emergence of subtle, noninstitutional forms of social coercion.

FREEDOM: COMMUNITY WITH WALLS

One might think that privacy undermines community, and that the problem with Anarres is that it still has some walls and does not live up to its ideals enough. I am suggesting, instead, that the ideals on Anarres are in conflict. To have a freely chosen community, as opposed to a collectivity that is an undifferentiated mob, individual autonomy must be preserved, and this requires privacy and some walls. Privacy is important for individual autonomy in a variety of ways. Privacy can provide an important emotional release from the effort we make to be civil and polite. A divide between the public and the private may help maintain our sanity and our integrity. Privacy can protect groups within a society, thereby enabling individuals freely to associate. There are of course dangers to privacy. Too much of it can inhibit personal development. Privacy can be a crutch for people who are not sufficiently autonomous, and crutches do not always help us develop what we lack.[24] Perhaps most importantly, privacy lets us maintain close ties to family and friends. While sometimes such commitments conflict with commitments to the state, on the whole they promote community.[25] Here one thinks of Hegel, for whom the modern family is an essential institution because it trains individuals to think beyond their own particular interests, to transcend the state of mind of possessive individualism and find their true meaning and worth as part of their state: "Through [the modern family], the state has as members individuals who in uniting to form a state, bring with them the sound basis of a political edifice, the capacity of feeling one with a whole."[26] For Hegel, transcending the state of mind of possessive individualism does not mean losing one's sense of self; one preserves it as part of a deeper and more adequate understanding of one's place in the world.

The Anarresti face obstacles to creating a strong sense of community. A strong attachment to place seems ruled out by the nondescript, even harsh environment. They do not like traditions, given their preference for change and negative liberty. What, then, can provide the basis for community? I have already considered two possibilities—commitment to the ideals of equality and liberty—

and found these wanting. The Anarresti appeal to a third abstract ideal, of brotherhood. This does not depend on traditions, or a shared sense of place. Yet Le Guin reveals it to be a somewhat empty ideal in one of the novel's most important scenes. At the end of chapter 4, Shevek is ill with fever and his mother Rulag visits. She had abandoned him for her career, and denies that they have a strong familial bond: they are merely biologically related. The bond they share, she says, is the Anarresti tie of brotherhood: "we are brother and sister, here and now. Which is what really matters, isn't it?" (4: 124). But this bond of brotherhood seems weak, as is evident from the ensuing exchange: Shevek replies, "I don't know"(4: 124). For a moment, Rulag's face breaks down, but she recovers; and then another patient also calls Shevek "brother," but this provides no solace: "Even from the brother there is no comfort in the bad hour, in the dark at the foot of the wall" (4: 125). At this point we perhaps see the political significance of Shevek's theory of simultaneity and sequentialism: you can not deny the past. There is a limit to the communal ideal of brotherhood when it is totalized, and replaces other commitments rooted in our historical past, in the relations that shaped us as individuals. Le Guin suggests that family, the consummate institution of private life, provides such a commitment and that Rulag and other Anarresti are mistaken to deny its significance.[27]

Le Guin has been accused of conservatism for espousing family values, as when she has her narrator preach about the homosexual Bedap having an empty life which he must change "if he would be saved."[28] If we read Le Guin's project as advocating an anarchist-communist libertarian society that breaks from all traditions, her apparent embracing of family, a traditional and private form of association, would be troubling. But if we understand her project as, rather, an exploration of the complex tensions one faces in building a community in which we are at home and free, then the encounter between Shevek and Rulag signals dissatisfaction with one-sided ideals and acknowledgment of the importance of traditional commitments such as family that preserve private life and individuality, so long as they do not undermine community. If the Anarresti are to establish meaningful commitments that will lead them freely to choose, rather than being shamed into, individual sacrifice, then they need some concrete basis for them.[29] Family is the foremost Terran and Urrasti institution demarcating private from public life. Concrete commitments to family can compete with an attachment to the abstract ideal of brotherhood. The Anarresti appear to think we must choose between these, and they outwardly reject family. But, on my reading, we come to see the limitations of one-sided ideals such as brotherhood, equality, and openness, and the need for some traditions, some privacy, some walls, both if we are to freely choose our commitments, and if they are to be meaningful. Of course not all families do well at providing meaningful commitments, and no one chooses their natal family so we might wonder how it provides a freely chosen commitment. However the families founded through marriage are, except in some traditional societies, freely chosen, as is, typically, the decision to have children. And while not all actual families provide privacy and nurture individuality, the fact that actuality can diverge from the ideal and that other means of protecting privacy and individuality, including the protection of privacy within families, are needed, is insufficient reason to reject the institution. Even the anarchist-communist Kropotkin, sometimes seen as a source for Le Guin, wants people to be able, should they choose, to take their meals with their family or friends, and rejects the "tyranny" of being forced to use communal kitchens.[30]

The problem with the ideal of brotherhood on Anarres is not that it is idealistic. As with the case of family, an ideal need not be thoroughly lived up to in every circumstance to still be feasible and worthy of our commitment. When Chifoilisk calls Anarres a "little commune of starving idealists," Shevek responds that in fact Anarres is practical, not idealistic: cooperation and mutual aid are the only means of staying alive (5: 135). Shevek still defends the ideal, telling Vea "we are all relatives" (7: 198). Yet he surely realizes that Anarresti can still be strangers, as on some of the rotational community labor groups (4: 106–7), and sometimes one needs protection from strangers. The problem is with the ideal itself, when totalized, and not with its feasibility. Sometimes there is a need for being by oneself, apart not only from strangers but loved ones. We are told that although Takver's "existence was necessary to Shevek her actual presence could be a distraction" (6: 188). Community doesn't demand the loss of individuality: "Sacrifice might be demanded of the individual, but never compromise: for though only the society could give security and stability, only the individual, the person, had the power of moral choice—the power of change, the essential function of life" (10: 333). An ideal of brotherhood that rejects competing commitments and privacy-preserving traditions such as family can threaten the individuality and autonomy necessary if we are to be free in, and freely choose, community. Preservation of the family alone is not sufficient to promote freedom. Hegel recognized that other institutions such as private property and the forming of contractual relations and corporate groups within civil society were also essential. But, contrary to critics who see pro-family sentiments as a capitulation and obstacle to achieving an anarchic communist utopia, on my interpretation they are an appropriate recognition of the need for institutions that mediate between the ideals of individuality and community.

The Dispossessed rejects one-sided and simplistic ideals that can lead only to hypocrisy. Le Guin's text points, in its very structure, to the limits of the Odonian's one-sided and conflicting ideals of an open society with negative freedom and no authority, and of brotherhood and community—or of the Urrasti's equally one-sided ideal of "possessive individualism," and to the need for reconciliation. The novel begins on both planets, and each successive chapter shifts from one to the other world, finally concluding back on both planets. Shevek's goal is to include and connect (9: 285), to reconcile difference (10: 322). He sees the need for both Anarres and Urras: "You will not achieve or even understand Urras unless you accept the reality, the enduring reality, of Anarres"(11: 349). The ship Shevek takes to return to Anarres in the final chapter, the *Davenant*, "had neither the opulence of Urras nor the austerity of Anarres, but struck a balance, with the effortless grace of long practice" (13: 381). A balance of conflicting ideals may ultimately constitute a political blueprint for freedom. Shevek wants to break down walls between the two planets to promote free exchange (5: 138). If he succeeds this may lead to the building of more walls on Anarres, or the making opaque the hidden and unacknowledged walls already present, walls needed to promote the individual autonomy essential for community.

The problem with Anarres's anarchic ideal that resists authority and emphasizes autonomy of conscience and challenging of conventions is that it cuts against another ideal in anarchist thought, an ideal also central to the Anarresti: the ideal of community. Shevek is torn: he rejects submission to authority, wanting to be his own person, yet he wants also to be a part of a community, a meaningful whole. Strict adherence to one or the other of their conflicting ideals leads to hypocrisy. The Urrasti Chifoilisk tells Shevek: "No need to pretend that all you Odonian brothers are full of brotherly love. . . . Human nature is human nature"(3: 69). Too much emphasis on autonomy, as in Bedap's forceful defense, leaves Shevek cold, lost, and without shelter (6: 172–73). Yet, I have argued, autonomy and privacy are important if one is to be free in a community. The Anarresti need some protective walls between public and private to shelter them from the coercive force of public opinion. It may be that this will lead to more possessiveness, and encourage conservative institutions like the nuclear family. But thanks to Shevek's journey and return, they can point to the excesses on Urras as a cautionary guide.

NOTES

I thank Laurence Davis for his careful reading of a previous draft and numerous important and thoughtful suggestions, Peter Stillman for inspiring me to take up this project, and Christian Weisser.

1. Ursula K. Le Guin, *The Dispossessed: An Ambiguous Utopia* (New York: Harper & Row, 1974), cited in the text by chapter and page to the 387-page Eos HarperCollins edition of 2001.

2. Tom Moylan, *Demand the Impossible: Science Fiction and the Utopian Imagination* (New York: Methuen, 1986), 91–97, 102, 113. Samuel Delany has also criticized Le Guin's conservatism, particularly her use of Bedap as a token homosexual, and is offended at Le Guin's implication that Bedap must shed his homosexuality and endorse traditional family values to be saved. See Samuel R. Delany, "To Read the Dispossessed," in *The Jewel-Hinged Jaw* (New York: Berkley Windhover, 1977).

3. Nadia Khouri, "The Dialectics of Power: Utopia in the Science Fiction of Le Guin, Jeury, and Piercy," *Science-Fiction Studies* 7, no. 1 (March, 1980): 49–61.

4. Karl Marx, "Theses on Feuerbach," in *The Marx-Engels Reader*, 2d ed., ed. Robert Tucker (New York: W.W. Norton and Co., 1978), 143–45.

5. Of course Marx was highly critical of utopians for ignoring the real material forces shaping society and for fancying that they could draw a blueprint of how the world ought to be that could be realized in practice simply by willing it. The anarchist Peter Kropotkin also distinguishes anarchy from utopia, utopia being a wished for ideal, anarchy being based on an analysis of existing tendencies—see Peter Kropotkin, "Anarchism," *Encyclopedia Britannica* (1910), http://dwardmac.pitzer.edu/Anarchist_Archives/kropotkin/britanniaanarchy.html (accessed 7 May 2004).

6. There are a wide variety of anarchist theories. Moylan (in *Demand the Impossible*, 96) points to Le Guin's sympathies with Peter Kropotkin, who emphasized mutual aid, the natural affinity for all species including man to help one another, and the ideal of decentralized voluntary associations that would realize an ideal of community without fettering individual initiative, though sometimes Kropotkin speaks of the "absorption of the I" by the clan or the tribe as the basis of ethics (Peter Kropotkin, *Ethics: Origins and Development* [New York: B. Blum, 1968], chaps. 1, 2, 9). Compare Robert Paul Wolff, *In Defense of Anarchism* (New York: Harper & Row, 1970), 81, on anarchism as a "local, community-based development of a consensual or general will" with emphasis on a decentralized idea of community. Other anarchists, such as Max Stirner, more emphasize the development of individuality rather than the flourishing of all members of the community; see April Carter, *The Political Theory of Anarchism* (London: Routledge and Kegan Paul, 1971).

7. For the classical liberal view see John Stuart Mill, *On Liberty*, and Immanuel Kant, *Metaphysics of Morals*; for a contemporary version see John Rawls, *A Theory of Justice*. This definition of freedom is used by Le Guin's omniscient narrator: doing "what he wanted to do when he wanted to do it for as long as he wanted to do it" (4: 112). But other definitions are given as well. For example, Shevek defines freedom as doing what's in your nature and carrying out your responsibilities, though Tirin seems unhappy with this definition (2: 45).

8. G. W. F. Hegel emphasizes the importance of a state of satisfaction (*Befriedigung*) in his *Phenomenology of Spirit*, trans. A. V. Miller (Oxford: Oxford University Press, 1977 [1806]), paras. 80, 163, 175. On the idea of freedom as "being at home" (*bei sich*), see G. W. F. Hegel, *Philosophy of Right*, trans. H. B. Nisbett (Cambridge: Cambridge University Press, 1991 [1821]), para. 7; *Phenomenology*, paras. 347, 533; and G. W. F. Hegel, *Philosophy of History*, trans. J. Sibree (New York: Dover, 1956), 39.

9. G. W. F. Hegel, *Reason in History*, trans. Robert Hartman (Upper Saddle River, NJ: Prentice-Hall, 1997), 55.

10. See Mark Tunick, *Hegel's Political Philosophy* (Princeton, NJ: Princeton University Press, 1992), chap. 3.

11. *Ur* means origin, as in the German "Ur-text."

12. Machiavelli, *The Discourses on Livy*, Book I, chap. 1.

13. Edmund Burke, "Speech on the Reform of the Representation of the Commons in Parliament, May 7, 1782," *Select Works of Edmund Burke, and Miscellaneous Writings*, www.econlib.org/library/LFBooks/Burke/brkSWv4c2.html (accessed 14 Jan. 2004).

14. Peter Kropotkin, "Must We Occupy Ourselves with an Examination of the Ideal of a Future System?" (1873), in *Selected Writings on Anarchism and Revolution*, ed. Martin Miller (Cambridge, MA: MIT Press, 1970), 48, 56–57.

15. The institutional mechanisms Anarres draws on in the event that someone causes harm to others are not made clear. It may be that "the right of the Odonian individual to initiate action harmless to others" (12: 357) is not enforced; yet presumably there are means of bringing nuchnibi or others to asylums.

16. Mill, *On Liberty*, chap. 1. Joseph Hamburger argues, controversially, that Mill favors such expressions of distaste for acts that are regarded as immoral though they do not cause harm. He regards Mill as illiberal, in *John Stuart Mill on Liberty and Control* (Princeton, NJ: Princeton University Press, 1999), 177.

17. Moylan, *Demand the Impossible*, 102, 110.

18. Michel Foucault, in *Discipline and Punish*, argues that Enlightenment penal reforms that marked an end to punishment as a public spectacle and attack on the physical body were even more nefarious in controlling and disciplining one's entire soul; discussed in Mark Tunick, *Punishment: Theory and Practice* (Berkeley: University of California Press, 1992).

19. "Ioti women did not go outside with naked breasts, reserving their nudity for its owners" (7: 213).

20. The lack of privacy in the mails on Anarres resembles the lack of privacy in colonial New England, where letters were also open to all. See David Flaherty, *Privacy in Colonial New England* (Charlottesville: University Press of Virginia, 1967), discussed in Tunick, *Practices and Principles* (Princeton, NJ: Princeton University Press, 1998), chap. 5.

21. Curiously Urras is the world in which there are public displays of affection, which Shevek looks down upon: "To caress and copulate in front of unpaired people was as vulgar as to eat in front of hungry people"(7: 226). But see 7: 213, cited in note 19 above.

22. Privacy is used interchangeably with private ownership on 6: 162–63.

23. In 2: 27: as an infant, Shevek was possessive, saying "mine"; cf. 2: 58: little children say "my mother" but with socialization soon learn to say "the mother."

24. See Gary Marx, "Privacy and Technology," *Whole Earth Review* 73 (Winter 1991): 90–95.

25. I develop the idea that privacy is needed for community in Mark Tunick, "Does Privacy Undermine Community?" *Journal of Value Inquiry* 35, no. 4 (December 2001): 517–34.

26. Hegel, *Reason in History*, 56; cf. *Philosophy of Right*, paras. 158–81.

27. Cf. 6: 152: only when married does Shevek's work progress. One should recognize that families take many forms not all of which may provide the sort of commitment that Le Guin or Hegel have in mind, although I doubt Le Guin or Hegel would essentialize the family by insisting that the concept refers to a single form.

28. 12: 298. Samuel Delany makes this criticism, see note 2, above.

29. This would be Burke's point. Burke is skeptical of commitment to abstract ideals: see Edmund Burke, *Reflections on the Revolution in France* [with Paine's *The Rights of Man*] (Garden City, NY: Anchor Books, 1973), 9, 72–74.

30. Peter Kropotkin, "Expropriation" (1882), in *Selected Writings*, 186. But see his *Ethics: Origin and Development*, chap. 4, where he criticizes Aristotle for confusing sociality with friendship and mutual love, perhaps implying a limited role for family in his anarchist-communist ideal; and of course Kropotkin argues in "Expropriation," "The Commune of Paris" (1880), and other works that private property should be expropriated,

further limiting his acceptance of privacy nurturing institutions within his anarchist-communist society.

WORKS CITED

Burke, Edmund. "Speech on the Reform of the Representation of the Commons in Parliament, May 7, 1782." *Select Works of Edmund Burke, and Miscellaneous Writings.* www.econlib.org/library/LFBoooks/Burke/brkSWv4c2.html (accessed 14 Jan. 2004).

Burke, Edmund. *Reflections on the Revolution in France.* Garden City, NY: Anchor Books, 1973.

Carter, April. *The Political Theory of Anarchism.* London: Routledge and Kegan Paul, 1971.

Delany, Samuel. "To Read the Dispossessed." Pp. 218–83 in his *The Jewel-Hinged Jaw.* New York: Berkley Windhover, 1977.

Flaherty, David. *Privacy in Colonial New England.* Charlottesville: University Press of Virginia: 1967.

Foucault, Michel. *Discipline and Punish.* New York: Pantheon, 1977.

Hamburger, Joseph. *John Stuart Mill on Liberty and Control.* Princeton, NJ: Princeton University Press, 1999.

Hegel, G. W. F. *Phenomenology of Spirit*, trans. A. V. Miller. Oxford: Oxford University Press, 1977 (1806).

———. *Philosophy of History*, trans. J. Sibree. New York: Dover, 1956.

———. *Philosophy of Right*, trans. H. B. Nisbett. Cambridge: Cambridge University Press, 1991 (1821).

———. *Reason in History*, trans. Robert Hartman. Upper Saddle River, NJ: Prentice-Hall, 1997.

Kant, Immanuel. *Metaphysics of Morals.*

Khouri, Nadia. "The Dialectics of Power: Utopia in the Science Fiction of Le Guin, Jeury, and Piercy." *Science-Fiction Studies* 7, no. 1 (March, 1980): 49–61.

Kropotkin, Peter. "Anarchism." *Encyclopedia Britannica* (1910). http://dwardmac.pitzer.edu/Anarchist_Archives/kropotkin/britanniaanarchy.html (accessed 7 May 2004).

———. *Ethics: Origins and Development.* New York: B. Blum, 1968.

———. "Expropriation." Pp. 160–209 in *Selected Writings on Anarchism and Revolution*, ed. Martin Miller. Cambridge, MA: MIT Press, 1970.

———. "Must We Occupy Ourselves with an Examination of the Ideal of a Future System?" Pp. 47–116 in *Selected Writings on Anarchism and Revolution*, ed. Martin Miller. Cambridge, MA: MIT Press, 1970.

Le Guin, Ursula K. *The Dispossessed: An Ambiguous Utopia.* New York: Eos, HarperCollins, 2001 (1974).

Machiavelli, Niccolo. *The Discourses on Livy.*

Marx, Gary. "Privacy and Technology." *Whole Earth Review* 73 (Winter, 1991): 90–95.

Marx, Karl. "Theses on Feuerbach." Pp. 143–45 in *The Marx-Engels Reader*, 2d ed., ed. Robert Tucker. New York: W.W. Norton and Co., 1978.

Mill, John Stuart. *On Liberty.*

Moylan, Tom. *Demand the Impossible: Science Fiction and the Utopian Imagination.* New York: Methuen, 1986.

Rawls, John. *A Theory of Justice*. Cambridge, MA: Harvard University Press, 1971.

Tunick, Mark. "Does Privacy Undermine Community?" *Journal of Value Inquiry* 35, no. 4 (December 2001): 517–34.

———. *Hegel's Political Philosophy*. Princeton, NJ: Princeton University Press, 1992.

———. *Practices and Principles*. Princeton, NJ: Princeton University Press, 1998.

———. *Punishment: Theory and Practice*. Berkeley: University of California Press, 1992.

Wolff, Robert Paul. *In Defense of Anarchism*. New York: Harper & Row, 1970.

8

Breaching Invisible Walls:
Individual Anarchy in *The Dispossessed*

Winter Elliott

$\mathcal{U}$rsula K. Le Guin's short story, "The Ones Who Walk Away From Omelas,"[1] written in 1972, considers the unattractive paradox of a seemingly perfect society corrupted by a single flaw. Although Omelas appears a perfect, and perfectly impossible, society for almost half of the story, its outward excellence necessitates an internal horror. Its citizens are not "simple folk" or "bland utopians," but what might instead be called complex—or ambiguous—citizens of a humanly imperfect, tragically flawed utopia. Omelas, this perfect society, depends upon and needs the suffering and misery of a single, innocent individual, representative of its most vulnerable, its most pure—brought to extremes of misery and suffering. Joy, happiness, beauty, material wealth or pastoral naiveté, an orgy or two—or not—all of these things compose Omelas, and all of these contradict a little, locked cellar room constraining a tortured child sacrificed for the pleasure and happiness of the city's other citizens. Le Guin's story recreates William James's theory of the scapegoat[2] in that lost child, intentionally opposing the possible permanent happiness of the many against the loss of just one, inconsequential child. In this short story, society and the individual are at odds, for Omelas survives as a whole through the unwilling sacrifice of a single part. But Omelas also loses the ethical few who cannot endure the price for their society's perfect happiness. These few walk away, perhaps to seek better worlds, perhaps to assuage guilty consciousnesses. Crucially, though, they do not return—and Omelas continues its blithe, blemished march to perfection.

In *The Dispossessed*,[3] written two years later, Le Guin constructs a still more ambiguous utopia, juxtaposing again the order and perfection of a carefully balanced society against the needs and desires of a single individual. Le Guin accomplishes many a careful balancing act within the novel, fluidly moving between times and worlds[4] to trace the personal evolution of that individual, the book's central character, the physicist Shevek. Shevek experiences two worlds, his own,

Anarres, and a mother planet seven generations removed, Urras. These two worlds provide both the backdrop and the philosophical underpinnings of the novel. In their own ways, both of these worlds are attempts at utopia; both are ultimately necessary to the successful development of Shevek's theory of temporal physics. Shevek also firmly believes that each world is essential to the survival of the other. Therefore, *The Dispossessed* is, on the surface, a mediation between two utopias, two worlds, two macrocosms of humanity, with differing goals, desires, and beliefs. However, *The Dispossessed* also maintains an unswerving, consistent focus on a single individual, Shevek. The book is not ultimately as interested in which world has the best, or even better, political system as it is in Shevek's role within those worlds. Instead, *The Dispossessed* depends upon a tension between the individual part and the social whole, a conflict most fully expressed by Shevek's relationship to and position within both Anarres and Urras.

The Dispossessed is, of course, a discussion of utopia, even a representation of an idealized utopia. Its subtitle, *An Ambiguous Utopia*, announces that intention even before the book's first words. But *The Dispossessed* does not carefully map guidelines for a perfect society; it does not advise roles and situations as if it were a very lengthy handbook on city planning. Nor does the book really depend upon utopia on a grand, social scale, though both Anarres and Urras are undeniably central to both the book and Shevek. Instead, *The Dispossessed* represents a personal utopia, an idea both experienced and realized by one person, Shevek. Societies, the book suggests, tend to stagnate, becoming comfortable in everyday routines and familiar customs, to the detriment of the exceptional. Because of this entropic tendency, a society can never realize even an imperfect utopia permanently; change, or anarchy, is requisite for even the cooperative communism of Anarres. That change, that anarchy, must occur on an individual level. Conversely, though, Shevek, the primary anarchist of *The Dispossessed*, is not isolated from either of the two societies in which he finds himself. If his individual rebellion is necessary to the evolution of both Anarres and Urras, the regulation and structure of both worlds, the interaction between people that each world promotes and allows in different ways, is equally essential to Shevek's growth and his scientific discoveries and theories.

Like the Omelas of Le Guin's short story, the utopian world of Anarres depends upon a central image of enclosure; unlike Omelas, not a single child, but entire societies, reside within walls. Shevek, the protagonist of *The Dispossessed*, walks away from this utopia too—but, more importantly, he eventually returns.[5] Urras also uses walls to uphold its social and political structure—the prison that once held Odo, the force behind the establishment of Anarres and its philosophy, walls between nations, walls that keep Shevek away from the common people, walls that isolate and regulate ideas. Yet, the walls of *The Dispossessed* are not, ultimately, impermeable, nor their prisoners finally victims—unlike the situation depicted in "The Ones Who Walk Away from Omelas." Instead, the walls of *The Dispossessed* are constructed and torn down invisibly, inside each person, before they are ever made tangibly real. *The Dispossessed* is, thus, a novel of individual anarchy, a depiction of a utopia secured through personal rebellion and renewal.

While the subtitle, *An Ambiguous Utopia*, identifies the book's subject as utopia, it also renders the identification of that utopia problematic—for there are two, not one, societies acknowledged as differing sorts of utopias within the book.[6] The Terran Ambassador Keng identifies Urras, a world beset by war, divided nations, and petty strife, as "the world that comes as close as any could to Paradise" (11: 347). Admitting her ignorance of Shevek's world, Anarres, she describes the planet merely as "arid and bleak," and its society as "an experiment in nonauthoritarian communism" (11: 342). While Shevek sometimes comments on his own distance from both worlds, pessimistically viewing himself as distinct and isolate from both Anarres—the world of his birth—and Urras—the world he had come to love (3: 88), Shevek does not, and cannot, have the sort of removed alienation that Keng embodies. Keng is, indeed, a true "alien" to both worlds; her status as Ambassador from a foreign planet grants her opinions both a distance and an impartiality that increases her credibility as an observer. Unlike Shevek, Keng's neutrality automatically allows her to distinguish the best, most favorable aspects of both worlds. To her, Urras is alive, a sharp contrast with the man-made desert of her native Earth; it is "the kindliest, most various, most beautiful of all the inhabited worlds" (11: 347). It is a "splendid world, this vital society, this Urras" (11: 348). In contrast, Anarres has nothing tangible to offer her—nothing but an idea, a certain philosophy of life, a working type of political system that seems to exist, for her at least, as an impossible dream. Keng is not, of course, truly impartial; the state of her native world shades her preferences and her dreams. Interestingly enough, though, Keng's characterization of Anarres and Urras is complementary to both.

Neither Anarres nor Urras can persist in perpetual isolation from the other; each has something to offer. In that sense, the two worlds, the two planets, are truly complementary, as Keng unintentionally implies. Reacting from intense stress, frustration, disappointment, and probably also loneliness, Shevek scathingly calls Urras "a box, a package, with all the beautiful wrapping of blue sky and meadows and forests and great cities" (11: 347). Inside that box, he sees nothing—nothing but corruption, death, and dust. But Shevek's box *is* alive—alive with the planetary wonder that Keng recognizes, filled with animals and plant life that, in less angry moments, Shevek admires and craves. Animals, such as the child Ini's otter or the horse he sees from the car soon after his arrival on Urras, inspire sadness in him, an unconscious recognition of that lack on Anarres, a deficit more severe than the simple absence of a furry pet or dark horsey eyes. Takver, Shevek's partner, "had always known that all lives are in common, rejoicing in her kinship to the fish in the tanks of her laboratories, seeking the experience of existences outside the human boundary" (1: 22). It is that commonality, that wellspring of natural life and abundance, that Anarres, as a planet, lacks.[7] Nor is it an absence fully recompensed by the vital bonds between humans that *do* exist on the world; Shevek also realizes that

Takver's "concern, feebly called 'love of nature,' seemed . . . to be something much broader than love. There are souls, he thought, whose umbilicus has never been cut. They never got weaned from the universe" (6: 185). Takver herself characterizes the possibilities of a more abundant natural world: "everywhere you looked animals, other creatures, sharing the earth and air with you. You'd feel so much more a *part*" (6: 186). Takver recognizes humankind's position within the universe, acknowledges that solely human relationships, while valid and necessary, cannot, and do not, completely satisfy the human impulse to experience life on a universal level—to be a part, not just of a particularly social species, nor just of a world, but of the universe.

In turn, Urras, despite its relative prosperity—as Keng comments, even the poor "are not so very poor" (11: 342)—and natural wealth, lacks substance. Its exterior is magnificent, rich with the opportunities denied its moon, Anarres. Urras lacks the true freedom and brotherhood that characterize Anarres's political system. But, while Odo's philosophy of justice and individual choice grows on the otherwise barren planet, little else does—suffering and difficulty typify life on Anarres. Indeed, Shevek and his small family survive a devastating drought that tears at the ties of brotherhood and, temporarily at least, separates him from Takver and their child. Anarres and Urras, therefore, represent different extremes of unrealized utopia; as Tifft and Sullivan remark, "The land (Urras) of possessed abundance, of natural beauty, where people have so much, is the land of surface pleasure and spiritual death. The land (Anarres) of surface dust, darkness, and scarcity is the land of spiritual life and fulfillment."[8] Each world lacks the very qualities that render the other most desirable, and each world manifests an isolationary impulse that not only makes the other world's wealth—whether natural or spiritual—unavailable, but also inhibits and damages individual potential and creativity.

Both Anarres and the nations of Urras depend upon authority and exert varying degrees of control over individual lives. Both worlds, intentionally or not, oppose themselves to the anarchist politics, ideals, and ideas maintained and expressed by Shevek. Despite the seeming opposition of their political systems—the authority and power upon which A-Io and the other nations of Urras depend; the Odonian nonauthoritarian communism of Anarres—both worlds grind toward hegemony and domination. Notably, both worlds attempt control on not just a physical but also a mental or spiritual level. Urras and Anarres manage not only bodies but also minds and ideas. Shevek experiences that regimentation on Anarres early on; the reader's first sight of the young Shevek shows him as a knobby baby staring up at beam of sunlight, soon displaced by a fat baby, whose only interest in the sun is its warmth. The nursery matron tells the baby Shevek that the sun "is not yours. . . . Nothing is yours. It is to use. It is to share. If you will not share it, you cannot use it" (2: 27). Shevek's father, with more gentleness, concurs: "Come on, you know you can't have things. What's wrong with you?" (2: 27–28). Both the matron and Shevek's father respond to the inconsequential, childish row with the common injustice and misunderstanding of adults toward young children; both miss Shevek's meaning. The sun, after all, is not a "thing," nor, really, can it be used as might any other tangible thing. And Shevek has, too, not refused to share the sunbeam's heat; he has been displaced by the other baby, who watches the scene with a fair degree of mindless ignorance.

More important than whether or not Shevek feels an infant inclination toward Odonian rites of sharing and brotherhood is the concept of the sun itself. *The Dispossessed* proceeds chronologically somewhat in the manner of stepping stones; forwards, backwards, forwards again. While the first chapter sees Shevek a seasoned man, with children and a partner, off on his journey to Urras, the second flips back in time, depicting the maturation of that man—literally from babyhood. This scene, then, is fundamental to Shevek's development—the first event in his life worthy of memory and representation. The baby Shevek is not merely being denied access to a warm spot on the floor; he does not express the same interest in the sunbeam as the other baby. To that baby, the warm spot on the floor may very well equate to a commodity, though he does not particularly want to share it. Shevek is not interested in the floor, or physical warmth, but in the sun, which cannot be owned and is not a thing. To him, the sun represents ideas, knowledge, something brilliant and far away, to be reached after struggle and challenge. A grown man, Shevek later finds himself again staring up at the sun, this time attaining the knowledge far out of a baby's grasp. When Shevek finally, after much despair and uncertainty, solves his General Temporal Theory, it comes to him as a "revelation. It was the way clear, the way home, the light" (9: 280). Shevek reacts to that revelation with awe: "And yet in his utter ease and happiness he shook with fear; his hands trembled, and his eyes filled up with tears, as if he had been looking into the sun" (9: 281). The sun of the baby Shevek and the light of the mature physicist are the same; both Sheveks pursue the clear light of knowledge, of ideas. Anarres, in the name of commonality, sharing, and brotherhood, consistently seeks to banish Shevek's sun, extinguish his ideas.

Urras also seeks control over ideas, as Shevek bluntly recognizes when he states "I came here from Anarres because I thought that here I could do the work and publish it. I didn't understand that here an idea is a property of the State" (9: 294). Urras also, unlike Anarres, has centralized governments—differing political systems, at war with each other in philosophy if not in fact. Such governments depend upon and require control. As Shevek tells Chifoilisk, a representative of a socialist country similar in a few ways to Anarres, "you are archists. The State of Thu is even more centralized than the State of A-Io. One power structure controls all, the government, administration, police, army, education, laws, trades, manufactures. And you have the money economy" (5: 136). It is this last point that appears to most acutely separate Anarres from any, or all, of the countries of Urras; Anarres does not depend upon property, profit, or money.

However, despite that crucial distinction, the free society of Anarres is in the process of becoming more dependent upon power, authority, and regulation of ideas and less supportive of free thought. Shevek's friend Bedap realizes that disagreeable fact long before Shevek himself. As he tells Shevek, "We've let cooperation become obedience. On Urras they have government by the minority. Here we have government by the majority. But it is government! The social conscience isn't a living thing any more, but a machine, a power machine, controlled by bureaucrats!" (6: 167). Bedap explains that

> stability gives scope to the authoritarian impulse. In the early years of the Settlement we were aware of that, on the lookout for it. People discriminated very carefully then between administering things and governing people. They did it so well that we forgot that the will to dominance is as central in human beings as the impulse to mutual aid is, and has to be trained in each individual, in each new generation. Nobody's born an Odonian any more than he's born civilized! But we've forgotten that. We don't educate for freedom. Education, the most important activity of the social organism, has become rigid, moralistic, authoritarian. Kids learn to parrot Odo's words as if they were *laws*—the ultimate blasphemy! (6: 167–68)

Bedap implies that the "impulse to mutual aid," upon which Anarres was founded, is in danger of succumbing to the inherent human "will to dominance," which, in turn, allows public opinion—or a particularly conniving and corrupt individual in a convenient position of power, like Sabul—to calcify social conceptions of good, bad and necessary and to obstruct innovation.[9] But Bedap's "will to dominance" might also be described as a "will to submission." An "impulse to mutual aid" implies that one person actively makes a choice to help another; it is social cooperation enacted consciously, willingly, by individuals. It necessitates free thought and obviates the need for governmental regulation and manipulation. But much of Anarres no longer makes that conscious choice; instead, its people happily conform, ignoring the very necessary Divlab computer that "runs their lives"[10] and the "giant, inchoate, and largely unrecognized bureaucracy [that] lurks behind the scenes"[11] in favor of compulsive obedience to a concept of social good. Shevek realizes that "the social conscience completely dominates the individual conscience, instead of striking a balance with it. We don't cooperate—we *obey*. We fear being outcast, being called lazy, dysfunctional, egoizing. We fear our neighbor's opinion more than we respect our own freedom of choice" (10: 330). Anarres lacks Urras's many centralized governments, but its people have grown comfortable with the blind obedience that governments typically encourage.

The social systems of Anarres and Urras, therefore, control the individual, by violence if necessary; both worlds, without the intervention, the rebellion, expressed by Shevek, would continue to move steadily toward a governed, centralized concept of a collective good that would dominate and diminish individual creativity—the light Shevek sees in the sun. Significantly, though, Anarres and Urras are not the only worlds described in *The Dispossessed*. Terran Ambassador Keng also gives Shevek a clear image of her world and its political system. Keng's

Earth was destroyed by human appetite and violence; its people "had saved what could be saved, and made a kind of life in the ruins, on Terra, in the only way it could be done: by total centralization. Total control over the use of every acre of land, every scrap of metal, every ounce of fuel. Total rationing, birth control, euthanasia, universal conscription into the labor force. The absolute regimentation of each life toward the goal of racial survival" (11: 348). Keng's Earth signifies government control carried toward an admitted—in this situation—extreme, and it also signifies the total obliteration of the individualist impulse implied in the Odonian concept of mutual aid.[12] Such total centralization also carries the communal or collective impulse to its logical destination; everything, everyone, is devoted to the whole, to the betterment of society, with a total disregard for any personal good.

Anarres, Urras, and Earth exemplify different types of political systems, each reflecting a tension between the individual and the collective. Each world also suggests a different stage in governmental development, a different degree of political control. What has begun on Anarres—power over individual choice—and characterizes the governments of Urras is a full-blown disease on the world of Earth. Indeed, Anarres and Urras, despite their ostensible differences, quite literally mirror each other; each world, to the other, is but a moon.[13] On Urras, sleeping in Demaere Oiie's guest room, Shevek dreams that he and his partner Takver were on the Moon: "They were on the Moon together, it was cold, and they were walking along together. It was a flat place, the Moon, all covered with bluish-white snow, though the snow was thin and easily kicked aside to show the luminous white ground. It was dead, a dead place" (5: 153). Significantly, Shevek does not identify *which* Moon his dream concerns; both Urras and Anarres may truly be considered Moons. Thus, his characterization of the Moon as dead and barren may easily apply to *both* Anarres and Urras; both worlds, like Earth, have constructed walls around individual creativity and have erected systems of social obedience that undermine their apparent utopias.

Seven generations after Odo's followers settled Urras's moon, Shevek endorses the same answer to the problem of control and dominance as his spiritual predecessor: anarchy.[14] However, although the Odonian society of Anarres is founded on the lack of control and regulation that anarchy would imply, anarchy cannot, finally, be perpetuated on a social level. Only on an individual basis can anarchy be achieved and maintained and the natural progression of societies toward laws and regulations—and power—be interrupted. Shevek's progression through his own life and the disjointed time frame of *The Dispossessed* thus implies a movement toward true anarchy; as he discovers his General Temporal Theory, Shevek must remove his ideas from social control. He undergoes an individual process of growth; though he has been educated in anarchy, he is not, initially, a true anarchist. As Smith accurately observes, "Shevek must face his own personal trials before he can achieve the knowledge and ability to work for the salvation and renewal of Anarresti society. This task can be accomplished only after

Shevek has broken out of the prison walls of his own cultural conditioning."[15] Shevek's first real words to his fellow physicists on Urras—and the last words of the book's first chapter—place him in the hands and control of others: "Well, you have me," he says to the Urrasti physicists. He continues, "You have your anarchist. What are you going to do with him?" (1: 25) A true anarchist, however, determines his own future, makes his own choices. An anarchist does; he is not done unto.

Shevek does not travel to Urras entirely ignorant of the cost to be paid, but he does, temporarily at least, succumb to its culture of profit and ownership. Shevek initially believes that he can fit into the nation of A-Io, deal with its leaders and rulers, its power structure, on its own terms. As he tells the Thuvian socialist Chifoilisk, he believes he can bargain with its profit economy. On Anarres, he says, "I acted. Here, I bargain" (5: 138). But Shevek finally concludes that instead of bargaining, he has instead almost been bought; as he tells Keng, "I am letting the propertarians *buy the truth* from me" (11: 345). Earlier, Shevek had made exactly the same mistake on his home planet, allowing an inferior scientist to judge his work, badly edit it, and attach his name to it. As Takver comments, "I was wrong, wasn't I, about the book. About letting Sabul cut it up and put his name on it. It seemed right. It seemed like setting the work before the workman, pride before vanity, community before ego, all that. But it wasn't really that at all, was it? It was a capitulation. A surrender to Sabul's authoritarianism" (10: 331). Shevek's initial impulse on both worlds, within both political systems, is cooperation; consciously or not, he tries to minimize the sense of alienation that stalks him all of his life. But by attempting participation within the power structures of either world, Shevek betrays both his own self and his ideas. In both cases, Shevek sublimates those ideas to the self-serving goals and desires of people in positions of power—Sabul on Anarres, the government of A-Io.

Shevek only truly realizes the ideal of anarchy through rebellion and individual choice. Importantly, Shevek's rebellion revolves around ideas and the promulgation and dissemination of those ideas to others.[16] On A-Io, ideas are currency; on Anarres, new ideas are feared for their novelty and the change and danger they represent. In each society, information is to be closely guarded, kept secret, and wielded against one's enemies or neighbors as a weapon. Thus, Rulag on Anarres reacts to Shevek and Bedap's Syndicate of Initiative with fear and anger, arguing that their communication with Urras is a betrayal and danger: "I don't propose to go again into the harm you've already done, the handing out of scientific information to a powerful enemy, the confession of our weakness that each of your broadcasts to Urras represents" (12: 355). The aged and presumably wise Urrasti physicist Atro feels much the same way about Shevek's General Temporal Theory, admonishing him to "think of your duty to your own people, your own kind" (5: 143). Atro wants scientific primacy for his world, commenting that "Scientific truth will out, you can't hide the sun under a stone. But before they get it, I want them to pay for it! I want us to take our rightful place. I want respect; and that's what you can win us" (5: 143). Both Anarres and Urras have a closed definition of "us." Even though Anarres depends upon a concept of brotherhood, it excludes all but the relative few who actually reside on the planet from that familial relationship. Likewise, Urras may be grudgingly willing to grant a relationship with Anarres, but all other worlds must be set aside, alienated, and considered enemy.

Shevek's General Temporal Theory is, like the sun or light itself, basically an idea. It is, however, a very useful idea, for its most immediate application is an ansible, a "device that will permit communication without any time interval between two points in space" (11: 344). As Bierman notes, "The ansible in Le Guin's stories is the correlative for immediately felt, simultaneously held knowledge, the goal of communication—to feel and think together across the spaces and times that separate humans."[17] Shevek's idea renders distance less meaningful and makes irrelevant the division between worlds, cultures, and people that both Anarres and Urras would foster. Shevek's rebellion, his anarchy, is not physical or violent; even the demonstration he joins on Urras is, on the part of the demonstrators, peaceful. But Shevek's anarchy is very much personal, and serves to isolate him from social institutions, though not from other people. His is very much the generative impulse, to be enacted alone, separately; as Tifft and Sullivan comment, "For only the individual can create, and only through moral choice does creation become possible."[18] Shevek produces his ideas, his theories, unaided, without the support or understanding of his brothers on Anarres; on Urras, the grasping greed of the other physicists instills in Shevek secretive tendencies. Too, his ideas are disruptive, insurrectionary, and uncomfortable to the power structures on both Anarres and Urras, leaving Shevek again an object of suspicion and concern. Ironically, the final product of Shevek's ideas, his General Temporal Theory, has the potential to draw people and worlds together, to facilitate instantaneous communication across great distance.

Shevek's recurring desire and need for communication with others, both physicists who can share in and understand his ideas and receptive people in general, appears at first contradictory; his pursuit of uncontrolled knowledge results in his initial detachment from both his own society and that of Urras. But Shevek's ideas are not troublesome in and of themselves. Their application is benign; even Keng, to whom physics are unintelligible, understands that Shevek's "temporal physics may make new technologies possible" (11: 343). It is only power itself, especially in the form of political systems and governments, that Shevek's ideas disrupt. To Shevek, anarchy is the annihilation of power, the abolition of the control one person or organization may exert over another. As Keng finally understands about the rebellion on Urras, "The revolutionists in Nio, they come from that same tradition. They weren't just striking for better wages or protesting the draft. They are not only socialists, they are anarchists; they were striking against power" (11: 342). Shevek's General Temporal Theory and his anarchist sensibilities exist in perfect accord. As an anarchist, he despises ownership,

even that inherent in one person's ability to mandate another's actions; as a physicist, his theories have the potential to equalize worlds and societies and make universal the limited brotherhood of Anarres.

Shevek consistently desires communication, a specialized kind of interaction—
one free of power. Shevek came to Urras "for the idea. For the sake of the idea. To
learn, to teach, to share in the idea" (11: 345). He ultimately gives his General Temporal Theory to all of the worlds for much the same reason—to share it, "so that one
of you cannot use it, as A-Io wants to do, to get power over the others, to get richer
or to win more wars. So that you cannot use the truth for your private profit, but
only for the common good" (11: 345). Shevek does not want to sell his ideas or to
guard them from others; nor does he wish his ideas to support a particular government or power structure. Instead, Shevek recalls the foundation of Anarres, Odonian tenets and theories; he comments, "But the ideas in my head aren't the only ones
important to me. My society is also an idea. I was made by it. An idea of freedom,
of change, of human solidarity, an important idea" (11: 345). By recalling the fundamental ideas behind his society, by freeing his own scientific theories and giving
them to all worlds, Shevek undermines the tendencies toward control and law that
have begun to regulate even the anarchist tendencies of Anarres. Thus, Shevek not
only shares his physics but also the theories of freedom and anarchy that motivate
his pursuit of ideas.

Shevek's ideas and his expression of those ideas ultimately represent intellectual and social freedom: intellectual, because Shevek does develop his General
Temporal Theory and release it to all; social, because his and Odo's idea of anarchy promotes autonomy and liberty. Shevek's ideas, thus, counteract the most
central image of *The Dispossessed*—walls. Physically, the wall with which *The
Dispossessed*—and Shevek's journey to Urras—begins is not very impressive; children can climb it, and it lacks a gate. That wall, however, exists on an intangible
level as well—it, like Shevek's temporal physics and Odo's anarchy, is primarily an
idea.[19] Indeed, "the idea was real. It was important. For seven generations there
had been nothing in the world more important than that wall" (1: 1). That wall
both encloses alien visitors and surrounds the entire planet. On Anarres, Shevek
realizes, "we have cut ourselves off. We don't talk with other people, the rest of
humanity" (11: 345). Whereas Shevek's abstract physics theory would have the
immediate result of allowing enhanced communication by breaking down the
barriers of space and time, the walls he sees all around in him on both Anarres
and Urras isolate each individual and each world, segregating and controlling
each small part of humankind. Drunken, exhausted, at Vea's party he still speaks
the truth as he knows it:

> Because our men and women are free—possessing nothing, they are free. And
> you the possessors are possessed. You are all in jail. Each alone, solitary, with a
> heap of what he owns. You live in prison, die in prison. It is all I can see in your
> eyes—the wall, the wall! (7: 229)

To breach those walls, the tangible one on Anarres and the more or less insubstantial ones he repeatedly encounters on both worlds, Shevek combats an idea of isolation and constraint with philosophical and scientific theories of freedom and free interaction.

Because both the wall and its solution are ideas, they must be understood by individuals and on an individual basis; Shevek can change worlds with his theories and beliefs, but only single people can choose whether or not to stay within the safe, limiting confines of their intellectual walls or to seek the frightening freedom Shevek envisions. As Cogell comments, the "relationship between the individual and society must be dynamic"[20]; the individual must actively choose to interact within and react to social precepts. Ketho, the Hainish ship officer who chooses to accompany Shevek back through Anarres's wall, does so of his own will, arguing that his people have "tried everything. Anarchism, with the rest. But *I* have not tried it. They say there is nothing new under any sun. But if each life is not new, each single life, then why are we born?" (13: 385). In his own language, Shevek responds, "We are the children of time" (13: 385). Ketho's and Shevek's attitudes suggest the value of individual life, of course, but they also imply singularity; each life is new and free to choose its own journey—as do Shevek and Ketho.

Ketho's and Shevek's comments also concur with the repetitive pattern of destruction and renewal enacted on individual and social levels throughout *The Dispossessed*. Shevek's theories and discoveries are based on time; Shevek sees the past, present, and future as equally real, equally valid. Shevek believes humans to be the children of time, but they are also creatures of it, subject to constant change. Although Shevek retraces, in reverse, Odo's footsteps, he does not do so pointlessly or in vain. His philosophic and scientific discoveries recall the past, validate the present, and affect the future. Societies, as wholes, progress toward the entropy and stagnation of authority and control; Shevek's individual revolt, his anarchy, permits individual choice, makes it possible to be a distinct part of the whole. As he tells Ketho, "It was our purpose all along—our Syndicate, this journey of mine—to shake up things, to stir up, to break some habits, to make people ask questions. To behave like anarchists!" (13: 384). Odo's people, seven generations before, also behaved like anarchists—were anarchists. That past provides a foundation for Shevek's present efforts; in the now, Shevek inspires the same sort of Odonian revolution, a continuous, "never pausing, but never pressing revolution,"[21] an upheaval that will, no doubt, again be necessary in the future. For the moment, Shevek has succeeded; his "unbuilding of walls implies that Anarresti culture can be liberated, to allow the creativity of freely adapting individuals to flourish."[22] The theological underpinnings and anarchist basis of Anarres are basically sound, and Shevek ultimately advocates the Odonian philosophy, the successful experiment enacted on Anarres, as the answer to both Urrasti and Terran problems.

But, as children of time, Shevek and Ketho necessarily live in the present; to them, Odo's theories, like Shevek's physics, can come as a revelation. The present,

Shevek believes, is individual to every person and every world and can be changed, must be changed. Paradise, Shevek observes,

> is for those who make Paradise. . . . The Settlers of Anarres had turned their backs on the Old World and its past, opted for the future only. But as surely as the future becomes the past, the past becomes the future. To deny is not to achieve. The Odonians who left Urras had been wrong, wrong in their desperate courage, to deny their history, to forgo the possibility of return. The explorer who will not come back or send back his ships to tell his tale is not an explorer, only an adventurer; and his sons are born in exile. (3: 89)

Utopia must be created anew each day or each generation, by those who engage their pasts and their futures, in a Tao-like cyclical process of disintegration and renewal.[23] Anarchy, too, which on Anarres promotes and equates to utopia, requires stimulus on an individual level—an anarchist society may only exist if it is composed of a very great many individual anarchists.

Anarchy does not, however, require an anarchist society. It may develop into a society of anarchists, as Anarres did and Urras at least has the possibility to do. Anarchy is Shevek's answer, and the anarchist society of Anarres his model and his goal; but Shevek becomes an anarchist of his own individual will, not because his society creates him. Indeed, it tries to destroy him, through violence when other forms of coercion fail. Like the government of A-Io, which sends its army to murder the escaped Shevek and his fellow demonstrators, the Anarresti mob at the beginning of *The Dispossessed* intends to kill Shevek, and fails only because it basically isn't a very practiced or competent mob, not because murder isn't really its goal. Societies, anarchist or no, tend to stagnate, develop written or unwritten rules, regulations, and methods of control. Shevek's anarchy fragments social order, destabilizing the innate human impulse to dominate—or obey—as part of a single-minded collective. His anarchy enables free choice, the true foundation of Odo's concept of mutual aid. But Shevek's anarchy must also be established individually, repetitively, constantly.

The motto carved on Odo's tombstone, "To be whole is to be part; true voyage is return" (3: 84), expresses that prime paradox of the successful Anarresti experiment; only individually can social anarchy be created and maintained. Shevek must be singular within the collective; he must also actively participate within his society. Unlike the unfortunate title characters of Le Guin's short story, "The Ones Who Walk Away From Omelas," Shevek does not truly walk away from Anarres, his own flawed society. He returns, having broken down the very walls, barriers and prisons that incarcerate the victimized child responsible for Omelas's tainted perfection. Those few who do leave Omelas do so with the knowledge of what they leave behind them—a city of happiness, based on the horrid exploitation of a child. They do not, presumably, return—and the simple fact of their departure serves to perpetuate Omelas's evil, its false perfection. Shevek returns, acting as an individual responsible to and aware of his society. At the end, Shevek attains his utopia, his "clear, unmixed happiness" (13: 386), by breaching those very invisible walls that constrain and destroy individuality. The realized utopia of *The Dispossessed*, then, is a personal one, attainable only through individual effort and psychological struggle.

NOTES

1. Ursula K. Le Guin, "The Ones Who Walk Away from Omelas," *The Wind's Twelve Quarters*. (New York: Harper & Row, 1975).

2. Charlotte Spivack, *Ursula K. Le Guin* (Boston: Twayne Publishers, 1984), 84.

3. Ursula K. Le Guin, *The Dispossessed: An Ambiguous Utopia* (New York: Harper & Row, 1974), cited in the text by chapter and page to the 387-page Eos HarperCollins edition of 2001.

4. See Spivack, *Le Guin*, 75 for a coherent description of the narrative pattern of *The Dispossessed*.

5. Interestingly, the founder of Shevek's Anarresti Odonianism, Odo, has been described by Le Guin as one of those who left Omelas. See the preface to Le Guin's short story, "The Day Before the Revolution," *The Wind's Twelve Quarters*. See also Bülent Somay, "Towards an Open-Ended Utopia," *Science-Fiction Studies* 11, no. 1 (March 1984): 36.

6. Many readers do identify either Anarres or Urras—and even Earth—as valid utopias. See John P. Brennan and Michael C. Downs, "Anarchism and Utopian Tradition in *The Dispossessed*," in *Ursula K. Le Guin*, ed. Joseph D. Olander and Martin Harry Greenberg, (New York: Taplinger, 1979), 152; Krishan Kumar, *Utopia and Anti-Utopia in Modern Times* (Oxford: Basil Blackwell, 1987), 414; and Warren G. Rochelle, *Communities of the Heart: The Rhetoric of Myth in the Fiction of Ursula K. Le Guin* (Liverpool, UK: Liverpool University Press, 2001), 73. Brennan and Downs clearly read Anarres as the ambiguous utopia of the subtitle, whereas Krishan Kumar, while preferring Anarres, sees Urras as a hopeful vision of industrial civilization. Even the Terran Earth has certain aspects in its favor; Rochelle comments that its vision of total centralization has been viewed as utopian by such writers as Plato and More.

7. It is also the barrenness of Anarres that renders it a surprising depiction of utopia. See Judah Bierman, "Ambiguity in Utopia: *The Dispossessed*," *Science-Fiction Studies* 2, no. 3 (Nov. 1975): 250 and Fredric Jameson, "World Reduction in Le Guin: The Emergence of Utopian Narrative" in *Ursula K. Le Guin*, ed. Harold Bloom, (New York: Chelsea House, 1986), 62, 66. Bierman comments that Anarres is truly ambiguous "because it shows us so many traditionally good institutions in a setting that imposes an absence of goods—traditional means to fulfillment," whereas Jameson sees Anarres's barrenness, including its lack of animals, as a release from "historical determinism" and as an indication of freedom.

8. Larry L. Tifft and Dennis C. Sullivan, "Possessed Sociology and Le Guin's *Dispossessed*," in *Ursula K. Le Guin: Voyager to Inner Lands and to Outer Space*, ed. Joe De Bolt (Port Washington, NY: Kennikat, 1979), 186.

9. See Victor Urbanowicz, "Personal and Political in *The Dispossessed*," *Science-Fiction Studies* 5, no. 2 (July 1978): 115. Urbanowicz comments that, when this happens, "the first

to suffer are likely to be those creative individuals whose work must be solitary—precisely those, in other words, who are the best justification of freedom. Such is the case on Anarres with Shevek and a number of creative artists."

10. Lynn F. Williams, "The Machine at Utopia's Center," *Utopian Studies III* (1991): 67.

11. William H. Hardesty, III, "Mapping the Future: Extrapolation in Utopian/Dystopian and Science Fiction," *Utopian Studies I* (1987): 163.

12. Notably, prior theorists and writers have relied on the State, not the individual, to promote and create Utopia—and the absolute regimentation of Keng's Earth might be considered very much in accord with the aims and desires of those earlier utopian theorists. As Brennan and Downs ("Anarchism and Utopian Tradition," 116) observe,

> The idea of an "anarchist utopia" would, on the face of it, seem to be a contradiction in terms. After all, anarchism is the antipolitical theory of politics, the one that rejects all authority, law, and government as being unnecessary and oppressive. On the other hand, in its search for order and justice in human affairs, the utopian tradition has, for the most part, looked to the state— hateful to the anarchist—as the key to reforming society.

13. See Carol McGuirk, "Optimism and the Limits of Subversion in *The Dispossessed* and *The Left Hand of Darkness*," in *Ursula K. Le Guin*, ed. Bloom, 244. McGuirk acknowledges that "Repeatedly in the 'Hainish' novels, the apparent alien becomes, on better acquaintance, really a repressed, rejected or earlier phase of the self" (244).

14. Commentators and critics of *The Dispossessed* generally recognize resonances between Le Guin's concept of anarchy and freedom and the writings of thinkers like Peter Kropotkin. Philip E. Smith II, for example, demonstrates Kropotkin's influence in his article "Unbuilding Walls: Human Nature and the Nature of Evolutionary and Political Theory in *The Dispossessed*," in *Ursula K. Le Guin*, ed. Olander and Greenberg. Victor Urbanowicz ("Personal and Political") also traces the similarities between Le Guin's political thought in *The Dispossessed* and other anarchist thinkers and writers.

15. At this point, it is very much worth repeating Le Guin's explanation of Odonianism and its relationship to the idea of the State, from her preface to the short story "The Day Before the Revolution," in *The Wind's Twelve Quarters*, 285. She states:

> Odonianism is anarchism. Not the bomb-in-the-pocket stuff, which is terrorism, whatever name it tries to dignify itself with; not the social-Darwinist economic "libertarianism" of the far right; but anarchism, as prefigured in early Taoist thought, and expounded by Shelley and Kropotkin, Goldman and Goodman. Anarchism's principal target is the authoritarian State (capitalist or socialist); its principal moral-political theme is cooperation (solidarity, mutual aid). It is the most idealistic, and to me the most interesting, of all political theories.

See also Smith, "Unbuilding Walls," 77.

16. Samuel R. Delany reacts against *The Dispossessed*, as an artifact of science fiction, in his study "To Read *The Dispossessed*," in *The Jewel-Hinged Jaw: Notes on the Language of Science Fiction* (New York: Dragon Press, 1977). Arguing that the book fails to live up to its ambitious intentions, he also remarks that "The science fiction novel—*The Dispossessed*— is a structure of words; any discourse it raises is raised by its words" (304). The book might also accurately be considered a novel of ideas.

17. Bierman, "Ambiguity," 251.

18. Tifft and Sullivan, "Possessed Sociology," 185.
19. See Suzanne Elizabeth Reid, *Presenting Ursula K. Le Guin* (New York: Twayne Publishers, 1997), 62, who comments that the wall "is more a mental barrier than a physical obstacle."
20. Elizabeth Cummins Cogell, "Taoist Configurations: *The Dispossessed*," in *Ursula K. Le Guin*, ed. Joe De Bolt, 178.
21. Tifft and Sullivan, "Possessed Sociology," 184.
22. Smith, "Unbuilding Walls," 96.
23. Cogell, "Taoist Configurations," 174–75.

WORKS CITED

Bierman, Judah. "Ambiguity in Utopia: *The Dispossessed*." *Science-Fiction Studies* 2, no. 3 (Nov. 1975): 249–55.
Brennan, John P., and Michael C. Downs. "Anarchism and Utopian Tradition in *The Dispossessed*." Pp. 97–115 in *Ursula K. Le Guin*, ed. Joseph D. Olander and Martin Harry Greenberg. New York: Taplinger, 1979.
Cogell, Elizabeth Cummins. "Taoist Configurations: *The Dispossessed*." Pp. 153–79 in *Ursula K. Le Guin: Voyager to Inner Lands and to Outer Space*, ed. Joe De Bolt. Port Washington, NY: Kennikat, 1979.
Delany, Samuel R. "To Read *The Dispossessed*." Pp. 239–308 in *The Jewel-Hinged Jaw: Notes on the Language of Science Fiction*. Elizabethtown, NY: Dragon Press, 1977.
Hardesty, William H., III. "Mapping the Future: Extrapolation in Utopian/Dystopian and Science Fiction," *Utopian Studies I* (1987): 160–72.
Jameson, Fredric. "World Reduction in Le Guin: The Emergence of Utopian Narrative." Pp. 57–70 in *Ursula K. Le Guin*, ed. Harold Bloom. New York: Chelsea House, 1986.
Kumar, Krishan. *Utopia and Anti-Utopia in Modern Times*. Oxford, UK: Basil Blackwell, 1987.
Le Guin, Ursula K. "The Day Before the Revolution." Pp. 286–303 in *The Wind's Twelve Quarters*. New York: Harper & Row, 1975.
———. *The Dispossessed: An Ambiguous Utopia*. New York: Eos, HarperCollins, 2001 (1974).
———. "The Ones Who Walk Away from Omelas." Pp. 275–84 in *The Wind's Twelve Quarters*. New York: Harper & Row, 1975.
———. *The Wind's Twelve Quarters*. New York: Harper & Row, 1975.
McGuirk, Carol. "Optimism and the Limits of Subversion in *The Dispossessed* and *The Left Hand of Darkness*." Pp. 243–58 in *Ursula K. Le Guin*, ed. Harold Bloom. New York: Chelsea House, 1986.
Reid, Suzanne Elizabeth. *Presenting Ursula K. Le Guin*. New York: Twayne Publishers, 1997.
Rochelle, Warren G. *Communities of the Heart: The Rhetoric of Myth in the Fiction of Ursula K. Le Guin*. Liverpool, UK: Liverpool University Press, 2001.
Smith, Philip E., II. "Unbuilding Walls: Human Nature and the Nature of Evolutionary and Political Theory in *The Dispossessed*." Pp. 77–96 in *Ursula K. Le Guin*, ed. Joseph D. Olander and Martin Harry Greenberg. New York: Taplinger, 1979.

Somay, Bülent. "Towards an Open-Ended Utopia." *Science-Fiction Studies* 11, no. 1 (March 1984): 25–38.

Tifft, Larry L., and Dennis C. Sullivan. "Possessed Sociology and Le Guin's *Dispossessed.*" Pp. 180–97 in *Ursula K. Le Guin: Voyager to Inner Lands and to Outer Space*, ed. Joe De Bolt. Port Washington, NY: Kennikat, 1979.

Urbanowicz, Victor. "Personal and Political in *The Dispossessed.*" *Science-Fiction Studies* 5, no. 2 (July 1978): 110–17.

Williams, Lynn F. "The Machine at Utopia's Center." *Utopian Studies III* (1991): 66–71.

IV

TEMPORAL POLITICS

9

Time and the Measure
of the Political Animal

Ellen M. Rigsby

$\mathscr{I}$s there a politics of time? And if one were to answer yes to that question, how is such a politics to be defined? Politics is often defined in terms of stable or unchanging concepts: as the regulation of institutionalized power or even as an ideology that structures thought and action. Politics, at least as it is studied in the social sciences, concerns stability: the institutions that allow government to function. But a politics structured on the human experience of time would have to entail fluidity at its core, which would make problematic the concepts that scholars have used to systematize politics for analysis. Even the often-quoted von Clausewitz statement "War is politics by other means" implies that there is a stable and continuous contest for power, in which individual states' power ebbs and flows.[1] Ursula K. Le Guin's *The Dispossessed* depicts just such a politics: a politics based on the human experience of being born into time. By reading the text of *The Dispossessed* through the lens of Hannah Arendt's writings on time, one can articulate a political theory based on human experience of time that entails radical freedom to act. Arendt maintains that humans are born into time, which is both linear and cyclical. Humans experience living, eating, sleeping, etc., in cyclical time, while in linear time they can form ethical decisions by looking into a future and remembering a past. The politics of time is dependent, though, on an active decision to enter into linear time as well as an active understanding that decisions can be interrupted by circumstance. This conception of time brings the capacity for will (and thus the freedom to act) to the center of politics, and defines free action in terms of the will. This chapter undertakes a close reading of Le Guin's protagonist Shevek's understanding of the relationship of time to ethics to articulate the politics of time sketched above. Before examining Le Guin's temporal politics from the text, this chapter will examine some relevant scholarship on *The Dispossessed* in order to counter the lack of complexity about politics and time displayed by that scholarship.

Usual ways of approaching politics would be to examine values or interests or institutions in an organized society.[2] Temporal politics cannot be articulated in this way, though other aspects of politics represented in *The Dispossessed* can be. For example, Werner Christie Mathisen looks for approaches that will speak to current political institutions. He writes:

> As a political scientist, it is easy to feel disappointed after reading [*The Dispossessed*. It] should have told us much more about the political system of the utopian societies! But the fact that we do not get much information about the political system . . . in question, at least not the formal and institutional aspects of them, is interesting in itself.[3]

The interest (and usefulness) of *The Dispossessed* for Mathisen lies in two places. On the one hand, Le Guin's strong criticism of the institutions of politics as a set of inequalities serves as a criticism of contemporary political institutions. On the other hand, he concludes that the worlds of Anarres and Urras are perceived ambivalently by Le Guin's protagonist, and thus warns against thinking too narrowly.[4] The criticisms that Mathisen points out can be confirmed in the text, but by emphasizing them, he neglects the opportunity to articulate any of the positive representations of politics that are implicit and explicit in the text. There are, contrary to Mathisen's thesis, several examples in Le Guin's text of regular decision making by Anarresti, particularly in the area of economic planning: the committees about the production and distribution of goods and labor (the PDC and Divlab). For local and less regular needs, syndicate meetings organized by any group plan and carry out projects that arise out of their need to be completed (3: 75–76). On the other hand, it does not follow that one must abstain from talk about politics because one is trying to describe a way of governing in which the state has been abolished. Nor does it follow that a system must be wrung from the text for it to describe a politics.

A careful analysis of the relationship of time to ethics is necessary to clearly articulate the Arendtian politics inherent in *The Dispossessed*. This approach has been used before by James Bittner to analyze Le Guin's temporality in a partial way, and the portion of his book on *The Dispossessed* will be discussed in the conclusion.[5] Nonetheless, simply interpreting the text brings its own problems. For example, James Bittner and Jim Jose both assume that Le Guin's understanding of time is limited in the same ways that they claim her narrative is limited. Both ignore the complex theory of time developed in the text, and fail to see how it escapes the criticisms they make of *The Dispossessed*'s narrative perspective and of its utopian structure. Unless one looks at time already from an Arendtian perspective, or is willing to consider the theory of time that Shevek articulates in the interpretation one offers, then the interpretation will miss the subtleties of the text's depiction of time. Naively, time is something that unfolds in narrative. Jim Jose, in doing a needed criticism of the limitations of the singular narrative voice in the text of *The Dispossessed*, misses the fact that the theory of time espoused by Shevek does not suffer from the same limitations as does the voice. Briefly, Jose is concerned that in *The Dispossessed* the narrative is told in third person through the eyes of Shevek. The first chapter depicts his journey to Urras, the last the journey back to Anarres, and the intervening chapters tell the chronology of Shevek's life up to the decision to go to Urras in the even chapters and the experience of his trip to Urras in the odd chapters. The narrative structure of *The Dispossessed* considers the importance of the past's relationship to the future, and vice versa, and Jose presumes that Le Guin wanted this structure to reproduce Shevek's temporal theory. However, when one looks at the narrative, one is limited to Shevek's perspective and his life. The way the narrative is put together creates a kind of directive to the reader: Shevek is made equivalent to the universal omniscient narrator by the focus on his life story, so while the narrative itself allows for some interesting interpretations of the ways Shevek's later decisions are shaped by earlier events (as well as the ways that themes recur in his life over and over again), it does not reproduce much of the genuine radicalism of Shevek's life or of Anarres: that society can exist in which everyone acts on his or her own initiative. The structure of *The Dispossessed*, as opposed to its content, does not itself produce any serious criticism of the state by using a universal narrator; in fact, at its most fundamental level, it strengthens it, by representing a singular subject who finds the answer that seems to be applicable to everyone.[6]

Jose is concerned that the limitations of the narrative described above prevent Le Guin from fully complicating the classical structure of a utopian novel. While the narrative of *The Dispossessed* avoids the trope of utopia being a foreign land to which a narrator travels, Le Guin nonetheless relates the narrative from one point of view, that of Shevek. Because of this, Jose concludes that Le Guin's narrative structure shores up the idea of the universal (western male) subject.[7] Le Guin herself agrees with Jose. She writes that her narrative in *The Dispossessed* fails to represent any perspective other than Shevek's.[8] Mario Klarer echoes this claim, though she lauds *The Dispossessed* because it "anticipates and evokes in its structure, symbolism and concern with simultaneity the thinking that informs a variety of schools in the late 70s and 80s, such as deconstruction, postmodernism, metafiction, feminist literary theory, and French feminist psychology."[9] In this reading, then, the way the narrative is related prevents *The Dispossessed* from being an entirely anarchist novel because its message is singular and directive. Nonetheless, the theory of time expressed by Shevek is, in fact, not mechanistic or modernist in its conception and for this reason *The Dispossessed* still belongs in the categories from which Klarer and Jose seek to exclude it insofar as one is talking about its conception of time.

Jose not only argues that Le Guin misses the opportunity to represent multiple narrative voices, but more strongly argues that the ansible (the practical application of Shevek's temporal physics) is the annihilation of time, because it allows faster than light speed communication. But he focuses inappropriately here only on linear time that unfolds in narrative. Jose asserts:

> The abyss of time can be abolished. Communication across space can be instantaneous, rendering past, present, and future irrelevant in the act of communication. . . . *The Dispossessed* retains the juxtaposition of mechanical progress and biological rhythm in which the latter remains shut off from the former. Process remains a function of structure rather than the other way around.[10]

Here Jose has reduced all time in the novel to a single linear narrative. From an Arendtian point of view though, the temporal interaction that the ansible allows is quite rich. The ansible actually highlights the interactions between cyclical and linear time by facilitating communication that distinguishes the two. In Jose's reading the ansible destroys past and future by making everyone (at least potentially) present. In his view anyone using the ansible is sharing the same experience in sequence, and thus time has lost its importance, and even its meaning. But from an Arendtian point of view time is not just events in sequence. It allows one to articulate one's relationship to one's past and future, including the recurring themes contained therein. So the ansible provides a way to connect human pasts and their futures to each other. It allows for ethics to be acted upon in any number of multiple narrative trajectories. Jose concludes here that the journey Shevek makes for the sake of completing his theory and its mechanical progress (and the impending reality of the communication device that Shevek's temporal physics will make possible) is not connected with the organic growth of Anarres that Shevek wishes to foster. But in fact the journey Shevek takes reminds his people on Anarres of their own past as revolutionaries. Jose reduces the text of *The Dispossessed* to his criticisms of its singular voice, missing the genuine radicalism of the text's temporality. Interpretations like Jose's make needed criticisms of the text or of previous secondary literature, but they also close off one of the most important ideas in the text: its temporal politics.

The rest of this chapter will be devoted to an analysis of Le Guin's temporal politics as articulated by the evolution of Shevek's conception of time. First it will discuss how Shevek articulates an Arendtian conception of time through his drive to understand the relationship of time to ethics; it will then explicate the limitations of Shevek's attempt to convert those he meets to his theory of time, and the possibility opened when Shevek recognizes these limitations; and finally it will conclude by offering an interpretation of the two central figures in the novel, the wall and the aphorism "true journey is return," in terms of Arendtian temporality.

One of Shevek's earliest formative experiences involves his wrestling with the differences between linear and cyclical time. As a schoolboy, Shevek tries to articulate a paradox he has just conceived to a group of students and the teacher. It is a version of Zeno's paradox, the situation in which the space between two points can be traversed (linear time), and yet is also a distance infinitely divisible by half, and thus unbridgeable if one continually goes half as far as one previously did, never reaching the other side (cyclical time). The teacher chastises him for wasting the group's time with nonsense. He requires him to leave the group, and Shevek begins to consider himself separate from his own community, especially when he chooses to pursue physics (2: 28–31). Shevek's feeling of separation or exile appears again and again in the text, guiding his decisions.

In his adult life, Shevek works out a general theory of time that takes account of the arrow reaching the tree and it never reaching the tree. He connects what he calls sequency with what he calls simultaneity. Sequency explains the event of the arrow reaching the target by connecting shooting the arrow with arriving: linear time in which an action is brought through a beginning to an end. Simultaneity explains the event of the arrow never reaching the target: cyclical time in which an action perpetuates itself infinitely. Such a theory of time grounds particular understandings of ethics and history as well. One can begin to see the connection to ethics in Shevek's explanation of the connection he and his partner maintain over a four-year separation brought about by the necessity to fight a drought.

> Fulfillment, Shevek thought, is a function of time. The search for pleasure is circular, repetitive, atemporal. . . . It comes to the end and has to start over. It is not a journey and return, but a closed cycle, a locked room, a cell.
>
> Outside the locked room is the landscape of time, in which the spirit may, with luck and courage, construct the fragile, makeshift, improbable roads and cities of fidelity: a landscape inhabitable by human beings.
>
> It is not until an act occurs within the landscape of the past and the future that it is a human act. Loyalty, which asserts the continuity of past and future, binding time into a whole, is the root of human strength; there is no good to be done without it. (10: 335)

In the quotation above, Shevek has enunciated a central Arendtian notion of time: that is, that willful human acts create linear time out of cyclical time. Instead of conceiving of a partnership as the means to achieve pleasure that always slips away and must be sought again, a partnership is a result of loyalty enduring over time. One can see the connection to Arendt here. She writes:

> Man is put into a world of change and movement as a new beginning because he knows that he has a beginning and an end; he even knows that his beginning is the beginning of the end. . . . In this sense, no animal, no species being, has a beginning or an end. With man, created in God's own image, a being came into the world that, because it was a beginning running toward an end, could be endowed with the capacity of willing and nilling.[11]

Will, the capacity to act by design, creates the possibility for a new beginning through the duration of action—ethics in both Le Guin's and Arendt's account.

Furthermore, Arendt's explication of time and human will in Augustine's *The City of God* elucidates what Shevek describes when he links time and human action by explaining the relevance of beginnings—the first step in a linear trajectory of time.

Arendt asserts that Augustine is the first philosopher to articulate how human ontology is fundamentally temporal. She argues that in *The City of God* Augustine states that time and man were created together, and she reads this to mean that man was created to make possible a beginning in linear time. "The very capacity for beginning is rooted in *natality*, and by no means in creativity, not in a gift but in the fact that human beings, new men, again and again appear in the world by virtue of birth."[12] Humans make new beginnings because they are born—they create linear time and the possibility of ethics out of cyclical time. Birth itself is cyclical, but each human life can be a ground for acting in linear time. Arendt concludes that this sounds like we are "doomed to be free by virtue of being born . . . no matter whether we like freedom or abhor its arbitrariness, are 'pleased' with it or prefer some form of fatalism."[13]

Freedom (the freedom to act) on this account is a human birthright, but it entails nothing other than a recognition that cyclical time may interfere with planned arcs of linear time. Of course, without the possibility to choose otherwise, individual initiative to act has no meaning. The short quotation above articulates the beginnings of a political theory that springs out of the freedom to act. Arendt secularizes Augustine's conception of free will to point out that human *natality*, the having-been-born-into-time that humans have by virtue of their being, creates the possibility of freely acting, that is, of acting ethically. While cyclical time has both the sense of repetition and innovation, it expresses the periodic repetitions or patterns human beings experience in their lives that may interfere with initiative through fate, happenstance, and so on. Nonetheless it also expresses the possibility of new beginning.

It is necessary to distinguish between patterns of behavior or repetition and genuine innovation for both Arendt and Le Guin. In *The Dispossessed*, Shevek tries to reunite Urras and Anarres to change the trajectories of their history. He worries that, because Urras is the Anarresti past and Anarres is a potential future of Urras (and for that matter, of anywhere else in the known universe), their continuing disavowal of each other will stagnate both societies in determinism. A history without possibility of return to a past golden age (or a past dark age for that matter) is stuck in linear narrative that Arendt would call determinism. This kind of determinism has no sense of cyclical time. It entails either a notion of entropy, in which the universe winds down to its end, or a notion of millennialism, in which one waits for the golden age to arrive.

> In its original integrity, freedom survived in political theory—i.e., theory conceived for the purpose of political action—only in utopian and unfounded promises of a final "realm of freedom" that, in its Marxian version at any rate, would indeed spell "the end of things," a sempiternal [sic] peace in which all specifically human activities would wither away.[14]

Thus a concept of linear time without cycles is ultimately determinism. The capacity to begin new cycles produces variation or contingency, which can be a threat to action. For the most part, the intellectual history of Europe demonstrates that its thinkers chose determinism over radical freedom by ignoring cyclical time as a means of avoiding contingency.[15]

If the intellectual history of Europe manifests the decision to give up freedom for determinism, Le Guin observes that Shevek chooses initiative. In the explication of this initiative, Shevek's thoughts move into an explicitly anarchist form. Arendt's radical republicanism remains almost identical to Shevek's understanding of the primary role of ability to act freely, but she grounds acting on one's own initiative in the distinction between the public and private sphere. Shevek's anarchism grounds it in the distinction between sacrifice and compromise.

> A healthy society would let him exercise that optimum function freely, in the coordination of all such functions finding its adaptability and strength. That was a central idea of Odo's *Analogy*. That the Odonian society on Anarres had fallen short of the ideal did not, in his eyes, lessen his responsibility to it; just the contrary. With the myth of the State out of the way, the real mutuality and reciprocity of society and individual became clear. Sacrifice might be demanded of the individual, but never compromise: for though only the society could give security and stability, only the individual, the person, had the power of moral choice—the power of change, the essential function of life. (10: 333)

It is useful here to substitute the terms of contingency for sacrifice and compulsion for compromise to understand this quotation. A society may demand sacrifice of the individual and similarly a moment of contingency may be unavoidable. Things get in the way of the best laid plans. But a society that compels individual action based on the optimal functioning of society is, in Le Guin's organic terms, unhealthy. To ask Shevek to do an emergency posting (even one as long as four years) is acceptable, but for Sabul to tell Shevek that his branch of physics is worthless is not. Contingency might interfere with a person wanting to do something appropriately, but a society asking someone to limit personal initiative permanently or a society that occludes it altogether, fails to promote the freedom to act, which is the highest ideal in Le Guin's and Arendt's temporal politics. The distinction here is the distinction made in Zeno's paradox between linear time and circular time. Society can interrupt personal action to tend to itself, as the source of security and stability. At this level it engenders contingency. But to deny someone freedom to act is to deny personhood and to create determinism at the level of government. The individual freedom to act on one's own initiative constitutes humanity. Thus it is society's role to foster human freedom because only beings born into time can initiate ethical acts. (Obviously they can do otherwise as well—the point here is not that beings will act ethically, but that healthy society fosters human initiative.) Another way of understanding this is to think of it in terms of the intellectual history of the west. Arendt outlines the evolution of Europe's conception of time and freedom to act, and articulates one exception in Augustine. Le Guin, dissatisfied with that evolution, creates a character who lives by Arendt's alternative conception of time that grounds the radical freedom to act.

Despite Shevek's satisfaction with his radical conception of temporality and ethics and his conviction that it is true, for most of the succeeding narrative he lives with a fundamental misapprehension that he can rationally convince the Urrasti of the truth of his ethics. He confuses living his ethics with understanding it. Throughout much of Shevek's journey to Urras he tries to convince the Urrasti there that his theory of time and ethics is the correct one. And yet it turns out that he can only teach his ethics by giving up the attempt to do so.

The following anecdote describes the height of Shevek's error before he realizes his confusion. At a party late in his stay on Urras, Shevek inadvertently articulates the ethical issues inherent in his understanding of the dual nature of time. He and a young man are discussing the implications of Shevek's theory of temporal physics, and the man asks Shevek if the practical applications of temporal physics were not actually in ethics. Shevek responds affirmatively:

> But it's true, chronosophy does involve ethics. Because our sense of time involves our ability to separate cause and effect, means and end. The baby, again, the animal, they don't see the difference between what they do now and what will happen because of it. They can't make a pulley, or a promise. We can. Seeing the difference between *now* and *not now*, we can make the connection. And there morality enters in. Responsibility. To say that a good end will follow from a bad means is just like saying that if I pull a rope on this pulley it will life the weight on that one. To break a promise is to deny the reality of the past; therefore it is to deny the hope of a real future. If time and reason are functions of each other, if we are creatures of time, then we had better know it, and try to make the best of it. To act responsibly. (7: 225)

Shevek still talks about ethics above as if it were self-evident. If ethics were really as simple as seeing that the pulley upon which one is pulling does not actually pull up the weight of the rope next to it, no one would act unethically. But that is not the mechanism by which ethics works. It does not function by mechanical or mathematical principles; there is no formula to apply. Ethics is merely a sustained action in time, or perhaps a series of such actions. One cannot step into the linear time of the pulley to act ethically, and in the same way describing ethics is not communicating it. Shevek is still trying to bring his temporal theory and the ethics it entails to Urras through argument. Later in the conversation he responded to another remark that the "solution" to Urras is Anarres (7: 227), once again, as if it were simply self-evident. At some level, Shevek wants to advertise for Anarres to Urras, yet Shevek's notable criticism of Machiavellian ethics (that the end justifies the means) is still empty for anyone in the conversation because no one in the room is open to anarchist temporal ethics. Right now there is nothing more than Shevek's admonition "to make the best of it." Communication does not imply persuasion.

By the morning after the party he attended, Shevek recognizes his error that he could simply convince the Urrasti to accept his ethics. In that recognition, Shevek can choose fatalism, in which he would retreat from the rest of the world to his home, or he can choose to continue his initiative to unbuild walls and share his temporal theory where he can. In fact Le Guin remarks in an interview that fatalism allows many in the west to choose determinism over radical free action.[16] The final part of this section of the chapter will discuss how Le Guin highlights fatalism by having the ambassador from earth embody it.

Shevek escapes to the Terran embassy, and asks Earth's help to return home from Urras. He offers the ambassador his temporal theory if she will broadcast it to all the worlds. The Terran ambassador, Keng, asks him what his theory will do and begins to anticipate the instantaneous speech that Shevek's temporal theory will enable as he describes it to her. Shevek can only ask her, "And what will you say?" (11: 344). The bitterness of Shevek's question arises out of his failure to communicate with even close scientific colleagues on Urras, never mind the audiences of the upper classes he spoke to when he first arrived, but his bitterness does not turn to fatalism: he gives Keng the equations to make the ansible, thereby offering people the chance to speak to each other.

Arendt's concept of fatalism, the result of a desire to deny the freedom that natality creates, ossifies into ideology in some, such as Keng. Despite Keng's optimism about the ansible, she does not believe that Anarres is a real possibility. She listened to the speech Shevek gave to the strikers, but did not understand him: "I heard you speak of Anarres, in the Square, and I wept listening to you, but I didn't really believe you" (11: 346). Keng is prevented from understanding what Shevek offers by her own assumptions, her own ideology. Shevek says to her:

> You don't understand what time is. . . . You say the past is gone, the future is not real, there is no change, no hope. . . . And least of all can you have the present, unless you accept with it the past and the future. Not only the past but also the future, not only the future but also the past! Because they are real. . . . You will not achieve or even understand Urras unless you accept the reality, the enduring reality, of Anarres. (11: 349)

Keng's experience has tricked her into thinking that because her past was so difficult, nothing can ever change. This is precisely Arendt's conception of being trapped in cyclical time. Keng's ideology of fatalism convinces her that her past has destroyed her future. Fatalism protects her from having to acknowledge that she has chosen fatalism because hope is too painful. To recall Arendt's quotation above, the western intellectual tradition often prefers fatalism to the idea that there is freedom to act; fatalism allows human beings to reassert archism and to avoid the radical freedom to act that is inherent in a dual concept of time. It is the same fatalism seen in Anarres when Sabul, a more senior physicist, uses guilt to try to force Shevek into admitting that his physics is irrelevant. He confronts

Shevek by claiming that his work isn't useful. "It doesn't get bread into people's mouths . . ." (8: 265). Sabul perverts the principle of mutual aid into determinism about what kind of physics is worthwhile (only survival-based occupations should be done), another kind of fatalistic ideology that the good of the whole outweighs the freedom of an individual to act.

At its worst, then, Anarres functions archistically as Urras does, or as Keng's reasoning does. While they are looking at a fur cloak of an ancient tyrant queen, Shevek has a conversation with the Urrasti Vea in which he argues that the Anarresti have left behind the barbarity associated with such a regime. Vea counters that if one doesn't have a tyrant to rebel against, then one cannot rebel against the internalized tyrant in one's head (7: 219–20). Vea speaks accurately when implying that the social conscience (Le Guin's terminology) on Anarres is capable of being perverted to tyranny. Conceiving time only in its linear form (as Arendt argues the west chose to do) or its cyclical form (as Le Guin's Keng chose to do) leaves one in determinism. Both concepts of time are in fact necessary for grounding the possibility for acting on one's own initiative.

The third and final part of this chapter will reconsider the two of the most mysterious figures in the text from an Arendtian perspective. Almost every textual analysis of *The Dispossessed* mentions the metaphor of the wall and the aphorism "true journey is return." It is beyond the scope of this chapter to interpret the image of the wall thoroughly, but the symbolism has an important relationship to the explication of Arendtian time. In its relevance to time, the metaphor of the wall expresses one way in which Shevek is caught up in cyclical time. The first sentence of the novel, "There was a wall," refers most directly to the physical barriers between Urras and Anarres, though such a fundamental metaphor cannot help but slip into other significations. To unbuild walls is literally to dismantle the apparatus of the state—that is what stands between Urras and Anarres most fundamentally. Nonetheless, images of the wall have haunted Shevek since his earliest memory (2: 33–34). In the quotation below, it is the image of the wall that drives him to Urras, and drives him to try to give his temporal ethics to Urras. Shevek voices his desire to go to Urras to his partner Takver in terms of ethics: "I am going to fulfill my proper function in the social organism. I'm going to go unbuild walls" (10: 332). But the charge of the wall as an image compels him to attempt a conversion of Urras that he cannot humanly do. Through most of the novel he remains stuck in his perceived necessity to unbuild walls. He mistakenly thinks that his inability to do his work on Anarres is related to his ability to offer his temporal ethics to Urras. His mistake is that in knowing that he needs Urras to finish his theory, he presumes that Urras needs his temporal ethics. When he recognizes his failure to teach the Urrasti his ethics, he can then think about trying to return from his journey.

Le Guin peppers her text with the aphorism "true journey is return." Grappling with this aphorism, James Bittner generalizes Le Guin's conception of utopia:

In order for a landscape to be inhabitable by human beings, it not only must permit, but also should encourage *human* acts, that is to say ethical acts, and those occur only in the present . . . not on Urras where the future is denied, nor on Anarres, where the past is denied, but in the process of a journey from one to the other and back again.[17]

Bittner equates Urras's denial of the future with Anarres's denial of the past, concluding that true journey is return for Le Guin, and so Shevek's position is the only functional one in the text (this mistake is similar to Jose's above). But Bittner forgets that Shevek's journey is successful regarding Anarres. One can see a potential affinity with Arendt's emphasis on acting freely in time in his analysis, but Bittner's interpretation is limited because it is posed in the idiom of Le Guin's fiction, in that he literally looks for what the journey is, and who returns, and leaves the aphorism there.[18] He focuses too much on Shevek. Rather than finish Shevek's narrative, Le Guin shifts to begin the story of Ketho. This change exemplifies the meaning of "true journey is return" from an Arendtian point of view.

On the surface Shevek returns to Anarres to find its citizens more willing to act on their own initiative. But upon taking a more careful look into the text one can see that there is something new in this return. Shevek's return is left out of the narrative, and instead the reader learns about an alien who wants to land with Shevek. Above, Arendt is quoted as writing that human natality presents the possibility of new beginnings. But beginnings mean nothing until they have sustained themselves in linear time. Rather than ending with the story of Shevek's homecoming, the narrative tells the beginning of Ketho's story, an alien pilot, who wants to travel to Anarres with Shevek to live there. By asking Shevek to let him land and live with the Anarresti he takes the first step toward understanding the society of Anarres. By acting out of his own initiative, Ketho begins something new, but does not know where it will lead. In the same way, Shevek did not know what the meaning or purpose of his journey would end up being until he returned home. The journey can only be understood when it is finished. Shevek thought that he could give the gift of his formula to Urras as a way of beginning to bridge the gap between the two worlds. What actually happened, the opening of his society, is quite different from his original idea. When Ketho requests to go to Anarres with Shevek, Shevek responds "maybe I can give you something in return [for being taken home]. An idea, a promise, a risk" (13: 386–87). What Shevek gives is a possible future. Until the future is followed through the present to its fruition, its effects are unknown. The application to time of the aphorism "true journey is return" is through its placement, into linear time, of cause and effect, or more aptly "effect/cause/effect" (6: 183). The aphorism is a statement that acting requires completion in order to render the act intelligible. Only when an act is understood can it be acted upon further. Without that understanding, the act remains stuck in cyclical time. In terms of the temporal politics of the text, past and future are brought together to create action in the present. In order to understand that action, though, another measure of time must pass to see what effects the action produces. Insofar as a journey is an act, the return from the journey gives the act meaning and makes it understandable.

Of course, Le Guin's text is explicitly about utopia, not about time. Le Guin's readers must actively seek for themselves to understand the utopian possibility of Anarres. The temporal politics implied in the text only go as far as suggesting that because Ketho has taken the first step, he now has access to a new future (13: 386). A possible future perhaps seems like a small reward for risking one's life; however, the realm of radical freedom made possible by the conception of time as linear and also cyclical makes no promises about outcomes. There is no stability at all in such a decision to act. Arendt writes at the end of *Life of the Mind* that it has been a device of western thought that the new is understood as the old: that revolutions are often thought of as renovations.[19] In *On Revolution*, she argues that founding something new requires a linear intervention into the cycle of political circumstance. And so one only knows that one has done something new retrospectively after it has sustained itself, or failed to do so. She makes no guarantees that any particular action will come out of the public sphere, merely that beings can act on their own initiative there.[20] Le Guin's ending, then, makes the point that in order to learn about Anarres, one has to seek it out. The character Ketho does this, initiating an act out of the wake of Shevek's decision to finish his temporal theory. Ketho measures out a new path of linear time by going to Anarres.

The temporal politics articulated in *The Dispossessed* cannot be understood within the conventions and methodologies of political science; nonetheless this politics does offer a theory of action and a concrete ethics that holds out an ideal way of relating individuals to their communities. While this politics may be conceived of as a function of time in a definitional sense, it cannot be represented stably in a system. The scale of temporal politics, or more precisely, its measure, exists within the bounds of natality—of being born into time. In Arendt's and Le Guin's understanding, without the measure that natals have, acting is forced into one of two determinisms: that of linear time preordained to occur in a set way, or that of cyclical time, in which nothing is new under the sun. The politics of time of *The Dispossessed* demonstrates that taking up both conceptions of time at once grounds the radicalism of acting on one's own initiative. It opens the possibility of begetting something new.

NOTES

1. Carl von Clausewitz, *On War*, trans. Michael Howard and Peter Paret (Princeton, NJ: Princeton University Press, 1989), 1.

2. Le Guin uses the term society in her text to refer to the organized community that cultures in the text have, and while this is not a neutral term for Arendt, this chapter will

follow Le Guin's usage rather than Arendt's. To expound and consider that difference is an important and useful project, but outside the scope of this paper. Ursula K. Le Guin, *The Dispossessed: An Ambiguous Utopia* (New York: Harper & Row, 1974), cited in the text by chapter and page to the 387-page Eos HarperCollins edition of 2001.

3. Werner Christie Mathisen, "The Underestimation of Politics in Green Utopias: The Description of Politics in Huxley's *Island*, Le Guin's *The Dispossessed*, and Callenbach's *Ecotopia*," *Utopian Studies* 25, no. 1 (2001): 59.

4. Mathisen, "Underestimation," 71.

5. James W. Bittner, *Approaches to the Fiction of Ursula K. Le Guin*. Ann Arbor, MI: UMI Research Press, 1984.

6. Jim Jose has done an interesting example of this analysis in his "Reflections on the Politics of Le Guin's Narrative Shifts," *Science-Fiction Studies* 18, no. 2 (July 1991).

7. Jose, "Reflections," 189. He refers here to Robert Elliott's *The Shape of Utopia* (Chicago: University of Chicago Press, 1970) to make the argument about utopian structure.

8. Ursula K. Le Guin, *Dancing at the End of the World: Thoughts on Words, Women, Places* (New York: Grove, 1989), 90.

9. Mario Klarer, "Gender and the 'Simultaneity Principle': Ursula Le Guin's *The Dispossessed*," *Mosaic* 25, no. 2 (Spring 1992): 120.

10. Jose "Reflections," 189. It is worth noting, though, that Le Guin also remarks in an interview that cyclical time is not the preferred mode of temporal thought in the western mind, and thus her mode of narrative is not simply an affirmation of the Universal (western male) subject ("Point of No Return," *Parabola* 23, no. 1 [Spring 1998]: 25). No hegemony is ever quite as hegemonic as its advocates or detractors would like to believe.

11. Hannah Arendt, *Life of the Mind: Willing* (New York: Harcourt Brace Jovanovich, 1978), 109.

12. Arendt, *Life of the Mind*, 217. One will find the appropriate passages from Augustine in *The City of God*, book 7, chap. 20.

13. Arendt, *Life of the Mind*, 216.

14. Arendt, *Life of the Mind*, 216. Arendt's analysis of Marxism here is somewhat pallid.

15. Arendt, *Life of the Mind*, 217. The state, in this model, is a form of fatalism to avoid free choice.

16. Le Guin, "Point of No Return," 25.

17. Bittner, *Approaches*, 122.

18. Bittner, *Approaches*, 125.

19. Arendt, *Life of the Mind*, 217.

20. Hannah Arendt, *On Revolution* (New York: Penguin, 1990), 239, and the whole of chap. 4 more generally.

WORKS CITED

Arendt, Hannah. *Life of the Mind: Willing*. New York: Harcourt Brace Jovanovich, 1978.
———. *On Revolution*. New York: Penguin, 1990.
Bittner, James W. *Approaches to the Fiction of Ursula K. Le Guin*. Ann Arbor, MI: UMI Research Press, 1984.

Clausewitz, Carl von. *On War*. Trans. Michael Howard and Peter Paret. Princeton, NJ: Princeton University Press, 1989.

Jose, Jim. "Reflections on the Politics of Le Guin's Narrative Shifts." *Science-Fiction Studies* 18, no. 2 (July 1991): 180–97.

Klarer, Mario. "Gender and the 'Simultaneity Principle': Ursula Le Guin's *The Dispossessed*." *Mosaic* 25, no. 2 (Spring 1992): 107–21.

Le Guin, Ursula K. *Dancing at the End of the World: Thoughts on Words, Women, Places*. New York: Grove, 1989.

———. *The Dispossessed: An Ambiguous Utopia*. New York: Eos, HarperCollins, 2001 (1974).

———. "Point of No Return." *Parabola* 23, no. 1 (Spring 1998): 19–27.

———. *The Wind's Twelve Quarters*. New York: Harper & Row, 1975.

Mathisen, Werner Christie. "The Underestimation of Politics in Green Utopias: The Description of Politics in Huxley's *Island*, Le Guin's *The Dispossessed*, and Callenbach's *Ecotopia*." *Utopian Studies* 25, no. 1 (2001): 56–78.

10

Fulfillment as a Function of Time, or the Ambiguous Process of Utopia

Jennifer Rodgers

In The Dispossessed, Ursula K. Le Guin provides the reader with a working model for utopia as evolution—not a place, but a process of becoming.[1] Process, in this instance, does not imply linear progression; even the structural level of the narrative, which moves from present to past and back again in alternating chapters, emphasizes a cyclical evolutionary movement. At the level of the story, this cyclical growth process is modeled by the character Shevek, whose life takes the form of a series of circular journeys. Some of these involve physical travel—to new places of work or study, to a new world. Some are intellectual journeys, as Shevek, a physicist, works to formulate a series of theories, culminating in a unified theory of time. And others are emotional journeys, as Le Guin's protagonist comes to new understandings of brotherhood, love, and personal fulfillment. Each cycle of outward voyage is completed by a return, each return affirming Shevek's conviction that "You *can* go home again . . . so long as you understand that home is a place where you have never been" (2: 55).[2] In Shevek, Le Guin unites the intensely personal journey toward fulfillment with the community journey toward utopia, uniting the two through an understanding of time that is linear and cyclical, as well as moral, ethical, and social.

When addressing a narrative that leaps back and forth through time and is constructed of circles within circles, there is a certain challenge in choosing a starting point. Although *The Dispossessed* centers around Shevek, the reader must understand the context to understand the individual. The physical form of the book underscores this point: the pages immediately preceding the novel's first chapter are occupied by maps. The novel is set on Urras and Anarres, a planet and its moon, in a solar system that Terran (Earth) scientists call Tau Ceti. These two planetary bodies are tied together as much by forces of history as by gravitational pull, and over the course of the novel the reader comes to understand that Shevek's individual journey out (away from home and to a foreign planet) is part of a homeward journey for his society (toward claiming the past, in the interest of continuing to build a future).

Shevek comes from an anarchic society based on Anarres, the moon. Nearly 170 years before the events of the novel's first chapter, Anarres was settled by a group of revolutionaries who agreed to an exile that would allow their homeworld to preserve its existing social structures. In Shevek's time, Anarresti society strives toward utopia as long as it includes a will to change and challenge; without that constant evolution, the society is diminished by a tendency toward stagnation and a harsh natural environment. Although the unforgiving climate and the resultant shortages of food and other resources have created a situation which rewards orthodoxy and resists change, a societal ideal nonetheless enjoins individuals to guard against "the way it's always been done" or "the way it has to be." Custom exists, and Shevek and his allies see an ever-present danger that ideals will become reified into laws, but Anarresti society places a heavy emphasis on individual initiative and responsibility, which has the potential to counteract these tendencies toward hierarchy.

Although Shevek intends for his journey to Urras to reunite his society with its past, Urras and Anarres appear in binary opposition throughout most of the narrative. Whatever their nationality, most Urrasti appear to share a belief in the immutability of tradition, the inevitability of social stratification, the inviolability of barriers between the sexes, and the need for a hierarchy of classes and nations. Those with whom Shevek speaks frame difference in terms of an evolutionary struggle for dominance, defining evolution as individual survival of the fittest, rather than cooperative survival of the community. The oldest and most respected Urrasti scientist in the novel, Atro, tells Shevek that "The law of existence is struggle—competition—elimination of the weak—a ruthless war for survival" (5: 143). Shevek, the only person in the novel who has first-hand experience of both worlds, steadfastly asserts, and manifests, the opposite value: mutual aid.[3] Although he admires the lush and bountiful natural landscape of Urras, he is horrified by the carefree materialism of A-Io, where the wealthy disregard the poor and thoughtlessly support "mass conscriptions" (9: 286) to staff a war whose sole purpose seems to be posturing. Shevek sees this, as well as the adamant exclusion of women from public and intellectual life, as a sign of death and decay. To him, the outwardly beautiful world is stagnant and hollow.

This contrast between the infinite potential nurtured by the harsh environment of Anarres and the corroding decadence at the heart of beautiful Urras is brought into relief by a third planet, which further contextualizes Shevek's experience and expands the cycle of journey and return. At many points in the novel, Urrasti and Anarresti characters make passing reference to the existence of other human-inhabited worlds outside of their solar system. One of these is given a particular predominance: Terra, our Earth, invisibly present from the start in the person of the unacknowledged but necessarily present reader. The narrator hints, continually, that Terra has special importance. Terrans coin the term "Cetian" to refer to those things common to Urras and Anarres; the theories of ancient Terran scientist Ainsetain help Shevek make the final breakthrough in his General Temporal Theory. And after a long and confusing journey to and on Urras, Shevek seeks sanctuary from Keng, the Terran ambassador.

Given the far-future frame of the novel in which the fact of interstellar flight is accepted, if not exactly commonplace, Keng's Terra is not precisely our own Earth. Keng's homeworld has been ravaged by war and environmental disaster, and supports only a fraction of the Earth's current population. Her perspective, therefore, compliments that of the reader; together, the representatives of Earth within and outside the text embody an external perspective that completes the careful social, political, historical, and planetary dance that binds Urras and Anarres. To Keng, Urras is "the world that comes as close as any could to Paradise" (11: 347). But Anarres, for all of its desolation, is something so far beyond Paradise that it has become a forfeited chance, so removed from possibility that it has become "nothing" (11: 349). While the reader may be supposed to anticipate possible futures for his or her own society, Keng sees her world as possessing only a past. To Shevek, Keng's view (which, in turn, seems to be a pale reflection of the attitudes of the Hainishmen who did their part to save Terra from destruction) is another trap, parallel to that of the Urrasti, brought on by a misconception of time. To him, life—the voyage toward utopia—is a matter of "working with time, instead of against it" (10: 335); for Keng to deny any possible future for her society is to declare her own death.

This idea of "working with time" provides one key to understanding *The Dispossessed*. In order to show, however, how a world or a species might work with time, the narrative begins with a focus on an individual. That individual, Shevek, receives his first lessons in working with time when he is very young. He first learns to wait. He waits for the mother who doesn't come back and for the father who returns as often as he can between work postings. The narrator tells us that as an eight-year-old, Shevek "asked why and how and what if, but he seldom asked when" (2: 31). Though he accepts time's inevitability, however, young Shevek demonstrates that he takes little else for granted. In a Speaking-and-Listening group with his peers, Shevek shares an idea that he has developed, an idea that readers may recognize as Zeno's paradox. But as he tries to explain why, theoretically speaking, a rock thrown at a tree should be unable to arrive at its destination, Shevek is interrupted by the group director, accused of egoizing and of stealing the idea from a book, and expelled from the group. Trying to keep from crying after being rejected by an adult as a direct result of his intellectual discovery, Shevek comforts himself with "the Square. It was made of numbers, and numbers were always cool and solid; when he was at fault, he could turn to them, for they had no fault" (2: 30).

Here the reader finds the deep roots of one driving impulse of Shevek's life, to give order to his experience through mathematics. At this point, and at other points in Shevek's life when he is isolated from physical and emotional contact with his fellows, mathematics becomes its own end. But even in these times, as when Shevek's father, Palat, shows him the Logarithmic Tables and teaches him to use a slide rule, Shevek's subconscious mind knows that there is something important beyond the numbers. Logarithms and slide rules are fascinating to Shevek, but they also mean time spent in comfort with his father. And in Shevek's dreams, mother and father are invisibly present as he encounters "the primal number, that was both unity and plurality . . . he was home" (2: 33–34). It will take years for Shevek to understand consciously what he has seen in his mystical dream, but this early glimpse gives the reader a background against which to measure the many homecomings that bring the novel's hero from childhood to maturity.

At age twelve, Shevek learns about the uncertainty of human perception of time when he and his friends, driven by curiosity and a spirit of perversity, craft a prison, and turn a volunteer into a prisoner. Haunted by the prisoner, Kadagv, Shevek learns how it feels to be possessed: "Every time he looked into his mind there was Kadagv in it" (2: 39). The power that he has assumed over another person, even as a shared game among friends, makes him feel "something like embarrassment, but worse than that . . . vile" (2: 39), and he terminates the experiment before its end. The Kadagv who emerges from the darkness is sick and covered in filth, visibly damaged by the hours he has spent deprived of agency. Although the other boys are disturbed by the outcome of their game, Shevek and Kadagv assume the most responsibility for their experiment. One acting as oppressor, the other as victim, they have come to a profound understanding of what it means to be possessed: one taking power over another, one relinquishing his own initiative to another's will. After the boys have helped their friend to get clean, Shevek becomes physically ill and vomits. From here forward, this illness appears whenever he faces or finds that he has participated in an action contrary to his ethics. While his experience of possession reveals to Shevek a human face of time, the illness that is the outward manifestation of internal disharmony gradually helps him to recognize a moral aspect of time. Both of these are vital to Shevek's attempt to bring together the apparently opposed Sequence and Simultaneity physics into a General Temporal Theory.

When he is older, Shevek consciously sees his actions reflecting the temporal theory that he studies. Working with other young people on a reforestation project in the plains region known as the Dust, Shevek sees his task as manifesting the principle of "Causative Reversibility," which he sees as a "tacit element of Odonian thought" (2: 46) as well as a theory of physics. Through their actions, the volunteers seek to reverse the natural evolutionary cycle of the planet, returning a barren desert to its former lush, forested state. In spite of his awareness of a greater principle at work, Shevek initially resents "being worked" (2: 49) while his friends back at the Institute work at what they want to do. Only later, first as he is leaving the Dust, and again, once he has had a chance to internalize the experience and get on with his physics, does Shevek start to see a point to his labors beyond the work itself. He recognizes that "to go was not enough for him, only half enough; he must come back" (2: 54). By taking a posting away from his comfort zone, working in miserable conditions, Shevek has broadened his experience and sacrificed for others he will never meet. As a result, he is able to return, finding that the changes within himself have transformed his understanding of the place he left behind, allowing him to find himself home, once more, in a place he has never been (2: 55). This experience of change and homecoming provides the basis for Shevek's first serious foray into physics, laying the groundwork for the eventual development of the theory that will change the way that humans understand time. Although he has yet, at the end of his teenage years, to find the balance between mutual aid and individual pursuit of happiness that will lead him to Urras, he finds the beginning of the social face of his theory, telling his friends that brotherhood "begins in shared pain" (2: 62).

When Shevek initially offers his theory about brotherhood to his friends, some try to argue that love, rather than shared pain, forms the basis for brotherhood. But as Thomas J. Remington explains in his essay "The Other Side of Suffering," pain often precedes love—one can begin with "the bond of fear" and, from the understanding born of shared suffering, create "a more human bond of love."[4] The first time that Shevek, as a young man, goes into the Dust, he believes his fellow workers to be "dull and loutish" (2: 48) and finds his sole pleasure in exchanging letters with friends back home. His attitude begins to change, however, when he is beaten up by a man, Shevet, who uses the excuse of their similar names to release some tension. A short time later, Shevek begins a sexual relationship with a young woman in the camp. In the misery of the situation, in positive ways and negative, Shevek finds that he is connected to others, even able to find companionship and pleasure. He has not yet discovered that "perfection of the human condition"[5] that love may represent, but the brotherhood underlying Anarresti society has become real to him. That experience remains with him even years later, when Shevek travels to Urras. Atro, a physicist whom he greatly admires, tries to justify the idea that there can be a Cetian bond of brotherhood between Urras and Anarres that excludes the Terrans, the Hainish, and other branches of humanity. "What defines brotherhood," Atro asks rhetorically, "but nonbrotherhood?" (5: 142). Having suffered the isolation of a brotherhood based on exclusion while studying physics as a young man, Shevek rejects Atro's idea of brotherhood for something more inclusive. He finds brotherhood on Anarres when he holds the hand of a man dying of severe burns. He finds it on Urras when he stays by the side of a man dying of a gunshot wound. He finds it in the Terran embassy in the fear of a forsaken future. And he finds it on the ship back to Anarres when a Hainishman named Ketho asks to accompany him home, hoping to find, perhaps, something new under the sun.

Shevek first articulates his concept of brotherhood at a farewell party thrown by his friends just before he leaves to study physics in the central Anarresti city of Abbenay. Ironically, while Shevek's time working in the Dust led him to brotherhood, this longed-for opportunity to devote himself to the physics he loves pulls him in the opposite direction. As he walks into Abbenay, Shevek is impressed by the openness and constant interaction of the multitudes of people that he sees. When he takes his place at the Institute, however, he is immediately cast into isolation. His ostensible mentor, Sabul, assigns him a private room—the first in his experience. The separation maintained by the four walls of that room is reinforced when Sabul tells him to study Iotic, one of the main languages of Urras, and to keep his study of the alien language to himself. Repulsed by the secrecy and exclusion, but intrigued by the possibility of an alien physics, Shevek accepts Sabul's conditions and loses all sense of brotherhood and connection to community. After a time, Shevek becomes so interiorized and alienated from everything outside his work that when he finally recognizes that Sabul has co-opted him and his work, he becomes seriously ill.

This illness helps Shevek to realize how far he has journeyed out—this time, into his mind and his work, rather than into the physical word—and prepares him to attempt a journey of return. As he reaches out to his community, it reaches back, and old friends reappear in his life. One of these, Bedap, plays two important roles. He provides Shevek with a friendship that is also a connection to the past—their shared childhood—and forces Shevek to acknowledge that Anarresti society is falling far short of its goals. For a time, Shevek and Bedap become lovers, though they "argued fiercely every time they met" (6: 172), and through Bedap, Shevek meets a number of unconventional individuals, all possessing an "independence of mind" (6: 173) that he admires. Although he is outraged to find that many of these talented people have been denied the opportunity to present their work to a larger audience, Shevek does not yet realize that he will be numbered among those blocked from exercise of his talents by jealousy and a lack of understanding. Still unwilling to admit the degree to which his society is beginning to stifle difference, or to recognize the shared pain that connects him to Bedap's friends, Shevek does take the first steps toward a sense of brotherhood that surpasses disagreement or difference. Bedap also helps to prepare Shevek emotionally to (re)encounter Takver, beginning the love partnership that provides the foundation for his future journeys.

Takver helps to balance Shevek. With her "hot temper" (6: 184), her art, and her love, she encourages in Shevek a stronger connection to his feelings, and to the world around him. As a biologist and a mother, Takver provides Shevek with an emotional connection to natural cycles on a planet where nature is more often an inimical force than a nurturing one. Watching her, Shevek thinks, "There are souls . . . whose umbilicus has never been cut. They never got weaned from the universe" (6: 185). During his later journey out to Urras, when Shevek is faced with the lush bounty of the alien world's natural environment, he finds himself reminded of Takver. After a first brief glimpse of a horse, which stares out of the darkness at a passing car, Shevek tells himself that "Takver would have known how to look back at that eye in the darkness under the trees" (1: 22). Takver possesses a mature human mind, an artistic sensibility, and a practical sense that leads her to value hard work and accept the need for compromise. But her affinity for nature and the lives she studies grounds her, allowing her to help Shevek, in turn, feel that he has put down roots.[6]

While Shevek is a physicist seeking a vast and encompassing understanding of time, Takver has a simpler relationship to time. She tells her partner, "I want to see [life] whole right in the middle of it, here, now. I don't give a hoot for eternity" (6: 190). This desire to live in the present is manifested in the work that Takver has chosen to pursue. Early in the partnership, when she shows Shevek around the laboratory where she works, he is transfixed by the fish, thinking of them as "small, strange lives . . . beings to whom the present is eternal" (6: 186). To Shevek, then, Takver and the animals that she studies come together to represent one facet of time, giving physicist and reader helpful insight into part of the complex equation that Shevek is pursuing.

At various times, Shevek tries to explain his ideas to nonphysicists and finds himself defining time in two ways, as "the arrow of time" and "the circle of time" (7: 223). Over the course of the novel, the reader learns that the circle of time includes, at least in part, *biotemporality* and *eotemporality*. The former is simply biological time, "the temporal reality of living organisms . . . characterized by a [limited] distinction among future, past, and present."[7] Biotemporality includes circadian rhythms, seasonal changes, and tidal variation. More cyclical than linear, this time is dominated by a continuous present, and only lightly bounded by the immediate past and future. In *The Dispossessed*, Takver articulates this view of temporality and helps Shevek to perceive it more clearly.

Shevek needs Takver's help to develop a better grasp of biological time before he can complete his theory, because he is most thoroughly versed in eotemporality, "'the physicist's t' . . . the temporal reality of the astronomical universe of massive matter . . . continuous but nondirected, nonflowing time to which our ideas of a present, future, or past cannot be applied."[8] Understanding eotemporality inspires Shevek to challenge Keng's idea of impossible futures; in the time belonging to physics, at least as physics is understood in our world at present, "all processes are reversible, the appropriate equations permit the exchange of cause and effects."[9] From childhood, Shevek has wanted mathematics and physics to have all of the answers. Early on, he tells himself, "If a book were written all in numbers, it would be true. . . . If you saw the numbers you could see . . . the balance, the pattern. You saw the foundations of the world. And they were solid" (2: 31). The pursuit of mathematical certainty becomes a Grail quest for Shevek, as he ventures into the realm where mathematics intersects with mysticism. When he at last comes to his theory, it appears in the form of a vision: "What he saw was simple, simpler than anything else. It was simplicity: and contained in it all complexity, all promise. It was revelation. It was the way clear, the way home, the light" (9: 280). This instant of enlightenment is sparked by inspiration from the distant past (in the form of Einstein) joined with inspiration from the recent past (from Saeba). The resolution of the equation's *t*, however, can come to Shevek only once he has also acknowledged his connection with the cycles of biological life, affirmed his relationship with ethics and morality, and lived with the human perception of passage.

The other dimension of time, outside or parallel to the circle, is time's arrow. The arrow of time is a human perception, also called noetic time, or *nootemporality*:

> This is the temporal reality of the mature human mind. It is characterized by a clear distinction among future, past, and present; by unlimited horizons of futurity and pastness; and by the mental present, with its changing temporal horizons, depending on attention.[10]

On Urras, Shevek is invited to a party hosted by Vea, a woman of his acquaintance. Dearri, one of the more obnoxious guests at the party, sees noetic time as "the *fact*" (7: 221). Seeking to challenge Shevek and show off his own wit for the benefit of the other guests, Dearri insists that "Simultaneity Theory denies the most obvious fact about time, the fact that time passes" (7: 221). Indeed, this human perception of time in movement helps to impel the drive toward utopia. To plan for the long-term betterment of the human race and its communities, one must have both the ability to contemplate the future and the awareness that present acts shape the future. Shevek, therefore, believes that this perception of time's passage, the aspect of the human mind that lets it contemplate both a distant past and a distant future—or even multiple possible pasts and futures—carries an ethical charge. The potential for awareness of consequences, of cause and effect, brings:

> Responsibility. To say that a good end will follow from a bad means is just like saying that if I pull a rope on this pulley it will lift the weight on that one. To break a promise is to deny the reality of the past; therefore it is to deny the hope of a real future. (7: 225)

In order to complete his equation, Shevek must also reconcile the ethical aspect inherent in the individual perception of time (as he sees it) and the moral facet of the social perception of time.

This social aspect of time, which compliments (and perhaps complicates) noetic time is *sociotemporality*, "the socialization of time and . . . the collective evaluation of time," constantly "in the process of being created."[11] This social aspect of time is a way to invent and reinforce community identity through shared experience. On Anarres, the social aspects of time are, in part, built into the calendar: on every tenth day, those who are able take a shift doing disagreeable work for the good of the community. Dangerous and unpleasant jobs that require a longer term of commitment are divided into half-year periods. Both of these divisions reinforce something both about the nature of the work to be done (unpleasant) and the importance of doing said work (in solidarity). There is a moral judgment implicit in the division of time about facing necessity with togetherness. The value of togetherness in a society that, at least theoretically, places individual judgment above all else is underscored by the communal meals that divide the day and the practice of ending all work and socialization when lights go out in the dorm. But social time is not simply about dividing up the days, the decads, the quarters, and the years; it is also about agreeing upon a history. "History," as J. T. Fraser explains, "is not something fixed to be discovered; it must be created and maintained in the social present."[12] Bedap tells Shevek, outraged, that children "learn to parrot Odo's words as if they were *laws*—the ultimate blasphemy" (6: 168). Earlier, an adolescent Tirin asks his friends how they know that the Urras that exists matches the Urras they are taught about. He recognizes the propaganda in the educational material which teaches young people to "detest Urras, hate Urras, fear Urras" (2: 43). The evolutionary internal process that motivates Shevek to attempt to disrupt the reifying tendency of Anarresti bureaucracy also drives him to shape the social aspect of time. To construct his unifying theory, Shevek must complete his own understanding of morality and social responsibility, and incorporate that understanding into his physics.

After Takver and Shevek recognize their partnership and have their first child, drought and Sabul's jealousy force them into crisis. Sabul blocks Shevek from teaching physics and has him, in essence, dismissed from the university. Shevek tries to stay near his family, but representatives of the Division of Labor can find no available postings in the fisheries where Takver is desperately needed. So he returns to the Dust for four more years of hard labor, far from Takver and the baby. The hardship of this experience changes Shevek enough that when he finally returns to his family and friends, he is nearly ready to journey out to Urras. This is heralded by the narrative as it describes Shevek and Takver's reunion; they are "like planets circling blindly, quietly, in the flood of sunlight, about the common center of gravity, swinging, circling endlessly" (10: 322). Uniting the suffering of separation and deprivation with the joy of the return home, Shevek is finally able to reach the conclusion that lets him form a new relationship with his society:

> If you evade suffering, you also evade the chance of joy. Pleasure you may get, or pleasures, but you will not be fulfilled. You will not know what it is to come home.
> [. . .]
> Fulfillment . . . is a function of time. The search for pleasure is circular, repetitive, atemporal. The variety seeking of the spectator, the thrill hunter, the sexually promiscuous, always ends in the same place. It has an end. It comes to the end and has to start over. It is not a journey and return, but a closed cycle, a locked room, a cell. (10: 334–35)

Pleasure seeking has never been a particular priority in Shevek's life, though his pursuit of physics, recognition, and belonging have included a certain amount of self-absorption. Fulfillment has come to him as a series of surprises: finding Urrasti physicists with whom he can converse and from whom he can learn, finding a life partner, rediscovering friendships that have endured years of separation. After each outward journey in Shevek's life, he returns, finding that by changing, learning, and growing—working with time—he has achieved another level of fulfillment in coming home. Each cycle is a new lesson. Shevek first learns to connect with others and willingly sacrifice for those he calls "brother." After seeing talented individuals, including himself, prevented from sharing their valuable skills in the name of a greater good, he learns to put individual conscience above social conscience. While society's survival may require a great deal from individuals, each individual has the responsibility to uphold "moral choice" (10: 333), refusing to waste human talent to preserve a system antagonistic to his or her ideals. Each journey, with the learning that it entails, has meant suffering. It has also involved emerging from the pain as part of a larger human family, as well as a better physicist. Shevek is fulfilled because he works *toward*—toward discovery, toward homecoming, toward the achievement of a personal vision and a social ideal.

As part of his commitment to fulfillment and working with time, Shevek, along with Takver, Bedap, and other friends, founds a Syndicate of Initiative, intended to counter the bureaucratizing and institutionalizing tendencies that the long drought has helped to reinforce in Anarresti society. Among other achievements, the Syndicate of Initiative begins expanded contact with Urras and publishes Shevek's unabridged work on temporal theory, regardless of how few people are capable of understanding his physics. The Syndicate of Initiative meets with serious and determined resistance, but to Shevek and his fellow syndics, it is necessary for Anarresti survival:

> Revolution is our obligation; our hope of evolution. "The Revolution is in the individual spirit, or it is nowhere. It is for all, or it is nothing. If it is seen as having any end, it will never truly begin." . . . We must go on. We must take the risks. (11: 359)

What began, for Shevek, in a new understanding of brotherhood arising from a shared condition of suffering has been transformed. As Shevek's feeling of connection with his society as a whole has encouraged him to form even closer bonds of friendship and love with those who share his life, those closer connections have in turn given Shevek the strength to turn back to his society. What began as a revolution of personal spirit, nurtured by both suffering and love, is transformed into an impetus toward social (r)evolution.

The formation of the Syndicate of Initiative is a major life achievement for Shevek, and a potential turning point for his society. But in spite of its early successes, it faces continual and mounting opposition, symbolized within the narrative as a wall. The novel opens, in fact, with one image of that wall. Because that image has been addressed at length by other scholars,[13] I will not belabor the point here, except to make note of this: "For seven generations there had been nothing in the world more important than that wall" (1: 1). Those seven generations have served to seal Urras in the past for Anarres. The two planets have so little communication that Anarresti students learning about the History of the Odonian movement have no context for what they learn about Urras. In the novel's second chapter, Tirin, a budding playwright, asks Shevek and a group of friends if they know whether the films and images they're shown are current. His point is that if the images they're shown of the excremental materialism of Urras "are a hundred and fifty years old, things could be entirely different now" (2: 42). Although several boys participate in the debate that Tirin foments, none of them are really able, at this point, to see where the question might lead. The idea that other members of the society might lie, or that there are restrictions—walls—in the society that exist as anything other than an individual will not to cross the line, is too foreign for the others to grasp all at once.

That wall, or better said, societal internalization of the division symbolized by the wall, has severed Anarres from its past and started a decline that threatens to deny its future. In Kingsley Widmer's words, "Seven generations of success have also produced anti[-]intellectual censoring, covert bureaucratization, punitive treatment of dissidence, and pervasive domination of individuals by the social ethic."[14] The refusal to examine—that is, think critically about—the past has led Anarresti society to complacency, so that the community's initial vigilance against centralization and bureaucracy has been lost. The Anarresti feel safe in the belief that the wall is a "barrier *for* survival,"[15] and therefore, most of them don't feel an urgent need toward self-examination. Safety has caused complacency, and complacency is leading to a stagnation that threatens the Odonian (r)evolutionary process. Shevek recognizes the wall as one manifestation of the drive that is turning his society toward what it claims to hate. He sees "this separation [as] a barrier *to* survival, reeking of a despair as desolate as the Anarres landscape."[16] Completing the picture, by allowing itself to be cut off from Anarres, Urras (and by extension the rest of the human universe) has cut itself off from the promise of utopia. Although an anarchic community on a desert moon may not be a universally desired goal, Anarres represents a struggle toward a better, more just, and fuller way of life. Even in the dark times, when its less positive tendencies are in ascension, Anarres can still produce a Shevek, an individual who can venture out, and in returning, carry in his empty hands the possibility of a never-ending process of revolution. In the novel, he leaves behind a regretful conclusion that is also a promise: "We cannot come to you. We can only wait for you to come to us" (11: 350).

Bernard Selinger sees the theory that Shevek pursues as "essentially a wish to stop time," to return to the time of "childhood, dreams, the unconscious, myths, legends, fairytales."[17] I would argue to the contrary that Shevek is heavily invested in time's movement. The Hainish, with their long history, appear to illustrate what happens to those stuck in time's circle. They have "tried everything. Anarchism, with the rest" (13: 385), which has meant a chance to reconnect the scattered strains of humanity and explore the universe. But there is a sense of finality about the sober and meditative Hainish, as though they are the end, seeking back to its beginning. Nonetheless, Shevek and his society have something to offer even to the "civil, considerate, [and] rather somber" (13: 381) Hainish, as one of their people, Ketho, returns to Anarres with Shevek, arguing that whatever his people's experience, *he*, in his living memory, has not tried it. This spark that Anarres represents for humankind will be spread by the invention of the ansible, a device based on Shevek's theory that will permit instantaneous communication between any two points in space. This gives an experiential dimension to the idea of simultaneity. The *now*, here, on Earth, can be matched to a *now* there on Anarres, which can be matched to other *nows*, wherever there are intelligent beings possessing ansibles. This makes possible an entirely new dimension of sociotemporality, the potential to speak of human, rather than Anarresti or Cetian or Terran, society. The past, the present, and the future can come together in continuous movement, whether that take the form of progress or ebb and flow. And movement, "the ever continuous breaking down of barriers, never pausing, but never pressing revolution . . . continuous change, a never-wavering commitment to risk," as Shevek discovers throughout his voyage, means "hope *for* survival."[18]

Early in this chapter, I framed the part of Shevek's individual outward journey that takes him to Urras as a societal homecoming. This societal experience of return is paralleled in the novel by Shevek's first return from the Dust. Delighted to be home, the young man nonetheless finds his former friends "rather callow" (2: 55) and goes his own way, no longer feeling connected to the patterns of the place. Although Shevek does not go to Urras as a representative of his people, he plays that role *de facto*, finding for all of Anarres that although Urras is a lovely and abundant world, it is still less than he had hoped. Urras is still the ancestral home, the place where Odo's revolution began and where her body lies. But while Anarres has toiled, suffered, and discovered the brotherhood born of shared pain, Urras has remained at play. It is not an evil world; the narrative makes clear that there is human kindness, intellectual and artistic achievement, concern for the environment, and all manner of goodness on Urras. Still, most social and governmental bodies on Urras continue to work against time, intent on maintaining the *status quo*. Where Anarres has struggled and must continue to struggle—now with the additional burden of intense internal conflict brought to the fore by the Syndicate of Initiative—it has also made possible the fulfillment of its ideals. In nurturing the potential for individual evolution, even imperfectly, it preserves a continual, never-ending (r)evolution—the process of utopia.

NOTES

I would like to acknowledge the generous and invaluable advice offered by Peter Stillman, who went above and beyond the call of duty to help me draw a chapter out of the germ of an idea. I would also like to thank Laurence Davis for his help with an elusive citation. And I am grateful to Maria Tymoczko and Daphne Patai for introducing me, once upon a time, to the study of *The Dispossessed*, and for their continuing support for my critical endeavors.

1. Ursula K. Le Guin, *The Dispossessed: An Ambiguous Utopia* (New York: Harper & Row, 1974), cited in the text by chapter and page to the 387-page Eos HarperCollins edition of 2001.

2. This home to which one returns in the course of life's voyage bears a certain resemblance to Utopia, "the one country," Oscar Wilde reminds us, "at which Humanity is always landing" ("The Soul of Man Under Socialism," *The Fortnightly Review* XLIX n.s., 1 February 1891: 303). Reflecting the individual's inner change and growth, "home" is a shifting target; likewise, the geography and contour of Utopia are in constant flux, according to the philosophies and knowledge of communities and nations.

3. Shevek's ideas about the principle of mutual aid bear a strong resemblance to those appearing in Peter Kropotkin's *Mutual Aid: A Factor of Evolution*, first published in 1902. For a thorough examination of Kropotkin's influence on Le Guin's novel, see Philip E. Smith II, "Unbuilding Walls: Human Nature and the Nature of Evolutionary and Political Theory in *The Dispossessed*," in *Ursula K. Le Guin*, ed. Joseph D. Olander and Martin Harry Greenberg (New York: Taplinger, 1979). See also John P. Brennan and Michael C. Downs, "Anarchism and Utopian Tradition in *The Dispossessed*," in *Ursula K. Le Guin*, ed. Olander and Greenberg.

4. Thomas J. Remington, "The Other Side of Suffering: Touch as Theme and Metaphor in Le Guin's Science Fiction Novels," in *Ursula K. Le Guin*, ed. Olander and Greenberg, 173.

5. Remington, "The Other Side of Suffering," 173.

6. See, for instance, Bernard Selinger's discussion of Takver's relationship with Shevek, in Bernard Selinger, *Le Guin and Identity in Contemporary Fiction* (Ann Arbor: University of Michigan Research Press, 1988); Elizabeth Cummins Cogell's commentary on the balance that Takver helps Shevek to achieve, in Elizabeth Cummins Cogell, "Taoist Configurations: *The Dispossessed*," in *Ursula K. Le Guin: Voyager to Inner Lands and to Outer Space*, ed. Joe De Bolt (Port Washington, NY: Kennikat Press, 1979); and Samuel R. Delany's discussion of Takver, biology, and women's sexuality in *The Dispossessed*, in Samuel R. Delany, "To Read *The Dispossessed*," in *The Jewel-Hinged Jaw: Notes on the Language of Science Fiction* (New York: Berkley Publishing, 1977).

7. J. T. Fraser, *Time, The Familiar Stranger* (Amherst: University of Massachusetts Press, 1987), 367. Dr. J. T. Fraser is the founder of the International Society for the Study of Time (1966) and is considered the foremost authority on the interdisciplinary study of time. He has written and lectured extensively on different aspects of the study of time.

In a 1975 interview for the *Portland Scribe*, Le Guin said of her use of Simultaneity theory that

> there are shelves of books about space and space-time, but there's one main reference for thinking about time, either from a physics point of view or from philosophy. It's called *The Voices of Time*, an anthology. [Fraser has] collected all the main articles. . . . Sequency and Simultaneity seem to be the basic question. As well as I understood it I tried to work it into the book. It got absolutely fascinating.

In Barry Barth, "Ursula Le Guin Interview: Tricks, Anthropology Create New Worlds," *Portland Scribe* 4, no. 8 (May 17–23, 1975): 8–9.

8. Fraser, *Time, The Familiar Stranger*, 368.
9. Fraser, *Time, The Familiar Stranger*, 288.
10. Fraser, *Time, The Familiar Stranger*, 367.
11. Fraser, *Time, The Familiar Stranger*, 368.
12. Fraser, *Time, The Familiar Stranger*, 202.
13. In addition to the relevant chapters in this book, see, for instance, the essays by Smith, "Unbuilding Walls," and Bernard Selinger, *Le Guin and Identity*.
14. Kingsley Widmer, *Counterings: Utopian Dialects in Contemporary Contexts* (Ann Arbor: University of Michigan Research Press, 1988), 51.
15. Larry L. Tifft and Dennis C. Sullivan, "Possessed Sociology and Le Guin's *Dispossessed*: From Exile to Anarchism," in *Ursula K. Le Guin*, ed. Joe De Bolt, 184.
16. Tifft and Sullivan, "Possessed Sociology," 184.
17. Selinger, *Le Guin and Identity*, 124.
18. Tifft and Sullivan, "Possessed Sociology," 184.

WORKS CITED

Barth, Barry. "Ursula Le Guin Interview: Tricks, Anthropology Create New Worlds." *Portland Scribe* 4, no. 8 (May 17–23, 1975): 8–9.
Brennan, John P., and Michael C. Downs. "Anarchism and Utopian Tradition in *The Dispossessed*." Pp. 116–52 in *Ursula K. Le Guin*, ed. Joseph D. Olander and Martin Harry Greenberg. New York: Taplinger, 1979.
Cogell, Elizabeth Cummins. "Taoist Configurations: *The Dispossessed*." Pp. 153–79 in *Ursula K. Le Guin: Voyager to Inner Lands and to Outer Space*, ed. Joe De Bolt. Port Washington, NY: Kennikat Press, 1979.
Delany, Samuel R. "To Read *The Dispossessed*." Pp. 218–83 in *The Jewel-Hinged Jaw: Notes on the Language of Science Fiction*. New York: Berkley Publishing, 1977.
Fraser, J. T. *Time, The Familiar Stranger*. Amherst: University of Massachusetts Press, 1987.
Le Guin, Ursula K. *The Dispossessed: An Ambiguous Utopia*. New York: Eos, HarperCollins, 2001 (1974).
Remington, Thomas J. "The Other Side of Suffering: Touch as Theme and Metaphor in Le Guin's Science Fiction Novels." Pp. 153–77 in *Ursula K. Le Guin*, ed. Joseph D. Olander and Martin Harry Greenberg. New York: Taplinger, 1979.
Selinger, Bernard. *Le Guin and Identity in Contemporary Fiction*. Ann Arbor: University of Michigan Research Press, 1988.
Smith, Philip E., II. "Unbuilding Walls: Human Nature and the Nature of Evolutionary and Political Theory in *The Dispossessed*." Pp. 77–96 in *Ursula K. Le Guin*, ed. Joseph D. Olander and Martin Harry Greenberg. New York: Taplinger, 1979.
Tifft, Larry L., and Dennis C. Sullivan. "Possessed Sociology and Le Guin's *Dispossessed*: From Exile to Anarchism." Pp. 180–97 in *Ursula K. Le Guin: Voyager to Inner Lands and to Outer Space*, ed. Joe De Bolt. Port Washington, NY: Kennikat Press, 1979.
Widmer, Kingsley. *Counterings: Utopian Dialects in Contemporary Contexts*. Ann Arbor: University of Michigan Research Press, 1988.
Wilde, Oscar. "The Soul of Man under Socialism." *The Fortnightly Review* XLIX n.s. (1 Feb. 1891): 291–319.

• *11* •

Science and Politics in *The Dispossessed*: Le Guin and the "Science Wars"

Tony Burns

INTRODUCTION

*A*lthough a great deal has been written about *The Dispossessed*, a survey of the literature indicates that not much has been written about it by those who have an interest in natural science or in the politics of science, even though the book is a work of science fiction and has a natural scientist, the physicist Shevek, as its central character.[1] This omission is quite surprising for there is some truth in Peter Koper's suggestion that the role of science in society is "the issue in *all* Le Guin's fiction."[2] This issue is undeniably a central concern for Le Guin in *The Dispossessed*, as it is in a number of her earlier short stories.[3] In what follows my central theme will be the way in which Le Guin's novel deals with this particular issue. I shall discuss the link between the novel's depiction of natural science on the one hand and its treatment of anarchist politics on the other.

Questions relating to the "politics" of science, broadly understood, have also been of interest to a number of twentieth-century theorists, especially those associated with the movement known as postmodernism, or what Paul Gross and Norman Levitt have misleadingly referred to as the "academic left."[4] The postmodern understanding of the nature of science and of the role of science in society has generated a considerable critical response and has led to the development of what, in the last ten years or so, has come to be referred to as "the science wars."[5] Given that Le Guin's *The Dispossessed* also deals with this issue, it is both interesting and enlightening to consider it in the light of the intellectual developments which have taken place in this area in the three decades since it was first published. A familiarity with the debates surrounding the "science wars" sheds new light on the way in which Le Guin deals with the relationship between science and politics in the novel, and on how the views on this subject expressed in the novel compare with those of the classical anarchist tradition.

THE "SCIENCE WARS"

As Gross and Levitt's *Higher Superstition: The Academic Left and its Quarrels with Science,* published in 1994, is a classic text in the debate over the "science wars," I shall use it as my main source in the account which follows. At first sight, this debate is a purely philosophical one. It is a debate between postmodernists and their view of science and the opponents of postmodernism, who like Gross and Levitt endorse a version of what might be described as the "modern" conception of science. Philosophically speaking, it is in effect two debates, having to do with questions of epistemology and ontology respectively. The epistemological debate has to do with the nature of truth. It is the debate between "perspectivists" or "relativists" on the one hand and "objectivists" on the other.[6] The ontological debate has to do with the nature of reality. It is the debate between "constructivism" on the one hand and scientific "realism" on the other.[7] The different positions adopted by those involved in these two debates tend to be associated with one another. The postmodernists of the "academic left," who embrace perspectivism or relativism, also embrace constructivism and therefore reject scientific realism. Their guiding principle is that of the linguistic construction of "reality." Their opponents, like Gross and Levitt, endorse both objectivism and scientific realism, and therefore reject constructivism.

It is evident from even a cursory reading of the relevant literature that this debate is also in some important sense a "political" one. According to Gross and Levitt, the "academic left" enthusiastically endorses Paul Feyerabend's "epistemological anarchism," the view that in science "anything goes,"[8] and is therefore unable to distinguish "reliable knowledge" or science from "superstition," that is to say, nonscientific or even antiscientific belief systems of the sort usually associated with mythology, religion, witchcraft, or magic.[9] Gross has claimed elsewhere that postmodernists believe that "authority is always wrong," and that they are opposed to any kind of "hierarchy," especially authority and hierarchy in science. In his view, the "academic left" is of the opinion that hierarchy and authority are, "in themselves, evil" and that it is possible for us to "have science without them." Given his insistence that "these beliefs are false" it is not surprising that Gross should go on to describe the "academic left" as "anti-science Luddites" who reject not just a particular approach to science and scientific explanation, or science as it is currently practiced, but the very idea of "science" and "scientific knowledge" as these terms are traditionally understood.[10]

Although Gross and Levitt do not themselves employ the term "anarchist" to describe the political outlook they criticize in their book, it does not seem inappropriate, in the light of their emphasis on the work of Paul Feyerabend as a source of philosophical inspiration for the "academic left," to describe as "anarchist" their depiction of the politics of postmodernism, it being understood that for them this type of politics is a bad thing. The remarks just cited suggest that Gross and Levitt do not like postmodernism in general and its approach to natural science in particular precisely *because*, in their view, postmodernists reject all forms of authority and all forms of hierarchy. For Gross and Levitt, the "academic left" are "the enemy within," who represent the forces of irrationality, chaos and moral nihilism in contemporary society.[11] Moreover, in *Higher Superstition* Gross and Levitt assume throughout that there is a close link between the politics of postmodernism and its understanding of natural science. They suggest that the commitment of the "academic left" to the former depends theoretically on its acceptance of the latter. Indeed, their basic strategy throughout the book is to seek to discredit the "anarchist" politics of postmodernism by exposing what they consider to be the obvious weaknesses of the view of natural science upon which that politics is based.

In what follows I will discuss Le Guin's *The Dispossessed* from the standpoint of the debates associated with the "science wars." When discussing the politics of the novel I will employ the term "politics" in a broad sense, such that it includes a reference to "morality" or "ethics," which terms I shall use interchangeably. Moreover, I shall assume that the political beliefs expressed by Shevek in *The Dispossessed* are also those of Le Guin, and that they reflect a commitment on her part to some form of anarchism.[12] Toward the end of *The Dispossessed* Le Guin has one of her minor characters suggest to Shevek that one of the most important practical applications of temporal physics "is in ethics" (7: 224).[13] Statements like this have led more than one commentator to observe that there is an homology between Shevek's views on science and his views on politics in the novel.[14] Nevertheless, there remains the question of the specific nature of the relationship which exists between the two. Is Shevek's approach to politics a reflection of his understanding of science because in both cases, as with postmodernism, his outlook is relativist and constructivist? Or alternatively is Shevek's approach to politics consonant with his view of science because in both cases his attitude is objectivist and realist? I will discuss first the "science" and then the "politics" of *The Dispossessed* in turn. In each case I shall argue that, contrary to the opinion of a number of commentators, there is evidence to support the view that Shevek's views on science and politics are not those associated with Gross and Levitt's "academic left."

NATURAL SCIENCE IN *THE DISPOSSESSED*

It has been rightly claimed on more than one occasion that the nature of truth is a key theme in Le Guin's work.[15] But is the understanding of truth in the natural sciences attributed to Shevek in *The Dispossessed* the same as that of postmodernism and the "academic left"? A number of commentators have suggested that Le Guin herself is a relativist, and therefore also by implication a constructivist.[16] For example, James Bittner relates Le Guin's view of science specifically to the work of T. S. Kuhn, who according to Gross and Levitt is one of the two main sources of intellectual influence for the "academic left," the other being Feyerabend.[17] In a judgment which now seems significantly out of date in the light of the recent furor surrounding the "science wars," Bittner insists that it is only "the most diehard mechanical materialist" today who would wish to argue against Kuhn, Feyerabend, and in his opinion also Le Guin, for an objectivist and a realist philosophy of natural science.[18]

Elizabeth [Cogell] Cummins has also argued that one of the core assumptions of *The Dispossessed*, insofar as it deals with the nature of scientific knowledge, is Shevek's commitment to cognitive relativism. One central theme of the book is Shevek's quest for a "General Temporal Theory," a new unified theory of time, which facilitates the technological development of the "ansible," a "device that will permit communication without any time interval between two points in space" no matter how distant, and thus "make a league of worlds possible" (11: 344). Such a league—the "Ekumen"—exists in Le Guin's "Hainish" science fiction writings, including *The Left Hand of Darkness*. According to Cummins, however, at the end of the novel Shevek is "finally able to create the unified temporal theory" which he has been seeking only because, unlike his contemporaries, both on Urras and on his own home planet of Anarres, so far as scientific knowledge is concerned, he "recognizes the relativity of truth."[19]

One argument which might be used to support the view that Shevek's understanding of science in *The Dispossessed* is relativistic would be to draw attention to his acknowledgment of the role which logical paradoxes and contradictions have to play in science and scientific explanation. For example, the General Temporal Theory which Shevek seeks throughout the novel involves a logical paradox relating to our understanding of the nature of time (2: 28–29; 7: 225–26). Time can be understood in a linear fashion, from the point of view of a "sequency theory" associated with the idea of the "arrow of time," or alternatively as being basically cyclical in character, from the point of view of a "simultaneity theory" (2: 54–55; 3: 79, 86; 4: 104, 112–13; 7: 223–25). These two ways of thinking about time are logically incompatible with one another. Consequently, for someone who believes that there is such a thing as objective truth, the sequency theory and the simultaneity theories cannot both be true. For an objectivist, if the sequency theory is true, the simultaneity theory must be false, and *vice versa*. Hence, if we are rational and commit ourselves to one of these theories, we ought to reject the other, precisely because we consider it to be false or "illusory." According to Shevek, however, despite the fact that they are logically inconsistent with one another, there are nevertheless good reasons for endorsing both of these two theories of time. Consider, for example, the following interchange that takes place toward the end of the novel:

> "You can't assert two contradictory statements about the same thing," said Dearri, with the calmness of superior knowledge. "In other words, one of these 'aspects' is real, the other's simply an illusion."

"Many physicists have said that," Shevek assented.

"But what do *you* say," asked the one who wanted to know.

"Well, I think it's an easy way out of the difficulty. . . . Can one dismiss either being or becoming as an illusion? . . . If the mind is able to perceive time in *both* ways, then a true chronosophy should provide a field in which the relation of the two aspects or processes of time could be understood." (7: 224; emphasis added)

For Shevek, then, there are good reasons for thinking that both of these two theories of time are true, or that they contain at least some "truth" and that neither is entirely false or "illusory." Whether one subscribes to the sequence theory or to the simultaneity theory is something that depends on the perspective or point of view which one chooses to adopt. Each of these theories has its uses, and there are no rational grounds or empirical evidence for preferring one of them to the other. It is, of course, for precisely this reason that Shevek attempts to incorporate them both in a more general "unified" theory of time. Shevek's understanding of the nature of time here is symptomatic of his attitude toward the world generally. Shevek refuses to think in the "either-or" terms of traditional Aristotelian logic. As a number of commentators have noted, he like his creator is a thoroughgoing "dialectical" thinker,[20] one whose first instinct is to think conjunctively rather than disjunctively. According to the hypothetical argument we are considering, however, in order for Shevek to "unify" the sequence and simultaneity theories of time he must reject the notion of objective truth and embrace the principle of cognitive relativism in science.

Readers familiar with the philosophical debates in twentieth-century physics and the impact which these have had on the postmodern understanding of natural science will recognize the similarity between Shevek's approach to the understanding of the nature of time in *The Dispossessed* and the way in which advocates of the Copenhagen Interpretation of quantum mechanics, like Niels Bohr and Werner Heisenberg, understand the nature of light and of electromagnetic radiation more generally—the so called wave-particle duality. According to the Copenhagen Interpretation, when asked to consider whether light is either a wave or a particle we should reject such a stark "either-or" choice and, despite the fact that these two ways of thinking about light are not logically consistent with one another, take seriously the possibility that light might legitimately be thought of as being both a wave *and* a particle. Given this attitude, it is not surprising that in *The Dispossessed* Le Guin has Shevek refer at one point to "the magnificent incoherences of quantum theory" (9: 229). Neither is it surprising, as Gross and Levitt note, that the Copenhagen Interpretation is often associated with the postmodern rejection of the "rationalistic" assumptions of modern physics and its endorsement of the principle of cognitive relativism.[21] It is for this reason that critics of postmodernism like Christopher Norris have recently turned their attention to problems of quantum theory in an effort to establish whether there is a credible "realist" alternative to the views of Bohr and Heisenberg.[22] This is important because in *The Dispossessed* Shevek's views do appear on numerous occasions to endorse the Copenhagen Interpretation. For example, the development of the "ansible" in the novel requires the theoretical possibility of "faster-than-light-speed" travel. This is something which, as Le Guin has Shevek point out, was rejected by Albert Einstein (Ainsetain), who throughout his life remained committed to the assumptions of the modern scientific world view and, as Le Guin has Shevek observe, with "endearing caution" believed that "his physics did indeed describe reality" (9: 279; also 2: 28–29; 5: 143; 7: 225–26; 9: 276; 11: 344). However, such "super-luminal" travel is accepted as a theoretical possibility by physicists who, like contemporary postmodernists but *unlike* Einstein, are sympathetic to the Copenhagen Interpretation.

At first sight, then, the claim that the "science" in *The Dispossessed* is premised upon a commitment on Shevek's part to the principle of cognitive relativism, and that this is something which Shevek shares with postmodernism and the "academic left," appears to be quite persuasive. Nevertheless, there are good reasons for finding it unconvincing. For example, consider Le Guin's characterization of Shevek's attitude toward mathematics, and hence also toward the theoretical principles which underpin his General Temporal Theory. Shevek's approach to mathematics is basically "realist" and not "constructivist." Shevek does not construct mathematical truths, rather he discovers them. He is, as Susan Wood has noted, a "truth seeking" and not a truth creating scientist.[23] Moreover, the truths associated with the General Temporal Theory which he seeks and which at the end of the novel he finally discovers are not truths for him alone or for those who happen to share his point of view at a particular moment in time. They are truths for anybody and everybody, at all times and in all places. They are objective, that is to say universal and permanent, truths which are in principle acceptable by all human kind. Shevek's attitude toward the truths of mathematics is similar to that of the character Ganil, in Le Guin's short story "The Masters," who is also a mathematician. For Ganil, "XVI and IXX don't make XXXVI (*sic*), never have, never can, never will, till the world ends."[24] In this respect Shevek's approach to mathematics in *The Dispossessed* is strikingly similar to Plato's. This is, of course, a reason for thinking that it is quite different from that of postmodernism.

Another similarity between Shevek's outlook and Platonism is Shevek's clear distinction between science and rhetoric. For Shevek as for Plato, when beliefs are expressed in words then the possibility of rhetorical manipulation immediately arises. Toward the beginning of the novel Le Guin has the young Shevek assert that "nothing said in words ever came out quite even." Beliefs expressed in words "got twisted and ran together, instead of staying straight and fitting together." But this does not happen in the fields of science and mathematics. For Shevek, "if a book were written all in numbers," like Galileo's book of the universe, "it would be true," that is to say, objectively true. In science therefore, if one could only see the numbers, "then one could see the foundations of the world." Moreover, one could also see that these foundations "were solid" (2: 31). This belief is so important for Le Guin that she has Shevek repeat these remarks, almost word for word, toward the end of the novel, once he has finally discovered the General Temporal Theory. At that point she has Shevek affirm that "he *had* seen the foundations of the universe, and they *were* solid" (9: 281; emphasis added). Needless to say at the heart of the postmodern view of natural science is not the acceptance but the rejection of the idea that scientific knowledge either has or needs any "foundations."

According to N. B. Hayles, with respect to any given question Le Guin's view is that the "perspective" from which the question is approached "will influence the answer" that is given. Consequently, for every statement Le Guin gives us, she invariably "supplies a counterstatement," which has an equal claim to be true or to represent the truth.[25] This account of Le Guin's attitude toward truth has a clear application to Shevek's reflections on the nature of time in *The Dispossessed*. Moreover, at first sight it does appear to imply that Shevek is committed to cognitive relativism. For it suggests, as Hayles also observes, that for Shevek, as for Le Guin, a given question will have "not one answer, but several." In fact, "it will have as many answers as there are perspectives from which to give an answer."[26] Nevertheless, again there are good reasons for not drawing this conclusion. One is that, as the discussion of the General Temporal Theory indicates, the question of the nature of time does not have "several" answers, or a multiplicity of answers. In fact, it has only two. In other words, Le Guin's treatment of Shevek's attitude toward this particular question in *The Dispossessed* demonstrates a tendency for him to think in terms of those "binary oppositions," such as that between the notion of "Being" and the notion of "Becoming," which have been central to the Western philosophical tradition from the time of the ancient Greeks, and which are rejected by Nietzsche, postmodernism, and the "academic left." Another reason, as Hayles goes on to observe, is that although in Le Guin's work "no truth is allowed to stand as the entire truth" and "every insight is presented as partial" and "subject to revision" by "another perspective," it does not follow from this that for either Shevek or Le Guin there could be no such thing as "*the* truth." In the case of *The Left Hand of Darkness*, for example, Hayles notes that all of these "multiple answers" are finally "subsumed into one holistic vision."

According to Hayles, Le Guin takes the view that although "all are true," nevertheless "each is only part of the final truth." It follows from this that for a "complete expression" of Le Guin's "holistic vision" or her view of "the truth" in that work, "nothing less than the entire structure of the book will suffice." In Hayles's account of Le Guin's view of truth, "the final whole that emerges" is "the book itself."[27] Hayles's account of Le Guin's attitude toward truth is reminiscent, not so much of Taoism, with which Le Guin is usually associated,[28] but of the philosophy of Hegel, which as Fritjof Capra has pointed out has an affinity with Taoism in respect of a number of its basic philosophical assumptions.[29] In Hegel's *Phenomenology of Spirit*[30] different partial and contradictory perspectives which have been adopted in the history of philosophy prior to Hegel are successively incorporated into Hegel's own philosophical system. The final outcome of this process is, of course, the *Phenomenology* itself, a book which for Hegel contains, not just at the end in the final section on "absolute knowledge," but in its entirety from beginning to end, what he considers to be *"the* truth." Indeed, it would be quite instructive to consider Le Guin's understanding of the nature of truth with that of Hegel.[31] For in Hegel's philosophy, we also find a rejection of the "either-or" thinking of traditional Aristotelian logic and a sensitivity to the idea that philosophical problems might be looked at from different points of view, combined with a commitment *not* to cognitive relativism but rather to the notion of objective truth. Moreover, as is well known, Hegel is one of the main targets of criticism for postmodernism and the "academic left," his philosophy usually being considered to be typically representative of the standpoint of "modernity."[32]

Ambiguity surrounds Shevek's understanding of the General Temporal Theory in *The Dispossessed*, and especially the specific nature of the *one* "truth" which is associated with his "unified" theory of time. One possibility is that Shevek's theory constitutes a logically coherent *third* doctrine which has been produced by combining the two contradictory perspectives associated with the sequency and the simultaneity theories of time. On this reading the logical paradox associated with these two opposed views of the nature of time is merely *apparent* rather than real, and hence not a genuine paradox at all. Here the General Temporal Theory demonstrates how these apparently contradictory perspectives on time can be "unified," in the sense of being incorporated into a logically self-consistent harmonious whole. To think of the theory in this way is to argue that at the end of the novel the older Shevek finally discovers what he has been seeking throughout his life, a coherent and systematic resolution of the logical paradox associated with the nature of time, the existence of which he had recognized as a schoolboy many years before.

A second possibility, however, is that for Shevek the logical paradox associated with the conjunction of the sequency and the simultaneity theories of time is a *real* and not just an apparent one. According to this second reading, although it remains the case that for Shevek there is indeed just *one* "truth" regarding the nature of time, nevertheless the General Temporal Theory is a logically incoherent framework of beliefs, and the one "truth" which it contains really *is* a paradoxical and self-contradictory truth. From the standpoint of this second interpretation, the sequency and the simultaneity theories of time can only be "unified" in the sense that it is possible for a scientist who is familiar with them both to appreciate their respective merits and therefore "rise above" them to a theoretical position which is able to see "both sides" of the question. On this second reading, Shevek's view is that with respect to any given question in science, although there is indeed such a thing as "*the* truth," nevertheless this can only be apprehended by those who like himself, with all of the wisdom of his older years, are able to reconcile themselves to the existence of such logical paradoxes, and indeed positively embrace them. From this point of view, the difference between the young and the mature Shevek is not that the latter finally achieves the objective which he has been seeking all of his life, it is rather that he abandons this objective altogether and his quest for the particular type of logical "certainty" which is associated with it (9: 279–81).

It is not clear which of these two interpretations of Shevek's understanding of the nature of scientific truth is to be preferred. For present purposes, however, the important point is that whichever of them we adopt the final outcome is an account of Shevek's view of truth which is "realist," rather than "constructivist" in terms of its basic philosophical assumptions. This is why, after finally discovering the General Temporal Theory, Shevek asks himself how he could "have stared at reality for ten years and not seen it?" (9: 280). According to this "realist" understanding of Shevek's views on science, the General Temporal Theory is a framework of objective truths which accurately reflects the real nature of time. It is true that at the heart of the General Temporal Theory there lies a logical paradox, either apparent or real. For Shevek, however, this is not a reason for denying the objective truth of the theory. Nor is it a reason for denying that the theory is true because it reflects the nature of a reality which is not linguistically constructed.

It is arguable therefore that Shevek's recognition in *The Dispossessed* that logical paradoxes have an important part to play in contemporary physics does not necessarily imply a commitment on his part to cognitive relativism in science. Consequently, it is also arguable that Shevek does not endorse views which today are associated with postmodernism and the "academic left." Shevek's views on science have much more in common with the doctrine in the philosophy of science known as "scientific realism" than they do with postmodernism.[33] In my opinion, therefore, despite the influence of the philosophy of Taoism upon Le Guin, there is at least something to be said for Patrick Parrinder's observation that *The Dispossessed* "incorporates all of the elements of the classic scientific world view,"[34] albeit modified in the light of theoretical developments in twentieth-century atomic physics. On this reading, so far as its understanding of natural science is concerned, the "realist" philosophical assumptions which underpin Shevek's views on science in *The Dispossessed* make it a "modern" rather than a "postmodern" work. In this respect Shevek's views on science fall firmly within the classical anarchist tradition.[35] As a seeker after "*the* truth," and from the ethical standpoint of anarchism, as Le Guin understands it, Shevek's main objection to Ioti society and its treatment of scientists is that "to be a physicist in A-Io was to serve not society, not mankind, not the truth, but the State" (9: 272). This brings us to the politics of *The Dispossessed*.

POLITICS IN *THE DISPOSSESSED*

How do Shevek's views on politics in *The Dispossessed* compare with those of post-modernism and Gross and Levitt's "academic left"? A great deal turns here on how one understands the postmodern approach to politics, something which has been interpreted in different ways. As Gross and Levitt associate postmodernism with moral nihilism, I shall first consider Shevek's attitude toward this issue. Consider, for example, the following interchange between Shevek and one of the main female characters in the novel, Vea, in which she criticizes the anarchist attitude toward morality:

> "Then it's true, you really have no morality?" she asked, as if shocked and de-lighted.
> "I don't know what you mean. To hurt a person there is the same as to hurt a person here."
> "You mean you have all the same old rules? You see, I believe that morality is just another superstition, like religion. It's just got to be thrown out. . . . I think you Odonians missed the whole point. You threw out the priests and judges and divorce laws and all that, but you kept the real trouble behind them. You just stuck it inside, into your consciences. But it's still there. You're just as much slaves as ever! You aren't really free." (7:219)

Assuming that Shevek's views on this subject are also those of Le Guin, this passage indicates that Le Guin is definitely not a moral nihilist. Nor, therefore, does she associate the type of anarchism of which she approves with moral nihilism. Indeed, as more than one commentator has suggested, it is arguable that far from being a moral nihilist Le Guin is in fact the very opposite.[36] For in all her writings—in her science fiction, fantasy, and "children's" literature—Le Guin always writes as someone who has an overarching concern with the ethical dimensions of human existence; she writes as a "moralist," whilst avoiding "moralizing" and preaching simple solutions to serious moral problems.[37] So far as her politics is concerned, then, if moral nihilism is the decisive issue Le Guin should not be associated with postmodernism and the "academic left."

Given Gross and Levitt's association of postmodernism in general with relativism and constructivism, a second possibility is that the "academic left" is committed, not as they suggest to moral nihilism, but rather to ethical relativism. So let us consider next Le Guin's attitude toward this issue in *The Dispossessed*. A number of commentators have claimed that Le Guin is indeed an ethical relativist, and once again it is often suggested that this reflects the influence of Taoist philosophy upon her thinking.[38] Moreover, as in the case of her understanding of science, it might be suggested that the reason why Le Guin endorses relativism in this area is her appreciation of the role which logical paradoxes have to play in the fundamental problems of ethics. Consider, for example, the way in which Le Guin deals with the question of whether the character Estraven in *The Left Hand of Darkness* should or should not be considered to be a "traitor," a question which might also, of course, be asked of Shevek in *The Dispossessed*. As Hayles points out, Le Guin is keen to show that whether one considers either Estraven or indeed Shevek to be a "traitor" will depend upon one's point of view. It is not the case, therefore, that there is just *one* correct answer to this question, by comparison with which all others answers may be shown to be false.[39] Indeed, what we have here is an ethical dilemma precisely because in each case there are good reasons for thinking that the individual concerned is both a "traitor" and not so at one and the same time. It is therefore arguable that Le Guin endorses the principle of relativism in ethics, just as Shevek endorses that of relativism in science, and for much the same reasons.

Nevertheless, there is counter-evidence, both in Le Guin's essays and in *The Dispossessed*, which points toward an alternative reading of her views on ethics and politics. There are times when Le Guin clearly endorses the doctrine of moral realism, according to which there are objective truths in ethics which possess a permanence and a universality of the kind which Shevek and Plato associate with the truths of mathematics and physics. For example, in one of her essays Le Guin draws a parallel between the realms of ethics and science, in each of which the "true laws—ethical and aesthetic, as surely as scientific—are not imposed from above by any authority, but exist in things and are to be found—discovered." The world is not chaotic or random but ordered, and the order to be discerned in the world is *not* "one imposed by man or by a personal or humane deity."[40] This is not the attitude of a moral relativist, a constructivist, or a contemporary postmodernist who, following Nietzsche, maintains that the only order in the world is imposed on it by human beings themselves. Rather, Le Guin's attitude is that of a moral realist and a humanist, who is committed to the idea that there is a universally valid ethical order, a moral law which applies to all human beings, a law which is in some sense "natural" rather than a purely social "construction," and which is therefore discovered by human beings rather than made by them. They also indicate that Le Guin actually agrees with the view expressed by Oiie, one of the Urrasti physicists in *The Dispossessed*, when at one point she has him say that "the politician and the physicist both deal with things as they are, with real forces, the basic laws of the world" (7: 203). It is true that when Oiie makes this statement Le Guin has Shevek criticize him for doing so, but it is clear from the context that the reason for this is because Oiie wrongly suggests that it is the laws of Ioti society which possess the same kind of universal applicability as "the law of entropy and the force of gravity" (7: 203), something which the anarchist Shevek is of course unable to accept. In other words, Shevek objects, not to the general principle enunciated by Oiie, but only to Oiie's specific formulation of that general principle.

In another of her essays, Le Guin tells us that what underpins her commitment to this one moral law is the assumption, which she considers to be "essential," that "we" human beings "are not objects" but "subjects." Hence, "whoever among us treats us as objects is acting inhumanly, wrongly, against nature."[41] And elsewhere she insists that "if you deny any affinity with another person or kind of person, if you declare it to be wholly different from yourself" then you inevitably deny its "spiritual equality" and hence also its "human reality."[42] Like the young Marx, whose ethical beliefs appear to have been inspired by Kant, Le Guin considers such "objectification" to be ethically unacceptable because it involves treating others instrumentally, as a means to our own ends rather than ends in themselves. Consequently, it violates the principle of natural equality or moral reciprocity. Moreover, also like the young Marx, Le Guin maintains that social relationships of this kind reflect a condition of "alienation," specifically the alienation of man from man. This is the attitude of those "propertarians" in *The Dispossessed* who attempt to own or "possess" others as if they were merely items of property or slaves rather than fellow human beings, free beings, their equals in the order of creation (2: 51, 53). Indeed, those who adopt this attitude are not only alienated from others, they are also alienated from themselves. In consequence they have, Le Guin insists, "fatally impoverished" their own status as human beings, as moral beings.[43] According to Le Guin, social relationships which are based on such a principle could only ever be power relationships, and not ethical ones.

These are the ethical beliefs which underpin *The Dispossessed* and which Le Guin associates with anarchism properly so called. For Shevek, the law of reciprocity or human equality (7: 194) is the "one law," the only law he acknowledges (1: 7). Like Kropotkin, Shevek considers this to be a law of "mutual aid" between individuals (9: 300). In the manner of a traditional natural law theorist, Shevek's commitment to this law leads him to criticize the political system of A-Io because it will "admit no morality outside the laws" (1: 15). It is his endorsement of this one moral law which compels him to object when the inhabitants of A-Io consider "foreigners" as "inferior, as less than fully human" (1: 14). Indeed, it is by appealing to this one law, that Shevek is able to condemn almost every aspect of life on A-Io, the social organization of which is based on the contrary principle of order, hierarchy and inequality. Shevek very quickly discovers, while voyaging to A-Io at the beginning of the novel that social status and the establishment of relationships of superiority and inferiority is a "central" issue in Ioti life (1: 18). For example in conversation with Pae, an Ioti physicist, Shevek is concerned that Pae refers to him as *Doctor* Shevek and not just Shevek. Pae's response is to apologize for having offended Shevek, but also to point out that in A-Io *not* to use the title in question would be considered to be offensive, as "in our terms, you see," to treat all other members of Ioti society as one's own equal "just doesn't seem right" (3: 81).

Last but by no means least, as in the case of *The Left Hand of Darkness*, the ethical vision of human equality underpins Le Guin's commitment to feminism and her attitude toward gender relationships in *The Dispossessed*.[44] Shevek is not long in contact with Ioti society before he reflects how wrong it is that in order to "respect himself" the doctor Kimoe "had to consider half the human race as inferior" (1: 18). Moreover, once again he is dismayed when he discovers that some Ioti women actually support the system of gender relationships in A-Io by apparently consenting to the reduction of themselves to the status of a "thing," an object or instrument to be used by others. At one point, for example, he notes that the character Vea "was so elaborately and ostentatiously a female body that she seemed scarcely to be a human being" (7: 213) and that, as such, "in the eyes of men" she was "a thing owned, bought, sold" (7: 215).

A second reason for thinking that Le Guin is not a moral relativist in *The Dispossessed* is that, as in the case of her views on science so also in ethics: rather than revel in the sheer multiplicity and diversity of the possible ethical judgments that might be made with respect to any given situation, she has a tendency to think "dialectically" or in "binary" terms. She recognizes that "good" and "evil," or "right" and "wrong," considered from one point of view may not simply be different but actually *reversed* when considered from another. Typically, Le Guin's attitude toward this type of situation is again to refuse to commit herself to just one of the two opposed points of view or to think in simplistic either-or terms. Rather, she encourages her readers to think for themselves and to engage with the complexities of the ethical dilemma in question. Le Guin enjoins the reader to rise above each of these limited and partial perspectives and to see the strengths and weaknesses associated with "both sides" of the story. In a manner similar to Hegel's interpretation of Sophocles's *Antigone*, in which Antigone faces the conflicting duties of burying her brother and obeying her city's ruler Creon (or toward family and city),[45] Le Guin is most interested in the ethical dilemmas confronted by her central characters and the conflicts of duties with which these are associated. From this point of view, the best way to read *The Dispossessed* is to see it not as a straightforward and relatively uninteresting conflict between the individual (Shevek) and society (Anarres), or between egotism and moral duty (2: 29; 6: 155, 157). In my view, Ian Watson is right to claim that "Shevek is no egoizer."[46] It is rather to see Shevek as an erstwhile "tragic" hero who is placed by Le Guin in a situation where he is confronted by two conflicting moral duties, one as a citizen of Anarres to uphold the values of his own society, the other as a scientist and citizen of the world to pursue "the truth" come what may for the benefit of all human kind.[47]

Le Guin's attitude toward ethics is one which denies that a judgment made from one of the two conflicting partial and one-sided perspectives associated with any particular ethical dilemma can legitimately claim to represent the truth in its entirety. This attitude does not deny that there is such a thing as "*the* truth" in ethics. On this reading, for Le Guin the purpose of ethics is to seek or discover an objective truth relating to the paradoxical character not of natural but of *social* reality. Moreover, Le Guin would not accept that this "*one* truth" is something which is relative or depends on one's point of view. Rather, she considers the dualities and oppositions associated with the ethical dilemmas which are fundamental to all human existence to be a part of the moral fabric of the universe and of the cosmic order of things. We cannot, therefore, distance ourselves from the categories associated with these dualities as we please, depending on our point of view. For Le Guin these categories are in some important sense fixed, immutable, objective, and natural. I am therefore, for these reasons, inclined to agree with the small minority of commentators who claim that there are good reasons for thinking that Le Guin is not an ethical relativist.[48]

Although it is undeniably "anarchist," then, Le Guin's approach to questions of ethics and politics in *The Dispossessed,* is quite different from the anarchism which Gross and Levitt associate with the "academic left." As in the case of Taoist philosophy, Le Guin believes in the existence of a cosmic ethical order, the "natural law" of which all human beings in all societies, in all places, and at all times have a moral duty to follow. Le Guin's moral outlook in this novel is therefore premised upon a rejection of nihilism, constructivism, and relativism. Because of its commitment to universalism, objectivism, essentialism, humanism, and the natural equality of all human beings, Le Guin's ethical vision makes *The Dispossessed* once again a fundamentally "modern" rather than a "postmodern" work.

CONCLUSION

Interestingly, Gross and Levitt comment on the work of Ursula K. Le Guin in their *Higher Superstition.* To be more specific, they comment not on *The Dispossessed* but on a later novel, *Always Coming Home,* which was published in 1985. In their remarks, they associate the ideas that in their opinion underpin the "message" of this later novel with postmodernism. They maintain that Le Guin's fondness for the seeming primitive simplicity of the lifestyle of the "Kesh" people in this later work is "emblematic," indeed "coextensive," with the type of "radical environmentalism" which they associate with the "anti-science" attitude of the "academic left" and its rejection of "modernity."[49] In my view, even in the case of *Always Coming Home* there are good reasons for doubting the validity of this judgment. For example, Le Guin indicates there that she is sensitive to any possible accusation of scientific "Luddism" of the sort that Gross and Levitt bring against postmodernism.[50] Moreover, as John Moore has observed, when asked in an interview to respond to the claim, made by critics that she is "anti-science" in *Always Coming Home,* Le Guin replied by saying that "I hope I have never been, and am never perceived as being in any way 'anti-science' in my work."[51]

As we have seen, whatever its merits in the case of *Always Coming Home,* my argument here has been that Gross and Levitt's association of Le Guin with the "academic left" certainly does not apply in the case of *The Dispossessed,* for a number of reasons. One is that *The Dispossessed* was written from a standpoint that is by no means "anti-science." Another is that *The Dispossessed* does not break with but rather continues the classical anarchist tradition so far as its understanding of the nature of science is concerned. As Moore has rightly argued, it might be said to constitute an endorsement of "the nineteenth century Western faith in secularism and scientific progress."[52] Finally, it is arguable that the views on science which Le Guin attributes to Shevek in the novel are as "realist" as those of Gross and Levitt. At the same time, however, this "realist" understanding of science is combined with a strong commitment on Le Guin's part to a form of "anarchist" politics, albeit of a type which is quite different from the nihilistic form which Gross and Levitt associate with postmodernism and the "academic left." At the core of Le Guin's anarchism (more accurately, her anarcho-communism) and hence of her critique of the ordered hierarchy associated with existing social institutions, is her commitment to the currently unfashionable doctrine of humanism, and her "essentialist" belief that human beings are by nature ethical animals. In my view, this is a strength and not a weakness. It is Le Guin's humanism, combined with her strong sense of the tragic dimension of human existence, which gives *The Dispossessed* its moral stature and which ensures that it will never be considered, at least by its more discerning readers, to be "merely" a work of science fiction.

NOTES

1. See James Bittner, "The Complementarity of Myth, Magic, and Science," in *Approaches to the Fiction of Ursula K. Le Guin* (Ann Arbor, MI: UMI Research Press, 1984), 55–84; Peter T. Koper, "Science and Rhetoric in the Fiction of Ursula Le Guin," in *Ursula K. Le Guin: Voyager to Inner Lands and to Outer Space*, ed. Joe De Bolt (New York: Kennikat Press, 1979), 66–88; Patrick Parrinder, "Science Fiction and the Scientific World View," in *SF: A Critical Guide*, ed. Patrick Parrinder (London: Longman, 1979), 67–89; M. Teresa Tavormina, "Physics as Metaphor: The General Temporal Theory in *The Dispossessed*," *Mosaic* 13, nos. 3–4 (Spring/Summer 1980): 51–62; Angus Taylor, "The Politics of Space, Time, and Entropy," *Foundation* 10 (1976): 34–44; Ian Watson, "What Do You Want—The Moon?" *Foundation* 9 (1975): 75–83.

2. Koper, "Science and Rhetoric," 67.

3. See, for example, Ursula K. Le Guin, "The Masters," in *The Wind's Twelve Quarters* (London: Panther Books, 1978), vol. 1, 46–63; Ursula K. Le Guin, "The Stars Below," in *The Wind's Twelve Quarters* (London: Panther Books 1980), vol. 2, 60–68; Ursula K. Le Guin, "Schrödinger's Cat," in *Universe 5*, ed. Terry Carr (New York: Random House, 1974), 26–33.

4. Paul Gross and Norman Levitt, *Higher Superstition: The Academic Left and its Quarrels with Science* (Baltimore: Johns Hopkins University Press, 1994). See also Paul Gross, Norman Levitt, and Martin W. Lewis, *The Flight from Science and Reason* (New York: New York Academy of Sciences, 1996).

5. Keith M. Ashman and Philip Baringer, eds., *After the Science Wars* (London: Routledge, 2001); Keith Parsons, ed., *The Science Wars: Debating Scientific Knowledge and Technology*

(Amherst, NY: Prometheus Books, 2003); Andrew Ross, ed., *Science Wars* (Durham, NC: Duke University Press, 1996); Ullica Segerstråle, ed., *Beyond the Science Wars: The Missing Discourse About Science and Society* (Albany, NY: SUNY Press, 2000).

6. Gross and Levitt, *Higher Superstition*, 38, 40.

7. In addition to Gross and Levitt, for a recent critique of constructivism and a defense of "scientific realism" see Noretta Koertge, *A House Built on Sand: Exposing Postmodernist Myths About Science* (New York: Oxford University Press, 1998); Christopher Norris, *New Idols of the Cave: On the Limits of Anti-Realism* (Manchester, UK: Manchester University Press, 1997); Christopher Norris, *Against Relativism: Philosophy of Science, Deconstruction and Critical Theory* (Oxford: Blackwell, 1997); Alan Sokal and Jean Bricmont, *Intellectual Impostures: Postmodern Philosophers' Abuse of Science* (London: Profile Books, 1998).

8. Paul Feyerabend, *Against Method: Outline of an Anarchistic Theory of Knowledge.* (London: Verso, 1978 [1975]), 23, 27–28; also *Higher Superstition*, 49, where Gross and Levitt refer to Feyerabend as being, "next to Kuhn," the philosopher of science who is "the most often cited" by the "academic left."

9. Gross and Levitt, *Higher Superstition*, 45.

10. Paul Gross, "Flights of Fancy: Science, Reason, and Common Sense," in Gross, Levitt, and Lewis, *The Flight from Science and Reason*, 81–82.

11. See, for example, the section entitled "The Face of the Enemy," *Higher Superstition*, 34–41. For the association of postmodernism with moral nihilism see Gross and Levitt, *Higher Superstition*, 72, 74, 85.

12. For the view that Le Guin sees *The Dispossessed* as an attempt to present her own commitment to anarchism in a literary form see Jonathan Ward, "Interview with Ursula K. Le Guin," in *Dreams Must Explain Themselves*, by Ursula K. Le Guin (New York: Algol Press, 1975), 34–35: "*The Dispossessed* . . . it's an anarchist novel"; "But anarchy is not anarchism. Anarchy means chaos and y'know sort of just take the lid off and let her blow; that is not what all the old anarchist political movements meant at all. It simply is anti-centralized-state"; and "My social activism is separate from my writing. Except, perhaps, for this last book, *The Dispossessed*, in which being utopian, I am trying to state something which I think desirable—which is a world with a lot less government, and a decentralized world, and a world without authoritarianism. Where people are allowed to act spontaneously instead of always being a part of a hierarchy directed from above."

13. Ursula K. Le Guin, *The Dispossessed: An Ambiguous Utopia* (New York: Harper & Row, 1974), cited in the text by chapter and page to the 387-page Eos HarperCollins edition of 2001.

14. Darko Suvin, "Parables of De-Alienation: Le Guin's Widdershins Dance," in his *Positions and Presuppositions in Science Fiction* (Kent, OH: Kent State University Press, 1988), 140; Victor Urbanowicz, "Personal and Political in *The Dispossessed*," in *Ursula K. Le Guin*, ed. Harold Bloom (New York: Chelsea House, 1985), 150.

15. Susan Wood, "Discovering Worlds: The Fiction of Ursula K. Le Guin," in *Ursula K. Le Guin*, ed. Bloom, 188; Dena C. Bain, "The *Tao Te Ching* as Background to the Novels of Ursula K. Le Guin," in *Ursula K. Le Guin*, ed. Bloom, 213.

16. Bain, "The *Tao Te Ching*," 213; Douglas Barbour, "Wholeness and Balance in the Hainish Novels of Ursula K. Le Guin," in *Science-Fiction Studies: Selected Articles on Science Fiction 1973–1975*, ed. R. D. Mullen and Darko Suvin (New York: Gregg Press, 1976), 154; Bittner, *Approaches*, 5–6; John H. Crow and Richard D. Erlich, "Words of

Binding: Patterns of Integration in the Earthsea Trilogy," in *Ursula K. Le Guin*, ed. Joseph D. Olander and Martin Harry Greenberg (New York: Taplinger, 1979), 221; Elizabeth [Cogell] Cummins, "Taoist Configurations: *The Dispossessed*," in *Ursula K. Le Guin*, ed. De Bolt, 158; Gerard Klein, "Le Guin's 'Aberrant' Opus: Escaping the Trap of Discontent," in *Ursula K. Le Guin*, ed. Bloom, 88–89; Erik S. Rabkin, "Determinism, Free Will, and Point of View in *The Left Hand of Darkness*" in *Ursula K. Le Guin*, ed. Bloom, 162–63, 166.

17. Gross and Levitt, *Higher Superstition*, 49, 56.

18. Bittner, *Approaches*, 20.

19. [Cogell] Cummins, Elizabeth, "Taoist Configurations," 171, 176.

20. Bittner, *Approaches*, 16–18; Rafael Nudelman, "An Approach to the Structure of Le Guin's SF," in *Science-Fiction Studies: Selected Articles on Science Fiction, 1973–1975*, ed. Mullen and Suvin, 249; Suvin, "Parables of De-Alienation: Le Guin's Widdershins Dance," 145; Donald Theall, "The Art of Social-Science Fiction: The Ambiguous Utopian Dialectics of Ursula K. Le Guin," in *Science-Fiction Studies: Selected Articles on Science Fiction, 1973–1975*, ed. Mullen and Suvin, 293–94.

21. Gross and Levitt, *Higher Superstition*, 51–52, 261–62.

22. Christopher Norris, *Quantum Theory and the Flight from Realism: Philosophical Responses to Quantum Mechanics* (London: Routledge, 2000).

23. Susan Wood, "Discovering Worlds," 204.

24. Le Guin, "The Masters," 50.

25. N. B. Hayles, "Androgyny, Ambivalence, and Assimilation in *The Left Hand of Darkness*," in *Ursula K. Le Guin*, ed. Olander and Greenberg, 114.

26. Hayles, "Androgyny, Ambivalence, and Assimilation," 112.

27. Hayles, "Androgyny, Ambivalence, and Assimilation," 114–15.

28. Dena C. Bain, "The *Tao Te Ching*," 211–24; Elizabeth [Cogell] Cummins, "Taoist Configurations," 153–79.

29. Fritjof Capra, *The Turning Point: Science, Society, and the Rising Culture* (London: Fontana, 1982), 16–17. See also Fritjof Capra, *The Tao of Physics: An Exploration of the Parallels Between Modern Physics and Eastern Mysticism* (3rd ed. London: Flamingo Press, 1992 [1975]). Le Guin cites Capra's *The Turning Point* in *Dancing at the Edge of the World: Thoughts on Words, Women, Places* (New York: Harper & Row, 1990), 89.

30. G. W. F. Hegel, *Phenomenology of Spirit*, trans. A. V. Miller (Oxford: Clarendon Press, 1977).

31. There is little discussion of this issue in the literature. Commentators like Bittner, Nudelman, Suvin, and Theall, who have noted the "dialectical" character of Le Guin's thinking generally (see note 20 above), rarely mention Hegel. A significant exception is George Edgar Slusser, *The Farthest Shores of Ursula K. Le Guin* (San Bernadino, CA: Borgo Press, 1976), 3. Slusser argues that any similarity between Le Guin and Hegel is superficial and that Le Guin is not a "dialectical" thinker in the Hegelian sense.

32. See, for example, Jean François Lyotard, *The Postmodern Condition: A Report on Knowledge* (Manchester, UK: Manchester University Press, 1984 [1979]), 33–34, 38, 81.

33. The *locus classicus* for scientific realism is Roy Bhaskar, *A Realist Theory of Science* (Sussex, UK: Harvester Press, 1978 [1975]).

34. Patrick Parrinder, "Science Fiction and the Scientific World View," 86.

35. The *locus classicus* for the anarchist understanding of natural science and the role of scientists in society is Michael Bakunin, "On Science and Authority," in *Selected Writings*,

ed. Arthur Lehning (London: Jonathan Cape, 1973), 155–65. See also Peter Kropotkin, *Modern Science and Anarchism* (London: Freedom Press, 1912); Herbert Read, *Anarchy and Order* (London: Souvenir Press, 1974), 41–43, 107, 235–37; and Paul Feyerabend, *Science in a Free Society* (London: New Left Books, 1978).

36. Wayne Cogell, "The Absurdity of Sartre's Ontology: A Response by Ursula K. Le Guin," in *Philosophers Look at Science Fiction*, ed. David Nichols (Chicago: Nelson Hall, 1982), 149; Susan Wood, Introduction to Ursula K. Le Guin, *The Language of the Night: Essays on Fantasy and Science Fiction*, ed. Susan Wood (New York: Perigee Books, 1979), 13.

37. See for example Ursula K. Le Guin, "On Norman Spinrad's *The Iron Dream*," in *Science-Fiction Studies: Selected Articles on Science Fiction*, ed. Mullen and Suvin, 157.

38. There is a tendency for commentators who claim that Le Guin is a cognitive relativist to also claim that she is an ethical relativist. See the references in note 16 above.

39. Hayles, "Androgyny, Ambivalence, and Assimilation," 112–14.

40. Ursula K. Le Guin, "Dreams Must Explain Themselves," in *The Language of the Night*, 49.

41. Ursula K. Le Guin, "Science Fiction and Mrs. Brown," in *The Language of the Night*, 116.

42. Ursula K. Le Guin, "American SF and the Other," in *The Language of the Night*, 99. In this respect, Le Guin's views have an affinity with those of Erich Fromm. See Erich Fromm, *To Have or to Be* (London: Abacus Books, 1979 [1976]).

43. Le Guin, "American SF and the Other," 97–100.

44. This and the following paragraph contain material which is duplicated from T. Burns, "Marxism and Science Fiction: A Celebration of the Work of Ursula K. Le Guin," *Capital and Class*, 84 (Winter 2004): 139–48. This material is reprinted here with the permission of the editors.

45. G. W. F. Hegel, *Hegel on Tragedy*, ed. Anne Paolucci and Henry Paolucci (New York: Doubleday, 1962).

46. Ian Watson, "Le Guin's *Lathe of Heaven* and the Role of Dick: The False Reality as Mediator," in *Science-Fiction Studies: Selected Articles on Science Fiction*, ed. Mullen and Suvin, 229.

47. John Huntington, "Public and Private Imperatives in Le Guin's Novels," in *Science-Fiction Studies: Selected Articles on Science Fiction*, ed. Mullen and Suvin, 267–68, hints at this, but sees the conflict as being one between "love" or Shevek's "personal attachments" as a private individual and his "public duty" rather than between two conflicting moral duties.

48. John P. Brennan and Michael C. Downs, "Anarchism and the Utopian Tradition in *The Dispossessed*," in *Ursula K. Le Guin*, ed. Olander and Greenberg, 123; Larry L. Tifft and Dennis C. Sullivan, "Possessed Sociology and Le Guin's *Dispossessed*: From Exile to Anarchism," in *Ursula K. Le Guin*, ed. De Bolt, 189.

49. Gross and Levitt, *Higher Superstition*, 149–50, 152.

50. Ursula K. Le Guin, *Always Coming Home* (London: Grafton Books, 1988 [1985]), 316.

51. John Moore, "An Archaeology of the Future: Ursula Le Guin and Anarcho-Primitivism," *Foundation: The Review of Science Fiction* 63 (Spring 1995): 36.

52. Moore, "An Archaeology of the Future," 33.

WORKS CITED

Ashman, Keith M., and Philip Baringer, eds. *After the Science Wars.* London: Routledge, 2001.

Bain, Dena C. "The *Tao Te Ching* as Background to the Novels of Ursula K. Le Guin." Pp. 211–24 in *Ursula K. Le Guin,* ed. Harold Bloom. New York: Chelsea House, 1985.

Bakunin, Michael. "On Science and Authority." Pp. 155–65 in *Selected Writings,* ed. Arthur Lehning. London: Jonathan Cape, 1973.

Barbour, Douglas. "Wholeness and Balance in the Hainish Novels of Ursula K. Le Guin." Pp. 145–55 in *Science-Fiction Studies: Selected Articles on Science Fiction 1973–1975,* ed. R. D. Mullen and Darko Suvin. New York: Gregg Press, 1976.

Bhaskar, Roy. *A Realist Theory of Science.* Sussex, UK: Harvester Press, 1978 (1975).

Bittner, James. "The Complementarity of Myth, Magic, and Science." Pp. 55–84 in *Approaches to the Fiction of Ursula K. Le Guin,* by James Bittner. Ann Arbor, MI: UMI Research Press, 1984.

Brennan, John P., and Michael C. Downs. "Anarchism and the Utopian Tradition in *The Dispossessed.*" Pp. 116–52 in *Ursula K. Le Guin,* ed. Joseph D. Olander and Martin Harry Greenberg. New York: Taplinger, 1979.

Burns, T. "Marxism and Science Fiction: A Celebration of the Work of Ursula K. Le Guin." *Capital and Class* 84 (Winter 2004): 139–48.

Capra, Fritjof. *The Tao of Physics: An Exploration of the Parallels Between Modern Physics and Eastern Mysticism,* 3rd edition. London: Flamingo Press, 1992 (1975).

Capra, Fritjof. *The Turning Point: Science, Society, and the Rising Culture.* London: Fontana, 1982.

[Cogell] Cummins, Elizabeth. "Taoist Configurations: *The Dispossessed.*" Pp. 153–79 in *Ursula K. Le Guin: Voyage to Inner Lands and to Outer Space,* ed. Joe De Bolt. New York: Kennikat Press, 1979.

Cogell, Wayne. "The Absurdity of Sartre's Ontology: A Response by Ursula K. Le Guin." Pp. 143–51 in *Philosophers Look at Science Fiction,* ed. David Nichols. Chicago: Nelson Hall, 1982.

Crow, John H., and Richard D. Erlich. "Words of Binding: Patterns of Integration in the Earthsea Trilogy." Pp. 200–224 in *Ursula K. Le Guin,* ed. Joseph D. Olander and Martin Harry Greenberg. New York: Taplinger, 1979.

Feyerabend, Paul. *Against Method: Outline of an Anarchistic Theory of Knowledge.* London: Verso, 1978 (1975).

———. *Science in a Free Society.* London. New Left Books, 1978.

Fromm, Erich. *To Have or to Be.* London: Abacus Books, 1979 (1976).

Gross, Paul. "Flights of Fancy: Science, Reason and Common Sense." Pp. 79–86 in *The Flight from Science and Reason,* ed. Paul Gross, Norman Levitt, and Martin W. Lewis. New York: New York Academy of Sciences, 1996.

Gross, Paul, and Norman Levitt. *Higher Superstition: The Academic Left and its Quarrels with Science.* Baltimore and London: John Hopkins University Press, 1994.

Gross, Paul, Norman Levitt, and Martin W. Lewis, ed. *The Flight from Science and Reason.* New York: New York Academy of Sciences, 1996.

Hayles, N. B. "Androgyny, Ambivalence, and Assimilation in *The Left Hand of Darkness.*" Pp. 97–115 in *Ursula K. Le Guin,* ed. Joseph D. Olander and Martin Harry Greenberg. New York: Taplinger, 1979.

Hegel, G. W. F. *Hegel on Tragedy,* ed. Anne Paolucci and Henry Paolucci. New York: Doubleday, 1962.

———. *Phenomenology of Spirit,* trans. A. V. Miller. Oxford: Clarendon Press, 1977.

Huntington, John. "Public and Private Imperatives in Le Guin's Novels." Pp. 267–72 in *Science-Fiction Studies: Selected Articles on Science Fiction,* ed. R. D. Mullen and Darko Suvin. New York: Gregg Press, 1976.

Klein, Gerard. "Le Guin's 'Aberrant' Opus: Escaping the Trap of Discontent." Pp. 85–97 in *Ursula K. Le Guin,* ed. Harold Bloom. New York: Chelsea House, 1985.

Koertge, Noretta. *A House Built on Sand: Exposing Postmodernist Myths About Science.* New York: Oxford University Press, 1998.

Koper, Peter T. "Science and Rhetoric in the Fiction of Ursula Le Guin." Pp. 66–88 in *Ursula K. Le Guin: Voyage to Inner Lands and to Outer Space,* ed. Joe De Bolt. New York: Kennikat, 1979.

Kropotkin, Peter. *Modern Science and Anarchism.* London: Freedom Press, 1912.

Le Guin, Ursula K. *Always Coming Home.* London: Grafton Books, 1988 (1985).

———. "American SF and the Other." Pp. 97–100 in her *The Language of the Night: Essays on Fantasy and Science Fiction,* edited by Susan Wood. New York: Perigee Books, 1979.

———. *Dancing at the Edge of the World: Thoughts on Words, Women, Places.* New York: Harper & Row, 1990.

———. *The Dispossessed: An Ambiguous Utopia.* New York: Eos, HarperCollins, 2001 (1974).

———. "Dreams Must Explain Themselves." Pp. 47–56 in her *The Language of the Night: Essays on Fantasy and Science Fiction,* ed. Susan Wood. New York: Perigee Books, 1979.

———. "The Masters." Pp. 46–63 in her *The Wind's Twelve Quarters,* vol. I. London: Panther Books, 1978.

———. "On Norman Spinrad's *The Iron Dream.*" Pp. 155–58 in *Science-Fiction Studies: Selected Articles on Science Fiction,* ed. R. D. Mullen and Darko Suvin. New York: Gregg Press, 1976.

———. "Schrödinger's Cat." Pp. 26–34 in *Universe 5,* ed. Terry Carr. New York: Random House, 1974.

———. "Science Fiction and Mrs. Brown." Pp. 101–20 in her *The Language of the Night: Essays on Fantasy and Science Fiction,* ed. Susan Wood. New York: Perigee Books, 1979.

———. "The Stars Below." Pp. 60–81 in her *The Wind's Twelve Quarters,* vol. 2. London: Panther Books, 1980.

Lyotard, Jean François. *The Postmodern Condition: A Report on Knowledge.* Manchester, UK: Manchester University Press, 1984 (1979).

Moore, John. "An Archaeology of the Future: Ursula Le Guin and Anarcho-Primitivism." *Foundation: The Review of Science Fiction* 63 (Spring 1995): 32–40.

Norris, Christopher. *Against Relativism: Philosophy of Science, Deconstruction, and Critical Theory.* Oxford: Blackwell, 1997.

———. *New Idols of the Cave: On the Limits of Anti-Realism.* Manchester, UK: Manchester University Press, 1997.

———. *Quantum Theory and the Flight from Realism: Philosophical Responses to Quantum Mechanics.* London: Routledge, 2000.

Nudelman, Rafael. "An Approach to the Structure of Le Guin's SF." Pp. 240–50 in *Science-Fiction Studies: Selected Articles on Science Fiction*, ed. R. D. Mullen and Darko Suvin. New York: Gregg Press, 1976.

Parrinder, Patrick. "Science Fiction and the Scientific World View." Pp. 67–89 in *SF: A Critical Guide*, ed. Patrick Parrinder. London: Longman, 1979.

Parsons, Keith, ed. *The Science Wars: Debating Scientific Knowledge and Technology*. Amherst, NY: Prometheus Books, 2003.

Rabkin, Erik S. "Determinism, Free Will, and Point of View in *The Left Hand of Darkness*." Pp. 155–69 in *Ursula K. Le Guin*, ed. Harold Bloom. New York: Chelsea House, 1985.

Read, Herbert. *Anarchy and Order*. London: Souvenir Press, 1974.

Ross, Andrew, ed. *Science Wars*. Durham, NC: Duke University Press, 1996.

Slusser, George Edgar. *The Farthest Shores of Ursula K. Le Guin*. San Bernadino, CA: Borgo Press, 1976.

Segerstråle, Ullica, ed. *Beyond the Science Wars. The Missing Discourse About Science and Society*. Albany, NY: SUNY Press, 2000.

Sokal, Alan, and Jean Bricmont, *Intellectual Impostures: Postmodern Philosophers' Abuse of Science*. London: Profile Books, 1998.

Suvin, Darko. "Parables of De-Alienation: Le Guin's Widdershins Dance." Pp. 134–50 in his *Positions and Presuppositions in Science Fiction*. Kent, OH: Kent State University Press, 1988.

Tavormina, M. Teresa. "Physics as Metaphor: The General Temporal Theory in *The Dispossessed*." *Mosaic* 13, no. 3–4 (Spring/Summer 1980): 51–62.

Taylor, Angus. "The Politics of Space, Time and Entropy." *Foundation* 10 (1976): 34–44.

Theall, Donald. "The Art of Social-Science Fiction: The Ambiguous Utopian Dialectics of Ursula K. Le Guin." Pp. 286–94 in *Science-Fiction Studies: Selected Articles on Science Fiction 1973–1975*, ed. R. D. Mullen and Darko Suvin. New York: Gregg Press, 1976.

Tifft, Larry L., and Dennis C. Sullivan. "Possessed Sociology and Le Guin's *Dispossessed*: From Exile to Anarchism." Pp. 180–97 in *Ursula K. Le Guin: Voyage to Inner Lands and to Outer Space*, ed. Joe De Bolt. New York: Kennikat Press, 1979.

Urbanowicz, Victor. "Personal and Political in *The Dispossessed*." Pp. 145–54 in *Ursula K. Le Guin*, ed. Harold Bloom. New York: Chelsea House, 1985.

Ward, Jonathan. "Interview With Ursula K. Le Guin." Pp. 30–37 in *Dreams Must Explain Themselves*, by Ursula K. Le Guin. New York: Algol Press, 1975.

Watson, Ian. "Le Guin's *Lathe of Heaven* and the Role of Dick: The False Reality as Mediator." Pp. 223–31 in *Science-Fiction Studies: Selected Articles on Science Fiction*, ed. R. D. Mullen and Darko Suvin. New York: Gregg Press, 1976.

———. "What Do You Want—The Moon?" *Foundation* 9 (1975): 75–83.

Wood, Susan. "Discovering Worlds: The Fiction of Ursula K. Le Guin." Pp. 183–210 in *Ursula K. Le Guin*, ed. Harold Bloom. New York: Chelsea House, 1985.

———. "Introduction." Pp. 11–18 in Ursula K. Le Guin, *The Language of the Night: Essays on Fantasy and Science Fiction*, ed. Susan Wood. New York: Perigee Books, 1979.

V

REVOLUTIONARY POLITICS

12

The Gap in the Wall:
Partnership, Physics, and Politics
in *The Dispossessed*

Everett L. Hamner

There was a wall. It did not look important.

—*The Dispossessed* (1: 1)

$\mathcal{A}$s other critics have suggested, walls are a central image in Ursula K. Le Guin's *The Dispossessed*. However, the potential of these walls to stifle utopia has been overemphasized. Certainly, some of the novel's walls merely imprison, but others make possible the very freedom the text celebrates. Although some walls enable exploitative relationships, others facilitate a dialectic through which interdependent opposites may be both distinct and unified. I read Le Guin's novel as presenting both possibilities, but favoring the latter: as in Taoism's *yin-yang* symbol, walls must be both strong and permeable, both firm and mobile, if they are to promote healthy relationships, insightful science, and societies that can approach (but never finally attain) the ideals of utopia.[1] This understanding of walls is useful for understanding not only *The Dispossessed*'s personal relationships, physics, and politics, but also the place of Le Guin's corpus within the utopian tradition.

When Le Guin portrays walls negatively, as mere obstacles, they separate two parties who view each other as objects for domination or manipulation. This is perhaps most starkly evident in the relationship between Shevek and Vea, which is motivated initially by simple curiosity but ultimately by Vea's seductive flirtatiousness and Shevek's surrender to her charms. Shevek's naïveté about Urrasti society contributes to this process, but it is largely the result of Vea's inability to know an other without assimilating him—she "collect[s] people" (7: 199). Even when Shevek first meets Vea at Oiie's home, we sense that her identity is divided: "she did not laugh with herself but at herself, the body's dark laughter, wiping out words" (7: 197). She offers glimpses of a subtle mind, but one thoroughly subjugated to her physical self. Shevek reflects, "she was so elaborately and ostentatiously a female body that she seemed scarcely to be a human being. She incarnated all the sexuality the Ioti repressed." In fact, she is "the woman in the table" (7: 213) that Shevek had recognized when exploring his cabin on *The Mindful*. Vea's internal compartmentalization is particularly evident in the absolute divisions she asserts between past and present and between her luxurious surroundings and those of A-Io's lower classes. She deflects Shevek's horror at Queen Teaea's cloak of human skins, for example, by saying, "But it's all just history. Things like that couldn't happen now!" (7: 217).

Most importantly, there is a formidable wall between Vea's theoretical ethics and her actual behavior. Objecting to Shevek's anti-Darwinist view that cooperation is more fundamental to survival than competition, she says, "I don't care about hurting and not hurting. I don't care about other people, and nobody else does, either. They pretend to. I don't want to pretend. I want to be free!" (7: 220). Vea believes that there can be a freedom without limits of any kind; she asserts a hedonism that acknowledges no distinction between temporary pleasures and lasting joy. However, when the influence of liquor causes Shevek to lose control and interpret her flirtation as sexual invitation, she suddenly qualifies her professed denial of ethical boundaries. "Listen, don't mess up my clothes, people will notice" (7: 230), she objects. Vea is entirely willing to have sex with Shevek—she is unconcerned about adultery—but she is obsessed with maintaining her social good name. Ironically, she wants "freedom," but she is enslaved to her public reputation. Appropriately, Shevek is capable only of ejaculating upon her dress. The wall that divides them allows each party to objectify the other.

Such absolute walls are also found in the novel's physics. Consider the working relationship between Shevek and Sabul, in which Shevek is warned from the beginning that he will be "[Sabul's] man" (2: 58). Sadly, Shevek finds in a university physics department the same overdependence on tradition that he experienced in his early schoolboy days, when a teacher reduced his independent creativity to "egoizing" (2: 29). Like Vea, Sabul is hindered by unnecessary intellectual barriers; he derides Gvarab's lectures on Simultaneity principles as "profiteering crap" and asserts that "we're working on physics here, not religion" (4: 104). To Sabul, the empiricism of Sequency physics is a more comfortable world than the explicit subjectivity of Simultaneity theory, and so he rejects the latter approach outright. His dependence on neat divisions is also apparent in his expectation that Shevek hide his knowledge behind walls like those separating products from their sources in A-Io, as if physics could be "a property, a source of power over his colleagues" (4: 109). Similarly unacknowledged inequities persist in the physics office, which "was of course communal, but Sabul kept this back room of the two littered with materials he was using, so that there never seemed to be quite room for anyone else" (4: 114). Finally, Sabul erects walls of false ownership by claiming primary credit for Shevek's work, creating a relationship that evokes one of Le Guin's most explicit references to Kropotkin's political theory: "a fundamental, unadmitted profit contract. Not a relationship of mutual aid and solidarity, but an exploitative relationship" (4: 117). Further examples of Sabul's domineering tendencies would only reinforce the point that both his physics and his interactions with others depend upon constructing absolute walls that limit both knowledge and freedom.

Beyond Shevek's relationships with Vea and Sabul, Shevek also finds walls being used as absolute barriers in the political relationships between A-Io and Thu and between Anarres and Urras. Neither A-Io nor Thu succeeds in dominating the other, but their attempts to do so and their respective capitalism and communism invite Cold War comparisons. We see this particularly in Chifoilisk's fear that Shevek's theories will enable "these fat Ioti capitalists" (5: 139) to acquire technology that will subjugate Thu to A-Io. Pae reveals the same concern in his smug reference to Chifoilisk's sudden departure from A-Io. Such suspicion also reigns in the relationship between Urras and its so-called moon, worlds separated by "the dry and terrible abyss" (4: 91). Even to fellow physicists like Atro who reach out to Shevek, the opportunity is as much about politics as science; it is a chance to upstage not only the Thuvians but also the Hainish, because "the law of existence is struggle—competition—elimination of the weak—a ruthless war for survival" (5: 143). Even to Urrasti who are less conscious of such maneuvers, Shevek is an object of curiosity but not a subject to be sincerely engaged. This is why Shevek finds himself locked in his room on *The Mindful*, encounters audiences that clap happily even when he directly insults their way of life, hears in Pae's public voice little more than "charm, courtesy, indifference" (3: 80), and tells the people at Vea's party, "It is all I can see in your eyes—the wall, the wall!" (7: 229). Like the feces-covered classmate who had been imprisoned under the learning center, Urras reeks of unsatisfied desires. Predicated on the assumption that "if people can possess enough things they will be content to live in prison" (5: 138), it leaves the individual "alone, solitary, with a heap of what he owns" (7: 229).

What we have seen thus far, then, is the accuracy of the unwitting prophecy that Shevek makes before departing for Urras. When Takver insists that he consider making the trip, he observes, "What a crazy idea! Like Tirin's play, only backwards. I'm to go subvert the archists" (12: 376–77). In Tirin's play, an Urrasti stowaway makes it to Anarres only to attempt to buy, sell, and possess things just as he would have at home; he even refuses a woman who would rather give than sell sex because taking it for free is "not good business!" (10: 327). Shevek's prediction before leaving Anarres that the story will be reversed is therefore more accurate than he knows. He will be a guest, not a stowaway, and he will try to copulate with a woman—Vea—who refuses *him*. Ultimately, he will help ignite a revolution in A-Io very much like the one two hundred years earlier. The only important aspect of Tirin's play not reversed is the moral that Shevek takes from it, that "those who build walls are their own prisoners" (10: 332).

Imprisoning, alienating walls are prominent in *The Dispossessed*, and so it is not surprising that they stand out in the novel's criticism. Sheila Finch rightly decries the prison walls of both *The Dispossessed* and "The Ones Who Walk Away from Omelas," and Carl Freedman accurately identifies Shevek's desire that "intellectual walls . . . be transcended."[2] Similarly, James W. Bittner and Tom Moylan both emphasize Shevek's valiant effort to "unbuild" walls, and Bülent Somay points out Le Guin's "militant opposition to isolation and enclosure."[3] Neil Easterbrook, Philip E. Smith II, and Susan Wood take similar views. Although full of valuable insights, these essays imply that the only important walls in the novel are those that Shevek is determined to destroy. Alternatively, M. Teresa Tavormina and Bernard Selinger[4] insist that some walls in *The Dispossessed* are *not* repudiated. In an excellent essay on the novel's physics, Tavormina observes that even with Shevek's discovery of formulas that will enable instantaneous communication across galaxies, "walls and abysses are not really taken away."[5] Widely separated peoples will now have the opportunity to communicate, but as Shevek recognizes, they will still have the problem of deciding what to say. Similarly, Selinger observes that "the unity that would come with closing the gap completely or unbuilding all walls is illusory; and the structure of the novel implies as much"; "total unity"[6] between Anarres and Urras is neither reached nor on the horizon. The closest the novel moves to such unity, he says, is the step that Ketho will take with Shevek in accompanying him onto Anarresti soil. "The novel does 'end,' the way it began," Selinger argues, "with the idea of the badness of walls and the need to remove them; but the conclusion we are forced to make is that no matter how bad walls are, they seem to be necessary."[7]

Tavormina's and Selinger's observations lead me to propose that there are actually two concepts of walls at work in the novel, not just one, and that *The Dispossessed* upholds "Taoist" walls over either absolute walls that enable abuse or any attempt to eliminate walls entirely. We must account in some way for the fact that while Shevek goes to Urras with the intention of unbuilding walls—and that in finding his General Temporal Theory he even sees that "the wall was down" (9: 280)—he also implicitly reasserts the need for walls by deciding that Urras is "hell" and returning to Anarres. Are walls such as the one around the landing field simply necessary evils, as Selinger calls them? I think the novel makes a more optimistic suggestion: although walls can merely obstruct justice, they are also a central component of freedom. Instead of being absolute, they must be sufficiently permeable and mobile to allow for change, but also solid and stable enough to protect that change as it occurs. In contrast to the negative walls on which I have focused to this point, such walls not only provide freedom *from* something, but also freedom *for* something.

Consider Shevek's partnership with Takver, a relationship that represents the novel's most thorough expression of the positive potential of walls. I consider it the novel's most explicit chronotope, a term coined by M. M. Bakhtin to emphasize the "inseparability of space and time (time as the fourth dimension of space),"[8] a relationship in which two categories are interdependent and neither is privileged above the other. Bakhtin explains that in a chronotope, "spatial and temporal indicators are fused into one carefully thought-out, concrete whole.

Time, as it were, thickens, takes on flesh, becomes artistically visible; likewise, space becomes charged and responsive to the movements of time, plot and history."[9] This is precisely what we see between Shevek and Takver, a couple Le Guin renders as inseparable but not assimilated into a single identity, a united whole even though half of the novel places them on separate planets. Their partnership is defined not by the objectification Shevek finds with Vea, but by mutual intersubjectivity: "sacrifice might be demanded of the individual, but never compromise" (10: 333).[10] Their "bond" (6: 180) is an active promise that protects rather than threatens their "distance, interval"—they can actively give themselves up to the other, but without losing their unique selves in the process. In essence, we see that in order to enjoy an authentic partnership rather than a never-ceasing battle for superiority, they need limitations. As Shevek puts it, "I'll die, you'll die; how could we love each other otherwise? The sun's going to burn out, what else keeps it shining?" (6: 190). Maintaining flexible walls allows Shevek and Takver to be distinct individuals, rather than one identity assimilated into another, and makes their partnership "not an institution but a function" (8: 244).

The enduring freedom that these partners give one another "ma[kes] the promise meaningful" even when they are separated for four years. Rather than being bound to a contractual abnegation of separate identities, "the self-limitation of choice" (8: 244) allows them "to maintain genuine spontaneous fidelity" (8: 246). They do not possess each other, but together "assert the wholeness of Time" (8: 252). Their wall of separation has a gap in which two can be one but also remain two. Nowhere is the difference between their relationship and Shevek's brief infatuation with Vea more evident than upon their reunion after years apart: whereas Vea is so overwhelmingly sensual that she seems incapable of anything else, Shevek finds Takver with two fewer teeth, "so that the gaps showed when she smiled. Her skin no longer had the fine taut surface of youth, and her hair, pulled back neatly, was dull" (10: 316). At the same time, there is a mutuality and balance in their partnership that Vea would not understand. Le Guin's astronomical metaphors when Shevek makes love with Takver allude powerfully to his work in physics and perhaps even his dream of an Anarres and Urras that respect each other. He and Takver "circled about the center of infinite pleasure, about each other's being, like planets circling blindly, quietly, in the flood of sunlight, about the common center of gravity, swinging, circling endlessly." As Takver reflects afterward, they have always come to each other "over great distances, over years, over abysses of chance" (10: 322). Perhaps this is what influences her to create a new mobile that she calls "the Inhabitation of Time"—a chronotope in itself—which has "two thin, clear bubbles of glass that moved with the oval wires in completely interwoven ellipsoid orbits about the common center, never quite meeting, never entirely parting" (12: 367–68). Through both sexual and artistic metaphors, Le Guin suggests that the authenticity of Shevek's and Takver's partnership, like that of any sustainable relationship, depends on the fact that both parties remain subjects orbiting a common center, rather than one party becoming a mere satellite of the other.[11]

These references to a "common center," "abyss of chance," and "center of infinite pleasure" are among the clearest images Le Guin provides of walls' positive potential. At times such "walls" are invisible boundaries rather than physical structures, but in every instance they provide both separation and unity at one and the same moment. This image of walls is also found in the novel's physics, especially between the historically divided scientific approaches that Le Guin names Sequency and Simultaneity. Through several glimpses of Shevek's boyhood, the novel introduces us very quickly to the problem—Zeno's Paradox—that will occupy him for years to come. As Shevek realizes, if he throws a rock at a tree, the rock must at some point be halfway between him and the tree, and then at some point halfway between *that* point and the tree, and so on into infinity. Theoretically, the rock should never reach the tree. Of course it does, though, so Shevek's General Temporal Theory has to account for both the Sequency of time (the succession of instants by which the rock's forward progress can be measured) and its Simultaneity (the larger perspective in which the rock-throwing and tree-hitting constitute a single action). No thinker to date has uncovered equations that satisfy this requirement, but this is the most important science fictional *novum* in this novel. As Tavormina recognizes, Shevek's discovery of a theory uniting Sequency and Simultaneity is not a "hard SF" device aimed principally at scientists; instead, like the partnership between Shevek and Takver, it is a search for an understanding of walls that serves both sides equally.[12]

The parallel with the novel's personal relationships is especially vivid in the fact that Shevek has to study both Sequency and Simultaneity theory in their separate domains before he can attempt a larger theory that might harmonize them. On one hand, he sees that Sequency explains our normal experience of time as linear progression, in which things can be born and die. However, "it speaks only of the arrow of time—never of the circle of time" (7: 223). To deal with the circle, he needs Simultaneity physics, which treats succession not as "a physically objective phenomenon, but as a subjective one" (7: 221) in which the movement of the interpreter is acknowledged. As Shevek explains to Dearri, "if you are a Simultanist the rock has already hit the tree, and if you are a Sequentist it never can. So which do you choose? . . . I prefer to make things difficult, and choose both" (7: 225). This rejection of binary thinking allows Shevek to devise a General Temporal Theory that at first glance might seem to eliminate walls—when Shevek finally reaches it, in fact, the narrator tells us that "the wall was down." What we must realize, however, is that the wall that falls is merely that of certainty. Shevek's "revelation . . . the way clear, the way home, the light" (9: 280) is not the elimination of the distinction between Sequency and Simultaneity, but the discovery of a relationship. Shevek realizes that the "arrow" of time and the "circle" of time together create an arrow that spirals forward, so that history can be both progressive and cyclical. The understanding of walls eschewed here is the one we observed earlier, in which walls uphold tradition but fail to provide shelter. The walls that Le Guin leaves standing provide protection with a purpose—

like those of Shevek's room in Abbenay, where he realizes that "privacy . . . was almost as desirable for physics as it was for sex" (4: 111).

The insight that emerges in the novel's physics metaphors, then, is that there is a fundamental relationship between our understandings of time and human beings—whether there are two or two million of them. Shevek realizes that even the physics of time, chronosophy, "involve[s] ethics": babies and animals cannot make a promise any more than they can make a pulley, because they recognize no wall between "*now*" and "*not now*"—a boundary necessary for morality. Shevek observes that "to break a promise is to deny the reality of the past; therefore it is to deny the hope of a real future" (7: 225). In other words, denying that there are walls between past, present, and future is as dangerous as making those walls absolute; either way both physics and ethics become impossible. We have seen already how Shevek and Takver's relationship depends on the promise, the fact as Takver puts it that Shevek "always come[s] back" (12: 379); we can now see how this is true of relationships between whole nations and even planets. There is a small difference here, in that the harmonious relationships between Shevek and Takver and between Sequency and Simultaneity reach full maturity, while a more ideal future relationship between Anarres and Urras remains a distant hope. Nonetheless, the novel's politics also drives us toward the ideal of a permeable, mobile wall rather than an absolute wall or the complete removal of walls.

Such a wall does not diminish Anarres's status as an anarchist experiment; Le Guin once observed that the political system she explores here is "the most idealistic, and to me the most interesting, of all political theories."[13] However, even Anarres's ideals depend upon limits. Originally settled by Urrasti revolutionaries who wanted a new start, the planet offers a space free from interference. The wall between the worlds, the abyss yawning between them, is in this sense a positive necessity, just like the privacy that Shevek appreciates for sex and physics. Two centuries later, however, Shevek slowly grasps that the wall has become nearly absolute. Children learn of Urras only as it was known by much earlier generations; Anarres is gradually slipping back toward the possessiveness repudiated by its founders. Upon traveling to Urras, Shevek realizes that a central problem in A-Io is that many people are maintained "in complete freedom from want, distractions, and cares," but "their freedom from obligation was in exact proportion to their lack of freedom of initiative" (5: 127). However, despite an environment harsh enough to lead a physicist to spend four years in manual labor and a mother to kill her starving child, Anarres is gradually developing the same inhibitions as its parent. As Bedap insists, the shift from "cooperation" to mere "obedience" (6: 167) is occurring quite subtly.

Both cooperation and obedience involve interaction with an other, but the former is predicated on walls that maintain communal and individual integrity, while the latter depends on walls that enforce hierarchy. Public opinion matters a great deal on both planets; whereas it is openly expressed on Anarres, however, it is repressed into such intangibles as "reputation" on Urras. Slavoj Zizek argues that "the real aim of ideology is the attitude demanded by it"[14] and that the most powerful ideologies are those that hide behind facades of complete utopia— exactly what we see in A-Io. Vea's society believes that its citizens enjoy true freedom, but in fact they are far more bound to convention and public expectation than even the most restrictive Anarresti. Gradually, though, Shevek sees that Anarres is capable of drifting back into such fundamentalism, and this motivates his observation that, while "the opinion of the neighbors" is a mighty force, it is a force defied "perhaps not often enough" (5: 150). In order for his world's anarchism to work, his society must not just honor its past but continue to be "a revolution, a permanent one, an ongoing process" (6: 176).

What sort of wall is required, then, if Anarres is to reclaim its founders' revolutionary ambitions? I suggest that it is not a new wall, but the wall the Anarresti already have, *properly understood*. In the novel's opening scenes at the landing site, this understanding is clearly absent. A mob attempts to block an individual's choice to leave his world behind, suggesting that Anarres is little different from A-Io or Thu. As Shevek tells Rulag, however, "we didn't come to Anarres for safety, but for freedom. . . . We are not subjects of a State founded upon law, but members of a society founded upon revolution" (12: 359). This is one reason why Shevek must go to Urras even when his Institute offers him a permanent posting: allowing himself and his syndicate to be domesticated would only make Anarres's boundary more difficult to cross. Unlike Shevek's mother, his partner understands this. Takver says, "If our society is settling down into politics and power seeking, then we'll get out, we'll go make an Anarres beyond Anarres, a new beginning" (12: 379). In her mind, a fundamental characteristic of Anarresti citizenship, like partnership with Shevek, is the individual's ongoing freedom to accept or reject it, and this is why the wall constructed around the landing site by the society's founders is so appropriate. The wall is not unbroken but has a gap "where the road cut through the wall" (1: 2). Rulag's and her followers' attempt to eliminate this gap is a mistake that would transform a wall enabling freedom into one that invites fundamentalism.

It is the permeability of this wall that Shevek reasserts as he dares the crowd in departing and returning to Anarres. However, even he only gradually understands that this wall, like those separating him from Takver and Simultaneity from Sequency, must be both respected and traversed. At the end of chapter 4, sick in Abbenay, Shevek is unable to reestablish a relationship with his mother, leaving him despondent "in the dark at the foot of the wall" (4: 125); at the end of the next chapter, years later on Urras, he dreams of "a distant line of something that looked flimsy and shiny, like plastic, a remote, hardly visible barrier" (5: 153). However, neither collapsing at the base of an absolute wall nor imagining that wall's withdrawal proves sufficient, whether what lies on the other side is a neglectful human mother, a disdainful mother planet, or one's own home world. Instead, Shevek has to reassert the gap in the wall, first alone and then alongside another alien. His invitation to the young Hainishman is significantly worded:

"You're sure you want to walk through this wall with me, Ketho?" (13: 386). Unlike most of his people, Shevek realizes that the wall around his world is dangerous only if rendered absolute or eliminated; it cannot be evaded or denied, but only passed *through*.

Initially, it may be tempting to assume that Shevek aims to *eliminate* the wall separating Anarres from Urras. That is indeed the case if we are discussing walls merely as obstructions that enable injustice. In this sense, Shevek deeply admires Tirin because "he never could build walls. . . . He was a free man" (10: 331). The same kinds of walls are demolished by Shevek's General Temporal Theory: "there were no more abysses, no more walls" (9: 281). Likewise, at the political level, Shevek's society is not an attempt to eliminate morality, but "to throw out the moralizing, yes—the rules, the laws, the punishments—so that men can see good and evil and choose between them" (7: 219). Each of these examples recognizes the capacity of walls to function simply as obstacles to freedom. However, we must also account for several of the novel's most crucial insights: that it is only through maintaining a wall between self and other that Shevek and Takver's relationship thrives, that Shevek's grand unifying theory is a harmonization rather than a mixture of Sequency and Simultaneity physics, and, most importantly, that Anarres can only pursue the freedoms it envisions by maintaining a wall between itself and Urras.

This last contention contains perhaps the most significant implications for studies of Le Guin, utopia, and borders in our own world. Considering *The Dispossessed* in the contexts of Le Guin's wider corpus and the larger utopian tradition, one is struck by the fact that Anarres's ambiguous utopia exists only as a departure from Urras's ambiguous dystopia. This is remindful of Le Guin's preface to the short story, "The Day Before the Revolution," in which she refers to Odo as "one of the ones who walked away from Omelas."[15] Her famous "Omelas" story suggests that the supposedly complete utopia depends upon some sort of repressed horror, even if it is contained within a small basement room, and that an ethical response is to renounce this injustice by "walking away." However, *The Dispossessed* takes this situation a step further by showing how righteous repudiation of an ambiguous dystopia can lead, ever so subtly and ironically, to blind celebration of a new one. Indeed, when Anarres begins to gloss over the reality of its history, attempting to wall itself off completely from its largely dystopian parent, this is the moment when it most dangerously resembles Urras.

The unavoidably intertwined fate of two cultures and the impossibility of a healthy future without an accurately understood past are themes characteristic of much of Le Guin's fiction. In *Always Coming Home*, the people of the Valley are never entirely free from the Condors; in *The Eye of the Heron*, those who leave Shanty Town for the wilderness are pursued by soldiers from the City; in *A Wizard of Earthsea*, Ged is chased by his shadow; and most recently, in *The Telling*, the people of the Telling exist in quiet defiance of the Corporation State, whose Monitor follows them even to their remote mountain library.[16] Inevitably, as is especially clear in the novella "Paradises Lost" (published in *The Birthday of the World*), any utopia that denies its history and seeks a self-encapsulated, unambiguous "bliss" ultimately degenerates into a dystopian nightmare. Le Guin specializes in imagining the revolutionary societies that emerge in defiance of such oversimplifications. One might even say that utopia is sustainable for her only through active, ongoing choices against the tangible possibility of dystopia—and that this is possible only if there remains a gap in the wall between worlds.

What does this mean for the literary and political possibilities of utopia? If we are to imagine or construct a good society, may we do so only by intentionally abandoning visions of complete, unambiguous utopia? As Kim Stanley Robinson commented in a recent interview, there is no easy recipe. Reflecting on Fredric Jameson's assertion that utopia does not exist to help us imagine a better future but to reveal "our own incapacity to conceive it in the first place,"[17] Robinson suggests that the greatest challenge is "imagining any plausible way of getting from here to there."[18] Robinson's observation points to one of the most important contributions of *The Dispossessed* to the utopian tradition: by setting the relationship of Anarres to Urras alongside *yin-yang* relationships on the most intimately personal and cosmically physical scales, the novel provides metaphors (but not formulas) by which we may understand walls in our own world. Le Guin does not show Urras become Anarres, and Anarres itself remains an incomplete utopia, but we see the beginnings of revolution in Thu and A-Io and the hope of renewed progress in the revolution on Anarres.

Finally, it is worth noting how unusual Le Guin's fiction is in its equal attention to utopian and dystopian spaces. Generally, utopian and dystopian novels focus on one world or the other: *Utopia*, *Looking Backward*, *News from Nowhere*, and *Herland* focus on visitors from our world spending time in a better one, while *We*, *Brave New World*, and *Nineteen Eighty-Four* invert this pattern by focusing on insurgents living in a terrible world that makes us better appreciate our own. Le Guin's approach, however, renders both "good" and "bad" societies quite ambiguously.[19] Her novel suggests that in a true utopia, there may be a "day before the revolution," but never a day after. Whether between individuals, theories of physics, or whole worlds, walls can be neither eliminated nor closed completely without assuring stagnation and the subtle reemergence of exploitation.

NOTES

Many thanks for thoughtful responses at various stages of this chapter's development by Ursula Le Guin, Loren Wilkinson, Florence Boos, Laurence Davis, and Peter Stillman.

1. For further insight into Le Guin's engagement with Taoist philosophy, see Dena C. Bain, "The *Tao Te Ching* as Background to the Novels of Ursula K. Le Guin," *Extrapolation* 21, no. 3 (Fall 1980) and Le Guin's own translation of Lao Tzu's text. Ursula K. Le

Guin, *The Dispossessed: An Ambiguous Utopia* (New York: Harper & Row, 1974), cited in the text by chapter and page to the 387-page Eos HarperCollins edition of 2001.

2. Carl Freedman, *Critical Theory and Science Fiction* (Hanover, NH: Wesleyan University Press, 2000), 113.

3. Bülent Somay, "Towards an Open-Ended Utopia," *Science-Fiction Studies* 11, no. 1 (March 1984): 32.

4. M. Teresa Tavormina, "Physics as Metaphor: The General Temporal Theory in *The Dispossessed*," *Mosaic* 13, nos. 3–4 (Spring/Summer 1980); Bernard Selinger, *Le Guin and Identity in Contemporary Fiction* (Ann Arbor: University of Michigan Research Press, 1988).

5. Tavormina, "Physics as Metaphor," 60.

6. Selinger, *Le Guin and Identity*, 125.

7. Selinger, *Le Guin and Identity*, 126.

8. M. M. Bakhtin, *The Dialogic Imagination*, ed. Michael Holquist, trans. Caryl Emerson and Michael Holquist (Austin: University of Texas Press, 1981).

9. Bakhtin, *The Dialogic Imagination*, 84.

10. The severity of the contrast between Takver and Vea is explicated helpfully in Robert M. Philmus's essay on the novel, which refers to Shevek's connection with Vea as "a travesty of a true bond." Robert M. Philmus, "Ursula Le Guin and Time's Dispossession," in *Science Fiction Roots and Branches: Contemporary Critical Approaches*, ed. Rhys Garnett and R. J. Ellis (London: Macmillan, 1990), 133.

11. Le Guin's use of couples as metaphors for other relationships in her fiction has also been noted by Naomi Jacobs, Tarya Malkki, and Heinz Tschachler. Jacobs views Le Guin's novels as using "marriage as a central metaphor" for both individual transformation and utopian revival (Naomi Jacobs, "Beyond Stasis and Symmetry: Lessing, Le Guin, and the Remodeling of Utopia," *Extrapolation* 29, no. 1 [Spring 1988]: 37); Malkki links "[Le Guin's] intimate pairs to her allied nations" in *The Dispossessed* (Tarya Malkki, "The Marriage Metaphor in the Works of Ursula K. Le Guin," in *Modes of the Fantastic: Selected Essays from the Twelfth International Conference on the Fantastic in the Arts*, ed. Robert A. Latham and Robert A. Collins [Westport, CT: Greenwood, 1995], 105); and Tschachler suggests that in the conclusion of *Four Ways to Forgiveness* the joining of two people is a step toward the reconciliation of two worlds (Heinz Tschachler, "'How to Walk with My People': Ursula K. Le Guin's Futuristic Frontier Mythology," *Western American Literature* 33, no. 3 [Fall 1998]).

12. Tavormina, "Physics as Metaphor."

13. Ursula K. Le Guin, "The Day Before the Revolution," in *The Wind's Twelve Quarters* (New York: Harper, 1991 [1975]), 360.

14. Slavoj Zizek, *The Sublime Object of Ideology* (New York: Verso, 1989), 83.

15. Le Guin, "The Day Before the Revolution," 360.

16. For an excellent essay on *The Eye of the Heron* that considers that novel's walls, see Richard D. Erlich and Diana Perkins, "Herons, Ringtrees, and Mud: Ursula K. Le Guin's *The Eye of the Heron*," *Extrapolation* 43, no. 3 (Fall 2002). Although Erlich and Perkins's essay is not entirely focused on this image, it recognizes that in this novel, too, Le Guin sees walls as potentially positive: "Shantih, too, has its walls, 'not visible but . . . very strong: companionship, cooperation, love'" (319).

17. Fredric Jameson, "World-Reduction in Le Guin: The Emergence of Utopian Narrative," in *The Jameson Reader*, ed. Michael Hardt and Kathi Weeks (Oxford: Blackwell, 2000), 380.

18. Imre Szeman and Maria Whiteman, "Future Politics: An Interview with Kim Stanley Robinson," *Science Fiction Studies* 31, no. 2 (July 2004): 187.

19. In making this observation, I want to be careful not to exacerbate the tendency to oversimplify the utopian tradition. Most utopias and dystopias, even those earlier than the twentieth century, are more ambiguous than is recognized generally. To cite just two examples, consider Thomas More's *Utopia* and William Morris's *News from Nowhere*. The former relies on multiple levels of narration to create complexity; a character named Thomas More, who has conveyed the testimony of "Raphael Nonsenso," concludes the text by observing, "I cannot agree with everything that he said, for all his undoubted learning and experience. But I freely admit that there are many features of the Utopian Republic which I should like—though I hardly expect—to see adopted in Europe." Likewise, although Morris's future society is rendered less ambiguously than Le Guin's, his world does suffer occasional killings and has not eliminated ungrateful grumblers.

WORKS CITED

Bain, Dena C. "The *Tao Te Ching* as Background to the Novels of Ursula K. Le Guin." *Extrapolation* 21, no. 3 (Fall 1980): 209–22.

Bakhtin, M. M. *The Dialogic Imagination*, ed. Michael Holquist, trans. Caryl Emerson and Michael Holquist. Austin: University of Texas Press, 1981.

Bittner, James W. "Chronosophy, Aesthetics, and Ethics in Le Guin's *The Dispossessed: An Ambiguous Utopia*." Pp. 244–70 in *No Place Else: Explorations in Utopian and Dystopian Fiction*, ed. Eric S. Rabkin, Martin H. Greenberg, and Joseph D. Olander. Carbondale: Southern Illinois University Press, 1983.

Easterbrook, Neil. "State, Heterotopia: The Political Imagination in Heinlein, Le Guin, and Delany." Pp. 43–75 in *Political Science Fiction*, ed. Donald M. Hassler and Clyde Wilcox. Columbia: University of South Carolina Press, 1997.

Erlich, Richard D., and Diana Perkins. "Herons, Ringtrees, and Mud: Ursula K. Le Guin's *The Eye of the Heron*." *Extrapolation* 43, no. 3 (Fall 2002): 314–29.

Finch, Sheila. "Paradise Lost: The Prison at the Heart of Le Guin's Utopia." *Extrapolation* 26, no. 3 (Fall 1985): 240–48.

Freedman, Carl. *Critical Theory and Science Fiction*. Hanover, NH: Wesleyan University Press, 2000.

Jacobs, Naomi. "Beyond Stasis and Symmetry: Lessing, Le Guin, and the Remodeling of Utopia." *Extrapolation* 29, no. 1 (Spring 1988): 33–45.

Jameson, Fredric. "World-Reduction in Le Guin: The Emergence of Utopian Narrative." Pp. 368–81 in *The Jameson Reader*, ed. Michael Hardt and Kathi Weeks. Oxford, UK: Blackwell, 2000.

Le Guin, Ursula K. *Always Coming Home*. New York: Bantam, 1985.

——. *The Birthday of the World*. New York: HarperCollins, 2002.

——. *The Dispossessed: An Ambiguous Utopia*. New York: Eos, HarperCollins, 2001 (1974).

——. *The Eye of the Heron*. New York: Harper & Row, 1978.

——. *The Telling*. New York: Harcourt, 2000.

——. *The Wind's Twelve Quarters*. New York: Harper, 1991 (1975).

———. *A Wizard of Earthsea*. New York: Bantam, 1968.

Malkki, Tarya. "The Marriage Metaphor in the Works of Ursula K. Le Guin." Pp. 100–109 in *Modes of the Fantastic: Selected Essays from the Twelfth International Conference on the Fantastic in the Arts*, ed. Robert A. Latham and Robert A. Collins. Westport, CT: Greenwood, 1995.

Moylan, Tom. "Beyond Negation: The Critical Utopias of Ursula K. Le Guin and Samuel R. Delany." *Extrapolation* 21, no. 3 (Fall 1980): 236–53.

Philmus, Robert M. "Ursula Le Guin and Time's Dispossession." Pp. 125–50 in *Science Fiction Roots and Branches: Contemporary Critical Approaches*, ed. Rhys Garnett and R. J. Ellis. London: Macmillan, 1990.

Selinger, Bernard. *Le Guin and Identity in Contemporary Fiction*. Ann Arbor: University of Michigan Research Press, 1988.

Smith, Philip E., II. "Unbuilding Walls: Human Nature and the Nature of Evolutionary and Political Theory in *The Dispossessed*." Pp. 77–96 in *Ursula K. Le Guin*, ed. Joseph D. Olander and Martin Harry Greenberg. New York: Taplinger, 1979.

Somay, Bülent. "Towards an Open-Ended Utopia," *Science-Fiction Studies* 11, no. 1 (March 1984): 25–38.

Szeman, Imre, and Maria Whiteman. "Future Politics: An Interview with Kim Stanley Robinson," *Science Fiction Studies* 31, no. 2 (July 2004): 177–88.

Tavormina, M. Teresa. "Physics as Metaphor: The General Temporal Theory in *The Dispossessed*," *Mosaic* 13, nos. 3–4 (Spring/Summer 1980): 51–62.

Tschachler, Heinz. "'How to Walk with My People': Ursula K. Le Guin's Futuristic Frontier Mythology," *Western American Literature* 33, no. 3 (Fall 1998): 254–72.

Tzu, Lao. *Tao Te Ching: A Book about the Way and the Power of the Way*, trans. Ursula K. Le Guin. Boston: Shambhala, 1998.

Wood, Susan. "Discovering Worlds: The Fiction of Ursula K. Le Guin." Pp. 183–209 in *Ursula K. Le Guin*, ed. Harold Bloom. New York: Chelsea House, 1986.

Zizek, Slavoj. *The Sublime Object of Ideology*. New York: Verso, 1989.

13

From Ambiguity to Self-Reflexivity: Revolutionizing Fantasy Space

Bülent Somay

$\mathcal{I}$t always seems to be an injustice to consider a work of literature solely from the point of view of its ideological content, by looking at what social or political message the author (who is supposed to be lurking behind their cunningly crafted creation) is trying to convey. There are, to be sure, a few authors who legitimately deserve such consideration, authors who write as if their natural habitat would have been the political/social/philosophical essay, but who chose a "more literary" form either for censorship reasons or simply because there is a bigger audience for it. We probably would not agree on *all* the names, but the first ones that come to *my* mind are Ayn Rand and, to a certain extent, Maxim Gorky, along with most of the socialist realist school. There are, however, times when a work of literature becomes an ideological beacon for a whole generation regardless of its author's intentions. Again, the first novel that comes to my mind in this respect would be Nikolay Tchernyshevsky's *What is to be Done?* Ursula K. Le Guin's *The Dispossessed* definitely belongs in this latter category.[1]

The Dispossessed was written in a period when the revolutionary wave of the 1960s—the first since the "success" of the Russian Revolution in 1917 and the following defeat of the European revolutions—was on the ebb. The "1968 Revolution" is, according to Arrighi, Hopkins, and Wallerstein, the most important world-historical revolutionary movement since the revolutions of 1848—curiously skipping both the Paris Commune of 1871 and the 1917 Bolshevik Revolution.[2] The importance of 1968 lies in the fact that it did not merely try subverting the economic foundation, but brought the entire political, cultural, ideological (super)structure into question. It involved a vast transformation in sexual traditions, national affiliations, religious and moral beliefs, and the conceptions of race, class, and gender. It also did not take place in a single country, nor was it limited to a region. It was the first truly transnational anti-systemic movement; it took place all over the world, in the United States, in almost all

233

Western Europe, and also in the "Socialist Bloc" and the Third World. It was not shaped by the existing subversive or anti-systemic ideologies only, but represented an amalgamation of the old and the new, combining elements of Marxism, anarchism, feminism, and national liberation ideologies, with psychoanalysis, sexual liberation, radical pacifism, and the first inklings of transnationalism (instead of the older "internationalism").

The Dispossessed was written (or at least conceived) in such an ideological atmosphere, but by the time it was published, the movement itself was almost over, with the end of the Vietnam War and the stabilization of world capitalism. It belonged to a generation of utopias which were rooted in the subversive movements of the sixties, were conceived in this period, but could only come to fruition after the circumstances that paved the way for their conception were almost completely gone. Other utopian texts that belong in this category, to name a few, are Joanna Russ's *Female Man*, Ernest Callenbach's *Ecotopia* and Samuel Delany's *Triton*. While Russ's and Callenbach's utopias were written from a singular ideological perspective—the former of feminism and the latter of ecologism—and therefore faced the risk of orthodoxy, Le Guin and Delany shared a more heterodox outlook despite the rather harsh polemic directed toward Le Guin by Delany.[3] Although Delany seems to have appropriated the rather postmodernist prefix "hetero-" in this polemic (proposing to replace "utopias" with "heterotopias," following Foucault), I argue that Le Guin is no less heterodox in her approach to utopianism. The main point of similarity between the two, however, is that their imagined *topoi* are both "ambiguous," although Delany's use of "ambiguity" may be due to the rhetorical necessities of the polemic.

"BOTH" IS MORE THAN TWO

We should start with Le Guin's subtitle, *An Ambiguous Utopia*. The term "ambiguous" has been met with more than a little enthusiasm, proving the nondoctrinaire approach of the author, entailing a criticism of ideology. The libertarian/anarchist/liberal critique of utopias has always stressed the hidden (and sometimes not-so-hidden) monolithic/totalitarian premise in utopianism: "Utopia is always totalitarian," Nicolas Berdyaev had said, "and totalitarianism, in the conditions of our world, always utopian."[4] The political problem with utopias is even worse than that: from Plato's *Republic* to Wells's early-twentieth-century work, *A Modern Utopia*, there are very few utopian designs, fictional or philosophical, that are not meritocratic, the exceptions being "Arcadias" or back-to-the-nature utopias which could neglect social division of labor completely and assert an absolute state of equality.[5] Most utopographers, however, have combined their criticism of any kind of oligarchy, be it economic or aristocratic, with an equally fervent dislike of democracy. The outcome of this two-edged criticism has been almost always a praise of meritocracy as a more objective and "scientific" way to rule and/or manage the affairs of society; but the important question, of who ("objectively") determined what merit was (and who the merited were), was always left unanswered, or answered by an appeal to abstractions ("philosophy") or, even worse, to positivistic pseudoscience (nominal IQ).

I have argued elsewhere[6] that the utopian tradition, up until the "open-ended" utopias of the 1970s, was authoritarian in style as well as totalitarian in content. Any social order, which is described as something final or something *finally achieved*, leaves no room for further change. As soon as change is excluded, however, any conflicts, differences, or even variations in style should be suppressed, since each of these may lead to a subversion of the existing (supposedly perfect) state of affairs. This exclusion necessitates a series of rules, regulations, laws, and conventions, breach of which may result in severe punishments, sometimes (and not very rarely) death. "Freedom" never has been (again, until the "open-ended" utopias of the 1970s) a favorite catchword of utopianism; the "greater social good," that is, the survival of the finally-realized utopia, has always been placed above individual freedom of choice: in this sense both Jacobinism and Bolshevism (at least after the expulsion of the Mensheviks and the mass assassination of the Anarchists) are "utopian," because they both place the "greater social good" (the former ethically and the latter "scientifically") above freedom of organization, expression, even above the right to live. This totalitarian content results in a narrative style that is also closed and authoritarian. Utopian narratives are usually what Barthes would call "writerly texts,"[7] and present their imaginary social orders to their audiences in the form of a referendum, a matter of "yes/no," rather than open-ended suggestions that would encourage the readers to "write" their own hopes, designs, and doubts into the texts. In short, therefore, until late twentieth century, utopia never left any room for ambiguity.

Le Guin's expression "ambiguous utopia," then, was some kind of an oxymoron, ascribing "two-ness" to something monolithic and bringing an element of doubt into something that was always philosophically or "scientifically" self-confident.

Still, we have to look further into the etymology of ambiguity in order to comprehend Le Guin's intention better. The prefix "ambi-" means "both," and in symbolic logic can only be reciprocated with a strict "and." The prefix "bi-" however, is just "two," and in symbolic logic it is an "ambiguous" and/or. A well-known "bi/ambi" argument in science is between Freud and Ferenczi: When Freud asserted that everybody is born bisexual, Ferenczi proposed to change the term to "ambisexual," meaning a presocial infant's sexual desire is directed toward both sexes as a totality, rather than an "I-don't-care-which!"[8] Ambiguity, in this sense, is more than an undecided state or a confused mind, as common usage suggests. It is an inclination towards *containing both*, and, as such, saves us from the illusory world of binary oppositions, coming closer to *aufheben*.[9] In the

Freud-Ferenczi discussion, "ambisexuality" implied a novel conception of sexuality, not delimited by the parameters of either "male" or "female" sexuality, quite different from the old term "bisexuality" which meant, "I may desire either males of females indiscriminately." I think that we are expected to make a similar effort in the case of Le Guin, rather than simply stating that she was (a) just making a cute oxymoron, or (b) just criticizing the totalitarian/monolithic utopian tradition from an anarchist/libertarian point of view.

We should start with the question whether Le Guin was "ambiguous" toward the Anarres/Urras binary opposition. "Binary" is the key word here because, apart from representing a binary opposition in the metaphorical sense, Anarres/Urras is a binary planetary system in the novel's fictional actuality. Le Guin is by no means ambiguous toward the Anarres/Urras dichotomy: she is wholeheartedly for Anarres, or at least what the Anarresti are trying to do, as she makes amply clear throughout the novel as well as in a later essay, in which she suggests that the whole enterprise was an effort "to embody [anarchism] in a novel."[10] Her main point, however, does not lie in a mere preference. If we are forced to choose, some (hopefully most) of us would choose Anarres, and yet some would remain ambiguous. The question is, however, are we forced to choose? Is it a matter of choice? The old world, with its capitalistic or state-capitalistic political-economical order, exploitation, unhindered class struggles, and sexual frustration, is not merely the *old* world. It exists *simultaneously* with the new one. The new world is not, as Enlightenment thinkers and modernist-cum-pseudo-Marxists would imagine, a simple progression from the old one. The relation between Anarres and Urras is not sequential, but simultaneous, as the main scientific (or pseudoscientific) novum in the novel would suggest. We can safely assume, then, that Le Guin's "simultaneity physics" is more than a pseudoscientific device to keep the plot going; she actually believes in her simultaneity theory, if not in the field of physics, then as a way of thinking and a mode of social and political analysis.

Le Guin, as a sympathizer of Taoism, can always subvert a binary opposition when she sees one. The Taoist attitude toward these binary oppositions is *not yet* that of Hegelian dialectics: Taoism, like most Oriental belief systems, is based on *acceptance* rather than negation; although it shares with Hegelian dialectics the "not only, but also" attitude, it does not seek transcendence in the negation of the basic premises of the dilemma. A Taoist is always inclined toward inclusion of both horns of a dilemma, and so Taoist inclusion is closer to Hegelian dialectics than to the Western/Enlightenment philosophical position which is grounded in "either/or" binary oppositions. The Yin/Yang system always stresses the unity or interdependence of opposites, Yin always being the precondition and *raison d'être* of Yang, and vice versa. Hegelian dialectics goes one step further and introduces a *third* element (which is the basis of *Aufhebung*) that both includes *and* negates the dilemma on a transcendent level. Knowing the Taoist inclination of Le Guin, it is not difficult to surmise that the Anarres/Urras system is actually based on Yin/Yang. But is it only that, or does Le Guin try to go one step further than simple acceptance or inclusion, toward negation (of the negation) and the introduction of the *third* element on a transcendent level?

The simultaneous existence of a capitalist (and state-capitalist) Urras and a postcapitalist Anarres brings the very idea of a "revolution" into question. It is true that Le Guin called the exodus from Urras to Anarres "revolution" in a later short story,[11] but a world-historical revolution that leaves the entire *ancien régime* intact is a contradiction in terms: of course the French and Bolshevik revolutions of 1789 and 1917 had to coexist with the *ancien régimes,* but they were national rather than world-historical revolutions, and, whether they chose to "export" the revolution or live in "peaceful coexistence," they were, in the long run, both limited to a single nation-state. In Le Guin's fictional world(s)-system, a similar situation exists on Urras, where the country of Thu deems itself post-revolutionary but is in fact nothing but state capitalist. In any case, an exodus-revolution is unheard of in known history (except maybe the exodus of Jews from Egypt, which was not a "revolution" in any sense of the word), and this fictional device creates an anomalous situation of coexistent pre- and post-revolutionary societies, one supposedly the "past" of the other. The "past" in this case, however, is not past, but alive and well and thriving.[12]

Shevek, who travels to the old world with an "idea," in order to be able to learn and teach and share, finds nothing but greed and exploitation there; nobody actually wants his gift, they want to buy it from him in order to own it, keep it from others, and use it for domination and possibly destruction. In the end he comes to the conclusion that

> there is nothing, nothing on Urras that we Anarresti need! We left with empty hands, a hundred and seventy years ago, and we were right. We took nothing. Because there is nothing here but States and their weapons, the rich and their lies, and the poor and their misery. . . . There is no freedom. It is a box—Urras is a box, a package, with all the beautiful wrapping of blue sky and meadows and forests and great cities. And you open the box, and what is inside it? A black cellar full of dust, and a dead man. A man whose hand was shot off because he held it out to others. I have been in Hell at last. Desar was right; it is Urras; Hell is Urras. (11: 346–47)

The answer to this statement, by an Earth woman, the Terran ambassador Keng is:

> To me, and to all my fellow Terrans who have seen the planet, Urras is the kindliest, most various, most beautiful of all the inhabited worlds. It is the world that comes as close as any could do to Paradise. . . . I know it's full of evils, full of human injustice, greed, folly, waste. But it is also full of good, of beauty, vitality, achievement. It is what a world should be! It is *alive,* tremendously alive—alive, despite all its evils, with hope. Is that not true? (11: 347)

The readers are, as in any *Bildungsroman*, supposed to identify with Shevek, the protagonist, whose growing-up process we have been following throughout the novel; but Keng is a curious personality, a sixtyish woman from Earth with a bad back, who is bitterly critical, even remorseful of her planet's past. It is very possible to assume that Le Guin expects us to identify at least partially in this instance with Keng, the bitter but wise woman from Earth, rather than Shevek, the confused, "ambiguous," hairy Cetian male. Keng seems to be the prototype of the "space crone," the woman whom Le Guin would propose to send to space to represent Earth in her later essay, "Space Crone."[13] Theall comments: "[Anarres and Urras] are juxtaposed within the broader framework of an interstellar community of planets containing a possible future world of Earth (Terra), and using the Terran ambassador as a choral commentator on the concluding action of the novel."[14] If we can identify with this "choral commentator" (who is supposed to represent the outside or "more objective" view) even partially, we have two conflicting statements about Urras: it is Hell, but it is also Paradise. Keng goes on to describe her (our) home planet:

> My world, my Earth, is a ruin. A planet spoiled by the human species. We multiplied and gobbled and fought until there was nothing left, and then we died. We controlled neither appetite nor violence; we did not adapt. We destroyed ourselves. But we destroyed the world first. There are no forests left on my Earth. The air is grey, the sky is grey, it is always hot. It is habitable, it is still habitable, but not as this world is. This is a living world, a harmony. Mine is a discord. You Odonians chose a desert; we Terrans made a desert. (11: 347–48)

So, Earth and Anarres are alike in being a desert, one chosen, the other one made. If Urras comes close to Keng's idea of Paradise, Anarres is definitely close to her visual image of Hell, her own planet, if not socioculturally, then at least as a landscape. We seem to have our "third" element here, in Terra, containing elements of both Anarres and Urras, but only the negative ones. Terra shares with Urras exploitation, greed, violence, and egoism, and with Anarres the desolation and infertility of a desert. The only problem is that this "third" element is not transcendent but rather represents some kind of a Kantian "Thing," a black hole in the symbolic order, a crack in which all hopes and attempts by humanity to create (or find) a meaning have failed. Terra is probably what Urras would have become if the twin planet Anarres had not existed, the revolution never took the form of an exodus, and the violent clash between the Odonian uprising and the establishment went on until one completely annihilated the other. This would mean annihilation for both and therefore for the planet which they shared. Urras therefore escapes the fate of Terra by splitting itself in the middle and exporting one half to a twin planet. Both halves, however, are Hell and Paradise both, with the imaginary (non-exodus, Terra-like) Urras representing pure Hell.

Resolving conflict by allowing one side to win absolute victory over the other can only end up in the destruction of both. The same point was made by Joanna Russ in her utopia/dystopia *The Female Man* only one year after *The Dispossessed*—one of the alternate/dystopian narratives in *The Female Man* is about men and women engaged in an endless war which can only result in the destruction of both.

"PHYSICIST, HEAL THYSELF!"

If the horns of the binary opposition are simultaneous and mutually exclusive (separated by a "wall," so to speak), and both are described as Hell and Paradise at the same time, neither can be construed as a utopia *in itself*, that is, in the tradition of hitherto existing utopias, as a locus that has finally achieved perfection. This is why Le Guin begins the depiction of Anarres with a series of criticisms. The baby boy who wants to appropriate a patch of sunlight is reproached for "egoizing." The boy who tries to be "original" or merely different is reprimanded for the same reason. The young physicist who tries out an original idea is ignored, reproached, demoted, or even conspired against. The critique is clear: Anarres, in trying to do away with class conflict and oppressive power, has done away with difference in general, ending up in impotence for all, except for a lucky (but not institutionalized) few who can use the bureaucratic loopholes for a temporary but not very satisfying power. So, when Delany, acting as the champion of Foucauldian heterogeneity (not to say Derridean *différance*), criticizes Le Guin in *Triton*, he is off to a false start, because Le Guin herself is precisely trying to criticize the disappearance of difference. When we identify Anarres with the concept of utopia, Delany sounds right: if Anarres is a utopia after all, albeit flawed, then Le Guin is in fact throwing the baby (difference) away along with the washwater (exploitation). But if we concede that Le Guin is trying to place the utopian horizon not on Anarres but elsewhere, then this criticism loses all credibility. Shevek, who denounced Urras to Keng in his last days on Urras (in chapter 11), had already denounced Anarres to Takver, shortly before he left for Urras (chapter 10):

> the social conscience completely dominates the individual conscience, instead of striking a balance with it. We don't cooperate—we *obey*. We fear being outcast, being called lazy, dysfunctional, egoizing. We fear our neighbor's opinion more than we respect our own freedom of choice. . . . We have created crime, just as the propertarians did. We force a man outside the sphere of our approval, and then condemn him for it. We've made laws, laws of conventional behavior, built walls all around ourselves, and we can't see them, because they're part of our thinking. (10: 330–31)

So, Anarres is "Hell" not only because it is a desolate, infertile desert, but also because it has excluded difference, heterogeneity. It has projected all the "otherness" that is inherent to itself onto the "old" world, Urras, walled itself away from it, and left no room for any "other" within. Anything that contradicts, or does not meet the approval of, the "social conscience" or the "neighbor's opinion" has achieved the status of the *jouissance* of the other.[15] In Zizek's words:

> The Id-Evil thus stages the most elementary "short circuit" in the subject's relationship to the primordially missing object-cause of his desire: what "bothers" us in the "other" (Jew, Japanese, African, Turk . . .) is that he appears to entertain a privileged relationship to the object—the other either possesses the object-treasure, having snatched it away from us (which is why we don't have it), or poses a threat to our possession of the object.[16]

On Anarres, where the "primordial lack" is epitomized by the structural lack of the planet ("We are poor, we lack," says Shevek to the Urrasti [7: 228]), the constant scarcity in everything material; any kind of "other," that is, any difference, any deviation from the norm, will take the form of a theft: the "different" person is the one who has caused the primordial lack; they have "snatched away" our "object-treasure." Thus everybody who gives in to this semi-institutionalized "social conscience" is inflicted by (in Zizek's terms) Id-Evil. It may camouflage itself as morality or a strict adherence to the tenets of Odonianism (Superego), but it nevertheless stems from the original lack.

Shevek, who rightly criticizes the social and cultural consequences of this situation, is still unable to detect its point of origin, as can be observed when he boasts to Keng that the Odonians took nothing from Urras when they left one hundred and seventy years ago. The primordial lack in Anarres's situation is Urras itself, the birthplace of its people, the spring of life and diversity, the mother. The Anarresti have given up their mother (planet) for a new life (as every child must do sooner or later), but by doing so they also have given up their object of desire and therefore must live in a constant feeling of lack, in which they conceive of this lack as something lost, something taken from them. So they cannot stand the idea of "difference," because every "other" that comes their way becomes an object onto which the "lost" *jouissance* is projected; every "other" is a potential "*jouissance* thief" who must be silenced, normalized, regularized.

This is why even Shevek, the first rebel in almost two centuries, cannot grasp the source of this "evil" breeding in his home, his utopia, until he is told by a complete stranger, an outsider, a Terran whose lack has taken the form of an absolute loss centuries ago. The realization of the primordial lack, that it is indeed a lack and not something lost or stolen, makes Shevek "free" for the first time. He is no more "ambiguous" but healed, because he has finally found a vantage point from which he can look at himself, his world, and the other world, finally free of the enclosed binary system in which each world is the other's "other." Difference from this vantage point ceases to be an object of lost *jouissance* and becomes mere difference; sharing and giving, which were already the basic tenets of Odonian ideology, gain a new meaning: the gift is no longer a catchword for the Anarresti, the true believers, the initiate, but is now for everyone, including but not limited to the Urrasti. The much-needed "third element" through which the enclosure of the Anarres/Urras binary system can be transcended is the whole universe "outside," embodied by a Terran woman whose race's one-time enclosure has ended in destruction.

The third element which transcends the actuality of the Anarres/Urras binary opposition is also the correct address for the utopian element we have been missing in Anarres, which, although first presented as a direct descendant and also an absolute negation of capitalist/state-capitalist Urras, cannot exist without its opposite. Because, if Urras had not existed, or if it had blown up in a cosmic accident, then the Anarresti would have had to invent their "other," on their own planet. The reasonable way to get rid of the "other" always seems to be to abolish or destroy it, but this only ends up in the creation of an "other" in a smaller scale. The unreasonable but practical way is to find or create another "other" outside the binary system, on a larger scale. It is only when we cannot get any larger, when we reach the absolute limit, that utopia becomes an actual possibility.

Wells had asserted in 1905, in his *A Modern Utopia*, that under the conditions of modern warfare and aeronautics, no less than a whole planet could serve as a location for utopia:

> We are acutely aware nowadays that, however subtly contrived a State may be, outside your boundary lines the epidemic, the breeding barbarian or the economic power, will gather its strength to overcome you. The swift march of invention is all for the invader. Now, perhaps you might still guard a rocky coast or a narrow pass; but what of that near tomorrow when the flying machine soars overhead, free to descend at this point or that? . . . World-state, therefore, it must be.[17]

In the universe of *The Dispossessed*, where interstellar travel is an actuality, a planet is not enough either. Not even a solar system could serve. Wells was right: utopia is either everywhere at the same time, filling all the space within an absolute limit, or it cannot exist at all. Unfortunately (or fortunately) we can never reach this absolute limit, and therefore utopia can never become an actual possibility. We can, however, still find a locus for utopia, if not on an island, a continent, a planet or a solar system, then in the void between islands, planets, solar systems, in short, in fantasy space.

UTOPIA AS FANTASY SPACE

Zizek, in trying to form a bridge between Lacan's concept of fantasy (and hence, of "traversing the fantasy") and the fantastic we find in SF or fantasy fiction, gives the example of Heinlein's "The Unpleasant Profession of Jonathan Hoag." In the short story, the private detective, while "tailing" his client, stumbles onto the fact of "the non-existent thirteenth floor." He follows the client as far as the thirteenth floor, but when he comes back to the building the next day, there is no thirteenth floor. As in many American buildings, the fourteenth floor is above the twelfth. So, where has this "extra floor" gone? In actual reality, the fourteenth floor is the thirteenth floor, and it is only we, in our superstition, who call it the fourteenth. But this still does not explain the disappearance, because when he inspects the fourteenth floor, it is not the thirteenth floor he had been in the day before. Zizek calls this nonexistent thirteenth floor "fantasy space":

> It seems that as soon as we wall in a given space, there is more of it "inside" than it appears possible to an outside view. Continuity and proportion are not possible, because this disproportion, the surplus of inside in relation to outside, is a necessary structural effect of the very separation of the two; it can only be abolished by demolishing the barrier and letting the outside swallow the inside. What I want to suggest, then, is that this excess of "inside" consists, precisely, in the fantasy-space—the mysterious thirteenth floor, the surplus space which is a persistent motif in science fiction and mystery stories.[18]

"To wall in a given space" is exactly what the Anarresti had done one hundred and seventy years ago. They walled themselves in, as the opening sentences of the novel tell us: "There was a wall. It did not look important. . . . For seven generations there had been nothing in the world more important than that wall" (1: 1). The existence of the wall generated a "surplus of inside," in Zizek's terms. But this is not all, because as Le Guin is quick to add, "Like all walls it was ambiguous, two-faced. What was inside it and what was outside it depended upon which side of it you were on" (1: 1). That means that in walling themselves in, the Anarresti also walled the Urrasti in, generating a surplus of inside for them too. These "surpluses" or excesses of inside can only find a place for themselves in the "thirteenth floor," the nonexistent floor between floors, or, in the case of Anarres/Urras, in the nonexistent space between the two planets. The interplanetary void between Anarres and Urras is precisely the fantasy space Zizek has been talking about.

If Anarres does not pretend to be a utopia, then the utopian horizon, which is walled inside and then excreted from Anarres, must be located somewhere. What Le Guin does is to locate this utopian horizon in the void between Anarres and Urras, in the fantasy space which has no actuality. This can be observed in the curious narrative structure of the novel: we start in between Anarres and Urras, then have eleven alternating chapters on Anarres and Urras, and then we end up again in between, but this time between Urras and Anarres. The beginning and the ending take place in between, that is, in the fantasy space which neither the *ancien régime* on Urras nor the presumed utopia on Anarres can rightly appropriate. The beginning of *The Dispossessed* is an escape *from* utopia, the exact opposite of almost all known utopian texts, which start with a journey *to* the utopia.

If nothing else, the mere fact that the hero is escaping from utopia intimates that there is something wrong with the utopia itself. But the author has already told us the problem: there is a wall. Like all utopias before it, Anarres is walled in, and precisely for this reason it is not a utopia, which is an implicit but very clear criticism of the hitherto imagined utopias: a utopia, when walled in, generates an excess, a surplus, which is the utopian horizon or the utopian ideal itself. What remains inside the wall is a series of rules, regulations, prohibitions, and arrangements; a symbolic order which is even more "ordered" than the one in the author's here and now. The utopian horizon, which is *excreted* from this order, can only find itself a locus outside the wall. It cannot, however, simply go to the other side of the wall, which represents another enclosure: the wall is ambiguous, two-faced. Urras, which represents the other side, cannot contain this utopian horizon: it has already thrown it out, excreted it one hundred and seventy years ago. Thus, the utopian horizon finds refuge in fantasy space, in the two-way journey between planets, which is described in the first and the last chapters.

The first chapter was about an escape, an escape from utopia that had done (or was doing) away with difference. The last chapter is a return ("True journey is return" [13: 386]), but at the same time another escape, from the oppressive, mass-murdering rulers of Urras. This time, however, Shevek is not alone, as he was in his initial escape. He is bringing somebody with him, a person neither from Urras, nor from Anarres, but from Hain. The Hainishmen, having neither been split in the middle like the Cetians nor devastated their home planet like the Terrans, are nevertheless subject to a monstrous sense of guilt, the reason for which we know nothing about. By giving away his theory to everybody who inhabits this universe without discrimination and by bringing somebody from the *real* outside (that is, outside the Anarres/Urras binary), Shevek practically "demolish[es] the barrier and let[s] the outside swallow the inside."

And Anarres rightly deserves to be swallowed as such, to be a part of the outside, a part of the universe it walled out when it was trying to protect itself from its opposite, because it is the only way to reverse the process of exodus/excretion. Enclosure breeds, in the Anarresti example as everywhere else, intolerance toward difference and diversity. To be swallowed by the binary opposite, Urras, would have meant destruction. To be swallowed by a heterogeneous universe, on the other hand, is the way toward self-reflexivity, toward seeing oneself in the mirror of others. The plural here is of primary importance, because two can never lead to self-reflexivity. Just as the child needs to have an intervening third element ("the name of the father"[19]) in order to be able to escape the enclosed mother/child binary and develop a proper self, Anarres needs a third element (Hain/Terra) in order to escape the Anarres/Urras binary. That is how it can become self-critical or, in another words, self-deconstructive. Binary oppositions, as well as binary planetary systems, subsist (in fact *thrive*) on the gravitational fields of each other. Exclusion becomes the main keyword, not only in the sense of excluding anything beyond the binary, but also of excluding anything within the binary not directly related to the substantial structure of the opposition. Self-reflexivity, contemplating on our own circumstances of being-here, becomes also contemplating on our complementary, the opposite without which our existence would be meaningless. In order to do this, we have to unstitch ourselves at the very seams that seem to hold us together, as well as cut the umbilical cord that ties us to our binary opposite. This, however, is a never-ending process, because as we unstitch, we have to rebuild our integrity, reconstruct another "other" (in the mirror of which we can reassert selfhood), and umbilically connect with it in order to retain our existence as a subject. We have to self-deconstruct and self-reconstruct at the same time.

Utopia, in this sense, is located in the (endless) process of self-deconstruction, or what Trotsky would have called a "permanent revolution."[20] Permanence in revolution is the only guarantee against the lure of the ever-unreachable object of desire, the primordial lack. Since this lack is structural, the desire for wholeness or completion will never be satisfied; and once the pursuit of completion stops, probably due to the illusion that it is already achieved (the basic *méconnaisance*[21] of all utopias), the lack which remains untouched assumes the form of a loss, something we possessed in the past, but is now taken away by some "other." Then the search for *jouissance* thieves will start anew, and "others" will be created again and again. The problem is, we never had completion: there never was a "Golden Age," except in our imaginations.[22] As long as this image is projected onto the past, as something once a reality but now lost, we tend to get stuck in our present identities, be they national, ethnic, religious, and so forth. If, however, this image is projected onto the future in the form of a utopian horizon, if, that is, revolutionary change never ceases, then permanent deconstruction and reconstruction of our "selves" (including and being included by a multiplicity of "others" in each de/reconstruction) will make the "inside" as diverse as the "outside," supplying us with an ever-changing inner mirror, in which self-reflection as well as self-reflexivity becomes a real possibility.

NOTES

1. Ursula K. Le Guin, *The Dispossessed: An Ambiguous Utopia* (New York: Harper & Row, 1974), cited in the text by chapter and page to the 387-page Eos HarperCollins edition of 2001.

2. See G. Arrighi, T. K. Hopkins, and I. Wallerstein, *Anti-systemic Movements* (London: Verso, 1989), chap. 2. This argument is later developed by Wallerstein in his books *After Liberalism* (New York: New Press, 1995) and *The End of the World As We Know It* (Minneapolis: University of Minnesota Press, 1999). According to Wallerstein, 1848 and 1968 are the only world-historical revolutions in the sense that only these two revolutions had

a universal project of radical change. All the other revolutions, including the 1917 Revolution and the national liberation movements of the nineteenth and twentieth centuries, were contained in the "liberal project," no matter how "leftist" they seemed. Their basic goal (either explicit or implicit) was to pave the way for (further or initial) capitalist development. This argument, which would seem quite "gauche" and out of place before the dissolution of the USSR in 1991, gains strength as the whole Bolshevik interlude seems to be a preparation for the quite brutal capitalism now reigning in Russia, passage to which happened without any kind of a counter-revolution.

3. Samuel Delany, "To Read the Dispossessed," in *The Jewel-Hinged Jaw* (New York: Berkley Windhover, 1977); Samuel Delany, *Triton* (New York: Bantam, 1976); Ernest Callenbach, *Ecotopia* (Berkeley, CA: Banyan Tree Books, 1975); Joanna Russ, *The Female Man* (New York: Bantam, 1975).

4. Robert C. Elliott, *The Shape of Utopia: Studies in a Literary Genre* (Chicago: University of Chicago Press, 1970), 90.

5. Needless to say, this is true for the utopian tradition, which is severed from its carnivalistic roots and translated to "high culture." The carnivalistic tradition, which goes back as far as the Saturnalian festival (see note 22 below), is egalitarian *and* libertarian at the same time, without any need for rationalistic or social/economic/political verisimilitude. Carnivalistic utopian fantasies like *The Land of Cokaygne*, "The Sugarcandy Mountains," or utopian paintings of Bosch and Bruegel represent a utopian horizon which cannot be rationalized or localized, and therefore have nothing to do with any kind of meritocratism. Most literary-Arcadian utopias retain this egalitarian/libertarian kernel, as can be observed in the inscription at the entrance of the Abbé de Thélème in Rabelais's *Gargantua and Pantagruel*: "Do what thou wilt!"

6. Bülent Somay, "Towards an Open-Ended Utopia," *Science-Fiction Studies* 11, no. 1 (March 1984): 24–25.

7. Roland Barthes, *S/Z* (New York: Hill & Wang, 1974), 4.

8. Adam Phillips, *Terrors and Experts* (London: Faber & Faber, 1995), 24.

9. I cannot bring myself to translate *Aufhebung* as mere "sublation": *aufheben* in the strict Hegelian sense means both to contain and to negate the horns of a seemingly binary opposition and to transcend both in a higher conceptual level with the introduction of a third term.

10. Ursula K. Le Guin, "Notes to 'The Day Before the Revolution,'" in her *The Wind's Twelve Quarters* (London: Harper & Row, 1975), 285. In the same essay she also points out that

> Odonianism is anarchism. Not the bomb-in-the-pocket stuff, which is terrorism, whatever name it tries to dignify itself with; not the social-Darwinist economic "libertarianism" of the far right; but anarchism, as pre-figured in early Taoist thought, and expounded by Shelley and Kropotkin, Goldman and Goodman. Anarchism's principal target is the authoritarian State (capitalist or socialist); its principal moral-practical theme is cooperation (solidarity, mutual aid). It is the most idealistic, and to me the most interesting, of all political theories. (Le Guin, "Notes," 285)

11. Le Guin, "The Day Before the Revolution."

12. From a Marxist point of view, such an exodus-revolution is actually impossible as well as impractical. After the exodus, the capitalist regimes on Urras would have lost most of their working class (it is safe to assume that most of the Odonian movement came from

the working classes), and therefore their principal source of surplus-value. This would result in a renewed crisis that would cause another (and probably more severe) revolt. The problem with the capitalist ruling class is that they cannot *let go* of the working class, nor can they completely destroy it. Destroying or losing it would mean destruction for itself too.

13. Ursula K. Le Guin, "The Space Crone" (1976), in her *Dancing at the Edge of the World: Thoughts on Words, Women, Places* (New York: Grove Press, 1989), 6.

14. Donald F. Theall, "The Art of Social-Science Fiction: The Ambiguous Utopian Dialectics of Ursula K. Le Guin," *Science-Fiction Studies* 2, no. 3 (Nov. 1975): 256.

15. "*Jouissance* of the other" is a Lacanian expression, extensively used by Zizek to denote the projection of a lack onto any (religious, sexual, national, ethnic) "other," in order to create the illusion that it is something *lost* rather than primordially missing. The myths that "all Jews are lustful," "all Turks have harems," or "all black men have huge penises," all belong in this category—they are created in order to be able to assume that the "other" enjoys something that we do not, something that is stolen from us. This projection, claims Zizek, is the basic drive behind all racism, bigotry, and xenophobia.

16. Slavoj Zizek, *The Metastates of Enjoyment* (London: Verso, 1994), 71.

17. H. G. Wells, *A Modern Utopia* (Lincoln: University of Nebraska Press, 1967), 11–12.

18. Slavoj Zizek, "The Undergrowth of Enjoyment," in *The Zizek Reader*, ed. Elizabeth Wright and Edmond Wright (Oxford: Blackwell, 1999), 20.

19. *The name-of-the-father* (*nom-du-père*) in Lacanian terminology should by no means be confused with the actual (genetic or otherwise) father, nor is it identical with the father *imago*. The name-of-the-father is the constitutive element behind all language (as the primordial name) and enters into a child's life as the main forbidding factor that serves to separate the child from the mother. Lacan's word play "name-of-the-father/no-of-the-father" (*nom-du-père/non-du-père*) indicates that the entry of language in a child's psychological constitution is always in the form of a prohibition. Anything that is within the symbolic order and is equipped to play the part of the prohibiting/intervening element that ends the mother/child symbiosis, can be properly called the "name-of-the-father."

20. Leon Trotsky, *The Permanent Revolution*, trans. Brian Pierce (New York: Merit Publishers, 1969).

21. *Méconnaisance* is a term invented by Lacan, meaning "mis-recognition."

22. Elliott traces the concept of utopia as far back as the Saturnalian festival (along with satire), which is the projection of the belief in the existence of a golden age in the past, into the future. "Utopia," he says, "is the secularization of the myth of the Golden Age, a myth incarnated in the festival of the Saturnalia" (Elliott, *Shape of Utopia*, 24).

WORKS CITED

Arrighi, G., T. K. Hopkins, and I. Wallerstein. *Anti-systemic Movements*. London: Verso, 1989.
Barthes, Roland. *S/Z*. New York: Hill & Wang, 1974.
Callenbach, Ernest. *Ecotopia*. Berkeley, CA: Banyan Tree Books, 1975.
Delany, Samuel. "To Read the Dispossessed." Pp. 218–83 in *The Jewel-Hinged Jaw*. New York: Berkley Windhover, 1977.

———. *Triton*. New York: Bantam, 1976; now published as *Troubles on Triton*. Hanover, NH: Wesleyan University Press, 1996.

Elliott, Robert C. *The Shape of Utopia: Studies in a Literary Genre*. Chicago: University of Chicago Press, 1970.

Le Guin, Ursula K. *The Dispossessed: An Ambiguous Utopia*. New York: Eos, HarperCollins, 2001 (1974).

———. "Notes to 'The Day Before the Revolution.'" Pp. 285–86 in her *The Wind's Twelve Quarters*. London: Harper & Row, 1975.

———. "The Space Crone." Pp. 3–6 in her *Dancing at the Edge of the World: Thoughts on Words, Women, Places*. New York: Grove Press, 1989 (1976).

Phillips, Adam. *Terrors and Experts*. London: Faber & Faber, 1995.

Russ, Joanna. *The Female Man*. New York: Bantam, 1975.

Somay, Bülent. "Towards an Open-Ended Utopia." *Science-Fiction Studies* 11, no. 1 (March 1984): 25–38.

Theall, Donald F. "The Art of Social-Science Fiction: The Ambiguous Utopian Dialectics of Ursula K. Le Guin." *Science-Fiction Studies* 2, no. 3 (November 1975): 256–64.

Trotsky, Leon. *The Permanent Revolution*, trans. Brian Pierce. New York: Merit Publishers, 1969.

Wallerstein, I. *After Liberalism*. New York: New Press, 1995.

———. *The End of the World As We Know It*. Minneapolis: University of Minnesota Press, 1999.

Wells, H. G. *A Modern Utopia*. Lincoln: University of Nebraska Press, 1967.

Zizek, Slavoj. *The Metastates of Enjoyment*. London: Verso, 1994.

———. "The Undergrowth of Enjoyment." Pp. 11–36 in *The Zizek Reader*, ed. Elizabeth Wright and Edmond Wright. Oxford: Blackwell, 1999.

• *14* •

Future Conditional or Future Perfect?
The Dispossessed and Permanent Revolution

Chris Ferns

*I*n 1858, writing in *La Revue Communiste*, Karl Marx warned of the potential dangers of emigration:

> If those honest people who struggle for a better future leave, they will leave the arena completely open to the obscurantists and the rogues. Europe would certainly fall. Europe is that part of the world where communal wealth can be put forward first and most easily, simply for statistical and economic reasons. Instead, fire and brimstone will descend upon suffering humanity for centuries to come.[1]

In *The Dispossessed*, Ursula Le Guin explores what is in many ways a similar scenario, where an anarchist revolution on Urras—a planet clearly analogous to Earth—culminates in the emigration *en masse* of the revolutionaries (the "honest people") to a new world, Anarres, leaving the old one to its own devices.

Le Guin's interest, however, is less in the fate of the old world, which is depicted as having existed in a kind of uneasy stasis for more than one hundred and fifty years since the anarchists' departure, than in what happens to a revolutionary society established in isolation from the world whose contradictions gave birth to it. Thus on Urras, a free-market capitalist state (A-Io), plainly modeled on the West, confronts an authoritarian socialist state (Thu), just as clearly based on the Soviet Union, with the two engaged in a power struggle largely waged in an analogue of the Third World (Benbili)—but not a great deal appears to have changed in the interim. On Anarres, by contrast, not only has a successfully functioning anarchist society been established on "the single principle of mutual aid between individuals" (9: 300) laid down by its founder, Odo, but it is depicted as having gradually evolved (or degenerated) over time to a point where, possibly as a result of its own internal contradictions, it is now in danger of turning into something far removed from the revolution's initial intent—a society where individual initiative is increasingly stifled by the pressure to conform to societal norms.

What emerges as a result, both from Le Guin's depiction of Anarresti society, and a series of alternating episodes in which the Anarresti physicist, Shevek, returns to Urras, provides an illuminating perspective on the frequently commented-upon tendency of revolutions to relapse into something all too similar to the social order they were designed to overthrow. This is not to say, of course, that what has happened on Anarres over the years since the Settlement constitutes as dramatic a reversal as the process whereby, say, the revolution which gave birth to the radical aspirations of the Levellers or the Diggers ended up with the restoration of the monarchy, still less that whereby a revolution ostensibly based on the principles of *The Communist Manifesto* gave rise to the rule of an autocrat more monstrous than any Tsar. Nevertheless, there are some parallels on which Le Guin's "thought experiment" sheds valuable light.

Numerous explanations have been advanced as to why revolutions lose their way. Trotsky, for example, in his analysis of the course of the Russian revolution in *The Permanent Revolution*, argues that what was at issue was in the first place a theoretical problem, which, in the course of the debates within the Bolshevik leadership, resulted in a strategic error—the adoption of the doctrine of socialism in one country, as opposed to the pursuit of permanent (in the sense of uninterrupted) revolution on a global basis. For Trotsky, while revolution might be possible in a developmentally backward country, such as Russia, its completion—its transformation into socialism—could only be achieved through international revolution, since "insofar as capitalism has created a world market, a world division of labor and world productive forces, it has also prepared [the] world economy as a whole for socialist transformation."[2] In order to maintain its momentum, in other words, the Russian revolution had to be the starting point for a larger process designed to transform the entire global economy of which Russia was merely a part—a process which would attain completion "only in the final victory of the new society on our entire planet."[3] In Trotsky's view, the decision of the Bolshevik leadership to turn its back on this possibility, not least because of the inherent risks involved, was one with disastrous consequences. Not only did it prompt the squalid compromises of Stalinist foreign policy, but it also led to a *structural* problem, as the exigencies stemming from the need to protect the gains already achieved all too predictably facilitated the replacement of what purported to be a bottom-up system of participatory democracy by a top-down authoritarian bureaucracy, as a result of the process of "substitutism" outlined in *The Revolution Betrayed*.

Beyond issues of theory and structure, however, there is also the question, raised by Herbert Marcuse among others, whether there is not also a psychological component involved:

> whether alongside the socio-historical Thermidor that can be demonstrated in all past revolutions there is not also a *psychic* Thermidor. Are revolutions perhaps

not only vanquished, reversed, and unmade from outside, is there perhaps in individuals themselves already a dynamic at work that *internally* negates possible
liberation and gratification and that supports external forces of denial?[4]

Just as, at the individual level, adults who were abused as children frequently grav-
itate toward relationships that are similarly abusive, inasmuch as they reproduce
a situation which, however unsatisfactory, is at the same time comfortingly familiar, at a collective level people experiencing the anxieties aroused by the possibility of the genuinely new may all too readily settle for something closer to what
they have been psychologically prepared for.

In the case of Anarres, however, it might seem (at least at first sight) that
everything possible has been done to preclude such an eventuality. At both the
theoretical and structural level, it is clear that the goal of the Odonian revolution
that founded Anarres was, not the seizure of power, but rather the dismantling, so
far as practically possible, of the mechanisms whereby power is exercised. While
on Urras there seems to have been no shortage of authoritarian rulers, such as the
infamous Queen Teaea, who wore a cloak made of the tanned skins of rebels who
had been flayed alive (7:217), Anarresti society is so structured as to prevent the
emergence of her revolutionary counterpart. At the psychological level, the influence of the family in perpetuating old patterns of dominance and repression has
been minimized by the institution of communal child-rearing, while even the language which shapes their experience of reality, Pravic, is an invented one, specifically designed to reinforce the break with past habits of thought and perception,
and to minimize the importance of both possession and hierarchy. (Where the
Urrasti "often used the word 'higher' as a synonym for 'better' in their writings
. . . an Anarresti would use 'more central'" [1:15]—although it is unclear why the
metaphor of center and margins is inherently any less hierarchical than that of relative height.) As well, given that the initial composition of the society may be assumed to have been self-selecting, consisting in its entirety of revolutionaries committed to Odonian anarchist ideals, there are none of the problems arising from
the continuing presence of counterrevolutionary forces within the new order, nor
any of the structural problems liable to arise from the emergency measures necessary to deal with them. Indeed, on Anarres, the only emergencies that arise are the
result of natural disasters, such as drought and famine, as opposed to those produced by the struggle between competing class interests.

Yet despite all the precautions taken to ensure that both structurally and psychologically the danger of relapse is minimized, it is clear the Anarresti nevertheless remain concerned about the risk of contamination by Urras. Under the Terms
of Settlement, we are told, it is stipulated that there would be "no Urrasti off the
ships, except the Settlers, then, or ever. No mixing. No contact" (12: 356). While
a limited amount of trade between the two worlds is permitted to continue, none
of the Urrasti freighter crews are allowed beyond the wall enclosing the Port of
Anarres where their space ships land, while communications with Urras are strictly

controlled by the coordinating body on Anarres, the PDC. (There would hence appear to be little danger of Anarresti youth being corrupted by the Urrasti equivalent of Coca-Cola commercials and advertisements for fast cars.)

Radical as such precautions may appear, however, they are actually perfectly consistent with the conventions of utopian narrative. While the decentralized social system may be atypical of all but a handful of earlier utopias (William Morris's *News From Nowhere* being a notable example), its emphasis on the rational organization of everything from food distribution to town planning is a standard feature of the traditional utopia, as indeed is the importance placed on the socialization of the individual through control of child-rearing practices and even through the language spoken—examples of which can be found as early as Campanella's *The City of the Sun* all the way through to the utopias of H. G. Wells and even Aldous Huxley.

Still more characteristic is the emphasis on the *separation* of the utopian society from the real world (or in this case, its analogue). Over and over again in utopian narrative we encounter examples of societies that are isolated from the rest of the world in space—as is the case with nearly all the utopias of the Renaissance from More on, and even such twentieth-century examples as Gilman's *Herland* or Huxley's *Island*—or in time, as increasingly becomes the case from the nineteenth century on, yet where that isolation is often reinforced by security measures that sometimes border on the pathological. In the case of *The Dispossessed*, the separation is actually both spatial *and* temporal, since the societies of Anarres and Urras are not only located on separate planets, but are also repeatedly identified as representing the future and the past respectively.

One consequence of such isolation is that one seldom finds in utopian narrative much evidence that the inhabitants of utopia have any real interest in the world to which their society constitutes an alternative. While visitors to utopia are generally portrayed as fascinated by the guided tour to which they are exposed, the utopians themselves rarely ask more than the most perfunctory questions about the world elsewhere or the world of the past (even where that past is their own), except insofar as it is used to confirm their belief in their own superiority. And in this regard, Anarres is no exception: while the PDC, through the educational supplies syndicate, does arrange for school children to be shown the contrasting images of conspicuous consumption and grinding poverty that characterized the world from which their ancestors escaped, this appears to be largely for propaganda purposes—to reinforce the sense of their own society's superiority—and any questioning of whether there may be a gap between the official version and the actual situation on Urras is portrayed as somewhat unusual. Tirin, the one character who thinks to ask how old the images they are shown are, and whether things might not have changed since then, ends up in a mental asylum following a public reprimand for failing to conform to Odonian orthodoxy.

In this respect, *The Dispossessed* has much in common with the dystopian parodies of the utopian ideal that emerge in the twentieth century. Taken by themselves, the Anarres chapters, which depict the process whereby a small group of individuals comes to rebel against the increasing conformity of their society, bear more than a passing resemblance to the narratives of dystopias such as Zamyatin's *We*, Huxley's *Brave New World*, or Orwell's *Nineteen Eighty-Four*, where similar struggles are in evidence. While the structure of Anarresti society may preclude the emergence of the tyrannical father figures who dominate the earlier narratives—Zamyatin's Benefactor, Huxley's Mustapha Mond, or Orwell's Big Brother—there are numerous other parallels. In all cases, dissidence is associated with an attempt to maintain contact with the past, which is something that the utopian/dystopian society systematically discourages; the goal of Pravic, which is to engineer language in such a way as to influence the ways in which people think, is (however well-intentioned) philosophically not so far removed from that of Orwell's Newspeak; while the very traditional commitment of the protagonist, Shevek, to heterosexual monogamy (to which so many of Le Guin's critics have objected[5]) is very much in keeping with the tendency of dystopian narratives to present as "natural" the sexual mores of our own society, in contrast to the norms of the dystopian future.

The central premise of dystopian narrative, of course, is that utopia does not work—that the aspiration to create a more perfect society inevitably leads to a conformist nightmare—and, while Anarres is a long way from becoming the kind of totalitarian state imagined by Zamyatin and Orwell, there is little doubt that it is headed in a less than desirable direction. Which in turn may be seen as a reflection of the fact that, for all the (highly utopian) precautions it has taken, Anarres has actually *failed* to solve the problem of how to prevent the Revolution losing its way—indeed, it seems to be in the process of falling victim to precisely those problems identified by theorists such as Trotsky and Marcuse. For example, despite the decentralized structural mechanisms designed to prevent it, increasing power does seem to be becoming vested in some of the coordinating bodies. The PDC, it appears, is more and more taking on the functions of a government, with a corresponding interest in preserving the status quo, while the principle that people should rotate between the tasks for which they are best qualified and more menial work is being violated on a regular basis by those in a position to make decisions about who does what. The founding principle of mutual aid, in other words, is being compromised by growing bureaucratization. Moreover, while the revolutionary society on Anarres may, at least in spatial terms, embrace the "entire planet," both the intention and the results are far removed from those envisaged in Trotsky's concept of permanent revolution. Indeed, in their efforts to preserve the separation of Anarres from Urras (which effectively serves as an analogue of the rest of the world), the Anarresti may be seen as reproducing contradictions similar to those stemming from the doctrine of "socialism in one country," with fears for their own security leading them to refuse to assist revolutionary movements on Urras, lest this should precipitate an Urrasti invasion (12: 355–56).

As well, it is clear that public opinion is becoming increasingly intolerant of difference. Besides the public shaming ritual that precipitates Tirin's mental breakdown, we learn that Shevek's elder daughter, though innocent of her father's allegedly antisocial conduct, is being persecuted by the other children in her communal dormitory. Likewise, the theoretical right of the individual to refuse the job postings they have been assigned is less and less observed in practice. As Shevek points out,

> the social conscience completely dominates the individual conscience, instead of striking a balance with it. We don't cooperate—we *obey*. We fear being outcast, being called lazy, dysfunctional, egoizing. We fear our neighbor's opinion more than we respect our own freedom of choice. (10: 330)

In fact, as Finn Bowring argues, the very reliance on the principle of mutual aid, without at the same time formalizing its operation in obligatory laws and regulations, seems to have had the unintended side-effect of rendering the actual power dynamics of Anarresti society invisible.[6] In the absence of laws and law-enforcement agencies, the Anarresti have become increasingly self-policing, acting in accordance with custom and habit, to the detriment of individual initiative. One Urrasti even goes so far as to suggest that, while the Odonians may have left Urras to escape the authoritarianism symbolized by the dreadful Queen Teaea, they still have a Queen Teaea of their own inside their heads, telling them what to do (7: 219).

All of which would seem to suggest that their socializing mechanisms are either failing to have the desired effect, or having an effect that is actually counterproductive. Through having made a fetish of their own superiority, and with the example of Urras as the Other which they must at all costs resist turning into, the Anarresti have created an environment where the prospect of any further change is seen as threatening. Psychic Thermidor, in this case, rather than being rooted in the specific historical conditions that produce any given revolution, might be seen as the psychological tendency to reproduce *any* familiar pattern, to shrink from any threat to its maintenance—and with the same result: stasis and ossification. The utopian measures which Anarres has adopted to preserve the Revolution, in other words, turn out to be part of the problem, rather than the solution. The only question left unanswered is when the rot set in, since, as is so frequently the case with utopian narratives, we actually learn very little about what happened in the period of more than one hundred and fifty years that have elapsed since the Settlement—which might be seen as a curious omission, in a narrative so preoccupied with time, and the relation between past, present, and future.

So far, one might then argue, so unsuccessful: Le Guin's narrative neither represents a society capable of sustaining ongoing revolutionary change, nor avoids the stasis inherent in both utopian narrative and (as I have argued elsewhere[7]) its dystopian parody—and if one were to take the Anarres sections of the novel in isolation, this might be a valid criticism. However, it is precisely here that Le Guin departs from the norms of earlier utopian (and dystopian) fiction by deliberately *not* maintaining the separation between utopia and reality; instead, the potentially dystopian narrative of Shevek and his comrades' growing resistance to societal conformity is juxtaposed with a counternarrative, in which Shevek returns to Urras to encounter at firsthand the society whose contradictions had given rise to the revolution that had founded his own. And, it may be argued, in thus resolving some of the *narrative* problems inherent in the traditional utopia, Le Guin also points to a possible way out of the political impasse in which Anarres finds itself.[8]

Through its juxtaposition of these two narratives, *The Dispossessed* reestablishes the connection that both the political policies of Anarres and the narrative devices of the traditional utopia seek to minimize. As well, whereas the implication of most dystopias is that the only real alternative to the nightmare futures they depict is something closer to the supposedly more "natural" values of our own society, Le Guin's dual narrative paradoxically serves to render Anarres's utopian ideals more, rather than less, appealing. What becomes apparent when the two narrative lines are seen in context is that the Odonian revolution that founded Anarres can only be understood in the context of the social inequities of Urras that created it, and, conversely, that Shevek's capacity to make a decisive intervention in the ongoing revolutionary struggle on Urras is actually the result of his socialization by the society that brands him a dissident.

What emerges as a result might be best described as a dialogic relationship between the alternating sections, whereby the developments in each episode take on a markedly different resonance in the context of their juxtaposition. On Anarres, Urras constitutes the past—a past represented as fixed and unchanging in the film footage shown in schools—but once Shevek comes into contact with Urras, Anarres becomes *his* past, and it becomes apparent that the revolutionary ideals which appear to be in danger of ossification back home immediately become reenergized in the context of the social realities from which they emerged in the first place. Throughout the narrative, it is stressed that the true meaning of events only becomes apparent in the light of their relation to the past, and moreover, that the true significance of the past can only be perceived in relation to the manifestation of its effects in the present. For the possibility of a future that is qualitatively *different* to emerge there has to be a dynamic relationship between past and present—and, as we shall see, this proves true at both the personal and the political level.

What becomes clear from the juxtaposition of the Urras and Anarres episodes is that the period of roughly a year that Shevek spends on Urras in many ways replicates, in microcosm at it were, the formative experiences of his previous forty years on Anarres. The learning process he goes through in chapter 1, during the flight to Urras and following his arrival there, is followed in chapter 2 by a more lengthy description of the learning processes that take place during the period from infancy to early adulthood on Anarres. The initial feeling of isolation he experiences on Urras, as described in chapter 3, is paralleled in the following chapter by the description of the terrible desolation he experiences on meeting his mother again while in hospital in Abbenay and reliving the sense of loss stemming from her abandonment of him as a child. In chapter 5, the account of Shevek's emergence from isolation as he begins to form social relationships with his Urrasti colleagues, which concludes with his spending the weekend at the home of Oiie (where he dreams of his partner Takver), is followed in chapter 6 by his emergence from social isolation in Abbenay, in the process of which he meets Takver, whom he had known only slightly before, and they take the decision to become partners.

One could multiply examples—these are only a few of the numerous parallels linking the alternating sections—and it might appear at first sight that what takes place in the Urras chapters constitutes merely a *repetition* of Shevek's earlier experiences on Anarres; or, in other words, that the future is *simply* determined by the past. What Le Guin suggests, however, is a rather more complex interconnection: that the relationship between past and future is not so much a simple matter of cause and effect, but rather one where the future (or indeed a variety of futures) may be seen as *latent* in the past, while any given future can only be realized through human action taken in the present—although here too the choices individuals may make are themselves inseparable from the past that has formed them. Thus, when Shevek and Takver become partners, he is forced to recognize that his past—even the period of unhappy isolation he experienced on first arriving in Abbenay—is not so much a cause as it is a part of the present:

> It was now clear to Shevek, and he would have thought it folly to think otherwise, that his wretched years in this city had all been part of his present great happiness, because they had led up to it, prepared him for it. Everything that had happened to him was part of what was happening to him now. (6:183)

Later, when he is reunited with Takver following their four years of separation during the famine, he comes to the realization that they were not wasted, but rather "part of the edifice that he and Takver were building with their lives" (10: 335).

What happens in the parallel episodes on Urras, however, has a very different outcome, determined as it is not merely by Urras's being a society both structurally and ideologically distinct from Anarres, but also by Shevek's having been shaped by what is now a longer and more complex past—a past of which his relationship to Takver is only one part. Whereas the ending of Shevek's isolation in Abbenay leads to his becoming Takver's partner, his entry into the social world of A-Io leads to his introduction to Oiie's sister, Vea, who flirts with him, and later invites him to a party where he inadvertently gets drunk, attempts to have sex with her, and ends up vomiting over a tray of canapés. This, of course, might be read simply as a rather crude binary opposition—with the virtuous, but rather plain, utopian Takver contrasted to the sexy Urrasti temptress Vea, and the latter's penchant for conspicuous consumption set against the decent austerity of life on Anarres—yet what emerges is again more complex. Whereas the schematic contrasts between wealth and poverty on Urras presented to Anarresti school children for educational purposes serve mainly to reinforce the status quo, persuading them their own society is superior and hence in no real need of further change, in the case of Shevek's experiences the effect of the contrasts is to establish a relationship between the two worlds, rather than merely reinforce a sense of their separation. In narrative terms, the chapter that concludes with the scene at Vea's party is followed by one describing the horrors of the famine on Anarres—a sequence that then makes sense of the sheer disgust Shevek feels, not merely at his own behavior, but at the excesses with which he now feels himself to be complicit. Instead of enhancing a complacent sense of Anarresti superiority, the contrast leads to action and engagement.

Indeed, it is this revulsion in turn that energizes him to take the final steps leading to his discovery of the General Temporal Theory that reconciles the two contrasting conceptions of time as linear and time as in a sense simultaneous. This then initiates another sequence through which the connections between his Anarresti past and Urrasti present become still further apparent, while at the same time leading to a future that seems by no means certain—yet which is for that very reason full of the renewed possibility of change. His possession of the Theory, which will make possible instantaneous communication across interstellar space and thereby spell an end to both spatial and temporal isolation, makes him all the more determined that it not become the property of any one nation or planet—a resolve that precipitates his involvement with the Urrasti revolutionaries, an act of resistance that turns out in the following chapter to have had its precursor in his decision to return to Abbenay to fight against the growing trend toward conformity by setting up the Syndicate of Initiative. His attempts to assist his dying comrade, fatally wounded in the massacre at the demonstration, may be seen to have their roots in his insight, gained while trying to help a dying fellow worker on Anarres, twenty years before, that brotherhood begins in "shared pain" (2: 62). And there are even links between the world of theoretical physics and the personal, as his realization that discovery is a form of homecoming in chapter 9 is followed in the subsequent chapter by his quite literal homecoming after his four-year separation from Takver. The theoretical, with all its political ramifications, ultimately proves to be intertwined with the personal.

In this context, Shevek's General Temporal Theory bears closer investigation. Very early in the novel, when he is still only a child, he arrives quite independently at his own version of Zeno's paradox, imagining a scenario where a rock thrown at a tree can never reach it, since it always has to traverse halfway the remaining distance, the number of halfways being infinite—and is promptly reprimanded by the teacher for showing off. Upset at the unfairness of his treatment, he comforts himself by taking refuge in thinking about numbers, always the same, always there. "If a book were written all in numbers," he reflects, "it would be true. . . . Everything could change, yet nothing would be lost. If you saw the numbers you could see that, the balance, the pattern. You saw the foundations of the world. And they were solid" (2: 31). It is here that the seed is planted of what turns out to be his life's work—the project of reconciling the endless process of change in linear time with the unchanging, eternal world of number, where all that happens is, in a sense, simultaneous. Elsewhere, Shevek compares time to a book: "all there, all at once, between its covers. But if you want to read the story and understand it, you must begin with the first page, and go forward, always in order" (7: 221). Time, which we *experience* in a linear fashion, is also, as it were, always already there. While the concept of time as linear is able to explain how things change, it is less able to explain the context within which they do so—the cyclical process whereby things recur, such as the seasons, or the orbits of the planets. Shevek's goal becomes to discover the connection between the two, sensing that neither can be understood in isolation. As he goes on to argue:

> So then time has two aspects. There is the arrow, the running river, without which there is no change, no progress, or direction, or creation. And there is the circle or the cycle, without which there is chaos, meaningless succession of instants, a world without clocks or seasons or promises. (7: 223)

Linear time and the events that take place within it, in other words, only have meaning in light of the larger pattern to which they belong, a pattern in which past, present, and future are all part of a single whole.

This insight, as we have seen, is one that also informs Shevek's personal life, in that the interconnectedness of their past, present, and future lives is what gives meaning to all of them, but it becomes clear, as the dual narrative unfolds, that it is equally relevant to the political realm. What becomes apparent, actually, is that for all the manifest differences between Urras and Anarres, one thing they have in common is a fear of change. For the Urrasti, the fear is of a future that might be different *in kind* from the past and present: experiencing time as merely linear, the only future they can conceive of is what Ernst Bloch calls the "false future," that is, "all that which repeats itself a hundred or a thousand times in the future. It is indeed a future but there is nothing really new in it."[9] The only future with which they are able to feel comfortable is one containing more of the same. On Anarres, by contrast, the future is something which they believe has been attained and, in their efforts to ensure that it does not revert to the past from whose contradictions it emerged, they are in the process of transforming it into something more sterile, lacking in the transforming vision and energy that was once capable of imagining the genuinely new. As Bloch goes on to argue,

> the genuine future contains a *Novum*, which always has a tendency, a possibility, or a probability that opens up the horizon. We are safe with the false fu-

ture, for it is like looking forward to going to sleep in a bed that we know is there. But the genuine future involves risk, because we are not certain what lies out there beyond us.[10]

And in this sense, both the Urrasti, persisting in their old ways, and the Anarresti, striving to preserve a future that was once genuinely new, are both committed to Bloch's "false future"—a future that is essentially static.

Yet it is precisely this stasis that Le Guin's dual narrative sets out to destabilize. In narrative terms, as we have seen, the juxtaposition of the Anarres and Urras sequences produces an effect far removed from either the static perfection of the traditional utopia or the standard dystopian narrative of heroic though doomed resistance to an artificially created human order in the name of the supposedly more natural values of our own society. Indeed, in this last regard, one of the most distinctive features of *The Dispossessed* is that dissidence is *not* associated with an attempt to restore the status quo. While Shevek's voyage to Urras may be seen as in one sense a return to the past, it is a return whose effect is ultimately to restore the possibility—on both worlds—of genuine change. On Urras, this is achieved politically by Shevek's ability to assist the rebels in recovering the sense of possibility that Anarres has always represented since its inception, thus providing a direction for the discontent arising from the same internal contradictions that had engendered the first Odonian revolution one hundred and seventy years earlier. On Anarres, by contrast, the possibility of Urras's changing is clearly the key to avoiding the stagnation that is increasingly apparent. So long as Urras remains unchanged—conforming to the stereotypical image shown to Anarresti school children—then the nature of the society on Anarres is still to a large extent governed by the example of the Other from which they are determined to remain different. Once Urras is shown to be susceptible to change, however, there is no longer a fixed point of reference by which the Anarresti can determine their difference. Equally, on a practical level, it might be argued that the reintegration of Anarres into the global economy of an Urras thrown into a process of radical change could have the effect of eliminating the negative consequences of the scarcity of resources on Anarres, which is the principal source of the recurring emergencies which Shevek cites as one of the main factors in producing an increasing tendency toward conformity (10: 330–31).

In this context, it is significant that part of Shevek's freedom from fear of the genuinely new stems from the paradoxical recognition that discovery is, at least in part, rediscovery—a return home after a voyage out, rather than merely a trip into the unknown, even though both the home and the voyager will have changed in the intervening period:

> You shall not go down twice to the same river, nor can you go home again. That he knew; indeed it was the basis of his view of the world. Yet from that acceptance of transience he evolved his vast theory, wherein what is most changeable

is shown to be fullest of eternity, and your relationship to the river, and the river's relationship to you and to itself, turns out to be at once more complex and more reassuring than a mere lack of identity. You *can* go home again, the General Temporal Theory asserts, so long as you understand that home is a place where you have never been. (2: 54–55)

To cling to the security of the known, for Shevek, is to forfeit the chance of that return, and significantly his great scientific breakthrough only becomes possible when he abandons his demand for certainty, his need to work from premises that must be proved incontrovertibly first. For as soon as he does this, we are told,

The wall was down. The vision was both clear and whole. What he saw was simple, simpler than anything else. It was simplicity: and contained in it all complexity, all promise. It was revelation. It was the way clear, the way home, the light. (9: 280)

Discovery, it turns out, also involves a sense of *recognition*, a sudden perception of what, in some ways, one has known all along, of a truth that was always latent until the moment of discovery.

It is this, it may be argued, that makes it possible for Shevek to commit himself to the original Odonian concept of the revolution as "a permanent one, an ongoing process" (6: 176). Viewed in such a light, ongoing change is not only not to be feared, but is the only way of avoiding the meaningless repetition of the past. Only in the abandonment of security lies the way home. While both the Urrasti and the Anarresti seem in their own ways to seek an End of History in the sense used by Fukuyama and his many precursors—a kind of steady state where all meaningful change has now run its course and where no more unpleasant surprises are to be anticipated, Shevek has a view of the End of History which is closer to Bloch's—the End as a goal in whose light alone the past and present acquire meaning. As Bloch puts it:

True genesis is not at the beginning but at the end, and it starts to begin only when society and existence become radical, i.e. grasp their roots. But the root of history is the working, creating human being who reshapes and overhauls the given facts. Once he has grasped himself and established what is his, without expropriation and alienation, in real democracy, there arises in the world something which shines into the childhood of all and in which no one has yet been: homeland.[11]

"Real democracy," as Bloch uses the term, necessarily involves a commitment to change, to the actualization of possibilities that have not yet been realized. In the face of the parody of democracy which Anarres is in danger of becoming, with meaningful individual choice increasingly stifled by the pressure to conform, it is Shevek and his comrades' commitment to change that prompts him to "grasp his roots"—to discover where he, and the revolution that formed him, came from.

Significantly, at the conclusion, the dual narratives merge into one, as Shevek prepares to return home, changed yet again, and to a home where we are told "things are . . . a little broken loose" (13: 384), with growing support for the Syndicate of Initiative. Revolution on both Urras and Anarres has once again become a real possibility. As Shevek prepares to land, we are told, the time is early morning.

NOTES

1. Karl Marx, *La Revue communiste*, 1858, no. 1, as cited by Louis Marin, *Utopics: The Semiological Play of Textual Spaces* (Atlantic Highlands, NJ: Humanities Press, 1990), 273. Ursula K. Le Guin, *The Dispossessed: An Ambiguous Utopia* (New York: Harper & Row, 1974), cited in the text by chapter and page to the 387-page Eos HarperCollins edition of 2001.

2. Leon Trotsky, *The Permanent Revolution*, trans. Brian Pierce (New York: Merit, 1969), 279.

3. Trotsky, *Permanent Revolution*, 279.

4. Herbert Marcuse, *Five Lectures: Psychoanalysis, Politics, and Utopia*, trans. Jeremy J. Shapiro and Shierry M. Weber (London: Allen Lane, 1970), 38.

5. See for example Samuel R. Delany, *The Jewel-Hinged Jaw: Notes on the Language of Science Fiction* (Elizabethtown, NY: Dragon Press, 1977), 239–308; Sarah Lefanu, *In the Chinks of the World Machine: Feminism and Science Fiction* (London: Women's Press, 1988), 140–44; and Tom Moylan, *Demand the Impossible: Science Fiction and the Utopian Imagination* (London: Methuen, 1986), 91–120.

6. Finn Bowring, "An Unencumbered Freedom: Ursula Le Guin's *The Dispossessed*," *Anarchist Studies* 6, no. 1 (March 1998): 32.

7. Chris Ferns, *Narrating Utopia: Ideology, Gender, Form in Utopian Literature* (Liverpool, UK: Liverpool University Press, 1999), 105–38.

8. A similar narrative strategy can be found in Marge Piercy's utopia, *Woman on the Edge of Time* (1976), first published two years later than *The Dispossessed*.

9. Ernst Bloch, as quoted in Jack Zipes, "Traces of Hope: The Non-Synchronicity of Ernst Bloch," ed. by Jamie Owen Daniel and Tom Moylan, *Not Yet: Reconsidering Ernst Bloch* (London: Verso, 1997), 11.

10. Bloch, as quoted in Zipes, "Traces of Hope," 11.

11. Ernst Bloch, *The Principle of Hope* (3 vols.), trans. Neville Plaice, Stephen Plaice, and Paul Knight (Cambridge, MA: MIT Press, 1986), 1375–76.

WORKS CITED

Bloch, Ernst. *The Principle of Hope*. 3 vols. Trans. Neville Plaice, Stephen Plaice, and Paul Knight. Cambridge, MA: MIT Press, 1986.

Bowring, Finn. "An Unencumbered Freedom: Ursula Le Guin's *The Dispossessed*." *Anarchist Studies* 6, no. 1 (March 1998): 21–37.

Delany, Samuel R. *The Jewel-Hinged Jaw: Notes on the Language of Science Fiction.* Elizabethtown, NY: Dragon Press, 1977.

Ferns, Chris. *Narrating Utopia: Ideology, Gender, Form in Utopian Literature.* Liverpool, UK: Liverpool University Press, 1999.

Lefanu, Sarah. *In the Chinks of the World Machine: Feminism and Science Fiction.* London: Women's Press, 1988.

Le Guin, Ursula K. *The Dispossessed: An Ambiguous Utopia.* New York: Eos, HarperCollins, 2001 (1974).

Marcuse, Herbert. *Five Lectures: Psychoanalysis, Politics, and Utopia.* Trans. Jeremy J. Shapiro and Shierry M. Weber. London: Allen Lane, 1970.

Marin, Louis. *Utopics: The Semiological Play of Textual Spaces.* Atlantic Highlands, NJ: Humanities Press, 1990.

Moylan, Tom. *Demand the Impossible: Science Fiction and the Utopian Imagination.* London: Methuen, 1986.

Trotsky, Leon. *The Permanent Revolution.* Trans. Brian Pierce. New York: Merit Publishers, 1969.

———. *The Revolution Betrayed: What is the Soviet Union and Where is it Going?* Trans. Max Eastman. New York: Pathfinder Press, 1972.

Zipes, Jack. "Traces of Hope: The Non-Synchronicity of Ernst Bloch." Pp. 1–12 in *Not Yet: Reconsidering Ernst Bloch*, ed. Jamie Owen Daniel and Tom Moylan. London: Verso, 1997.

VI

OPEN-ENDED
UTOPIAN POLITICS

15

Ambiguous Choices:
Skepticism as a Grounding for Utopia

Claire P. Curtis

*T*he idea of utopia, the wholly good (and yet absent) place, has been a constant theme in Western political thought. Yet with the twentieth century the idea of dystopia,[1] the worst possible place, was introduced and, alongside it, the theoretical framework for criticizing the idea of utopia itself.[2] This criticism has become almost standard: the three most prominent twentieth-century Anglo-American political philosophers, Michael Oakeshott, Isaiah Berlin, and John Rawls, have all, in their own ways, criticized the idea of utopia and established prescriptive theories consonant with this criticism. Yet in their criticism they seem to have shortchanged (or misunderstood) the possibilities inherent in the idea of utopia. And they seem not to have noticed that their own critical arguments may themselves establish a new foundation for utopia. These authors are criticizing dogmatic utopia yet they do not recognize the possibility for the skeptical or ambiguous utopia, a utopia that responds to the need for hope in an increasingly ambiguous world. But it is a hope tempered by a skeptical attitude toward the world in which we live. This is a utopia that counters the passivity of both complacency and pessimism.

To read *The Dispossessed* is to encounter a utopia that is immune from the criticisms of these political philosophers, a utopia that breaks new ground for thinking about the ideal. Tellingly Le Guin subtitled *The Dispossessed*, an ambiguous utopia. Capturing the nature of that ambiguity is essential for understanding the framework for a skeptical utopia. It is this notion of ambiguity and its implications for thinking about politics that I explore in this chapter. The argument is in four parts: first, a presentation of the anti-utopianism of twentieth-century Anglo-American political thought in the work of Oakeshott, Rawls, and Berlin, with a brief discussion of Le Guin's utopia; second, a comparison of Oakeshott's critique of rationalism to the problem of Anarres's increasing bureaucratization; third, a comparison of Rawls's concern with teleology to the goal-oriented nature of Urras, and Shevek's initial attraction to that system; and fourth, an analysis of Berlin's advocacy of pluralism and the necessity of compromise in relation to Shevek's discussion of suffering and hope.

I

Oakeshott, Rawls, and Berlin all agree that utopian thinking has three dangerous tendencies. First, the utopian assumes a dogmatic rationalism: any problem can be solved and no obstacle is insurmountable. Second, the utopian is likely to let the ends justify the means: once the ideal society is envisioned, the utopian will do anything to create that society. Third, the utopian presumes that everyone will be attracted to the utopian vision, so that compromise is unnecessary and even self-defeating. Oakeshott, Rawls, and Berlin endorse all of these criticisms, although they prioritize the criticisms differently and thus develop different prescriptive theories stemming from these criticisms. Each affirms that presuming a single answer to achieving universal happiness is flawed at best and a recipe for disaster at worst, that humans are not all made happy in the same way, and that avoiding dystopian disaster means focusing on the means and not merely the ends of a society. Oakeshott rejects the rationalist outlook in politics, Rawls focuses on process-oriented rather than end-oriented thinking, and Berlin criticizes the demand for agreement on a single set of values. Each develops prescriptive theories that differ both from one another and from Le Guin. The visions are comparable precisely because Le Guin does build a utopian society that withstands their criticisms. Because she builds a society with a utopian spirit that embraces skepticism, all three political philosophers could, with differing emphases, consent to her vision.

Oakeshott criticizes what he called rationalism in politics, arguing that politics is best understood as a civil association and not an enterprise association.[3] Oakeshott argues that the mode of problem-solving is destructive to politics, which should be about determining the conditions under which humans (who have different ends) should live. He identifies enterprise association as a "relationship in terms of the pursuit of some common purpose, some substantive condition of things to be jointly procured, or some common interest to be continuously satisfied."[4] While this is appropriate for some human activities (including such diverse activities as meat inspection and religious communities), it is not appropriate for politics. There are two reasons to divide the two kinds of activity. First, not every activity has either a common purpose or a known method for achieving that purpose; and second, to categorize all possible human activity purposively is to posit a singular purpose for the very activity of human living. Our lives cannot be described in such a singularly rational, purposive mode (although, as with the members of religious communities structured as enterprise associations, one may wish to designate a single purpose for one's own life).

Politics, understood broadly, is the mode of human activity that designates a community, a civil association in which humans are "related solely in terms of their common recognition of rules which constitute the practice of civility."[5] Oakeshott is thus contrasting the mode of thinking that aims to solve all problems (and that designates the world as a series of problems to be solved) with a mode of thinking that concerns the desirability of sets of conditions under which we could live. In other words, politics is the mode by which we deliberate over rules under which we want to live. Those conditions include the role that enterprise associations will play in our lives. But the conditions are not themselves subject to the rationalist mode. In other words, the conditions under which we live are not perfectible, although they are surely more or less desirable.

> The laws of civil association . . . are not imposed upon an already shaped and articulated engagement; they relate to the miscellaneous, unforeseeable choices and transactions of agents each concerned to live the life of a man like me, who are joined in no common purpose or engagement, who may be strangers to one another.[6]

Oakeshott thus criticizes a politics of rationalist problem-solving in favor of a politics properly understood as the place where these miscellaneous choices are made. I contend that these choices establish the need for a utopia sensitive to ambiguity.

John Rawls's *Theory of Justice* famously argues against the end-oriented thinking of utilitarianism and sets out two principles of justice chosen by individuals who do not know any particular facts about themselves. No one in Rawls's original position can choose principles that will benefit any particular person or group in a society since the individual choosing might turn out to be anyone. Rawls's two principles of justice are: first, equality in the assignment of basic rights and duties; and second, allowing inequality in status and wealth only where that inequality benefits the least advantaged of society. These principles provide a framework for a just society, but they do not dictate any good toward which society or the individuals in it should aim. By contrast, a utilitarian approach focuses on the good of the whole society and is thus willing to sacrifice the good of one for the good of the whole. Rawls specifies that in utilitarian or end-oriented thinking "the good is defined independently from the right, and then the right is defined as that which maximizes the good."[7] He goes on to say that "teleological theories have a deep intuitive appeal since they seem to embody the idea of rationality."[8] This rationality (as in Oakeshott's enterprise association) results from the identification of an overriding principle to organize society (the good) and a method for achieving that good (the right). The proper relationship between the identification of the good and the identification of the right is crucial for Rawls. He acknowledges that the good is something that differs among people ("a person's good is determined by what is for him the most rational long-term plan of life given reasonably favorable circumstances"[9]). Thus it would be better to organize a society around the principle of the right (how should people act) and to let people seek out their own good (what should they do) within the limitations of this right procedure.[10] Individuals can "bring together into one scheme all individual perspectives and arrive together at regulative principles that can be affirmed by everyone as he lives by them, each from his own standpoint. Purity of heart, if one could attain it, would be to see clearly and to act with grace and self-command from this point of view."[11] Rawls is thus criticizing the utopian who posits a highest good and demands agreement from everyone to the fact of that good, as the inhabitants of Plato's *Republic* are to agree with the decisions made by philosopher rulers who know the Form of the Good. But Rawls is also acknowledging the possibility for what I would call a utopian perspective, one whereby the above-mentioned "purity of heart" has been attained—a purity that affects how you see and not what you see.

Berlin's criticism of utopia focuses explicitly on this Platonic ideal. Berlin defines this ideal as embracing three claims: first, that for all "genuine" questions there is only one answer; second, that there is a way to find the answers to those questions; and third, that all the answers, when put together, will form a compatible whole.[12] Berlin criticizes each of these claims, suggesting that different individuals and cultures have differing answers to questions about the good life, that some questions cannot be answered, and most importantly that certain values conflict. This conflict of values necessitates that compromises be made. For Berlin, utopias deny the possibility of compromise. "I can only say that those who rest on such comfortable beds of dogma are victims of forms of self-induced myopia, blinkers that may make for contentment, but not for understanding what it means to be human."[13] Berlin challenges each of the contentions within the Platonic Ideal. But it is the last—the compatibility of values—that concerns him most. For ultimately, perfect compatibility demands dogmatism and uniformity. "To force people into the neat uniforms demanded by dogmatically believed-in schemes is almost always the road to inhumanity. We can only do what we can: but that we must do, against difficulties."[14] We act, for Berlin, within a human horizon that dictates the limits of human activity. These limits (and he includes slavery and torture, which establish where there is "no justification for compromise"[15]) are determined deliberatively within and among communities.

Oakeshott, Rawls, and Berlin are all concerned with the dogmatism that might seem to be implicit in utopia. This dogmatism, understood in Oakeshott's criticism of rationalism, Rawls's criticism of teleology, and Berlin's criticism of single-mindedness, is rejected in favor of a messier world of rules, procedures, and deliberation with no guarantee of success. It is just such a world that Le Guin has created in Anarres. *The Dispossessed* presents an extended analysis of Anarres through Shevek's struggles on his home planet and his travels to Urras. Le Guin rejects the dogmatism of Urras in favor of the messier and more difficult Anarres. Yet in doing so Le Guin does not deny that Anarres is a utopia. Rather she rewrites[16] the very idea of utopia with her presentation of Anarres.

Anarres is and always should be a work in progress; it cannot rest on its laurels and presume to have achieved perfection. Anarres denies Berlin's own understanding of utopia in the essay "Decline of Utopian Ideals in the West":

> Broadly speaking, western Utopias tend to contain the same elements: a society lives in a state of pure harmony, in which all its members live in peace, love one another, are free from physical danger, from want of any kind, from insecurity, from degrading work, from envy, from frustration, experience no injustice or violence, live in perpetual, even light in a temperate climate, in the midst of infinitely fruitful, generous nature.[17]

Berlin's understanding of utopia—the notion of a static, perfect world that either existed somewhere in the past or exists in a near-present future—is surely a vision that describes some utopias. And yet Berlin is not describing Anarres. It is as if Le Guin read Berlin's description and then chose to create a utopian society precisely by turning that description on its head.

Anarres must come to terms with its own tendencies toward dogmatism and learn (or relearn) to embrace the ambiguous. This ambiguity is its only route back to utopia. "For her [Takver] as for him [Shevek], there was no end. There was process: process was all. You could go in a promising direction or you could go wrong, but you did not set out with the expectation of stopping anywhere" (10: 334). Anarres must affirm one of the key conditions under which Anarresti have decided to live: one cannot promote one person's happiness on the basis of another's degradation, even if the happiness is easy to achieve and the degradation equally easy to ignore. Acknowledging this as the condition of Anarresti life differs radically from any utopian claim about universal happiness. Rather, this condition sets out a limitation on *how* individuals may seek their own happiness.

Anarres is an ideal society whose ideal must be constantly struggled for. Harmony may be a goal, but it is surely not yet attained. Love is present between some, but surely not between all. Life is difficult, work is hard, the climate is harsh, food is sometimes scarce, human mistakes are sometimes made. Compromise is constant, although the issue of where one should and should not compromise is still pressing. Shevek faces numerous conflicts of values: between his desire to do his own work in his own way and the communal values of Anarres, between the egalitarian values of his society and the hierarchical ones of Urras. And yet, in Anarres, Le Guin has created a utopia. In this utopia, happiness is ultimately the responsibility of the individual, while the conditions for attaining happiness (conditions that include education, sustenance, housing, health, family, and work) are the responsibility of the community. So either Berlin is wrong about the nature of utopia (which in part he is) or Le Guin is responding to the criticisms of utopia by building an ideal society that is not static, not perfect, not heaven on Earth, and yet vibrant, real and, in an important sense, right.

Anarres is familiar in the frustrations of its daily life and yet deeply compelling in its vision for a society committed to the idea that no one should benefit from someone else's degradation. It is precisely through the frustrations of life on Anarres that Le Guin answers the criticisms of Oakeshott, Rawls, and Berlin. The principles of Odonianism and Shevek's understanding of them reflect Oakeshott's distinction between enterprise and civil association; the presentation of Urras as the site for teleological thinking offers Anarres as the criticism of this teleology, reflecting Rawls's concerns; and Shevek's understanding that suffering is the key human experience reflects Berlin's acknowledgment that perfection is unattainable (and likely undesirable).

II

Oakeshott's concern with the spread of rationalism beyond its bounds within enterprise association is present in Shevek's recognition that Anarres has been straying off course. Bedap's complaints to Shevek concerning the direction that Anarres is taking illustrates the division between the two ways of thinking:

> We've let cooperation become obedience. On Urras they have government by the minority. Here we have government by the majority. But it is government! The social conscience isn't a living thing any more, but a machine, a power machine, controlled by bureaucrats! . . . And its not just PDC [Production and Distribution Coordination]. It's anywhere on Anarres. Learning centers, institutes, mines, mills, fisheries, canneries, agricultural development and research stations, anywhere that function demands expertise and a stable institution. But that stability gives scope to the authoritarian impulse. In the early years of the Settlement we were aware of that, on the lookout for it. People discriminated very carefully then between administering things and governing people. (6: 167)

Bedap recognizes that some functions demand expertise: for example, the very creation of Pravic, the Anarresti language, was a rationalist attempt to create a language that would deny the possibility of both hierarchy and ownership. However, the organizing function, the very job of the PDC, is not one for which there is any appropriate expertise other than the expertise of the bureaucrat. What the PDC requires (and this is further reflected in its lack of parliamentary procedure) is simply deliberation, messy and argumentative. In its ideal form the PDC simply decides, as Oakeshott has it, the conditions under which the Anarresti will live. The PDC engages in the necessarily skeptical attitude that questions Anarresti assumptions. Its members (volunteers on rotation) will decide, for example, the desirability of maintaining the Terms of the Settlement, which are the rules concerning relations with Urras, and they may decide, based on those conditions, that no Urrasti may come to Anarres.

To work appropriately the PDC must reject any rationalist problem-solving role for itself. It must also see the limits to its own reach. The PDC must see certain decisions as off limits. For example, the PDC cannot give a rationalist verdict of true or false for the question of whether to continue the Terms of the Settlement. Furthermore it cannot decide that Shevek may not go to Urras; that decision is entirely up to Shevek himself, because "the Terms of the Settlement do not forbid it. To forbid it now would be an assumption of authority by the PDC, an abridgement of the right of the Odonian individual to initiate action harmless to others" (12: 357). To forbid Shevek's journey to Urras might seem wholly rational, but this decision is recognized by the PDC as outside of the purview of their discussions. And while they argue that Shevek may not return (for once he is coming from Urras he is, according to one interpretation of the Terms, an Urrasti), this argument has no necessarily correct decision.

Shevek acknowledges that this process of deciding how to organize the functions of the Anarresti is the key to fulfilling the needs of the individual and to producing a progressive society.

> He recognized that need, in Odonian terms, as his "cellular function," the analogic term for the individual's individuality, the work he can do best, therefore his best contribution to society. A healthy society would let him exercise that optimum function freely, in the coordination of all such functions finding its adaptability and strength. That was a central idea of Odo's *Analogy*. That the Odonian society on Anarres had fallen short of the ideal did not, in his eyes, lessen his responsibility to it; just the contrary. (10: 333)

The PDC is to coordinate such functions, yet Le Guin (unlike Plato) is clear that individuals decide for themselves what their own activity is. Shevek refuses to be swayed from his commitment to physics, even when criticized that his work is neither essential nor sharable. Shevek asserts that one's work is one's "duty and [one's] right" (12: 359). Doing physics is the only way Shevek knows to fulfill his function, a function that he sees as wholly connected to the principles of Anarres as it seeks "to organize everything comprehensible to the human mind" (8: 265).

But Shevek must recognize that when he is on Urras his function changes, despite his claim to Takver before his departure that his effect on Urras will be minimal. ("I might make a little revolution in their physics again, but not in their opinions. It's here, here that I can affect society, even though here they won't pay attention to my physics" [12: 377].) On Urras he is more than a physicist; he is an Anarresti, an Odonian, on a hostile world. Thus on Urras, as on Anarres, he embraces the revolutionary mode. "The Odonian society was conceived as a permanent revolution" (10: 333). But what it means to act in a revolutionary way changes when Shevek goes from Anarres to Urras.

> On Anarres he had chosen, in defiance of the expectations of his society, to do the work he was individually called to do. To do it was to rebel: to risk the self

for the sake of society. Here on Urras, that act of rebellion was a luxury, a self-indulgence. To be a physicist in A-Io was to serve not society, not mankind, not the truth, but the State. (9: 272)

On Urras, as on Anarres, he is taking risks for his society. On Anarres he takes risks in persisting to work on the theories he believed to be right despite the lack of support he received from Sabul. On Urras, Shevek's risk-taking goes beyond doing physics. Yet, importantly, his are not the self-sacrificial risks of the martyr.

Shevek is not seeking to bring Odonianism to Urras (although he is pleased to be an example of Anarresti success on Urras); he is trying to renew the Odonian spirit of Anarres. Thus Shevek's function is particular to Anarres (and on Anarres his function does go beyond that of physics: he is also a partner, a father, and a member of the community). Whatever he *might* bring to Urras or to the Council of World Governments in the form of transilience is done *not* for the sake of the universe, but for Anarres, and for himself ("I am no altruist!" he declares to Keng, the Ambassador from Terra, while asking her to help him return to Anarres [11: 350]). In this Le Guin presents a kind of realist utopia; it is a utopia that acknowledges the necessity of self-interest. It is not Shevek's place to change the conditions under which Urrasti live—only they can do that. But it is his place to question and change the conditions under which Anarresti live. Shevek is not called to altruism, but to brotherhood. But he determines the bounds of this brotherhood—Anarres. Even while on Urras, Shevek is engaged in doing Anarresti politics for Anarres.

On Urras, Shevek must do what the Anarresti would do as a matter of course: share. He will ultimately share the very scientific information that the government of A-Io has been trying to take from him—instantaneous travel through space. This sharing might well be considered by a materialist Urrasti as the height of altruistic nonsense. But Shevek does not share to save the universe. He shares because that is who he is. He also shares precisely to defeat, in some small part, the materialism of the Urrasti. Furthermore, he will share his very presence with those who need it most: the workers of A-Io, but he need not become their martyr. On both planets Shevek must think about the society that *he* wants to live in, and that is a society where he can be and do what he is (a physicist, a partner, a father, a brother). But this being and doing does not make him a cog in a machine. "If we must all agree, all work together, we're no better than a machine" (12: 359). Both Anarres and Urras have tried to force his hand. Urras does so to make a profit, it does so because profit-making is the central function of the state of A-Io. Anarres does so by valuing the rationality of the mechanism over the unpredictability of an organism. So Anarres is learning why the rationalist mode is hierarchical management masked as efficiency. The rationalism of Anarres is being criticized from within, by Shevek and Bedap, and it is arguably apparent at the end when things "are . . . a little broken loose" (13: 384) that the purely rational has been undermined. (Although, appropriately enough, Le Guin has left ambiguous how successful the undermining of this rationalist mode will be.)

III

But even if Anarres is working to avoid the trap of rationalism, it might well be susceptible to the charge of teleology. As Anarres itself has a guiding set of principles in Odonianism, one might argue that the end of the society is simply to bring about those principles. But, as seen above, the principles of Odonianism, the idea of the constant revolution, do not imply an end in the usual teleological sense. Appeals to Odonianism are not appeals to a future shared outcome; rather they are attempts to find common ground. But it is a common ground always open to interpretation. Le Guin clarifies that Odonianism is not to be seen as mere teleology by establishing Urras as the teleological world, focused on the achievement of the good.

Both A-Io as a nation and the university that hosts Shevek are built along teleological lines. A-Io is clearly a nation focused on the goal of ensuring its wealth and beauty through great central planning. For example, while A-Io is clearly an individualist community, it is also one that is restricted in such a way to avoid environmental degradation. "All such luxuries which if freely allowed to the public would tend to drain irreplaceable natural resources or to foul the environment with waste products were strictly controlled by regulation and taxation" (3: 82). What individuals might do with their wealth on A-Io is limited by government control. The teleology is even more evident at Ieu Eun University, which is single-mindedly oriented toward the attainment of knowledge. The students Shevek taught

> were superbly trained. . . . Their minds were fine, keen, ready. When they weren't working, they rested. They were not blunted and distracted by a dozen other obligations. They never fell asleep in class because they were tired from having worked on rotational duty the day before. Their society maintained them in complete freedom from want, distractions, and cares. (5: 127)

They were free to be nothing other than students and this freedom cuts them loose from both communal ties and individual responsibility (as evidenced in their response to Shevek's decision to let students grade themselves). Shevek is clearly attracted to the efficiency, the rationality, of the hierarchy apparent in Urrasti meritocracy. Furthermore he recognizes the university as a kind of brotherhood (he says that it "*felt* like a community" [3: 81]). Yet this is a brotherhood without women and limited to only students and professors. It is a brotherhood of equals built on a foundation of inequality.

His initial experience talking to other physicists reflects further the attractions of this world:

> It was a revelation, a liberation. Physicists, mathematicians, astronomers, logicians, biologists, all were here at the University, and they came to him or he went to them, and they talked, and new worlds were born of their talking. It is of the nature of idea to be communicated: written, spoken, done. The idea is like grass. It craves light, likes crowds, thrives on crossbreeding, grows better for being stepped on. (3: 72)

This revelation is wholly real. For Shevek this is the first time he can interact completely as a physicist, thus fulfilling his cellular function. The intellectual exchange denied him on Anarres (because no one could do physics at his level, because no one would let him teach the physics he had realized to others) is provided on Urras. But the enlightenment of sharing ideas with like-minded scientists is dimmed by the realization that the freedom of students and faculty at Ieu Eun University to study, think, and share ideas necessitated that others cook, clean, build, labor, and ultimately *serve* those whose function is simply to think.

The consequences of such hierarchy have not always been evident to Shevek. Shevek had been tempted as a young man to think that his abilities justified special treatment for himself:

> Shevek's first decades in the afforestation project had been spent in silent resentment and exhaustion. People who had chosen to work in centrally functional fields such as physics should not be called upon for these projects and special levies. Wasn't it immoral to do work you didn't enjoy? The work needed doing, but a lot of people didn't care what they were posted to and changed jobs all the time; they should have volunteered. . . . He found the workmates dull and loutish, and even those younger than himself treated him like a boy. (2: 48)

However Shevek is ultimately made ill by life at the Institute in Abbenay where he is allowed a kind of special status. He is given a single room, something usually reserved for those with whom others refuse to live, the cafeterias provide dessert every day; and he is told to learn Iotic (the language of A-Io) and to keep the knowledge of that learning a secret. He embraces this privacy and does not join with others in recreation or meals. But this treatment has its own consequences. Shevek must deal with Sabul, his superior who expects to be stroked, validated, and admired. Shevek's success as a physicist on Anarres depends on his ability to massage Sabul's ego. For example, his publications are only accepted with Sabul as coauthor. This violates the principles of Anarres in a number of ways: Sabul is not to be seen as above Shevek, Shevek's ideas are not to be subject to Sabul's whims, and the publication of those ideas should not need the inclusion of Sabul's coauthorship to pass editorial muster. Anarres is a non-hierarchical place, and

Shevek's need to learn how to manipulate Sabul denies the brotherhood implicit in Odonianism. Shevek becomes ill at the recognition that he is "Sabul's man." After this illness he recognizes his need to connect with others in Abbenay. "He had been keeping himself for himself, against the ethical imperative of brotherhood" (6: 155). Shevek, who is described at this point in his development as "not a prig, exactly" is using "the simplistic Odonianism taught to children by mediocre adults, an internalized preaching" (6: 155). The voice of this internal preacher is the Odonianism made teleological that, like the appeal to rationalism, is leading Anarres away from its anarchist foundation.

Sabul appeals to the same simplistic Odonianism in his rejection of Shevek's *Principles of Simultaneity*. Sabul knows that he cannot challenge Shevek's physics. But he can abuse Odonianism and punish Shevek through a moral rejection of the direction in which Shevek's physics is taking him: "That Sequence Physics is the high road of chronosophical thought in the Odonian Society has been a mutually agreed principle since Settlement" (8: 238). Here Sabul's rejection of Shevek's work (a rejection Sabul will withdraw once he becomes coauthor) is clearly ideological and appeals to a merely mechanical Odonianism that one would use like a catechism. The vibrancy of Anarres to which Shevek will appeal later in his life is dependent on the common foundation that all learn in Odo's writings. When these writings are used teleologically to simply mold Anarresti into one shape, the principles fail. It is only when the principles themselves become the subject of who and what Anarres is that their vibrancy is rediscovered. Urras has no such issue with the teleological mode. This mode is the most efficient means to justify the hierarchical structure of the society.

On Urras, Shevek's brothers are fellow intellectuals, and he initially hides from himself that this brotherhood of those at the top of the hierarchy must deny the brotherhood of all. Shevek finds at the university in A-Io the advantages of being at the top of the hierarchy: there is seemingly no one to whom he must bow, and ideas seem free to go where they will. But of course he is subject, not to the small-minded Sabul, but to the State of A-Io itself. Thus when he rejects Urras, he rejects the whole package: the meritocracy, the single-minded pursuit of knowledge, the teleological spirit that focuses on the goal and sees the means as merely steps from here to there. Urras is not ambiguous; it is complex, but wholly predictable.

When Shevek ultimately rejects Urras he does so in contrast to the ambassador from the Earth and her alternative view of the Urrasti world. Shevek, who has escaped from A-Io's crackdown on striking workers, has sought refuge in the Terran Embassy. There he meets the ambassador and explains why he has learned to detest Urras:

> We left with empty hands, a hundred and seventy years ago, and we were right. We took nothing. Because there is nothing here but States and their weapons, the rich and their lies, and the poor and their misery. *There is no way to act*

rightly, with a clear heart, on Urras. There is nothing you can do that profit does not enter into, and fear of loss, and the wish for power. (11: 346, emphasis added)

On Anarres, Shevek has been able, through the formation of the "Syndicate of Initiative," to respond to the problems arising from Sabul and the encroaching bureaucracy of his system. On Urras this is an impossibility. The goal of profit-seeking is ever-present. To learn to live on Urras is to become Urrasti (thus recognizing, perhaps, that Rulag and other members of the PDC were right that Anarres cannot open its borders to Urrasti). The ambassador from Earth, Keng, replies:

> Let me tell you how this world seems to me. To me, and to all my fellow Terrans who have seen the planet, Urras is the kindliest, most various, most beautiful of all the inhabited worlds. It is the world that comes as close as any could to Paradise. . . . I know it's full of evils, full of human injustice, greed, folly, waste. But it is also full of good, of beauty, vitality, achievement. It is what a world should be! It is *alive*, tremendously alive—alive despite all its evils, with hope. Is that not true? (11: 347)

Keng's perspective is colored by the contrast she is making between Urras and Earth, which has at this point almost died out:

> My world, my Earth, is a ruin. A planet spoiled by the human species. We multiplied and gobbled and fought until there was nothing left, and then we died. We controlled neither appetite nor violence; we did not adapt. We destroyed ourselves. But we destroyed the world first. (11: 347–48)

Urras is not to be understood as Earth today, but as a rationalist, teleological response to the problems of our Earth. Keng's Earth is our future unless we act. The question is whether we act to choose the hierarchy of Urras or the equality of Anarres. Shevek rejects Urras because its own ideology justifies the denial of brotherhood. Keng admires Urras because its rejection of brotherhood has itself been controlled in such a way that it can maintain itself. The inequality of Urras is wrapped up in a package of beauty, technology, and excess whereas the equality of Anarres is wrapped in a stark, arid world of effort. Keng admits that Anarres is no longer a possible future for her Earth ("we forfeited our chance for Anarres centuries ago" [11: 349]), and yet this very claim awakens Shevek's ire, for he rejects both the nature of the hope that Keng claims Urras has (hope for Keng, perhaps, whose vision is so narrowed) and Keng's own denial of hope for Earth. But, ultimately Shevek is not concerned with either Keng or Earth. Shevek seeks to return to Anarres to break down its walls of entrenched behavior. But the reader is being chastised along with Keng. Anarres *is* a possible future, as the final exchange between Shevek and Keng indicates. Shevek: "Dead anarchists make martyrs, you know, and keep living for centuries. But absent ones can be forgotten." "'I thought I knew what "realism" was,' Keng said. She smiled. But it was not an easy smile." "'How can you, [Shevek replied,] if you don't know what hope is?'" (11: 351). The hope that Shevek wants us to acknowledge is the hope that effort and will might bring about positive change. The death of hope is found in both the pessimism that says nothing can be done and the complacency that says nothing needs to be done.

IV

Shevek's choice of Anarres is a choice for compromise.[18] It is a Berlin-like choice to recognize that "it is on earth that we live, and it is here that we must believe and act."[19] But compromise over what? Early on in *The Dispossessed*, as Shevek is preparing to leave for Abbenay, he declares in a fit of youthful pique, and against his society's own self image, that suffering is the core human experience:

> Suffering is the condition on which we live. And when it comes, you know it. You know it as the truth. Of course it's right to cure diseases, to prevent hunger and injustice, as the social organism does. But no society can change the nature of existence. We can't prevent suffering. This pain and that pain, yes, but not Pain. A society can only relieve social suffering, unnecessary suffering. The rest remains. The root, the reality. (2: 60)

A brief exchange occurs when one of the girls present argues that it is not suffering but "Love is the true condition of human life." Shevek then argues again for suffering, recounting the story of a man who died of burns in an accident, a man for whom nothing could be done. But if suffering is the key to human existence, the girl asks, "What have you left, then? Isolation and despair! You're denying brotherhood, Shevek!" And he answers, "No—no, I'm not. I'm trying to say what I think brotherhood really is. It begins—it begins in shared pain" (2: 60–62).

If Shevek is right then we have a necessary starting point without which any feasible utopia is clearly lost. If there are compromises to be made we cannot compromise on doing what we can about that suffering that is under our control, social suffering. But how can one maintain the hopeful legacy of utopian thinking while arguing for the fact of a human suffering about which we can do nothing? And how do we avoid fetishizing suffering itself? In the short story "The Day Before the Revolution," which focuses on the last day of the life of Odo, the anarchist revolutionary who wrote the principles upon which Anarres is founded, Odo muses:

> She had never feared or despised the city. It was her country. There would not be slums like this, if the Revolution prevailed. But there would be misery.

There would always be misery, waste, cruelty. She had never pretended to be changing the human condition, to be Mama taking tragedy away from the children so they won't hurt themselves. Anything but. So long as people were free to choose, if they chose to drink flybane and live in sewers, it was their business. Just so long as it wasn't the business of Business, the source of profit and the means of power for other people.[20]

Individual suffering, misery, is unavoidable. To try and avoid misery is to create a world of parents hopelessly trying to keep their children from skinning knees and losing friends. Shevek divides suffering into that which can be alleviated (social suffering or "unnecessary suffering") and that which cannot (individual suffering). He also recognizes that the starting point of suffering is the recognition that it is shared. Shevek is making two key points here. First, the fact of suffering does not necessitate "isolation and despair." Rather once we see that such suffering is shared we see the only basis for universal shared experience. Second, Shevek recognizes that we must do what we can about "unnecessary suffering," for which he gives three examples: disease, hunger, and injustice (2: 60).

Social suffering is the appropriate realm of rational problem-solving. Individual suffering is not available to such problem-solving (and dystopias emerge when individual suffering is abolished, as with Huxley's *soma*). Politics is the realm whereby we determine the conditions of our lives. Politics is the arena where we deliberate over what kinds of suffering are acceptable and what kinds are not. It is the place where we decide which problems shall be given over to rational problem-solving (although it is not the arena whereby we discover or promote solutions). For example, the PDC may decide to explore the possibility of new food sources; but it is Takver and her colleagues at the algae processing plant who will decide what to grow, how to grow it, and whether it will make an acceptable food source. Politics is the place where we deliberate over how we understand the very idea of suffering. For Shevek we cannot compromise on our attempts to decrease that suffering that we *can* fix; nor must we compromise on our acknowledgment that society *cannot* fix the suffering of individuals. As Efor (his Urrasti manservant) learns when he asks Shevek about life on Anarres:

"Nobody ever out of work, there."
There was a faint edge of irony, or question, in his voice.
"No."
"And nobody goes hungry?"
"Nobody goes hungry while another eats."
"Ah."
"But we have been hungry. We have starved. There was a famine, you know, eight years ago. I knew a woman then who killed her baby, because she had no milk, and there was nothing else, nothing else to give it. It is not all . . . all milk and honey on Anarres, Efor."
"I don't doubt it, sir. . . . All the same there's none of *them* there!"

"Them?"

"You know, Mr. Shevek. What you said once. The owners." (9: 285)

Le Guin is clearly not making it easy here. If we are to see Anarres as a utopia we can only see it that way with open eyes. We must recognize it as a place where violence will occur, and the only reassurance that we will have is that violence is not the result of the State. No one will try to justify societal violence or degradation and call it a necessary part of human existence.

Anarres is attractive for a number of reasons, not the least being that in its movement away from the rationalism that Shevek and Bedap discuss throughout the novel, it realizes a self-consciousness about its own values that is essential for any utopia. Anarres is trying—trying to be itself and to discover what it is to be itself. Anarres is not trying to achieve perfection. It is trying to stay true to the principles that its inhabitants have endorsed: brotherhood, equality, freedom. Here we can return to Isaiah Berlin's own ambiguously utopian dream.

> Of course social or political collisions will take place; the mere conflict of positive values alone makes this unavoidable. Yet they can, I believe, be minimized by promoting and preserving an uneasy equilibrium, which is constantly threatened and in constant need of repair—that alone, I repeat, is the precondition for decent societies and morally acceptable behavior, otherwise we are bound to lose our way. A little dull as a solution, you will say? Not the stuff of which calls to heroic action by inspired leaders are made? Yet if there is some truth in this view, perhaps that is sufficient.[21]

Le Guin challenges her readers on a number of levels and, as with all utopias, her challenge is a direct criticism of our own world at this time. We have three options. First, there is Keng's Earth and the human and environmental degradation that accompany it. Second, there is Urras, a world clearly modeled on Earth, although improved in certain ways. Urras is wholly hierarchical: men over women, rich over poor, educated over uneducated. Its hierarchy is essential to its structure and the arguments given to justify or explain away the hierarchy (particularly the gender hierarchy) are wholly familiar to us. Third, there is Anarres, materially limited although communally rich. Anarres is striving to uphold the egalitarian, nonauthoritarian vision imagined by Odo. It refuses to rationalize the unacceptable. Although it also recognizes that sometimes the unacceptable happens. Anarres is not perfect. It is an ambiguous utopia, not because its utopian nature is ambiguous, but because it accepts that skepticism is simply the ground from which we must work.

Le Guin is demanding of her reader that she makes choices about the world in which she lives. All three options are available to us. We could recognize the possibility of the worst-case scenario and become immobilized by pessimism; this is a choice present in the proliferation and popularity of doomsday scenarios.[22] We could celebrate the wealth and beauty that exist in our society and work to control society (through environmental regulation, for example) such that we maintain that wealth and beauty. However, this choice demands that we ignore the fact that our wealth and beauty are limited to certain layers of society and are often attained at the expense of other layers. Or we could choose to change radically, change how we see ourselves as members of a human community, change the very notion of what it is that we desire and where we are willing to compromise.

Criticisms of utopia get their force from the depiction and the reality of dystopia. It is no accident that the strongest criticisms of utopianism emerge from post–World War II writers. Yet we cannot let our fear that someone's vision is in fact a theory of debasement turn us away from the very idea of vision itself. Once someone sets up a blueprint for a more perfect society, someone else will show how that society will inevitably fail or has within it the seeds of the worst possible society. Rather than deny the idea of vision and simply accustom ourselves to what we already know, we should consider visions such as Le Guin's. For Le Guin is neither offering a blueprint nor a utopia written from the perspective of Truth. There is no set of guidelines that we can simply enact to produce our Anarres. But she has created a utopia that provides a principle from which to build: one cannot justify the happiness of one by the degradation of another. And she has created a utopia that sets out a framework for what is desirable: self-chosen work, vibrant (self-chosen) communal ties, commitment to oneself and one's community, and commitment to both the idea of a vision and the skeptical attitude necessary to keep that vision alive.

NOTES

I would like to thank Laurence Davis, Phil Jos, and Larry Krasnoff for their excellent and insightful comments on earlier drafts.

1. Eugene Zamiatin's *We* is the first of the twentieth century's totalitarian dystopias. *We* was written in the USSR in 1920–1921 and read to a disapproving audience of the All-Russian Writer's Union in 1923. *We* depicts a totalitarian state where citizens are known by numbers and privacy is destroyed; it was enormously influential for both Huxley's *Brave New World* and Orwell's *Nineteen Eighty-Four*. More recent dystopias (such as Margaret Atwood's *Oryx and Crake* or the *Parable* series by Octavia Butler) have moved away from totalitarianism as the source of our greatest fear, and toward the fear of apathy in the face of rapid environmental and political change. Ursula K. Le Guin, *The Dispossessed: An Ambiguous Utopia* (New York: Harper & Row, 1974), cited in the text by chapter and page to the 387-page Eos HarperCollins edition of 2001.

2. This is not to say that prior to the twentieth century there were no criticisms of utopia. Many earlier political philosophers—for example, Aristotle, Pyrrhonian skeptics, Machiavelli, Montaigne, Hobbes, and Hume—all challenge the premises of utopian writers. But their criticisms are not self-consciously anti-utopian, as these three twentieth-century political philosophers are.

3. An example of the rationalism Oakeshott is criticizing can be found in utopias such as Charlotte Perkins Gilman's *Herland* or Edward Bellamy's popular *Looking Backward*.

4. Michael Oakeshott, *On Human Conduct* (Oxford: Clarendon Press, 1975), 114.

5. Oakeshott, *On Human Conduct*, 128.

6. Oakeshott, *On Human Conduct*, 128.

7. John Rawls, *A Theory of Justice* (Cambridge, MA: Harvard University Press, 1971), 24.

8. Rawls, *Theory of Justice*, 24.

9. Rawls, *Theory of Justice*, 93.

10. Oakeshott would understand Rawls as promoting our adverbial relations over our imperative or commanded relations. One should act well (and we are the ones to determine what that means) before one does good. Furthermore politics is about deciding what it means to act well. Politics is not about determining what it means to do good.

11. Rawls, *Theory of Justice*, 514.

12. Isaiah Berlin, "Pursuit of the Ideal," in *The Crooked Timber of Humanity* (New York: Alfred A. Knopf, 1991), 5–6.

13. Berlin, "Pursuit," 14.

14. Berlin, "Pursuit," 19.

15. Berlin, "Pursuit," 18.

16. As many authors within the feminist science fiction genre have done. The skeptical utopia is also presented by Octavia Butler and Marge Piercy. See Claire Curtis, "Rehabilitating Utopia: Feminist Science Fiction and Finding the Ideal," in *Contemporary Justice Review* 8, no. 2 (June 2002), 147–62.

17. Isaiah Berlin, "Decline of Utopian Ideas in the West," in *The Crooked Timber*, 20.

18. A choice for compromise despite Shevek's own distinction between compromise (which he rejects) and sacrifice (which he accepts [10: 333]).

19. Berlin, "Pursuit," 13.

20. Ursula K. Le Guin, "The Day Before the Revolution," in *The Utopia Reader*, ed. Gregory Claeys and Lyman Tower Sargent (New York: New York University Press, 1999), 417–18.

21. Berlin, "Pursuit," 19.

22. The popularity of Tim LaHaye's *Left Behind* series may be the best example of how we are tempted by a vision of the end, a vision that LaHaye dresses up as inevitable and leading to salvation for (the few) believers. More secular versions of this are present in the recent spate of apocalyptic novels and films (the most recent being *The Day After Tomorrow* [2004]).

WORKS CITED

Berlin, Isaiah. "Decline of Utopian Ideas in the West." Pp. 20–48 in *The Crooked Timber of Humanity*. New York: Alfred A. Knopf. 1991.

———. "Pursuit of the Ideal." Pp. 1–19 in *The Crooked Timber of Humanity*. New York: Alfred A. Knopf, 1991.

Curtis, Claire. "Rehabilitating Utopia: Feminist Science Fiction and Finding the Ideal." *Contemporary Justice Review* 8, no. 2 (June 2002), 147–62.

Le Guin, Ursula K. "The Day Before the Revolution." Pp. 407–20 in *The Utopia Reader*, ed. Gregory Claeys and Lyman Tower Sargent. New York: New York University Press, 1999.

———. *The Dispossessed: An Ambiguous Utopia.* New York: Eos, HarperCollins, 2001 (1974).

Oakeshott, Michael. *On Human Conduct.* Oxford: Clarendon Press, 1975.

Rawls, John. *A Theory of Justice.* Cambridge, MA: Harvard University Press, 1971.

16

Empty Hands: Communication, Pluralism, and Community in Ursula K. Le Guin's *The Dispossessed*

Avery Plaw

> My father felt very strongly you can never get outside your own cul-
> ture. All you can do is try. I think that feeling sometime comes out
> in my writing. My father studied real cultures and I make them up—
> in a way it's the same thing.
>
> —Ursula Le Guin[1]

> But [Shevek] felt more strongly the need that had brought him
> across the dry abyss from the other world, the need for communica-
> tion, the wish to unbuild walls.
>
> —Ursula Le Guin, *The Dispossessed* (3: 75)

It is a critical commonplace that the invented worlds of science fiction offer an especially fertile ground for exploring contemporary political and social issues. In this chapter, I will briefly examine an exemplary case—Ursula K. Le Guin's Hugo and Nebula award-winning winning novel *The Dispossessed* (1974)—particularly in terms of its treatment of the possibilities of communicating with, understanding, and evaluating profoundly different cultural and political worlds. In a rapidly glob-alizing world increasingly threatened by what Samuel Huntington has termed "the clash of civilizations" the topicality of these themes needs hardly to be belabored.[2]

Le Guin's novels generally are deeply concerned with the possibilities and limits of communication and understanding between different worlds (both liter-ally and figuratively[3]); for example, her other Hugo and Nebula award-winning novel, *The Left Hand of Darkness*, tells the story of Genly Ai's solitary and ulti-mately failed embassy from the Ekumen (a peaceful interstellar federation) to the unique "ambisexual society" of the newly discovered world Gethen/Winter.[4] In *The Dispossessed*, Le Guin modulates this theme to focus on the limits of commu-nication and understanding within a single species (Cetians) split into profoundly different political societies located on sister planets, Urras and Anarres.

Almost two hundred years before the novel begins, A-Io, the leading industrial nation on Urras, was convulsed by a widespread general strike inspired by the revolutionary anarcho-syndicalist thought of Laia Odo.[5] The conflict was ultimately resolved by an agreement to allow the revolutionaries to colonize the desolate and virtually uninhabited sister planet Anarres. There the Odonian revolutionaries established a society based on Odo's principles of free association and mutual aid between individuals. In accordance with the mutually-agreed Terms of Settlement, however, virtually all communication (and all immigration) between the worlds was cut off. When the novel opens, Anarres has been isolated for a century and a half.

The novel tells the story of the physicist Shevek's groundbreaking visit from the Odonian settlement on Anarres back to Urras. Shevek feels compelled to make the voyage because he is convinced that "We must know each other" (3: 75). The author presents the voyage as an "exploration . . . into the extremes of the comprehensible" (2: 54). A central concern of the novel is the degree to which Shevek succeeds in communicating with, and understanding, his Urrasti hosts. In this chapter I will argue, contrary to Le Guin's self-description, that Shevek does succeed in "getting outside his own culture" by learning to understand the Urrasti; he also helps them to see beyond their culture by communicating something of himself and his society to the Iotians on Urras. If this reading is persuasive, then Le Guin's story challenges a central assumption shared by anthropological relativists, postmodernists, and cultural conservatives like Huntington—that individuals are captive of their own cultural backgrounds, and by consequence are sharply limited in their capacities to intimately communicate with, or to deeply understand, other cultures.

This possibility of genuine inter-world/cultural communication and understanding invites reflection on the question of which world is, on the whole, better or more desirable—the (utopian/dystopian?) Anarresti anarcho-syndicalist community or the Iotian (proxy for our own?) plutocratic-capitalist political society?[6] Le Guin's critics have disagreed sharply on how the book resolves this question. Many, like Elizabeth Cummins and Jim Jose, have seen *The Dispossessed*'s portrayal of Anarres as, in Carl Freedman's words, "the reinvention of the positive utopia."[7] Others, like John Brennan and Michael Downs, have seen the portrayal as essentially dystopian—as "a penetrating critique of all utopian experience, even that of anarchism";[8] André Gorz describes it as "the most striking description I know of the seductions—and snares—of self-managed communist, or in other words, anarchist society."[9] One point on which most critics are agreed, however, is that the book is, in one way or the other, "didactic," "moralizing," and "monistic."[10]

By contrast, it is my contention that the understanding of the worlds that Shevek's journey permits is pluralistic rather than monistic, and persuasive in tone rather than didactic or moralizing.[11] What Shevek reveals is that each society realizes its own ultimate human goods at its own human costs, which makes them difficult to assess comparatively. The contrasting constellations of values and flaws embodied in the two societies pose a genuine ethical dilemma: choosing either involves irremediable loss, and the correct choice cannot be determined with rational certainty. The issue must finally rest on individual conviction. That does not mean that Shevek might not have good personal and political reasons for preferring Anarres, reasons which warrant serious consideration. It does, however, reflect the fact that he also recognizes genuine goods on Urras absent on Anarres (even if he personally finds them unnecessary). Moreover, Shevek is portrayed from the beginning of the novel as an exemplary Odonian, and so the fact that he is little troubled by the choice does not diminish the difficulty confronted by those less deeply committed. Indeed, Le Guin carefully follows Shevek's most powerful denunciation of Urras with a far more disinterested and favorable account from the Terran Ambassador which draws attention to some of the real ethical difficulties of comparison.

However, even if the book is more persuasive than didactic, Shevek's words and actions still do suggest some forceful reasons for choosing Anarres over Urras.[12] Anarres provides at least the potential for a kind of open community which promotes human solidarity and ensures an equal freedom to realize individual potential. A-Io, by contrast, offers a home only for some of its citizens at the price of suppressing and alienating others. A-Io, in short, is a fractured community. In illuminating this contrast, Le Guin develops a powerful and original, although not necessarily conclusive, argument for the pursuit of anarcho-syndicalist ideals.[13]

I

The Dispossessed opens with the statement that "There was a wall" surrounding the Port of Anarres, and that although "It did not look important. . . . It was important" (1: 1). Le Guin describes it as "like all walls . . . ambiguous, two-faced" (1: 1). It protected the Anarresti community from outside influences, but also trapped the Anarresti in their own hermetically-sealed environment, cutting them off from the rest of the nine known worlds. This image of a wall as an obstacle to communication and understanding, as a sort of trap, recurs throughout the book. The image haunts Shevek in his dreams (4: 125; 5: 153). It comes as no surprise then that the purpose of Shevek's journey to Urras, which forms the narrative focus of the book, is, in his words, "to unbuild walls," to establish "free exchange between Urras and Anarres" (3: 75; 5: 138; 10: 332; 11: 346). As he puts it dramatically shortly after his arrival on Urras:

> We ignore you; you ignore us. . . . I want to learn, not to ignore. It is the reason I came. We must know each other. We are not primitive men. Our morality is no longer tribal, it cannot be. Such ignorance is a wrong, from which wrong will arise. So I come to learn. (3: 75)

One critical question raised by the text is whether his, or any such mission be-tween worlds, can succeed. This section argues that Shevek's mission does suc-ceed, at least in part.

Of course, "speech," as Shevek is reminded early in the book, is "a two-way function" (2: 30), "a cooperative art" (2: 29). For communication to occur, under-standing has to run in both directions. So there are really two facets to the ques-tion of Shevek's success. First, what is communicated to him about Urras that he did not already know? And second, what does he communicate to the Urrasti about Anarres that they did not already know?

Shevek's challenge in understanding the Urrasti is foreshadowed by the first words that he speaks in the book. During the launch from the Port of Anarres, Shevek, staring out a port at the diminishing planet, declares "I don't understand" (1: 6). Of course, at this point he is merely surprised by the experience of space-flight, but his bafflement before the Urrasti technology anticipates the deeper challenge of understanding their culture. As the book's narrator shortly explains, "it is hard . . . for people who have never paid money for anything to understand the psychology of cost, the argument of the marketplace" (4: 92).

Le Guin reinforces the gulf between the cultures of the two worlds by em-phasizing a divergence of language. The Odonian revolutionaries who settled on Anarres wanted to make a wholesale break with their Urrasti past, and so in-vented a new language for themselves—Pravic—that reflected the kind of com-munity they hoped to build. In the new language, for example, articles are typi-cally general rather than possessive (so "the mother" rather than "my mother") in order to avoid suggesting the idea of possessions (2: 58). At the direction of Sabul, his senior at the Anarresti Central Institute of the Sciences, Shevek is able to teach himself sufficient Iotic to read and write physics and to conduct normal conversations, but as Le Guin emphasizes, it remains a foreign tongue (11: 339; 13: 382). Shevek repeatedly notes Iotic words, such as "bastard," "splendor," and "propertied class," that have no equivalent in Pravic (1: 3, 23; 2: 42). He is not even able to establish a referent for these words until he has actually spent time on Urras.

Nonetheless, a hopeful note is quickly struck through Shevek's exchanges with his one real companion on the voyage to Urras, Dr. Kimoe: "All their con-versations were like this, exhausting to the doctor and unsatisfying to Shevek, yet intensely interesting to both" (1: 15). The conversations are exhausting and un-satisfying because all they can discern of one another are fragments of their over-all worldviews (such as their sharply differing attitudes on the place of women in society), not the whole consciousness that makes sense of particular attitudes. Yet they were intensely interesting because these fragments at least suggested the strange landscape of the other's world.

Even after months on Urras, however, there remain crucial aspects of Iotian culture that Shevek cannot bring himself even to contemplate. For example:

He tried to read an elementary economics text; it bored him past endurance, it was like listening to somebody interminably recounting a long and stupid dream. He could not force himself to understand how banks functioned and so forth, because all the operations of capitalism were as meaningless to him as the rites of a primitive religion, as barbaric, as elaborate, and as unnecessary. In a human sacrifice to deity there might be at least a mistaken and terrible beauty; in the rites of the moneychangers where greed, laziness, and envy were assumed to move all men's acts, even the terrible became banal. (5: 130–31)

Shevek's understanding of Iotian society and motivations remains incomplete—as dramatically demonstrated, for example, by his misunderstanding of social and sexual signals at Vea Oiie's *soirée*, eventuating in a thankfully bungled attempt to rape her (7: 228–31).

Despite clear limitations, however, Shevek's understanding of the Iotians develops and evolves over time. Indeed, the pattern of its development mirrors one of Odo's dictums in combination with the central insight of Shevek's General Temporal Theory: "true journey is return," said Odo; "You *can* go home again, the General Temporal Theory asserts, so long as you understand that home is a place where you have never been" (2: 55). In short, true journey is a return to a home that is no longer as you left it; it is return to a home transformed.

Shevek's developing understanding of Urras follows just this pattern of a return to a point of origin transformed. On arrival in A-Io, he is quickly disabused of the reductive and antagonistic attitudes about Urras he had been taught as a child:

But they were not the gross, cold egoists he had expected them to be: they were as complex and various as their culture, as their landscape; and they were intelligent; and they were kind. . . . And he did feel at home. (3: 77)

Indeed, the prejudices Shevek brought with him to Urras (such as Desar's characterization of Urras as hell) are quickly turned on their head. His own first-hand observations, at least during the initial phase of his trip, compel him toward a very different set of conclusions:

The beauty of the land and the well-being of its people remained a perpetual marvel to him. . . . the Urrasti knew how to use their world. He had been taught as a child that Urras was a festering mass of inequity, iniquity, and waste. But all the people . . . he saw, in the smallest country village, were well dressed, well fed, and, contrary to his expectations, industrious. (3: 82)

Shevek is also surprised to discover that the Iotians excel in "ecological control and the husbanding of natural resources" (3: 82). Moreover, beyond the "grace and comfort" (5: 133) of their world, he finds an unexpected freedom among the Iotians. When, for example, he visits the family of his reserved and elusive colleague

Demaere Oiie, he discovers that "In fact, at home, [Oiie] suddenly appeared as a simple, brotherly kind of man, a free man" (5: 147). Urras too, like Anarres, provides for a sort of individual freedom. Altogether Shevek feels compelled to "revise his understanding" (3: 83). Gradually, he comes to recognize Urras as a "paradise" from which he and his fellow Anarresti have excluded themselves (3: 89; 5: 129).

The inversion of Shevek's initial expectations, however, represents only the first stage in his growing understanding of Urras. Following the "ludicrous and abominable . . . scene with Vea" (9: 273), he begins to perceive something behind Urras's gorgeous veneer, something hidden. In the course of an illness he is able to establish a genuine connection with his servant, Efor. Efor then shares some chilling personal experiences that reveal a very different face of Urras, a face that Shevek is able, despite having no similar experience, to understand quite vividly:

> Shevek had to exercise his imagination and summon every scrap of knowledge he had about Urras to understand them at all. And yet they were familiar to him in a way that nothing he had yet seen here was, *and he did understand.*
> This was the Urras he had learned about in school on Anarres. This was the world from which his ancestors had fled. . . . This was the human suffering in which the ideals of his society were rooted. (9: 284, emphasis added)

At this point, it might appear as if Shevek had simply come full circle back to his original (home) understanding of Urras, but the home to which he returns has also changed under the weight of his initial insights. He thus continues:

> It was not "the real Urras." The dignity and beauty of the room he and Efor were in was as real as the squalor to which Efor was native. To him a thinking man's job was not to deny one reality at the expense of the other, but to include and to connect. It was not an easy job. (9: 284–85)

Urras thus contains both the wealth, beauty, energy, accomplishment, ecological balance, and the dignity that he perceived on his first arrival, and also the brutal class hierarchy he was taught about as a child. Like his own world, it is a complex intertwining of mutually dependent goods and evils.

While this insight by no means comprises a complete understanding of Urras, a good deal of the moral balance of Iotian culture is communicated to Shevek in the course of his journey. From an Odonian perspective, the Urrasti trade-off was not an attractive one for reasons that will be examined below, but Shevek also discovers that the Odonian truth is not necessarily the only one. He acknowledges that his own system of belief is anchored in an article of faith: he declares that the Iotians "think if people can possess enough things they will be content to live in prison. But I will not believe that" (5: 138). He believes that people can only realize contentment if they can choose their work free of economic constraint—if "work is done for work's sake" (5: 150). Individual choice can and should be freed from the prison of property. If, however, the core of Shevek's be-liefs is individual freedom, then people must be allowed to discover the truth for themselves and make their own choices. Shevek's deepening understanding of Urras reveals a genuine choice. Shevek himself certainly chooses Anarres—and comes to regard Urras as a hellish prison—but after all, he is an Odonian and his intention in traveling to Urras from the beginning was to "go subvert the archists" (12: 377). His own final rejection of Urras does not impinge on either his grow-ing understanding of it or the complexity of comparing the worlds.

If Shevek then is able in the course of his journey to gain a deepened, if not wholly complete, understanding of A-Io, the question remains of what he is able to communicate to his hosts in exchange. During his lengthy stay at Ieu Eun University, his colleagues express little interest in life on Anarres, and Shevek ends up keeping his thoughts mainly to himself. As he nears the end of his stay, "he felt that he had not touched anything, anyone, on Urras all these months" (5: 145). When Efor finally opens up to him, however, Shevek also seems able to communicate something of life on Anarres (9: 285). This conversation leads in turn to his escape from the "gracious prison cell" (9: 278) at the university, and his contact with the revolutionary movement in the nearby capital city of Nio Esseia.

Shevek then begins to write about Anarres for radical newspapers and pam-phlets. He finally makes contact with the Iotian poor. Even in this work, however, there is little actual dialogue and he has scant sense of the impact he is having:

> He did not read over what he had written. He did not listen closely to Maedda and the others who described the enthusiasm with which the papers were read . . . the effect his presence at the demonstration would make in the eyes of the world. (9: 297)

It is only at the demonstration itself, speaking spontaneously from the center of his being to a crowd of tens of thousands, that he has a clear sense of delivering his message. The end of his speech, however, is cut off by the brutal intervention of the Iotian security forces, and he is forced to run and hide before he can feel the impact, if any, his words have had.

It is only later, in the relative security of the Terran embassy, that Shevek gets a clear sense that his message, or at least some part of it, has been received. The Terran ambassador Keng tells him, "I heard you speak. I was very moved" (11: 341). Even the ambassador, however, has only partially understood. She tells him:

> I heard you speak of Anarres, in the Square, and I wept listening to you, but I didn't really believe you. Men always speak so of their homes, the absent land. . . . But you are *not* like other men. (11: 346)

Her personal interview with Shevek, however, forces her to concede that she has been wrong in thinking Anarres unimportant: "It is important. Perhaps Anarres

is the key to Urras" (11: 342). She begins to see that the social and political possibilities embodied on Anarres shape the political dynamics on Urras.

Shevek points out, however, that this possibility is only part of his message—
Anarres is not just a possibility, not just an ideal, but an accomplished fact:

> You are right, we are the key. But when you said that, you didn't really believe
> it. You don't believe in Anarres. You don't believe in me, though I stand with
> you, in this room, in this moment. . . . My people were right, and I was wrong,
> in this: We cannot come to you. You will not let us. You do not believe in
> change, in chance, in evolution. You would destroy us rather than admit our re-
> ality, rather than admit that there is hope! (11: 349–50)

Shevek perceives that both the Terrans and the Urrasti are in denial about the fact
of Anarres because it conflicts with a deeply embedded belief they have about human nature. They believe that human beings are necessarily lazy, greedy, and envi-
ous creatures—self-interested, acquisitive animals. This belief arises as a concomitant of market society, of property and power, and blinds people to real human
potential, to where their hope really lies. Urras's leading physicist, Atro, insists, for
example, that "the law of existence is struggle—competition—elimination of the
weak—a ruthless war for survival" (5: 143). Chifoilisk, the Thuvian physicist, implies much the same thing when he declares, "Human nature is human nature" (3:
69). Vea tells Shevek:

> Life is a fight, and the strongest wins. All civilization does is hide the blood
> and cover up the hate with pretty words. . . . I don't care about hurting and not
> hurting. I don't care about other people, and nobody else does, either. . . . I want
> to be free! (7: 220)

Vea desires freedom and intuitively understands that it is the truth that sets you
free. For Shevek, however, the truth that she reveals, that human beings just are
this way, is a delusion—an ideological by-product of a market society based on
ownership of property (including women). This delusion forms a psychological
wall that protects other core beliefs but only at the cost of obstructing human solidarity, and the authentic freedom that follows. Because Vea is herself "a thing
owned, bought, sold" (7: 215), she can feel nothing but resentment, contempt,
and disregard for her owners, and so for people in general. She seems to Shevek
not only intellectually but emotionally stunted. This insight reflects Shevek's
deepening understanding of Urras, but the wall he perceives in the Urrasti system
of beliefs remains an obstacle to communication with most Iotians he meets.

Nevertheless, despite all of the difficulties, Shevek is eventually able to communicate something of what he is and of what Anarres is to those Urrasti who are
willing to listen. Most importantly perhaps, he shows the Urrasti who are dissatisfied with their own culture and society a real alternative in which they can believe. He is also able to at least begin to understand them—both their strengths

and their often frustrating limitations. Consequently, both then in terms of what he communicates and what is communicated to him, Shevek's journey can be termed at least a partial success. Le Guin's story suggests then that the veil of anthropological relativism can be partially lifted, at least where four criteria are met: (1) where the person making the effort is a genuinely gifted and well-intentioned communicator, (2) where a great and sustained effort is made, (3) where the effort includes a journey to the other world or culture, and (4) where the other world or culture is receptive (and perhaps even responsive).

II

If some genuine communication and understanding of one another's communities develops in the course of *The Dispossessed*, at least between Shevek and those who are open to his message, then the next question is how do the two worlds actually compare. On this point many critics have found the novel didactic or monistic, a book with a one-note message that too often gets in the way of the story. In this section, I will contest this widely held view, maintaining by contrast that the book offers a genuinely pluralist perspective on the two worlds, and that its tone is persuasive rather than didactic.

Here I employ the term pluralist in the sense that writers like Isaiah Berlin, Bernard Williams, and John Gray have developed it in political and ethical theory—the two worlds realize incompatible but equally ultimate goods.[14] The question of which goods, and therefore which world, should be preferred is not one about which reason alone can give us a clear and definitive answer.[15] The question depends in large part on which goods a particular individual values most, and on what possibilities they recognize in human nature. This pluralism does not mean, however, that there is no possibility for genuine discussion or persuasion regarding which goods an individual does or should value. The book opens such a discussion by offering a thought experiment concerning what an anarcho-syndicalist society might actually feel like. The novel itself is an attempt to stimulate readers' imaginations and alert them to the possibility of realizing neglected values (like human solidarity). It invites readers to compare this possibility with a society (A-Io) organized around the pursuit of more conventional values, albeit with more advanced technology. It neither denies that the comparison presents a real ethical dilemma nor purports to establish certainty about the right answer. It is perhaps for this reason that Le Guin subtitles her book "An Ambiguous Utopia," and why critics have been divided over whether its intention is utopian or dystopian. Her thought experiment is in fact pluralist rather than monist.

The main burden of a pluralist reading is to show two things: first, that Urras, and Iotian political society in particular, realizes certain ultimate goods; and second that these goods are absent on Anarres.[16] A number of textual points can be raised in an effort to discharge this burden, but probably the most important is simply this: as Shevek and Takver, his life partner, both observe, Shevek can only complete his General Temporal Theory on Urras. In trying to convince Shevek to undertake his journey, for example, Takver urges "Go to Urras. . . . Why not? They want you there. They don't here! . . . You do need appreciation, and discussion, and students—with no Sabul-strings attached" (12: 376). A few minutes later, Shevek declares, "Here I'm walled in. I'm cramped, it's hard to work, to test the work, always without equipment, without colleagues and students. And then when I do the work, they don't want it" (12: 378). Much later, in conversation with the Terran ambassador, Shevek describes his theory as "the work I could not do on Anarres" (11: 343). A few moments later he explains:

> I could not finish my work there. And if I had been able to finish it, they did not want it, they saw no use in it. So I came here. Here is what I need—the talk, the sharing, an experiment in the Light Laboratory that proves something it wasn't meant to prove, a book of Relativity Theory from an alien world, the stimulus I need. And so I finished the work, at last. (11: 345)

In short, A-Io's capitalism and cultivation of individual excellence produce a dynamic scientific community absent on the more ideologically hidebound and egalitarian Anarres.

Strictly speaking, the great good of scientific progress, of unraveling the truth of the natural universe, is enough to establish a genuine trade-off between the virtues of A-Io and Anarres, but Le Guin also takes trouble to note a whole further range of goods that impress and astonish Shevek on his arrival from Anarres. It has already been noted, for example, how "The beauty of the land and the well-being of its people remained a perpetual marvel to him," along with the surprising "industry" and "coordination" of its workers, and its practice of conservation (3: 82–85). Shevek also discovers at Demaere Oiie's home that the Iotians enjoy a vital, if "very small range of freedom" (5: 147). Moreover, he finds that in spite of the hierarchical character of Iotian society, it provides important room for social mobility: Oiie's grandfather had been a janitor, his father a self-made man, while Oiie himself became an intellectual, a leading Iotian physicist (5: 151). He is even impressed with the "chivalry" Oiie shows his wife (5: 147).

In light of these qualities, Shevek is compelled to admit to himself that A-Io, or at least Ieu Eun University, "*felt* like a community" and he even comes to "feel at home" in it (3: 81, 77). All of these relatively positive aspects of Iotian society tend to fade into the background, however, as Shevek is exposed to the deep inequities of Iotian society. Toward the end of his stay he becomes increasingly hostile to A-Io and Urras in general, and this has likely contributed to the impression of the book as one-sided and moralizing. In his interview with the Terran ambassador, for example, Shevek declares that there is nothing, nothing on Urras that we Anarresti need! We left with empty hands, a hundred and seventy years ago, and we were right. We took nothing. Because there is nothing here but States and their weapons, the rich and their lies, and the poor and their misery. There is no way to act rightly, with a clear heart, on Urras. . . . You cannot act like a brother to other people, you must manipulate them, or command them. . . . It is a box . . . a package with all the beautiful wrapping of blue skies and meadows and forests and great cities . . . and what is inside it? A black cellar full of dust, and a dead man. A man whose hand was shot off because he held it out to others. I have been in Hell at last. Desar was right; it is Urras; Hell is Urras. (11: 346–47)

This diatribe certainly sounds damning enough, but Le Guin carefully juxtaposes it with a sharply opposed opinion from Keng, the Terran Ambassador:

"Let me tell you how this world seems to me. To me, and to all my fellow Terrans who have seen the planet, Urras is the kindliest, most various, most beautiful of all the inhabited worlds. It is the world that comes as close as any could to Paradise. . . .

"I know it's full of evils, full of human injustice, greed, folly, waste. But it is also full of good, of beauty, vitality, achievement. It is what a world should be! It is *alive*, tremendously alive—alive, despite all its evils, with hope. Is that not true?"

He nodded. (11: 347)

Critics have been apt to take one of these descriptions very seriously and to dismiss the other. What Le Guin presents, however, is a balanced picture. Iotian society (and the other archist or state-centered societies, Thu and Benbili) are deeply flawed, but also exhibit distinctive strengths, many of which appear absent from the community on Anarres. Moreover, these strengths seem intimately connected with their faults. For example, both the Iotian cultivation of individual excellence (albeit primarily among its elite) and the dynamism of its economy seem to be intimately connected with its market economy and its hierarchical social organization. Le Guin's insight here seems to be that these goods may potentially be realized by a society, but only at a steep price in terms of equality, a narrowing of individual freedom and a loss of community. There is a genuine trade-off here. The fact that Shevek rejects the trade-off embodied by A-Io does not mean that others might not reasonably accept it. After all, many (although not all) of the diverse Iotians that Shevek encounters are intelligent and kind and enjoy a real, if limited, range of freedom, but do not seek after escape or social transformation. As Shevek himself stresses, the job of a thinking person is to try to recognize and reconcile both the good and the bad of a society. Moreover, as Shevek himself shows, the recognition of social vice is as important in thinking about Anarresti society as it is in thinking about Urras.

While Shevek fully embraces (rather unquestioningly) the Odonian ideals he was taught in his youth, he still recognizes deep flaws in his society's actualization of them. For example, the organization of Anarresti society places tremendous burdens on conventional love relations, which for many people form their most basic and intimate experience of community. It is through his relationship with Takver, for example, that Shevek discovers the joy of full communion with another person, and the sense of freedom that comes with it (6: 177–91). On Anarres, however, "a couple that undertook partnership did so knowing that they might be separated at any time by the exigencies of labor distribution" (8: 246). Takver and Shevek are at one point unable to even see one another for more than four years (10: 311, 320). Moreover, parents are encouraged to move their children as early as possible into dormitories to be raised collectively. Indeed, Shevek's own deeply embittered relationship with his mother, Rulag, is a result of her being posted far away to Abbenay throughout his youth while he was left in a dormitory in Northsetting, never seeing or hearing from her between the age of three and his early twenties. In short, on Anarres the collective is sharply prioritized over individual needs at great cost to individual relationships. Indeed, Shevek himself protests early on in the book that any sort of permanent partnership is contrary to Odonian ideals (2: 50). Le Guin's depiction of Anarresti society persistently reveals deep personal scars resulting from its distinctive form of social organization.

Anarresti society also invites forms of individual power and domination that are, as Shevek himself points out, even harder to confront and uproot than Iotian social stratification because they are informal or conventional, "because they're part of our thinking" (10: 331). This threat is most vividly represented in the novel by the influential Anarresti physicist Sabul who exploits Shevek for his own aggrandizement, and blocks all Shevek's efforts to do and publish work he cannot use to his own ends (4: 109–10, 116).

Anarres is also a society that is easily exploited by the lazy who desire to do nothing but live off the labor of others. This tendency is clearly exhibited through unsympathetic characters like Desar, the unproductive mathematician, and Bunup, the repellent neighbor, who deftly exploit the social system. Anarresti society struggles to deal with the problem of free riders—or those, for example, who simply seize for themselves food resources desperately needed elsewhere (10: 311–13).

The most important challenge confronting the Anarresti society's realization of Odo's ideals, however, is the tremendous expectations it imposes on individuals. Odonian ideals call on individuals to be continuous revolutionaries—to reject established conventions and norms and only to "act from the center of one's soul" (6: 176). The burden is on the individual to reactualize the revolution in each successive generation, regardless of the risks it imposes on them. Shevek argues that:

> The Odonian society was conceived as a permanent revolution. . . . Revolution is our obligation: our hope of evolution. "The Revolution is in the individual

spirit, or it is nowhere. It is for all, or it is nothing. If it is seen as having any end, it will never truly begin." We can't stop here. We must go on. We must take the risks. (10: 333; 12: 359)

But to be a genuine revolutionary, as Shevek's friend Bedap poignantly recognizes, involves enormous sacrifice (12: 359–61). Takver, for example, is hounded out of her job, just as Shevek's oldest child is driven from her dormitory, just as his friend Tirin, who Shevek describes as the most natural revolutionary of them all, is driven mad and broken as a man:

> You realize then what Tirin is, and why he's a wreck, a lost soul. . . . We force a man outside the sphere of our approval, and then condemn him for it. We've made laws, laws of conventional behavior, built walls all around ourselves, and we can't see them, because they're part of our thinking. Tir never did that. I knew him since we were ten years old. He never did it, he never could build walls. He was a natural rebel. He was a natural Odonian—a real one! He was a free man, and the rest of us, his brothers, drove him insane in punishment for his first free act. (10: 330–31)

The burden that Odonian ideals places on individuals is simply too heavy for many to bear, and in some cases it destroys them. Indeed, the social pressure to conform is so strong that Takver winds up talking about the possibility of renouncing Anarresti society and founding a new community to carry on the revolution: "we'll go make an Anarres beyond Anarres, a new beginning" (12: 379).

None of this is, of course, to say that the anarcho-syndicalist community is presented as a failed solution to the problem of human social organization, as some critics have suggested. It is only to say that Le Guin presents it as offering a trade-off, like the Urrasti societies, balancing certain distinctive goods against certain unique burdens. Far from being one-sided or didactic, the worlds that Le Guin presents in *The Dispossessed* are genuinely pluralistic, realizing different but equally ultimate human goods at different, but similarly heavy, human costs. The choice to be made is a genuine one, not one that is stacked wholly to one side.[17]

Faced with this genuine choice of leading values, however, it seems clear enough where Shevek's and Le Guin's sympathies lie. The final section of this chapter draws out the central argument Le Guin develops in the text to explain her and Shevek's preference for Anarres.

III

The main rationale Shevek offers oppressed Urrasti for preferring Anarresti society is that it promotes a good that is characteristically neglected in market societies, human solidarity, which he sees as the basis of genuine community. Genuine community creates the opportunity for full freedom and equality.[18] Shevek prefers these great goods to those realized by the Iotian community, such as wealth, beauty, dynamic science, and stable political order and family life. This choice involves a genuine sacrifice of ultimate human goods. In a pluralistic universe, however, we cannot have it all. We are, in Berlin's words, "doomed to choose, and every choice may involve an irreparable loss."[19] Shevek believes that, all things considered, Anarres provides the best opportunity for fulfilling human beings, even if it entails irreparable loss. The force of his argument, however, is anchored in a distinctive understanding of community.

What most strikingly distinguishes Shevek's understanding of community is the emphasis it places on respecting and celebrating the plurality of individuals that compose it. Le Guin signals this distinctive view of community from the opening scene of the novel when a crowd gathers outside the Port of Anarres to confront Shevek and, if possible, to prevent his departure. Because the individuals composing the crowd were "Members of a community, not elements of a collectivity, there were not moved by mass feeling; there were as many emotions there as there were people" (1: 4). Community should not be confused then with the subsumption of individuals into a collective identity, but is rather defined by the open recognition and communication of their individuality, their diversity. Thus Le Guin describes, for example, the Anarresti managerial debate during which Shevek's voyage to Urras is hotly contested as follows: "It was like an argument among brothers, or among thoughts in an undecided mind" (12: 353). Even when the Anarresti deeply disagree, as long as they are wholly open with one another their community is uncompromised. In the terms of Odo's analogy, they remain cooperative organs or cells within a single organism, revealing the real range of choices that are open to it.

For Shevek, community can be sustained through the celebration of individual diversity as long as individual participation remains wholly voluntary, and the collectivity remains open to the perspective of each individual member. It requires, as Shevek suggests to the Thuvian physicist Chifoilisk, "free exchange," communication without walls, without vested interests to protect, without seeking for domination (5: 138). Property, power, and competition render communication instrumental to ulterior purposes, and thus isolate and imprison those who seek them. As Shevek puts it in a rapidly advancing state of inebriation at Vea's party:

> On Anarres nothing is beautiful, nothing but the faces. The other faces, the men and women. We have nothing but that, nothing but each other. Here you see the jewels, there you see the eyes. And in the eyes you see the splendor, the splendor of the human spirit. Because our men and women are free—possessing nothing, they are free. And you the possessors are possessed. You are all in jail. Each alone, solitary, with a heap of what he owns. You live in prison, die in prison. It is all I can see in your eyes—the wall, the wall! (7: 228–29)

As Odo put it succinctly, "To make a thief, make an owner; to create crime, create laws" or, in Chifoilisk's vernacular, "where there's property, there's theft" (5: 139). Theft breaks the bonds of human solidarity and forms a permanent impediment to open communication and community. The same is true of seeking after domination—as exemplified in the secretive Sabul, enclosed in the office he has appropriated for himself at the Institute. All of these things pit human beings against one another, and motivate them to use speech instrumentally to advance their purposes rather than simply to share. Power and property build walls, encourage a distorted perception of human nature as inherently competitive, inhibit trust, and therefore restrict the potential range of free choices. Correspondingly, Shevek perceives distorting walls interfering with the clear thinking of every Urrasti he meets from Dr. Kimoe through to Saio Pae. Toward the end of his stay he (symbolically) tells the Urrasti "You are contemptible. . . . You cannot keep doors open. You will never be free" (9: 304). It is for this reason that Shevek stresses, both in his speech at the demonstration and on his own return to Anarres, that anyone who wishes to join the Anarresti community (or indeed to form any genuine community) must come with "empty hands"—without property or purposes which wall them off from their fellows (9: 301; 13: 387).

A final distinctive quality of Shevek's understanding of community is the importance of shared pain in forging it: "I'm trying to say what I think brotherhood really is. It begins—it begins in shared pain;" (2: 62). "It is pain that brings men together" (5: 144–45). By struggling and suffering together, people learn to value one another for the distinctive qualities they can contribute to the common life, rather than for some arbitrary characteristic they share such as place of birth or race.

Shevek's account of the roots of community contrasts sharply with the more familiar conception advanced, for example, by Atro. According to Atro, it is "Definition by exclusion, my dear," that "defines brotherhood and nonbrotherhood" (5: 142). In other words, a community is defined by what it rejects as alien—in Atro's case, the Hainish and Terrans. Here the criteria of exclusion are quite likely to be place of birth or race. On this familiar conception of community, however, there is no need for a celebration of what makes each individual member unique—indeed, an emphasis on diversity tends to undermine the force of a systematic distinction between communities based on an arbitrary point of exclusion like race. Definition by exclusion rather tends to homogenize its community to illustrate its contrast with the aliens.

Shevek's own experience on Urras provides at least some support for his belief in the importance of open communication and community for the realization of human potential. His communication with the Urrasti physicists and his reading of the work of the Terran Ainsetain (Einstein) finally permit him to overcome the lacunae in his own thinking and complete the general field theory linking sequency and simultaneity for which everyone is so desperate. Indeed, the train of thought which leads him to his revelation begins with an insight into the weakness of Pae's work (9: 278). Appropriately, the immediate practical consequence of this discovery is the ansible, permitting direct and immediate communication between worlds. As the Terran ambassador puts it in astonishment, "It's as if you had invented human speech! We can talk—at last we can talk together"[20] (11: 344). Moreover, Shevek insists on giving his theory to all of the planets at once, so that it cannot be transformed into property and a basis of power and domination[21] (11: 350). He thus provides a forceful example of the kind of open communication that he believes emancipates human beings and establishes the condition for genuine brotherhood and community. Although the point is not emphasized in the novel itself, in the long run in Le Guin's imaginary universe the General Temporal Theory that Shevek disseminates, and the ansible that results, permit the development of the Ekumen, the peaceful federation of planets that will in the distant future send Genly Ai as a peaceful ambassador to the isolated planet of Gethen/Winter.

In the final chapter of *The Dispossessed*, Le Guin describes Shevek's return trip to Anarres. As the Hainish ship carrying Shevek prepares for landing at the Port of Anarres, Le Guin ends the novel by observing "he had not brought anything. His hands were empty as they'd always been" (13: 387). Shevek returns as he departed, "the Beggarman" (3: 70), depending on the openness and kindness of others. But as Odo's dictum and the General Temporal Theory predict, home had changed. In the first place, Shevek is pleased to hear that he and the Syndicate of Initiative now have more "friends" or supporters than when he left. The campaign against creeping bureaucratization and institutionalized power has drawn new inspiration from his gesture of opening communication with Urras. His hope is being rewarded.

Shevek's attitude to his home has also evolved. On his departure, he resented and perhaps even feared the resistance his campaign was inspiring, not so much for himself perhaps but in terms of its consequences for his family (and especially his daughter, Sadik) (12: 367–77). On his return, he laughs when warned of the likelihood of a conflict at the Port of Anarres. He accepts the conflict as part of the pain that makes the Anarresti an authentic community, a necessary concomitant of growth and evolution.

Finally, Shevek himself brings home with him a source of further transformative change on Anarres. Ketho, a Hainish officer on the ship transporting him, indicates an interest in landing on Anarres with him. Shevek asks him the reason for his interest, and Ketho explains that he's curious, and that although the Hainish have experimented with anarchy in the distant past that he himself has never seen it. He wants to learn (13: 382–87). Shevek predictably accepts his request. Ketho's individual initiative and his willingness to accept the risks of his choice fulfill in one important part Shevek's purpose of unbuilding walls and making Anarres "a society among others, a world among others" (11: 346). It also meets the revised conditions that Shevek specifies in his talk with the Terran ambassador, that others must come to Anarres and not in a spirit of competition or domination, but cooperatively, with empty hands. Finally, Ketho's offer seems to fulfill at least some of the criteria for successful communication between worlds that Shevek's own journey suggests: he is well-intentioned and he is ready to make an extended trip to the other world. It remains to be seen whether Ketho will prove a gifted communicator, whether he will be able to sustain his effort, and whether the world to which he journeys will prove receptive. As they prepare to land together, however, all indications look promising. What Shevek then finds so late and unexpectedly in Ketho seems to be what his quest was in search of, a voice from space with which he can speak as a brother.

As the story closes, then, Shevek has good reason to feel some sense of joy and release (13: 381–82). He has completed his general theory and given it to humanity as he had always planned; he has unbuilt some walls (albeit not necessarily the right ones) and now has a prospect of unbuilding more both at home and abroad; he has seen Urras and he knows why it is not for him, but he has also been able to give his brothers on Urras some hope; and he has escaped and is returning home to his family. He will sleep with Takver that night. Le Guin then gives Shevek a quiet moment of triumph, but Shevek responds with caution, pointing out to Ketho the magnitude of the task still ahead and the burden of success, the continual risk of freedom. But the prospects encourage hope. The resolution of the story lends gentle affirmation to Shevek's project, his ideas, and the life he creates for himself. Le Guin does not, however, follow the story into the landing, and the violence likely to follow, and show whether Shevek even survives the showdown, whether Ketho is permitted across the low brick wall with which the book opens, or whether Anarres will finally be able to overcome institutional inertia. She does not show us whether Shevek's permanent revolution is ultimately viable, and hence she leaves open the question of what political order is finally best. But she suggests hope for Anarres, and some argument in its favor.

Le Guin's argument for Anarres is suggested both in the story she tells and the way she tells it. Her novel persistently portrays private property and political power interfering with human self-realization by disrupting genuine community, undermining equality, and constraining freedom—in part by blocking open communication. Only a society which relieves individuals of property and relations of power can permit the kind of open communication which allows human beings to freely realize themselves.

The argument is ambitious and obviously provocative. It draws its power from a concept of human nature that is at least partially romantic, emphasizing the human capacity to create and suggesting that human beings are only fully realized in becoming free artists of themselves. Their potential is blunted when they are subject to political rule or the exigencies of the market. The novel also draws attention to the rational aspect of human nature, for example through its central motif of scientific discovery. The core of the argument is that the full realization of both of these basic human capacities—for reason and for creativity—require an environment of genuinely open communication, an environment which governments and markets necessarily stifle. However, two key elements in the argument remain highly contestable: the distinctive conception of human nature Le Guin invokes and the realism of Odonianism as a political alternative, even in a distant future. The plausibility of these elements ultimately rests, as it should, on the truth of the novel for the individual reader.

Le Guin's *The Dispossessed* offers a thought experiment designed to stimulate the imagination and encourage a reexamination of basic political commitments.[22] It is a fantasy which, by offering the reader insight into distant, imaginary worlds, seeks to reveal the hidden potential of our own. To do more, to dictate a solution to the reader, as if it could be known with certainty, would be to lecture, not to communicate openly. It would run against the theme of the book. Le Guin, true to her theme, comes to the reader with empty hands.

NOTES

Special thanks to Laurence Davis and Gilbert Plaw for their helpful comments on this chapter.

1. Quoted in Joe De Bolt, "The Voyager: A Le Guin Biography," in *Ursula K. Le Guin: Voyager to Inner Lands and to Outer Space*, ed. Joe De Bolt (Port Washington, NY: Kennikat, 1979), 15–16; Ursula K. Le Guin, *The Dispossessed: An Ambiguous Utopia* (New York: Harper & Row, 1974), cited in the text by chapter and page to the 387-page Eos Harper-Collins edition of 2001.

2. Samuel Huntington, *The Clash of Civilizations and the Remaking of World Order* (New York: Touchstone, 1997). Of course, Le Guin's book, written and published in the mid-1970s, was probably more a reflection on the Cold War's East-West division than on tensions between the Western and Islamic or Sinic worlds.

3. See, for example, Susan Wood, "Discovering Worlds: The Fiction of Ursula K. Le Guin," in *Voices for the Future*, ed. Thomas D. Clareson (Bowling Green, OH: Bowling Green University Popular Press, 1979).

4. I take the phrase "ambisexual society" from Fredric Jameson, "World-Reduction in Le Guin: The Emergence of Utopian Narrative," in *Ursula K. Le Guin*, ed. Harold Bloom (New York: Chelsea House, 1986), 63.

5. Le Guin provides a glimpse of this movement in her story, "The Day Before the Revolution," which tells of Laia Odo's death on the eve of the revolution: www.d.umn.edu/cla/faculty/tbacig/hmcl3230/3230anth/day.html

6. I use the expression "invites reflection on" because I think that the first question (is communication or understanding possible between worlds?), or its resolution, does not entail the second question (which world is better?). The point is rather that the second question is obviously an interesting and important one, both in the book and in normal life, but only becomes a viable subject of inquiry once the first question has been answered in the affirmative. After all, if there is no possibility of communication or understanding between worlds, how can one go about comparing them? One's perspective would necessarily be limited, as Tirin puts it at one point, to "the hill one happens to be sitting on" (2: 41). So

the resolution of the first question makes it possible to inquire seriously into the independently interesting second question.

One other connection between the questions, or at least their answers, is worth noting. Both are integral to a pluralist outlook: values and the basic models that link them are fundamentally distinct but comprehensible, at least to a large extent, from one another's perspectives. The resolution of the first question thus supports the resolution of the second by lending additional credibility to the pluralist perspective, and illustrating how deeply anchored it is in the text.

7. Carl H. Freedman, *Critical Theory and Science Fiction* (Hanover, NH: Wesleyan University Press, 2000), xvii, also 113–15; see also Elizabeth Cummins, *Understanding Ursula K. Le Guin* (Columbia: University of South Carolina Press, 1990), 103–8; Jim Jose, "Reflections on Le Guin's Narrative Shifts," *Science-Fiction Studies* 18, no. 2 (1991): 183–85; Le Guin herself calls her book a utopian novel in her "Science Fiction and Mrs. Brown," in *The Language of the Night*, ed. Susan Wood (New York: HarperCollins, 1992), 108–10; on the other hand, she problematizes this characterization by subtitling her book *An Ambiguous Utopia*.

8. John P. Brennan and Michael C. Downs, "Anarchism and the Utopian Tradition in *The Dispossessed*," in *Ursula K. Le Guin*, ed. Joseph D. Olander and Martin Harry Greenberg (New York: Taplinger, 1979), 117.

9. André Gorz, *Capitalism, Socialism, Ecology*, trans. Chris Turner. (London: Verso, 1994), 81. Kingsley Widmer sees the book as unmasking the inherent flaws in both forms of government; see his "Utopian, Dystopian, Diatopian Libertarianism: Le Guin's *The Dispossessed*," *The Sphinx* 4, no. 1 (1981): 62.

10. See, for example, Donna Glee Williams, "The Moons of Le Guin and Heinlein," *Science-Fiction Studies* 21, no. 2 (1994): 164; George Edgar Slusser, *The Farthest Shore of Ursula K. Le Guin* (San Bernardino, CA: Borgo Press, 1976), 47–48; Neil Easterbrook, "State, Heterotopia: The Political Imagination in Heinlein, Le Guin, and Delany," in *Political Science Fiction*, ed. Donald Hassler and Clyde Wilcox (Columbia: University of South Carolina Press, 1997), 68; Warren Rochelle characterizes the book as reproducing a traditional "monomyth" into which all the book's facets are ultimately assimilated (Warren G. Rochelle, *Communities of the Heart: The Rhetoric of Myth in the Fiction of Ursula K. Le Guin* [Liverpool, UK: Liverpool University Press, 2001], 43–48); Victor Urbanowicz is troubled by Le Guin's "strong partisanship" in the novel ("Personal and the Political in *The Dispossessed*" in *Ursula K. Le Guin*, ed. Bloom), 145; Bloom himself suggests that it is less well balanced than *The Left Hand of Darkness* ("Introduction," *Ursula K. Le Guin*, 5–6). Susan Wood suggests that Le Guin suffers from a general tendency to "impose moral and ethical patterns on her work" ("Discovering Worlds: The Fiction of Ursula K. Le Guin," in *Ursula K. Le Guin*, ed. Bloom, 185). Le Guin herself characterizes the book as "didactic" in "Science Fiction and Mrs. Brown," 109; see also "The Book is What is Real," *The Language of the Night*, 124.

11. In advancing this argument I follow the suggestion of a minority of critics who insist, in the words of Gérard Klein, that "Le Guin, for her part, challenges all orthodoxy in advance, in the sense that in all her works she posits a diversity of solutions or rather of responses, a plurality of societies, and furthermore that history is made where cultures come into contact: in *Rocannon's World* as in *The Left Hand of Darkness*, and more clearly in the recent *The Dispossessed*." See Gérard Klein, "Le Guin's 'Aberrant' Opus: Escaping the Trap of Discontent," in *Ursula K. Le Guin*, ed. Bloom, 86.

12. In Charles Nicol's ("The Good Witch of the West Gets Processed," *Science Fiction Studies* 29, no. 1 [March 2002]: 127) words, "Le Guin writes to *persuade* the reader of a particular moral view."

13. I do not mean to say, of course, that the book is merely a vehicle for disseminating this argument. My point is simply that some of the features of the story, worthwhile in itself, suggest an argument that could be made in favor of an anarcho-syndicalist community. Moreover, some of the narrative elements that can form points in this argument are original and insightful and deserve closer examination. Still, the case for these political ideals represents only one aspect of a complex story whose value can in no way be reduced to the force of the argument.

14. Some readers may, quite understandably, perceive a tension here produced by invoking Berlinian value pluralism as a framework for reading Le Guin's utopian novel. As has been observed by George Crowder (*Liberalism and Value Pluralism* [London: Continuum, 2002], 78–102), amongst others, Berlin's pluralism is strongly anti-utopian. In this light, Berlin's view might provide a stronger basis to critique Le Guin's book than to interpret it. While this is a perfectly legitimate concern, I think that it relies on a misunderstanding of the relationship between value pluralism and utopianism, as well as at least partial misreadings of both Berlin and Le Guin. First, as Laurence Davis has argued persuasively ("Isaiah Berlin, William Morris and the Politics of Utopia," *Critical Review of International Social and Political Philosophy* 3, nos. 2/3 [Summer/Autumn 2000], 56–86), a sweeping and unqualified rejection of utopian radicalism by no means follows from value pluralist premises. Second, as both Davis and Crowder note, Berlin has no problem with utopias as thought experiments designed to encourage political reflection. Indeed, his problem is really with monistic utopias as real political agendas, particularly insofar as they effectively encourage the suppression of political dissent and discussion and are used to justify extreme (that is, violent) political actions. These objections need not apply, for example, to a pluralist utopia that ensures maximum opportunity for dissent and disputation within a just and secure environment. Third, I think that Le Guin's depiction of Anarres is not meant to be utopian, at least in the conventional sense of a perfect (and usually static) political society. Shevek, for example, challenges the established Anarresti order, demanding a permanent revolution, a continual challenging and testing of ideas and order, a continually evolving society. I am not really sure whether such a society would be properly described as utopian or "ambiguously utopian" or as anti-utopian in rejecting any vision of final perfection. What I think is clear, at any rate, is that it would not fall prey to Berlin's concerns about the preclusion of dissent or the justification of political violence in the name of a final political solution.

15. Isaiah Berlin, "Two Concepts of Liberty," in *The Proper Study of Mankind*, ed. Henry Hardy (London: Pimlico, 1998), 213–14; for a brief summary of the position see Isaiah Berlin and Bernard Williams, "Pluralism and Liberalism: A Reply," *Political Studies* XLII, no. 2 (June 1994): 306–9; and John Gray, "Where Pluralists and Liberals Part Company," in *Pluralism: The Philosophy and Politics of Diversity*, ed. M. Baghramian and A. Ingram (New York: Routledge, 2000), 85–102.

16. I say the "main" burden here because a full pluralist account would require at least two more steps: first, it would have to show that Anarresti society also realized some distinctive political values (such as equality, community, individual freedom); and second, that the realization of these values was incompatible with the realization of some Urrasti values

(like wealth and power, rapid scientific progress, or glory). However, it seems to me that the first additional point is simply obvious in the novel, and is at any rate dealt with in the final section of this chapter concerning the reasons Le Guin suggests for preferring Anarres to Urras. Finally, once it is clear that the Urrasti are presented as realizing their own distinctive values, the second point—that the realization of these values is incompatible with at least some Odonian values—also becomes fairly self-evident. That is presumably why the Odonians embraced the idea of establishing their own society on Anarres. The hinge of the case then is the question of whether the Urrasti do realize any genuine distinctive values, and it is for this reason that I present it as the main burden of the pluralist case.

17. As may be argued about at least some of Le Guin's other novels, such as *The Word for World is Forest*.

18. For a good discussion of the centrality of the theme of community in Le Guin's work, see Warren Rochelle, *Communities of the Heart*, 148–50; also see Le Guin, "The Child and the Shadow," in *The Language of the Night*, 58–67.

19. Isaiah Berlin, "The Pursuit of the Ideal," 11.

20. The structure of the book reflects just this integration of the sequential and the simultaneous: the (sequential) stories of two distinct periods of Shevek's life are told simultaneously to form a distinctive and complete whole. For a good discussion of this structure as a reflection of the General Temporal Theory, see Elizabeth Cummins, *Understanding Ursula K. Le Guin*, 108–13.

21. For a good discussion of the theme of a gift-giving in Le Guin see W. A. Senior, "Cultural Anthropology and Rituals of Exchange in Ursula K. Le Guin's 'Earthsea,'" *Mosaic* 29, no. 4 (December 1996): 101–13.

22. Jim Jose characterizes it in similar language, in his "Reflections," 181.

WORKS CITED

Berlin, Isaiah, "The Pursuit of the Ideal." Pp. 1–16 in *The Proper Study of Mankind*, ed. Henry Hardy. London: Pimlico, 1998.

———. "Two Concepts of Liberty." Pp. 191–242 in *The Proper Study of Mankind*, ed. Henry Hardy. London: Pimlico, 1998.

Berlin, Isaiah, and Williams, Bernard. "Pluralism and Liberalism: A Reply." *Political Studies* XLII, no. 2 (June 1994): 306–9.

Bloom, Harold. "Introduction." Pp. 1–10 in *Ursula K. Le Guin*, ed. Harold Bloom. New York: Chelsea House, 1986.

Brennan, John P., and Downs, Michael C. "Anarchism and the Utopian Tradition in *The Dispossessed*." Pp. 116–52 in *Ursula K. Le Guin*, ed. Joseph D. Olander and Martin Harry Greenberg. New York: Taplinger, 1979.

Crowder, George. *Liberalism and Value Pluralism*. London: Continuum, 2002.

Cummins, Elizabeth. *Understanding Ursula K. Le Guin*. Columbia: University of South Carolina Press, 1990.

Davis, Laurence. "Isaiah Berlin, William Morris, and the Politics of Utopia." *Critical Review of International Social and Political Philosophy* 3, nos. 2/3 (Summer/Autumn, 2000): 56–86.

De Bolt, Joe. "The Voyager: A Le Guin Biography." Pp. 13–28 in *Ursula K. Le Guin: Voyager to Inner Lands and to Outer Space*, ed. Joe De Bolt. Port Washington, NY: Kennikat, 1979.

Easterbrook, Neil. "State, Heterotopia: The Political Imagination in Heinlein, Le Guin, and Delany." Pp. 43–75 in *Political Science Fiction*, ed. Donald Hassler and Clyde Wilcox. Columbia: University of South Carolina Press, 1997.

Freedman, Carl H. *Critical Theory and Science Fiction*. Hanover, NH: Wesleyan University Press, 2000.

Gorz, André. *Capitalism, Socialism, Ecology*, trans. Chris Turner. London: Verso, 1994.

Gray, John. "Where Pluralists and Liberals Part Company." Pp. 85–102 in *Pluralism: The Philosophy and Politics of Diversity*, ed. M. Baghramian and A. Ingram. New York: Routledge, 2000.

Huntington, Samuel. *The Clash of Civilizations and the Remaking of World Order*. New York: Touchstone, 1997.

Jameson, Fredric. "World-Reduction in Le Guin: The Emergence of Utopian Narrative." Pp. 57–70 in *Ursula K. Le Guin*, ed. Harold Bloom. New York: Chelsea House, 1986.

Jose, Jim. "Reflections on Le Guin's Narrative Shifts." *Science-Fiction Studies* 18, no. 2 (July 1991): 180–97.

Klein, Gérard. "Le Guin's 'Aberrant' Opus: Escaping the Trap of Discontent." Pp. 85–98 in *Ursula K. Le Guin*, ed. Harold Bloom. New York: Chelsea House, 1986.

Le Guin, Ursula K. "The Child and the Shadow." Pp. 54–67 in *The Language of the Night*, ed. Susan Wood. New York: HarperCollins, 1992.

———. *The Dispossessed: An Ambiguous Utopia*. New York: Eos, HarperCollins, 2001 (1974).

———. "Science Fiction and Mrs. Brown." Pp. 97–117 in *The Language of the Night*, ed. Susan Wood. New York: HarperCollins, 1992.

Nicol, Charles. "The Good Witch of the West Gets Processed," *Science Fiction Studies* 29, no. 1 (March 2002): 127–28.

Rochelle, Warren G. *Communities of the Heart: The Rhetoric of Myth in the Fiction of Ursula K. Le Guin*. Liverpool, UK: Liverpool University Press, 2001.

Senior, W. A. "Cultural Anthropology and Rituals of Exchange in Ursula K. Le Guin's 'Earthsea,'" *Mosaic* 29, no. 4 (December 1996): 101–13.

Slusser, George Edgar. *The Farthest Shore of Ursula K. Le Guin*. San Bernardino, CA: Borgo Press, 1976.

Urbanowicz, Victor. "Personal and the Political in *The Dispossessed*." Pp. 145–54 in *Ursula K. Le Guin*, ed. Harold Bloom. New York: Chelsea House, 1986.

Widmer, Kingsley. "Utopian, Dystopian, Diatopian Libertarianism: Le Guin's *The Dispossessed*." *The Sphinx* 4, no. 1 (1981): 55–65.

Williams, Donna Glee. "The Moons of Le Guin and Heinlein." *Science-Fiction Studies* 21, no. 2 (July 1994): 164–72.

Wood, Susan. "Discovering Worlds: The Fiction of Ursula K. Le Guin." Pp. 154–79 in *Voices for the Future*, ed. Thomas D. Clareson. Bowling Green, OH: Bowling Green University Popular Press, 1979.

A Response, by Ansible, from Tau Ceti

Ursula K. Le Guin

I've spent a good deal of vehemence objecting to the reduction of fiction to ideas. Readers, I think, are often led astray by the widespread belief that a novel springs from a single originating "idea," and then are kept astray by the critical practice of discussing fiction as completely accessible to intellect, a rational presentation of ideas by means of an essentially ornamental narrative. In discussing novels that clearly deal with social, political, or ethical issues, and above all in discussing science fiction, supposed to be a "literature of ideas," this practice is so common—particularly in teaching and academic texts—that it has driven me to slightly lunatic extremes of protest.

In reaction to it, I find myself talking as if intellect had nothing to with novel writing or novel reading, speaking of composition as a pure trance state, and asserting that all I seek when writing is to allow my unconscious mind to control the course of the story, using rational thought only to reality check when revising.

All this is perfectly true, but it's only half the picture. It's because the other half of the picture is so often the only one shown and discussed that I counter-react to the point of sounding woowoo.

When treated—even with much praise—as a methodical ax grinder, I am driven to deny that there's any didactic intention at all in my fiction. Of course there is—I'm dead set against preaching, but the teaching impulse is often stronger than I am. Even in quite sophisticated criticism, the naïve conflation of what a character (particularly a sympathetic one) says with what the author believes will drive me to deny that I agree with what the character says, even when I do. It's the only way I can assert that the fact that I agree is never— never—to be taken for granted. "Je suis Mme Bovary," said Flaubert, groaning, as usual. J'aime Shevek mais je ne le suis pas. I envy Homer and Shakespeare, who by being only semi-existent evade such impertinent assimilations. They retain effortlessly the responsible detachment that I must consciously, and never wholly, earn.

So *The Dispossessed*, a science-fiction novel not only concerned with politics, society, and ethics but approaching them via a definite political theory, has given me a lot of grief. It has generally, not always but often, been discussed as a treatise, not as a novel. This is its own damn fault, of course—what did it expect, announcing itself as a utopia, even if an ambiguous one? Everybody knows utopias are to be read not as novels but as blueprints for social theory or practice.

But the fact is that, starting with Plato's *Republic* in Philosophy 1-A when I was seventeen, I read utopias as novels. Actually, I read everything as novels, including history, memoir, and the newspaper—I think J. L. Borges is quite correct, all prose is fiction. So when I came to write a utopia of course I wrote a novel.

I wasn't surprised that it was treated as a treatise, but I wondered if the people who read it as a treatise ever wondered why I had written it as a novel. Were they as indifferent as they seemed to be to what made it a novel—the inherent self-contradictions of novelistic narrative that prevent simplistic, single-theme interpretation, the novelistic "thickness of description" (Geertz's term) that resists reduction to abstracts and binaries, the embodiment of ethical dilemma in a drama of character that evades allegorical interpretation, the presence of symbolic elements that are not fully accessible to rational thought?

You will understand, perhaps, why I approached this collection of essays with my head down and my shoulders hunched. Experience had taught me to expect a set of intellectual exercises which, even if not accusing me of preaching, moralizing, political naivety, compulsive heterosexuality, or bourgeois cowardice, even if interested in or supportive of what the book "says," would prove essentially indifferent to how it says it.

If fiction is how it says what it says, then useful criticism is what shows you how fiction says what it says.

To my grateful surprise, that's what this collection does. These essays are not about an idea of the book. They are about the book.

Perhaps I can express my gratitude best by saying that reading them left me knowing far better than I knew before how I wrote the book and why I wrote it as I did. By seldom exaggerating the intentionality of the text, they have freed me from exaggerating its nonintentionality, allowing me once more to consider what I wanted to do and how I tried to do it. They have restored the book to me as I conceived it, not as an exposition of ideas but as an embodiment of idea—a revolutionary artifact, a work containing a potential permanent source of renewal of thought and perception, like a William Morris design, or the Bernard Maybeck house I grew up in.

These critics show me how the events and relationships of the narrative, which as I wrote the book seemed to follow neither an arbitrary nor a rationally decided course, do constitute an architecture which is fundamentally aesthetic and which, *in being so,* fulfils an intellectual or rational design. They enable me to see the system of links and echoes, of leaps and recurrences, that make the narrative structure work. This is criticism as I first knew it, serious, responsive, and jargon free. I honor it as an invaluable aid to reading—my own text as well as that of others.

Though I had pretty well saturated my mind with utopian literature, with the literature of pacifist Anarchism, and with "temporal physics" (insofar as it existed), before I wrote the book, my knowledge of relevant theoretical thinking was very weak. When I read recurrent citations in these essays—Hegel above all, Bakhtin, Adorno, Marcuse, and many more—I hunch up a bit again. I am embarrassed. My capacity for sustained abstract thought is somewhat above that of a spaniel. I knew and know these authors only by name and reputation; the book was not written under their influence, and they can't be held responsible, positively or negatively, for anything in my text. At most (as with the "shadow" in Carl Jung and in *A Wizard of Earthsea*) it is interesting to observe parallels or intersections of thought. On the other hand, I was glad to see my thought experiment tested against the writers who did contribute to its formation—above all Lao Tzu, Kropotkin, and Paul Goodman.

A good many of the writers of this volume treat *The Dispossessed* as if it stood quite alone in my work. This ahistorical approach seems odd, since the book has been around so long, and isn't an anomaly among my other works. It was followed in 1982 by a fairly lengthy discussion of utopias ("A Non-Euclidean View of California as a Cold Place to Be"), which forms a clear link to a second, if radically different, utopian novel, *Always Coming Home* (1985). It's hard for me to put these out of my mind when thinking about *The Dispossessed.* Both offer a chance to compare some of the things I did in the earlier novel with things I said in the essay, or did in the later novel—testing for consistency, change of mind, progress, regress, aesthetic and intellectual purpose. And also, the unanimity with which these writers refuse to read *The Dispossessed* as a single-theme, monistic, closed-minded text makes me long to see some of them take on *Always Coming Home,* which has been read, or dismissed unread, as a naively regressive picture of a sort of Happy Hunting Ground for fake Indians. The narrative experimentation and the postmodernist self-conscious fictionality which some of these essayists point to in *The Dispossessed* are carried a great deal further in *Always Coming Home.* I for one am curious as to why I play these particular tricks only when writing utopias, or anyhow semi-utopias with flies in them. In some of these chapters I began to catch a glimpse of why, and I'd very much like to learn more.

I found nothing really to correct—nothing I thought simply wrong, a misreading—in all these pages. I would point out that Hainish guilt is not unmotivated or mysterious; in other stories one finds that the Hainish, everybody's ancestors, have a terribly long history which is, like all human histories, terrible. So Ketho, who comes in at the end, is indeed cautious in his search for hope. But whether he finds it or not the book does not say. And here I felt in a few of the essays a slight tendency to wishful thinking. The book doesn't have a happy ending. It has an open ending. As pointed out in at least one of the chapters, it's quite possible that both Shevek and Ketho will be killed on arrival by an angry mob. And it's only too likely that Shevek's specific plans and hopes for his people will come to little or nothing. That would not surprise Ketho.

In speaking of the end of the book I must once again thank its first reader and first critic, Darko Suvin, who brought to my Anarchist manuscript the merciless eye of a Marxist and the merciful mind of a friend. It had twelve chapters then, and a neat full-circle ending. Twelve chapters? he cried, enraged. It should be an odd number! And what is this—closure? You are not allowed to close this text! Is the circle open or not?

The circle is open. The doors are open. In order to have doors to open, you have to have a house.

To those who helped me build my drafty and imaginary house, and to those who have brought to it their generous comment and keen perception, making its rooms come alive with resounding and unending arguments, I am grateful. Be welcome, ammari.

—August 2004

Further Reading on
The Dispossessed

$\mathscr{R}$eaders interested in delving further into some of the topics explored in this book may wish to consult the works cited by individual chapter authors, as well as the following recommended readings. This list is intended merely as a starting point for further research, a selective guide to some of the most thought-provoking work in the field. A helpful recent bibliography is James F. Collins's "The High Points So Far: An Annotated Bibliography of Ursula K. Le Guin's *The Left Hand of Darkness* and *The Dispossessed*," *Bulletin of Bibliography* 58, no. 2 (2001): 89–100.

Bittner, James. *Approaches to the Fiction of Ursula K. Le Guin*. Ann Arbor: University of Michigan Research Press, 1984, and Essex, UK: Bowker, 1984, chap. 4.

———. "Chronosophy, Aesthetics, and Ethics in Le Guin's *The Dispossessed: An Ambiguous Utopia*." Pp. 244–70 in *No Place Else: Explorations in Utopian and Dystopian Fiction*, ed. Eric S. Rabkin, Martin H. Greenberg, and Joseph D. Olander. Carbondale: Southern Illinois University Press, 1983.

Brennan, John P., and Michael C. Downs. "Anarchism and Utopian Tradition in *The Dispossessed*." Pp. 116–52 in *Ursula K. Le Guin*, ed. Joseph D. Olander and Martin H. Greenberg. New York: Taplinger, 1979.

Bucknall, Barbara J. *Ursula K. Le Guin*. New York: Frederick Ungar, 1981, 102–24.

Cogell, Elizabeth Cummins. "Taoist Configurations: *The Dispossessed*." Pp. 153–79 in *Ursula K. Le Guin: Voyager to Inner Lands and to Outer Space*, ed. Joe De Bolt. Port Washington, NY: Kennikat Press, 1979.

Ferns, Chris. *Narrating Utopia: Ideology, Gender, Form in Utopian Literature*. Liverpool, UK: Liverpool University Press, 1999, 219–30.

Freedman, Carl. *Critical Theory and Science Fiction*. Hanover, NH: Wesleyan University Press, 2000, 111–29.

Le Guin, Ursula K. "The Day Before the Revolution." Pp. 359–82 in her *The Wind's Twelve Quarters*. New York: HarperCollins, 1991 [1975]; pp. 285–303 in the edition from London: Victor Gollancz, 2000.

———. "A Non-Euclidean View of California as a Cold Place to Be." Pp. 80–100 in her *Dancing at the Edge of the World: Thoughts on Words, Women, Places*. New York: Grove Press, 1989.

———. "Science Fiction and Mrs. Brown." Pp. 13–33 in *Science Fiction at Large*, ed. Peter Nicholls. London: Gollancz, 1976.

Smith, Philip E, II. "Unbuilding Walls: Human Nature and the Nature of Evolutionary and Political Theory in *The Dispossessed*." Pp. 77–96 in *Ursula K. Le Guin*, ed. Joseph D. Olander and Martin Harry Greenberg. New York: Taplinger, 1979.

Urbanowicz, Victor. "Personal and Political in *The Dispossessed*." *Science-Fiction Studies* 5, no. 2 (July 1978): 110–17.

Index

1968, 22, 34n28, 98, 103, 233

Adorno, Theodor, 76, 78, 84
Ainsetein, Einstein, 4, 5, 19, 65, 183, 187, 200, 297
A-Io. *See* Urras
alienation, 171, 206, 221; from objects, xiii, 95–106; Keng's, 151; in labor and work, 78, 80, 83, 87, 95–106; Marxist, 95–97, 206; Shevek's, 9, 11–15, 19, 22, 63, 156, 171, 186, 260, 272–75
altruism, altruists, 119–20, 127n18, 272
anarchy, anarchism, anarchist, 38, 182, 191, 275–77, 284–85, 295, 298; anarchist community, xxii, 65–66, 86, 111–25, 129–43, 149–61, 222–23; anarchist individuality and freedom, 68, 85–90, 102, 111–25, 129–43, 149–61; decentralization, xx, 21, 33n20, 116–17, 120–21, 153–55, 158; and environmental issues, xii, 33n25, 55–70, 86; to Keng, 28–29, 276–77; Le Guin on, xxiv–xxvi, 111, 225, 236, 245n10, 307; post-consumerist, 85–89; and science, xvii, 156–58, 195–97, 203, 209; Shevek's anarchism, 8–10, 12, 18–19, 21, 23,

26–27, 30–31, 90, 105, 152–53, 155–61, 173–74, 226; theory of, xiii–xv, 34n27, 85–90, 93n35, 111–25, 129–43, 144n5–n6, 149–61, 162n15, 203–9, 210n12, 225, 236, 249. *See also* Odo
Anarres, 55–70, 88–91, 111–25, 284, 294–300; in relation to Urras, xiii–xv, xvii–xix, xxi–xxii, 8–9, 13, 46, 57–59, 61–63, 65–70, 95, 106, 129, 132–35, 137, 140–43, 150–57, 172, 175–76, 182, 221, 225–27, 236–38, 240, 255–56, 285–86, 291, 293; in relation to Urras and Terra, 182–83, 192, 238–44, 276–77; shortcomings of, xiii–xv, 10–12, 26, 102, 105, 129, 131–35, 137, 190–91, 239, 249–54, 270–72, 294–95; as utopia, xiii, xx–xxi, 69, 191–92, 236, 268–70, 277–80
ansible, 27, 91, 157, 169–70, 175, 192, 198, 200, 257, 298
Arendt, Hannah, xvi, 48, 167–78
Arnold, Matthew, 47
art, aesthetic, xiii, 44–45, 58–59, 84, 95–97, 101–6, 205
Atro, 131, 156, 182, 185, 221, 290, 297
Atwood, Margaret, 38
Augustine, on time, 171–73

311

Bacon, Francis, 39

Bakhtin, M. M., 26, 222

Bakunin, Mikhail, 111

Barthes, Roland, 100–101, 106

Baudrillard, Jean, 77, 99–100, 104, 106

Bedap, 28, 30, 42, 45, 65, 86, 139, 143; criticisms of Anarres, 10–11, 26, 44, 59, 68, 102, 134–35, 154, 189–90, 225, 270–272, 279; friendship with Shevek, 62, 69, 186; genuine revolutionary, 295; homosexuality, 62, 141, 143n2

Bellamy Edward (and *Looking Backward*), 4, 228

Benbili, 15, 27, 30, 67, 249

Berdyaev, Nicolas, 234

Bergson, Henri, 5

Berlin, Isaiah, xx–xxii, 265–66, 268–70, 277, 279, 291, 302n14

Beshun, 62, 185

birth control, 71n10

Bittner, James, 4–5, 7, 168–69, 176–77, 198, 222

Bloch, Ernst, 258–60

Borges, J. L., 306

Brotherhood. *See* community

Bunup, 294

Burke, Edmund, 132

Campanella, Tommaso (and *The City of the Sun*), 4, 13, 252

certainty, mathematical, 11, 19, 183–84, 187–88, 203, 224, 258, 260

change, x, xvi–xix, 9–13, 17–19, 23, 27–31, 44, 63–64, 67–69, 102, 106, 113, 122, 124–25, 133, 142–43, 150, 160, 171–73, 175, 182, 185, 189–92, 222, 235, 244, 255–61, 269, 277, 280, 294–95

Chifoilisk, 14, 142, 143, 153, 156, 221, 290, 296–97

Clausewitz, 167

communication, 11, 23–24, 60, 158, 192, 222, 257, 283–300; cross-cultural, xxi, 20, 157, 283–84; and

persuasion, 29, 174–75; and time, 24, 169–70, 192. *See also* ansible

community (and brotherhood); based on exclusion, 157, 185, 297; based in love, 185, 190; based in shared pain, suffering, 20, 90, 114, 185–86, 189, 257, 277, 297; based in trust, 115–17, 171–72; and individuality, xiv–xv, 69, 85–86, 112–25, 130–43, 150–61, 173, 271–73, 295–300; result of journeys and returns, 189–90; in Leopold, 64–65; in Marcuse, 82–84, 87; meaning of, xxii, 22–25, 30, 38, 65–66, 68, 86–88, 112–21, 123–25, 130–43, 152–60, 171–72, 181, 186, 190, 269, 275–77, 280, 284–85, 294–99; in Oakeshott, 266–67; Urras and, 9, 273, 292–93. *See also* mutual aid, promise

conflict, political or social, 3, 15, 18, 20–27, 60–61, 112–13, 123–25, 277–79; exists in Le Guin's utopia, 27–28, 30–31, 120, 125, 192, 235, 298

consumerist society, consumerism, capitalist consumer society, xi–xiii, 14–15, 58, 67, 69, 76–77, 85–86, 91, 95, 98–100, 102–4, 116, 135–36

Darwin, Darwinism, social Darwinism, 15, 65, 162n15, 220, 245n10

Davenant, 7–8, 29, 30, 143

Dearri, 6–7, 42–43, 188, 198, 224

death, 24, 42, 79, 85, 87–88, 151–52; in utopian tradition, 235

Delany, Samuel R., xix, 143n2, 162n16, 234, 239

Derrida, Jacques, 239

Desar, 136, 237, 287, 293–94

design theorists, xiii, 96–106

dialectic (and dialogic relations), xiv–xv, xvii–xviii, 8–9, 28, 32n8, 41–43, 48, 78–80, 90, 101, 137, 199–202, 207, 211n31, 219, 228, 235–37, 254–260

About the Contributors

Tony Burns is a Lecturer in the School of Politics, University of Nottingham, UK. He is the author of *Natural Law and Political Ideology in the Philosophy of Hegel* (Aldershot: Ashgate, 1996) and coeditor, with Ian Fraser (Nottingham Trent University), of *The Hegel Marx Connection* (London: Palgrave, 2000). He has published a number of articles relating to various aspects of political theory and the history of political thought in a variety of academic journals, including *Utopian Studies, Political Studies, History of Political Thought, Sociological Review, History of the Human Sciences*, and *Science and Society*. In the present context, the most relevant of these is an article entitled "Zamyatin's *We* and Postmodernism," *Utopian Studies* 11, no. 1 (2000).

Claire P. Curtis is Assistant Professor of Political Science at the College of Charleston, where she teaches political theory. She received her B.A. from Bowdoin College and her Ph.D. from Johns Hopkins University. She is the author of a forthcoming paper in *Contemporary Justice Review* titled "Rehabilitating Utopia: Feminist Science Fiction and Finding the Ideal." Her research work centers on the interplay between skepticism and perfectionism that is found in much of twentieth-century political philosophy and feminist science fiction. She is currently working on a book titled *The Loss of Utopia* that questions the conventional claim by twentieth-century political philosophers that teleological thinking is a recipe for disaster.

Laurence Davis studied for his B.A. in political science at Columbia University and earned his D.Phil. in politics at Oxford University. He has taught political and social theory at Oxford University, Ruskin College, and University Colleges Galway and Dublin. His current research interests include radical and utopian political thought, anarchism, social radicalism and the arts, the politics of work and time, and the utopian writings of William Morris and Ursula Le Guin. He currently lives in Dublin, Ireland.

Winter Elliott received her Ph.D. from the University of Georgia. Her research interests include medieval literature and popular culture, especially fantasy and science fiction. She is particularly interested in the construction of the individual, both social and literary, and has taught a course entitled "The Individual in Society."

Chris Ferns is Professor of English at Mount Saint Vincent University in Halifax, Nova Scotia. His research interests include historical fiction, gender studies, and utopian thought. His publications include *Narrating Utopia: Ideology, Gender, Form in Utopian Literature* (1999), *Aldous Huxley: Novelist* (1980), and "The Value/s of Dystopia: *The Handmaid's Tale* and the Anti-Utopian Tradition," as well as articles on Walter Scott, J. G. Farrell, and Charlotte Perkins Gilman.

Everett L. Hamner earned Masters degrees at Johns Hopkins University and Regent College (Vancouver) before becoming a Presidential Fellow in English at the University of Iowa. His special interests include the fantastic, especially science fiction; relationships between religion, literature, and film; Latin American and Latino/a culture; the American South; and theories of time and place. Previously published essays on Walker Percy and Hans-Georg Gadamer may be found in *Christianity and Literature* and *Renascence*.

Ursula K. Le Guin's Earthsea books have sold millions of copies in sixteen different languages. Her Hainish cycle is one of the most critically acclaimed constructs in science fiction. An honored author of short stories, children's books, poetry, and criticism, she is the recipient of numerous literary prizes, including the National Book Award, the Newbery Silver Medal, five Hugo and six Nebula Awards, and the PEN/Malamud Award for Short Fiction. She lives in Portland, Oregon.

Avery Plaw is Assistant Professor of Political Science at Concordia University in Montreal, Quebec. He grew up in Montreal, earned his B.A. at Trinity College, Toronto, his M.A. at the University of Toronto, and his Ph.D. in political philosophy at McGill University (2002). He is currently finishing his first book, *Precarious Equilibrium and Moral Imagination: The Politics of Isaiah Berlin's Value Pluralism*.

Andrew Reynolds is a Ph.D. candidate in the Department of English at the University of Florida. His research interests include twentieth-century American literature, critical theory, the theory of the novel, literary utopias, and science fiction. He has recently taught courses on American postmodern literature and American postwar suburban literature and culture. He is currently completing a dissertation analyzing the American suburban novel. This study begins with the genre's late nineteenth-century roots in the writings of William Dean Howells and discusses works by Vladimir Nabokov, Joyce Carol Oates, and Octavia Butler.

Ellen Rigsby is Assistant Professor of Communication at Saint Mary's College of California. Her teaching interests include American political theory, constitutional law, American political and legal cultures, and American utopian thought. Her research focuses on the study of political fantasies—that is, the intersections of utopian literature, speculative fiction, and utopian communities. She is interested in constructions, both real and imaginary, of governments, politics, constitutions, and reform. She published an article in *Theory and Event* in 2002 entitled "The Failure of Success: Arendt and Pocock on The Fall of American Republicanism."

Jennifer Rodgers received her Ph.D. in comparative literature from the University of Massachusetts, Amherst in 2002, where much of her teaching focused on utopian fiction, fantasy, and science fiction. Her current research focuses on the social implications of the fantastic in literatures of the Americas, and she is finishing a book based on her dissertation, which explores the connections between magic realism and social protest in Spanish America and the United States.

Dan Sabia is Associate Professor in the Department of Political Science of the University of South Carolina. His teaching areas of specialization lie in political philosophy, especially political ethics, utopian political thought, democratic theory, and modern and contemporary political thought. He has edited *Changing Social Science: Critical Theory and Other Critical Perspectives* and *Dissent and Affirmation: Essays in Honor of Mulford Q. Sibley*, contributed chapters to those books, and published articles on topics in political theory from Machiavelli to the present.

Bülent Somay received an M.A. in English Literature in 1981 from Bosphorus University, Istanbul, and returned to Turkey after an incomplete Ph.D. study at McGill University, Montreal. From 1995 to 2002 he worked in the publishing house Metis as the Editor-in-Chief for Science Fiction and Fantasy. Since 1999 he has been teaching at Bilgi University, Istanbul. He has published two collections of his essays, *Geriye Kalan Devrimdir* (*What Remains is the Revolution*, 1997) and *Sarki Okuma Kitabi* (*Song Reader*, 2000). His most recent book, *Tarihin Bilincdisi* (*The Unconscious of History*, 2004), is a collection of essays on psychoanalysis, historiography, and popular culture. His current project, *L'Orient n'existe pas*, is a book (in English) on psychoanalysis and Orientalism/postcolonialism to be published in late 2005.

Douglas Spencer gained his first degree in history of art, design, and film studies at Sheffield City Polytechnic and his Masters in cultural studies at Thames

Valley University. He has worked as a visiting lecturer at a number of universities teaching historical, theoretical, and philosophical approaches to architecture and design. His published work includes essays on architecture, urbanism, science fiction, film, and social theory, and he is currently preparing a Ph.D. on the subject of architecture's engagement with the body.

Peter G. Stillman is Professor of Political Science at Vassar College, where he teaches courses in modern political theory and participates in the environmental studies and American culture multidisciplinary programs. In addition to editing *Hegel's Philosophy of Spirit* and a new translation of Rousseau's *Confessions*, he has published numerous articles and book chapters on utopian and dystopian thought, Hegel's political philosophy, Marx's ideas, and ecological issues.

Simon Stow is Assistant Professor in the Department of Government at The College of William and Mary. He is interested in the intersection of literary theory and contemporary political thought. He has published articles on Richard Rorty's reading of Vladimir Nabokov, the politics of ethical criticism, and the recent novels of Philip Roth. He is currently at work on his first book.

Mark Tunick is Professor of Political Science and Interim Associate Dean at the Harriet L. Wilkes Honors College of Florida Atlantic University. He teaches courses on political theory, law, and moral philosophy. He has published three books: *Punishment: Theory and Practice* (1992), *Hegel's Political Philosophy* (1992), and *Practices and Principles: Approaches to Ethical and Legal Judgment* (1998, paperback 2000), as well as a number of articles on Hegel, Kant, constitutional law, and morality. In addition to Le Guin's *The Dispossessed*, his current interests include J. S. Mill; privacy; legal punishment; culture and law; politics and ethics in film (especially film noir); and Hegel.